The French Book Trade in Enlightenment Europe I

Also available from Bloomsbury

The French Book Trade in Enlightenment Europe II: Enlightenment Bestsellers, by Simon Burrows
The Foreign Political Press in Nineteenth-Century London: Politics from a Distance, edited by Constance Bantman and Ana Cláudia Suriani da Silva
London Calling: Britain, the BBC World Service and the Cold War, by Alban Webb

The French Book Trade in Enlightenment Europe I

Selling Enlightenment

Mark Curran

BLOOMSBURY ACADEMIC
LONDON • NEW YORK • OXFORD • NEW DELHI • SYDNEY

BLOOMSBURY ACADEMIC
Bloomsbury Publishing Plc
50 Bedford Square, London, WC1B 3DP, UK
1385 Broadway, New York, NY, 10018, USA
29 Earlsfort Terrace, Dublin 2, Ireland

BLOOMSBURY, BLOOMSBURY ACADEMIC and the Diana logo are trademarks of Bloomsbury Publishing Plc

First published in Great Britain 2018
Paperback edition published 2021

Copyright © Mark Curran, 2018

Mark Curran has asserted his right under the Copyright, Designs and Patents Act, 1988, to be identified as Author of this work.

For legal purposes the Acknowledgements on p.ix constitute an extension of this copyright page.

All rights reserved. No part of this publication may be reproduced or transmitted in any form or by any means, electronic or mechanical, including photocopying, recording, or any information storage or retrieval system, without prior permission in writing from the publishers.

Bloomsbury Publishing Plc does not have any control over, or responsibility for, any third-party websites referred to or in this book. All internet addresses given in this book were correct at the time of going to press. The author and publisher regret any inconvenience caused if addresses have changed or sites have ceased to exist, but can accept no responsibility for any such changes.

A catalogue record for this book is available from the British Library.

A catalog record for this book is available from the Library of Congress.

ISBN: HB: 978-1-4411-7890-9
PB: 978-1-3502-5083-3
ePDF: 978-1-4411-1169-2
eBook: 978-1-4411-8460-3

Typeset by Deanta Global Publishing Services, Chennai, India

To find out more about our authors and books visit www.bloomsbury.com and sign up for our newsletters.

For Marie, Benjamin and Lucy

Contents

List of Figures	viii
Acknowledgements	ix
Preface	x
Introduction – The French Book Trade in Enlightenment Europe	1
1 A Printing Shop across the Border	15
2 The Myth of the Mountain Dwellers	49
3 The Republic of Books	83
4 The Storm Will Pass	97
5 Conclusion: Selling Enlightenment	135
Epilogue – The End of the STN	151
Appendix Essay – Decoding and Coding the French Book Trade	155
Notes	161
Bibliography	207
Index	227

List of Figures

Figure 0.1	FBTEE database schema, by Sarah Kattau and Henry Merivale	6
Figure 1.1	The Swiss Romand	18
Figure 1.2	Group-Stacked Bar Chart displaying the annual repartition of STN sales for the geographic zones of Switzerland, France and the rest of Europe	24
Figure 1.3	Map of STN envois 1 October 1771 to 26 January 1780	29
Figure 1.4	Surviving STN archive	38
Figure 1.5	Sources used to construct the FBTEE 'core data stream'	40
Figure 1.6	Typical day book entry	40
Figure 2.1	Books sourced by the STN, 1769–94 (including printings)	52

Acknowledgements

During the years that I have spent working on this volume, I have amassed so many intellectual debts, and benefited so much from conversations with colleagues and friends, that it would make little sense to simply here present a long list of names. Many of the findings discussed in the following pages represent some of the first spoils of a research agenda and programme conducted entirely collaboratively. Any faults are my own, any strengths the work of an extraordinary and dedicated team. I have repeatedly expressed my gratitude to those kind individuals who spent many long months, even years, helping to see this book through to publication in its current form. The selflessness of some individuals is heartening. Finally, I would like to add a word of thanks to all of the many libraries and institutions that assisted, financially and practically, the research behind this work. Without the generosity and support of the Arts and Humanities Research Council, the Bibliothèque publique et universitaire de Neuchâtel, the University of Leeds, Queen Mary University of London, Darwin College Cambridge and Cambridge University Library, this book would not exist. This research was supported by the British Arts and Humanities Research Council's Research Grants (Standard) Scheme AH/E509363/1.

Preface

A lurch of fancy might transform a single number buried deep inside a set of eighteenth-century bookseller's accounts into an intriguing image. Having completed a survey of the unbound books crammed into their lakeside storeroom in June 1786, the Société typographique de Neuchâtel (STN) recorded a grand total of 1,805,427 sheets in stock.[1] Printed *feuilles* were relatively large, with each side capable of carrying eight or twelve pages of pocket-sized text. Laid end to end, as a result, this remarkable pile would have sufficed to pave a literary path through the town and far beyond the Jura Mountains to Paris, across northern France to the great book-trade centres of the Low Countries and, eventually, back home to Neuchâtel via a meandering trail through the Rhineland. Hypothetical travellers could have wandered along a ribbon of bad novels and self-help guides; delighted in social and political accounts of most of the settlements and regions that they passed; dined on science, history, botany and philosophy; and laid their heads along kilometres of sermons and scripture. And yes, by starlight, a fortunate few might even have spotted some salacious *libels* – weapon texts devised to bring the high and mighty down a peg or two – cut randomly into the narrative.

What was this mountainous stack of paper doing in sleepy Neuchâtel? From where did the books come and to whence were they sent? Which authors, genres and discourses were popular? Might an analysis of such texts help us to better understand the world in which they circulated? Could we use them to confirm or challenge our interpretations of the Enlightenment? Does our imaginary road mirror the literary path said to have issued onto the French Revolution of 1789? What, more prosaically, was a commercial business situated in a provincial Swiss backwater doing with so much capital tied up in stock?

Responding to such queries will take a more informed image, painstakingly constructed from the hundreds of thousands of additional numbers found within the STN's crumbling account books. Picture an interactive map of the STN's entire pan-European client network charged with real-time purchase and sales information that details the movements of almost every book that this late-Enlightenment printing and mail-order bookselling business handled. At the click of a button, we might use this chart to investigate the trade conducted by the Society during any stretch of time or across any geographical region. And through sustained investigation we might outline the history of the Society, discern bestselling authors and titles, and examine the functioning of the French-language book industry on the eve of the French Revolution. Thanks to the French Book Trade in Enlightenment Europe (FBTEE) project, this map exists. It is the star of the current volume, but far from its only source. For the STN account books do not yield their secrets easily and contain some intriguingly problematic numbers. Like the number 1,805,427 – the number of printed sheets that the Neuchâtelois had in stock in 1786. Does it matter if the STN was not very good at selling books? We should start at the beginning …

Introduction – The French Book Trade in Enlightenment Europe

Late in the spring of 2006, punch drunk with excitement and aspiration, Simon Burrows and I sat down in his unruly Leeds University office to draft the funding application for the French Book Trade in Enlightenment Europe (FBTEE) project. Weeks earlier, in the archives of the eighteenth-century French-language printer booksellers the Société typographique de Neuchâtel (STN), located in the provincial Swiss Bibliothèque publique et universitaire de Neuchâtel (BPUN), we had made a quite remarkable discovery. Although the STN's account books had only partially survived, a miracle of double-entry bookkeeping meant that few of the Society's trading transactions were actually lost. By jumping between the various manuscripts and capturing their scattered secrets in a relational database, we could potentially recover, interrogate and understand almost all of the Society's 1769–94 book dealing history. Further, because the Neuchâtelois traded extensively throughout Europe, our imagined electronic resource might lay bare the functioning of the Enlightenment francophone book trade and give precious insight into what excited readers on the eve of the French Revolution. Little wonder, then, that the research questions flowed so readily. How far did patterns of demand differ over time and across space? Which authors, books and subjects sold best? What might we learn about the popularity of Jean-Jacques Rousseau and Voltaire and the other leading lights of the Enlightenment? Do books cause revolutions? Ah, so many lines of enquiry! So much lofty ambition!

A full decade and a completed Arts and Humanities Research Council funded project later, the resultant database is now fully and freely available for online interrogation, hosted by the University of Western Sydney.[1] It is the product of an extraordinary collaborative effort between Simon and me as historians and a number of technical specialists, most notably Sarah Kattau and Henry Merivale of the now defunct Leeds Electronic Text Centre, and Vincent Hiribarren.[2] Unlocking previously inaccessible facets of the Neuchâtel collection, the FBTEE database records the production, acquisition and distribution of nearly 450,000 physical copies of 3,987 different single-volume and multivolume editions in 70,584 distinct STN transactions. Each transaction is fleshed out in the fullest possible manner, from the enhanced bibliographical details of the editions traded – their authors, editors, translators, publication dates, format, genre and so forth – to the precise geolocated business address of the buyer and even the shipping references stamped onto the outbound books crates.[3] Because this information is stored in a complex MySQL database comprised of almost 100 interrelated tables, each containing multiple fields, scholars can expediently output more query results than they might ever hope to analyse.

Any researcher interested in how many novels the STN sold to Burgundy, or how rapidly stocks of each separate volume of Voltaire's *Questions sur l'Encyclopédie* (n.p. [Neuchâtel]: [Société typographique de Neuchâtel], 1771–2) were exhausted, will quickly find their prize! In part due to this scope and flexibility, the FBTEE database has already attracted considerable attention and generous praise from scholars, digitally focused and otherwise, from across the humanities.[4]

Publicizing and discussing the broad utility of the database led us to Cambridge, Chicago, Copenhagen, Edinburgh, Helsinki, Neuchâtel, Oxford, Sydney, Washington and beyond.[5] The longer these travels continued the more, without always quite feeling qualified, we found ourselves being introduced as database specialists, 'digital' humanists, and speaking from podiums about interfaces and data streams. I swotted up on Graphical Information Systems (GIS), fretted over the nature of 'born digital' resources and data preservation techniques, and turned my reading attention towards curious new journals like *Information Visualisation* and *Digital Humanities Quarterly*. I got drawn into blogosphere debates and exchanged tweets. Despite spending my weekends retracing the steps of Jean-Jacques Rousseau in the wooded mountains that loom over Neuchâtel, the closest I got to brushing with his great texts was through data and metadata. Grasping for the rim of this digital rabbit hole, on stage at the Baird Auditorium of the American Museum of Natural History in Washington, DC, during the Society for the History of Authorship, Reading and Publishing's annual conference for 2011, I attempted to make a stand. I confessed that this was all too much, insisted that our database was a mere tool, and assured the audience that the things that really mattered were *these* twin monographs about the Enlightenment book trade.[6]

The conference twitter stream ran red. Fellow panellist Matthew Kirschenbaum, author of one of the most important contributions to the field of digital humanities of recent times, smelt a dinosaur and suggested that equating a database to a dumb tool was unhelpful.[7] He was right. The core FBTEE archival data stream is not a digital surrogate of any set of BPUN documents, but a unique and original object pieced together selectively from fragments of information scattered throughout the STN account books. Its construction required the regular taking of interpretive decisions concerning, say, the meaning of irregular accounting practices or the relative reliability of conflicting sales records. And the post-archival refinement and enrichment that was necessary to turn this stream into the final FBTEE dataset drew upon shelves of secondary literature and required the detailed investigation of hundreds of problematic cases. The database that emerged from this work is, in short, as lovingly and *subjectively* shaped as any work of academic scholarship, only with logs and fields in the place of paragraphs and pages. Further, freed from the constraints of narrative and the desire to impose meaning, the FBTEE database boasts a level of objective rigour that oftentimes proves difficult to achieve in research monographs. By design it encourages users to manipulate temporal, spatial and source information in order to probe their research questions from multiple perspectives. And it houses a concentration of bibliographic and bibliometric discovery – important new data concerning thousands of authors, texts, themes, actors and book-trade centres – that could never find a practicable home in print. It captures and celebrates complexity and comprehensiveness.

Nonetheless, the FBTEE database suffers from certain shortcomings that are best addressed by more traditional scholarly forms. A typical simple database query output reveals that, say, 500 copies of the first volume of the STN's printing of the baron d'Holbach's atheist *Système de la nature* (London [Neuchâtel]: [Société typographique de Neuchâtel], n.d. [1771]) were sent to the Brussels book dealer Jean-Louis de Boubers, via the middlemen Luc Preiswerck in Basle and 'Leclerc' in Metz, on 7 March 1771. But without more contextual information than the database can straightforwardly provide – without, for example, some understanding of the STN's early 1770s growth strategies and the unique role that all Swiss printers played in the European trade in mail-order books – it is difficult to derive *meaning* from such precise data points. Further, because the database contains no knowledge of the current state of scholarly enquiry, even where query outputs can be adequately interpreted it is impossible for all but the keenest of specialists to discern which of them *matter*. With well over a million discreet pieces of data housed, those illuminating sales and purchases and exchanges that most challenge, extend or confirm our current understanding of particular authors, works or trading relationships are frightfully well hidden! Advanced queries – perhaps of the 'top-selling' scientific works to the Italian Peninsula during the 1780s or the principal cities to which the STN sold novels – certainly reveal more telling snapshots and provoke more searching questions than does the raw data. But only by analysing lengthy strings of purposely chosen queries and by setting them in conversation with both comparable contemporary sources and the fruits of modern historical enquiry – only, in short, by forging scholarly argument from its normal stuff – can the most important secrets of the FBTEE database be revealed.[8]

Through its focus on the history of the STN and the functioning of the European francophone book trade, the current volume aims to both unveil some of these secrets and offer a platform from which others might see still further. Many readers, of course, will be familiar with the STN from the evocative sketches of shady scandalmongers and moonlit smuggling runs across the Swiss border that litter Robert Darnton's rich body of work on early modern publishing and the circulation of clandestine literature in pre-Revolutionary France.[9] If here some of Darnton's grander narratives will be put to question, every paragraph is nonetheless profoundly indebted to the experimental spirit, encyclopaedic understanding and pitch-perfect tone of joyous writings like 'The High Enlightenment and the Low-Life of Literature in Pre-Revolutionary France' and *The Business of Enlightenment*.[10] From the work of Darnton and the dozens of fellow *dix-huitièmistes* that have graced the BPUN's lakeside reading room over the past half-century – Jeffrey Freedman, Renato Pasta, Michel Schlup, Jacques Rychner and Dominique Varry among them – we already know a lot about the STN and its clients. A clutch of writings has explained the quotidian functioning of the Neuchâtel presses and revealed how the Society negotiated with its suppliers, authors, intermediaries and censors.[11] Numerous studies have pieced together the STN's trade with groups of clients based in specific cities or regions, including Italy, Lyon, Poland, Saint Petersburg and Moscow.[12] Bibliographical grind has uncovered the significant majority of the works that the STN published.[13] And several meticulous treatments have detailed the production and reception of the Society's most noteworthy publishing ventures, including its expanded re-edition of the Academy of Science's *Descriptions des arts et métiers* (Neuchâtel, Société typographique de Neuchâtel, 1771–83) and the quarto third edition of Diderot and d'Alembert's famous *Encyclopédie* (Neuchâtel and Geneva: Jean-Léonard Pellet and Société typographique de Neuchâtel, 1778–9).[14]

Many of these important writings share a case study-based methodological approach that owes much to the contours of the extant sources and their organization in the BPUN archive. Regrettably, the STN's directors left no formal records of their strategic decision making, no diaries or memoirs, and the entire run of the Society's overview 'Grand livre' account books are missing. And because the many subsidiary account books that have survived are extremely fragmented and impossible to fully decipher without specialist knowledge of early modern bookkeeping, they have rarely been used by historians.[15] Scholarly attention, instead, has generally focused upon the substantially complete collection of 24,000 letters that the STN received from its correspondents, which are organized into dossiers for each individual client and meticulously described in a card-index system that gives that client's location and profession, the volume and dates of their correspondence with the Neuchâtelois, the presence of supplementary documents such as trade catalogues or legal argument in the dossier, and so forth.[16] Researchers on the hunt for, say, the STN's dealings with the booksellers of Lyon, find upon hundreds of letters brimming with valuable information about many aspects of the trade. But what the letters do not readily yield – and what, by consequence, fifty years of intermittent archival work has yet to satisfactorily furnish – is a clear view of the history and purpose of the STN.[17] What were its directors trying to achieve? How did their plans change over time? What sorts of books did the Society sell? How important was the much-discussed illegal sector to its plans? Why did the STN fail? There is so much still to know.

The FBTEE database provides a new backbone – a near complete series of enriched and geolocated sales and purchase records – that helps us to understand the evolution of the STN's primary business from its first shipments in 1769 to its protracted liquidation during the early 1790s. This data spine lays bare the Society's strategic manoeuvres, from its attempts to profit from the popularity of certain authors, genres and book formats to its constantly evolving efforts to tap specific regional markets, on a day-by-day and volume-by-volume basis. In the softness of the STN's sales to its core customer base, and in its total failure to profitably and sustainably ship its products to key book-trade cities including Paris and Amsterdam, we can begin to understand the difficulties that led to its slow decline and ultimate liquidation. And in the evolution of the volumes held in Neuchâtel – for the database allows us to examine exactly what the Society stocked at any given moment – we can clearly see what sort of book business the STN was. For sure, the new data spine has its limitations and brings its own set of potential distortions to our reading. It fails, for example, to satisfactorily include important products of the Neuchâtel presses – news sheets, ephemera (from lottery tickets to fire regulations) and larger subscription projects like the *Descriptions des arts et métiers* – that the STN declined to account for in its standard fashion. And where the granularity and flexibility of the database encourages the user to anachronistically apply modern techniques of enterprise analytics to an early modern business it must be treated with some caution. The STN's directors, it must be remembered, considered monitoring even bottom line profitability an unnecessary distraction. But if treated carefully and if seen as a spine that helps us to contextualize and bring together decades of formidable scholarly work drawn from the STN letter collections, then the FBTEE database represents a promising route towards a new telling of the quite extraordinary history of the STN.

Better knowing the STN is of particular interest, of course, because its story can further our understanding of how the eighteenth-century French-language book trade functioned. The approach taken in this volume builds upon a body of great work concerning historical geographical book trade networks that has emerged since the seminal sixth chapter of Lucien Febvre and Henri-Jean Martin's *L'apparition du livre* (Paris, 1957-8) and, more recently, Bertrum MacDonald and Fiona Black's GIS blueprint 'Using GIS for Spatial and Temporal Analysis in Print Culture Studies: Some Opportunities and Challenges'.[18] The geographers of the book of this school have generally focused upon pinpointing trade actors, assets, infrastructures and institutions in time and space: the setting up of new presses and printing shops; the numbers of booksellers active in particular towns, cities, regions or states; the forms and locations of guilds, inspection chambers and customs barriers; the roads and waterways down which books travelled; and so forth. Their method has proved most thrilling when delineating the frontiers of printing – from the explosive growth seen in post-Gutenberg Europe to the arrival of presses in Canadian towns alongside cases of chocolate or rum – where the formation of new networks can be caught in motion.[19] Yet it has shown itself no less valuable when applied to historical periods and places, including our own, where printing was well established and print infrastructures and institutions were firmly embedded. Thierry Rigogne's exceptional study of French booksellers and printers lays bare the state's unexpectedly coherent and successful push to ensure a contraction in the number of print shops in operation over the course of the century of lights.[20] In the process Rigogne, if read alongside a number of previous writings, gives us a detailed and coherent view of the shape of France's bookselling and printing networks.[21] And, although we lack broadly focused studies of French-language publishing networks beyond the kingdom's borders, the work of the likes of Georges Bonnant, Silvio Corsini and Paul Hoftijzer provides much hard detail concerning the publishing infrastructures that were established in specific Dutch and Swiss towns, cities and regions.[22]

This large and important body of scholarly work, then, means that we already understand a great deal about the remarkable density and connectedness of eighteenth-century Europe's French-language book trade networks. We know, too, much about the legal and custumal frameworks that underpinned the trade in France and elsewhere, with particular attention having been focused upon the question of censorship and the century-long search to find an equitable and productive balance of power between the Parisian, provincial and extraterritorial presses.[23] What we lack, however, is even a rudimentary understanding of how books really flowed around these networks. Almost every book or article ever written about the eighteenth-century book trade, from expansive and ambitious projects like Darnton's *The Business of Enlightenment* to detailed microstudies such as Gilles Eboli's *Livres et lecteurs en Provence au XVIIIe siècle*, does, of course, contain valuable information about the flow of French books around Europe. But issues of scope and representativeness have left critical questions beyond the reach of these studies, both individually and collectively. Of course French-language books could and did regularly travel between Amsterdam and Paris, between London and Lausanne and between Lyon and Rome during the Enlightenment. But which books? In what relative volumes? Via which routes? And through which trade actors? If the FBTEE database and the current volume might hope to extend the rich body of existing scholarship concerning the eighteenth-century francophone book trade, it is by providing a model to show the value of reorienting our enquiries towards questions of flow.[24]

The complex structures of the FBTEE database were designed by the project team to capture the flow of books in and out of Neuchâtel, as detailed in the STN account books, as completely as possible. The first of three principal interlinked sections shown in Figure 0.1, comprised of 'clients' tables and denoted 'A', allows for the full desciption of the vast network of interconnected businesses and private individuals that interacted with the STN. These tables contain information about the location and commercial purpose of each of the Society's 2,895 contacts, as well as biographical details (gender, profession, social status and so forth) relating to named individuals and the number of business letters held in the BPUN archives for each correspondent. The data has been structured in such a way as to reflect the reality that actors moved between partnerships and changed location as their fortunes developed over time. A second section, marked 'B', enables the full bibliograhical description – dozens of fields of authorship and publication details as well as keyword *and* issue tree categorization – of the books that the STN sourced from and dispatched to this client network. Each individual volume of a book 'set' is treated independently, so to allow the database to deal elegantly with the reality that early modern books were often sent to clients in stages. The final section and true heart of the FBTEE database, designated 'C', links these richly described books to the flexible client network graph by enabling an exhaustive

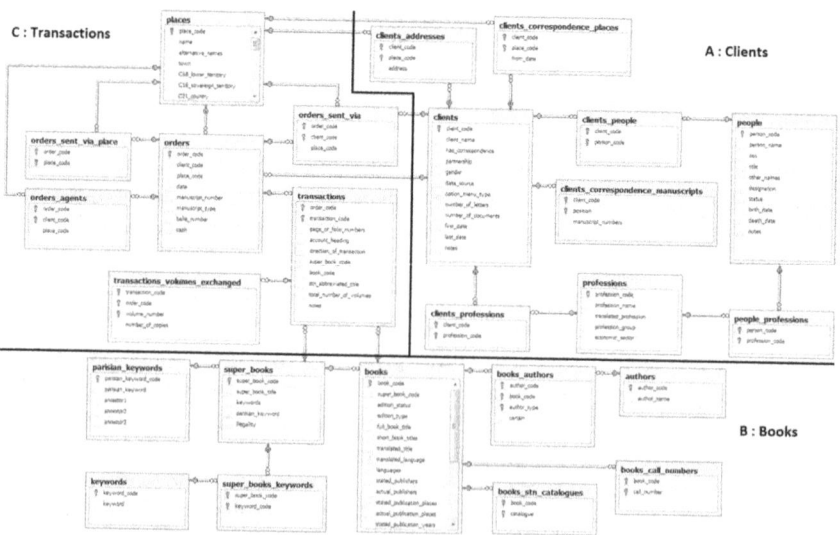

Figure 0.1 FBTEE database schema, by Sarah Kattau and Henry Merivale.

description of the STN's extensive trading transactions. Populated with details of over 70,000 transactions, it tracks the movement across space and through time of 445,496 copies of 3,987 different editions that were exchanged between the STN and their clients between 1769 and 1794.[25] It reveals from where almost every individual volume that the STN traded was sourced, to where the Society's printings and purchases were dispatched, and precisely when and with whom all of those transactions were made. Where the manuscript information allows, the precise route via which the Society's books reached their final destination, often involving several staging posts and named middlemen, is also described.

It will be shown throughout this volume that better knowing how books flowed around the STN's networks extends our understanding of the European trade in fundamental and surprising ways. Robert Darnton bet the methodological validity of his award-winning 1995 *The Forbidden Best-Sellers of Pre-Revolutionary France* on the 'hunch' that French booksellers around Europe each traded in more-or-less the same 'floating' stock of books. In order to diversify their offerings and reduce commercial risk, Darnton suggested, European French-language publishers from Amsterdam to Geneva swapped large proportions of their new publications as soon as they left the presses.[26] The STN, then, traded in more-or-less the same books as its European competitors and, as such, its order books could be taken as more-or-less representative of the wider trade. Early in the process of constructing the FBTEE database, however, it became very clear that the STN's purchase and sales patterns were actually very different from those predicted by Darnton. Most strikingly, the Neuchâtelois appeared to have almost exclusively stocked Swiss editions sourced locally, and seemed to have sent intriguingly little to key book-trade towns including Paris, Amsterdam and London. Where the nodes of the STN's network of contacts suggested a thoroughly cosmopolitan business, then, the sales and purchase data flowing down the network's edges and paths suggested a more limited and complicated reality.

The data also indicated that most of those books held public attention for a remarkably limited amount of time. Because the STN only traded for a relatively short period – officially 1769–94, although the Society was being wound down from 1784 and did almost no business after 1788 – their account books cannot provide direct answers to expansive questions concerning how the Enlightenment book trade changed over the course of the eighteenth century. Nonetheless, because the ledgers contain information pertaining to the complete and partial exhaustion of hundreds of individual editions, they do give us an unprecedented insight into the temporal life of books on the eve of the French Revolution. Most of all, they reveal the extent to which the international francophone Enlightenment book trade was organized to shift *nouveautés* and, by extension, they show the difficulty with which the STN found placing works that were even only a few years old. Some specific types of books – certain religious texts and school books most notably – were in regular demand over a sustained period of time. But almost all of the STN's regular 'Enlightenment' editions – from popular histories to travelogues to the philosophical works of Voltaire and Rousseau – became devilishly difficult to shift after only a couple of years on the market. Even the very best of late-eighteenth-century best sellers, the STN wholesale channel data suggests, enjoyed limited commercial longevity.

With this clearer view of the temporal and spatial flows of the francophone book trade, it might be noted, we are still some distance from proposing answers to some of the more ambitious questions that inspired the construction of the FBTEE database. Of course, no superabundance of data – not even a perfect dataset of every volume bought and sold across Europe from every printer across the entirety of the eighteenth century – could ever settle complex humanistic debates such as those concerning the nature of the Enlightenment or whether books cause revolutions. Knowing that readers of the 1770s and 1780s delighted in the middlebrow novels of Madame Riccoboni more regularly than the epoch-defining philosophical writings of Montesquieu or Hobbes, as is perfectly obvious from the bibliographical record of works printed, hardly convinces literary scholars or intellectual historians that her works were particularly influential or important. And significant issues surrounding the definition of books and their contents – how a two-page pamphlet may be compared to a full set of the *Encyclopédie* or what might be considered a 'religious' or 'Enlightenment' text – will forever render statistical approaches to book history problematic. Further, the extant hard data residing in Europe's archives and rare book rooms manifestly fails to give us an even view of early-modern informational culture, and falls still further short of allowing us to understand the mental worlds of eighteenth-century readers. Once sold, how did books circulate between private individuals, such as family members, and in formal and informal spaces of exchange, from reading rooms to coffee houses? How might we account for the fact that some books sold well despite offending and disappointing both reviewers and general readers? And were not books, anyhow, just one small part of a wider early-modern information economy made up of several competing forms of print, including newspapers, pamphlets and periodicals, and an even wider world of oral exchange that took place in academies, salons, pubs and cafés, public places, churches, educational establishments, in the home and at the workplace?

Historians of early-modern information culture, of course, regularly wrestle with each of these issues, and understand the limitations of using 'best-sellers' figures to address the field's most intriguing questions.[27] Still more problematically, or at least more immediately disquieting for our purposes, the archives of the STN do not allow us to straightforwardly produce such lists, as was once hoped. Because he mistakenly believed that Europe's francophone booksellers traded in more-or-less the same 'floating stock' of books, Robert Darnton saw the STN papers as a source sufficiently representative to uncover the forbidden best sellers of pre-Revolutionary France. Alas, the Swiss only sold Swiss books and most of France's books, illegal or otherwise, were not printed in Switzerland. The FBTEE database reveals that books never floated gracefully around Europe, they ground their way down highways and waterways haemorrhaging profitability and approaching fierce competition by the kilometre. If that insight goes some way towards justifying the FBTEE project's exhaustive digital methodological approach to the sources, it also problematizes its wider purpose by bringing the question of the representativeness of the STN squarely into focus. If the STN only sold Swiss books, then can its archives really tell us much about the wider course of European history? Further, the extraordinary detail captured by the FBTEE database allows for an unprecedented and, at times, alarming view of the inadequacies and biases of the source upon which it is constructed. The STN underwent such an extreme cycle of growth and decline – the Society's stock holdings, for example, exploded from just 10 titles two years after its 1769 establishment to over 1,500 by 1785 – as to render many sales comparisons over time, or to competitors enjoying a more sedate existence, largely meaningless. Its business ambitions and market orientation changed markedly as the years passed. And the fortunes of the STN's editions owed as much to a backdrop of massive instability in the Swiss market, as well as changing international regulatory environments, as to their intrinsic value as saleable products. A representative source and a shortcut towards knowing European reading tastes on the eve of the French Revolution? Not likely!

And yet, the spatial and temporal reappraisal of the European francophone book trade that the FBTEE database encourages reveals more profound truths than we might have ever hoped. For sure, books represent just one constituent part of the eighteenth-century public sphere and, when addressing the influence of the circulation of ideas and information on contemporary events and mentalities, we must never lose sight of the crucial roles played by cafés, law courts, salons, sermons, academy-sponsored essay competitions and many other forms or forums of intellectual exchange. But the authors of books were so thoroughly embedded within the overlapping networks that underpinned and nourished each of these spaces and types of media, that their works betray a luxuriant, if admittedly sometimes unbalanced, view of the entire public sphere. Essay prize entries, trial briefs and sermons were directly published and the contents of many a private conversation held in the hallways of Versailles, on the streets of Paris or in some exclusive salon worked their ways, in one form or another, into books. Further, because a relatively small number of late-eighteenth-century French-language books are lost – of the many thousands of works mentioned in the STN papers, at least one copy of one edition of only a handful cannot now be located somewhere in the world's library systems – the record that they provide is not only rich, but sufficiently comprehensive to invite systematic study. Far from marginalizing books as symbols of a rarefied *philosophe* Enlightenment current only among certain circles of intellectual historians, then, a broad approach to information exchange and the public sphere cements their place at the centre of our understanding. And while it would be wholly unreasonable to expect the STN archives to provide an uncomplicated way of knowing about a large part of this world, they do provide an exhaustive view of one of its important constituent parts. If the specific editions that bounced around the STN's segment of the trade were not entirely and exactly representative of the broad whole, it is the contention of this volume that the Society's travails in selling books in a European marketplace that was regionally variegated, obsessed with *nouveautés*, fickle and capricious, and in the thralls of power and money, betray much about the fabric of the wider Enlightenment. More, indeed, than could any list of best sellers.

This book's efforts to begin to chart the flows of the eighteenth-century French-language book trade unfold across five principal argumentative chapters, each of which is more broadly focused than its predecessor. They examine, in turn, the history of the rise of the STN; the Society's role in the Swiss book production nexus; the international markets served by that productive zone; the turbulent trading conditions that brought Swiss publishing to its knees during the 1780s; and, finally, the intellectual geography and temporal rhythms of the Enlightenment book trade. Chapter 1, 'A Printing Shop

Across the Border', then, locates the STN in space and explains the commercial and political circumstances of their 1770s ascent, so as to provide the contextual grounding necessary for any use of the FBTEE database's bibliometric data. Neuchâtel, situated in a relatively central part of the European book market's long-established heartlands – a western diagonal running from London to Venice through the Low Countries – was well placed to profit from buoyant international demand for French-language books. Yet despite burgeoning watchmaking and lacemaking industries, the town and its regional dependencies remained relatively underdeveloped and, even by Swiss standards, somewhat off the beaten track. Despite many efforts, the establishment of a book-producing printing shop in Neuchâtel had never quite proven sustainable, and the STN came into being at a moment of particular crisis in the Swiss book trade. During its first decade of trading, changes in leadership, an increasingly mature understanding of the trade, and the demands of investment capital led the Society towards several strategic shifts. The amateurishness of its directors' first moves, it will be argued, slowly gave way to a measured and insightful approach that allowed the STN to grow towards the point of genuine European significance.

What the STN's directors and their trade counterparts in the Swiss Romand understood, Chapter 2, 'The Myth of the Mountain Dwellers' contends, was how to work together to produce a compelling product in broad demand across Europe. They sold cheap, French-language, of-the-moment, locally produced books. They largely avoided technical and scientific works likely to attract only limited and distant audiences and specialized in novels and travelogues and collections of sermons that publics everywhere devoured. Bound together by their mutual interest in the success of this common product, these Swiss *maisons d'édition*, despite constant skirmishing over specific deals, operated as an informal cartel. They shared information, coordinated publication decisions and worked together to promote their wares. And because they regularly swapped stocks among themselves, they all offered more-or-less the same books to their international clientele. It is the story of these cheap, contemporary, Swiss books that the FBTEE database most straightforwardly reveals.

And what a story! Current scholarly understanding of the eighteenth-century francophone book trade, based largely on static network models, has given the impression that few areas were beyond the Neuchâtelois' reach. The STN, the story goes, effortlessly sold and swapped books to London and Amsterdam and Paris and Rome. Where local or national authorities were so bold as to attempt to intervene, they were outwitted by an army of brave and wily smugglers strapping packs to their backs and heading off across moonlit mountain trails or sowing printed sheets into the hems of their dresses. Chapter 3, 'The Republic of Books' offers a tour of the STN's entire sales around Europe so as to reveal how much harsher the grind of the international francophone book trade proved in reality. The Society never managed to conduct lucrative business in Paris and failed to establish profitable ties with the traders of the book-producing cities of the Low Countries. The printers of those places fiercely protected their own interests and repelled the threat of Swiss books with quite astonishing efficacy. And their influence over the booksellers of significant hinterlands across Northern Europe left the STN starved of sales to the continent's most profitable literary markets. The commercial space of the republic of books was shaped not by a 'war of all against all', as one contemporary suggested, but by actions of powerful competitive trading blocks that have hitherto largely gone unnoticed.[28]

The 1780s, Chapter 4, 'The Storm Will Pass', reveals, were ruinous times for the Swiss book industry. Squeezed by a collapse in the market for Latin works in Southern Europe and hard competition for French books from their northern rivals, one by one long-established businesses were failing. Unencumbered by large stocks of unsaleable old books, the STN had achieved rapid growth during the 1770s in direct defiance of the broader industry trend. But with growth came mounting debts, operational complexity, enormous stockpiles of printed paper and, increasingly, an acute realization that the business was unsustainable and would collapse without change. After years of experimentation with journal and prestige publishing, and following a spell formalizing ties with fellow Swiss publishers for mutual protection, the STN's directors tried something radical. Alongside several other newly formed Neuchâtelois publishing ventures linked to the former STN director Samuel Fauche, they started to find arrangements that allowed the Society to print enormous runs of editions of dubious legality by the likes of Jacques-Pierre Brissot and Louis-Sébastien Mercier to be sold on the streets of Paris. The works touched upon dangerous themes, not least the unsustainable burden of France's public debt and the despotism of France's political elites. And the timing of their publication was particularly perilous. In London, the slanderous publications of a clique of blackmailer *libellistes* were also proving enough of a nuisance as to invite direct repressive measures.[29] Rattled and pressurized, through directives passed in 1783 and 1784, the chapter shows, the French state did something that most historians of the trade contend was beyond their powers: they closed the Swiss border to book imports. Mercier advised the STN to hold its nerve – the storm would surely pass. Instead it gathered force. The entire international French book trade, bound together by complex credit arrangements, dipped into a prolonged crisis from which only the very strongest houses survived. The STN, under administration, looked eastwards for several years, chasing down demand in unlikely markets and limping towards collapse. At least it enjoyed good company. The Bourbon monarchy that was partially to blame for the Society's undoing, crippled itself by terrible debt and answering public accusations of despotism with provocatively despotic actions, was taking the first steps of its own dance with death.

This book's conclusion, Chapter 5, 'Selling Enlightenment', orients us back towards the wider goals of the FBTEE project. It argues that while the limits of the STN's business and its turbulent history complicate the task of employing FBTEE data to discern broad Enlightenment reading tastes, they reveal much about the nature of the Enlightenment on the eve of the French Revolution. First, the chapter suggests that the remarkably small window of time for which even the most popular works held public attention kept Enlightenment debate dynamic and relevant and limited the inclination to fetishize great writing of the past. That even the most popular books of the 1770s were of little interest to STN buyers during the 1780s, it contends, adds support for approaches to the Enlightenment focused upon transfer and intertextuality and casts further doubt upon the value of narrow academic approaches obsessed with a small group of *grands hommes* and their clever writings. Second, it argues that the reality that Europe's bookshops were not all stocked with the same books amounts to something important. The Swiss Enlightenment revealed by the FBTEE database was different enough to that read and spoken in Paris, Marseille, London or Amsterdam to have subtly altered the way that different individuals and populations viewed the world. And third, it argues that the Enlightenment's fabric was both subject to manipulation by those with capital or influence and prone to sudden and significant ruptures. The process of selling enlightenment was not an exercise in selecting the most commendable texts for the purpose of the equitable advancement of society; for the STN, at least, it proved an object lesson in the emergence of deep proto capitalist tensions between commercial worth and literary worthiness, between free trade and protectionism and, ultimately, between acting with moral integrity and surviving. It was quite an art!

The narrative argument that unfolds across these five principal chapters is broken up by two supportive case studies. The first employs an analysis of the production and dissemination of a typical STN printing, the *Histoire de François Wills, ou Le triomphe de la bienfaisance* (Neuchâtel, 1773) to broach questions of how the STN's business integrated into the wider European book industry. A faithful translation of an undistinguished and anonymously published English novel, this French-language edition was marketed as a new work by Oliver Goldsmith, the author of the spectacularly popular *The Vicar of Wakefield* (Salisbury, 1766). Despite the text demonstrating little of the Irishman's charm, the Neuchâtelois quickly shifted their entire 1,500-copy print run. By comparing the publishing history of *François Wills* to both other STN editions and our wider understanding of the trade, this chapter shows the remarkable contemporaneousness of the book business and suggests that the publishing profiles of European *maisons d'édition* varied subtly across space. The second case study, for contrast, reminds us that while searching for the typical is important, it should not prevent us from learning from the truly exceptional. During the course of 1779, as messy divorce proceedings began to unfold, the brilliant Genevan economist and market speculator Théodore Rilliet de Saussure hatched a dastardly plan that led him to a watery grave. He accused his wife Ursule of having confessed, on their very wedding night, to having previously borne an incestuous love child to her brother the baron de Planta. After serving time in prison and being stripped of his citizenship, Rilliet decided, during 1782 and 1783, to employ the STN's presses to take his ill-advised fight to one last tribunal – the international court of public opinion. The editions that emerged – impossibly incendiary, printed in an innovative and unusual format and marketed by blackmail – show the STN at their worst, as the financial pressures of the 1780s mounted. And they take us to the heart of what was really considered beyond the pale in the international pre-Revolutionary European publishing industry. How many of Enlightenment's leading lights, after all, ended up floating face down in Lake Geneva for their toils?

Finally, also interspersed into the narrative are two chapters that explain the methodological approach employed by the FBTEE project, as well as the archival sources used. The first of these, 'Bookkeeping Made Simple', discusses the historical circumstances of the remarkable, but not actually unique, survival of the STN account books. It explains the nature of early modern accounting and the benefits and limitations of the system of double-entry accounting that the Neuchâtelois employed.

It describes how the FBTEE team managed to piece together a trail through the surviving documents that led to the reconstruction of the STN's extensive bookselling activities. For many readers, this methodological explanation of the foundations upon which the FBTEE database was constructed might prove more than enough academic naval gazing! But for the more intrepid, and especially for committed enthusiasts of the digital humanities, a supplementary appendix essay, 'Coding and Decoding the French Book Trade', provides further methodological particulars. It details how considerable challenges faced during the conception, construction and utilization of each of the major parts of the FBTEE database – clients, transactions and books – were overcome.

All of this – these arguments and chapters and methodological interludes – amounts to a somewhat traditional scholarly monograph, albeit one designed to accompany an online resource. After I had outlined some of the features of the FBTEE database at a small Cambridge book history workshop held in the spring of 2012, William St Clair rhetorically challenged me to list the digital humanities projects that have really transformed our field in the manner that printed academic books have done so regularly and with so much less bluster. The comment was good humoured and meaningful: 'Well, you certainly *talk* a good game!' And it drove home the important point that scholarly monuments like St Clair's *The Reading Nation in the Romantic Period* draw upon such a rich variety of sources, as well as lifetimes of scholarly endeavour and hard-won insight, that their continued place at the top of the learned tree is unlikely to be threatened by digital upstarts anytime soon.[30] So what might, I wondered, beyond the gratitude of a few university bean counters happy to see research money being spent and 'impact' clicks garnered, justify the effort and expense of creating a resource as limited in overall scope as the FBTEE database? I would like to suggest that the current volume, and the FBTEE project more generally, should be judged not only according to its success in advancing our understanding of our chosen research questions – that is a given, and the standard to which all scholarly work must be held – but also on the extent that its major arguments could not have been reasonably arrived at without recourse to its digital methodological approach. And so if the conclusions presented here are sometimes modest, they might at least hint at the transformational potential of digital approaches that will, given the necessary time and funding to mature, feed into the next wave of great works of book history, Enlightenment studies and many more fields.

Most of all, this volume aims simply to do justice to the richness of the STN ledgers. *Selling Enlightenment* is an early-modern business saga – of supply and demand, risk and reward, ambition and collapse – that played out across the entire European canvas. It is a political and economic story – of contraband, credit and realpolitik – that foreshadowed revolutionary change. And finally, it is a tale of multiple Enlightenments, with a bankruptcy, a suspicious death and a cankerous horse. Ah, so much lofty ambition!

1

A Printing Shop across the Border

Guidebook in hand, on 9 September 1776 the British traveller William Coxe entered the Prussian-governed Swiss principality of Neuchâtel from the direction of Lausanne and Lake Geneva.[1] The slender sloping plain along which he travelled was, and remains, hemmed in between the heavily forested southern slopes of the Jura mountain range and the forty-kilometre-long Lake Neuchâtel. Like an ever-increasing stream of tourists, Coxe had come to see at first-hand the peculiar inventiveness and enlightenment of the region's inhabitants. The watchmaking and lacemaking industries were booming, examples of the technological and organizational advances beginning to revolutionize European commerce, and stories of underground water mills and clavier-playing automata intrigued. Jean-Jacques Rousseau had lived in the Neuchâtelois' mountains during the 1760s, and had there placed the 'Arcadie' of his 1758 classic *Lettre à d'Alembert sur les spectacles*. For sure, the Enlightenment literary landscape was littered with such fantasies of paradise, but most came from traveller's tales of the South Seas, harked back to an idealized past or dared to imagine a different future.[2] A utopia located in the heart of contemporary Europe demanded first-hand investigation.

Along the lakeside road, Coxe passed the castle at Grandson where Charles the Bold of Burgundy's mercenary army had famously been routed by the Swiss in 1476. He admired the 'pleasantness' of the vineyards, meadows and cornfields that covered the inclines – the terrain criss-crossed by low stone walls and mountain streams and dotted with hamlets and villages. He dined in little Colombier, home to the pioneering writer and *salonnière* Isabelle de Charrière and her husband Charles-Emmanuel, with a couple who he considered personified the good breeding of the Swiss gentry. He crossed Serrières with its river-hugging sliver of forges and foundries buried in a gorge so steep-sided as to be practically invisible from the plain. Eventually, he arrived at the western gate of the town of Neuchâtel with a single objective in mind: to understand how several generations of progress had elevated this region from a witch-hunting backwater to an exemplar of new ways of thinking and doing business. His reading matter, the STN director Samuel Ostervald's *Description des montagnes … de Neuchâtel et Valangin*, suggested that his travels would be rewarded with insights into how the freedom of the Neuchâtelois fortified their morality, and how their isolation bred creativity and industry. Yet pinning down exactly *why* this region was so special would not be easy; Ostervald concluded that there was just something in the air.[3]

From the western gate, positioned forebodingly between dungeon and prison tower, a handful of streets cascaded down towards the river Seyon, along which Neuchâtel's dense medieval core was crowded. These streets rose steeply on the Seyon's far banks, dramatically corseting the town into a narrow canyon. Yet Neuchâtel's 3,000 strong population would hardly have felt claustrophobic. Towards the lakeside the town's streets fanned out to reveal spacious public places, a tree-lined waterfront boulevard, a small port and 100-kilometre vistas across the lake, the Fribourgeois plateau and towards the perennially snow-capped Alps. Occupying a plum waterfront location stood the print shop of the STN.

Had Coxe paid a visit, he would have found freshly pressed sheets of the *Feuille d'avis de Neuchâtel* and the *Nouveau Journal helvétique*, as well as the latest parts of the 'complete' works of Claude-Joseph Dorat, hanging drying from the rafters. Approaching 34,000 copies of over 500 different works filled the STN's stock room at the time, and the Society was advancing towards its 100,000th book sale.[4] The Englishman might have witnessed straw-lined crates of unbound sheets being packed and unpacked, since the Neuchâtelois processed fifteen orders during his stay. On 9 September, for example, they received shipments of highly illegal works from Gabriel Grasset and Jean-Samuel Cailler in Geneva, including fifty copies of the baron d'Holbach's wickedly anticlerical mock-theological dictionary *Théologie portative* and 100 examples of the underground pornographic classic *La fille de joie* (John Cleland's *Fanny Hill*). They sent consignments of books to the French towns of Bar-le-Duc, Dôle and Salins-les-bains, to the Swiss towns of Berne, Lausanne and Soleure and to the Austrian-Italian territory of Milan. Not that Coxe cared. Print shops were hardly exceptional and the STN, although large, was hardly an exceptional print shop. Anyhow, the Englishman was looking to create rather than consume literature; his account of this voyage around Switzerland later became an international bestseller. Its French translation was published in the nearby Swiss town of Lausanne in the spring of 1781 by François Grasset.[5]

Coxe's travelogue, Ostervald's guidebook, Cailler and Gabriel Grasset's subversive texts and the complete works of Dorat were all sold by the STN. They represent just a small subset of the 3,987 editions recorded in the FBTEE database. This bibliometric treasure trove commands attention, but, true to the account books it draws upon, its richness can overwhelm and its data can be difficult to interpret. What should be made, for example, of those fifty copies of d'Holbach's *Théologie portative* that arrived from Geneva in early September 1776? We can see that thirty-two among them were quickly dispatched to the modest French towns of Autun, Bar-le-Duc, Besançon, Melun and Tours. Perhaps this is worthy of further investigation or comment. But why preference these envois above others? The database, after all, records the shipment of 413,710 books. Perhaps, likewise, it is significant that François Grasset's edition of Coxe's travels was a steady seller throughout the 1780s. By the end of that decade, the STN had dispatched over 200 copies to Dublin, Hamburg, Lyon, Moscow, Paris and three dozen other towns across Europe. But, viewed at the 314th place in the Society's overall bestsellers table, registering 0.05 per cent of their total sales, the work appears unexceptional. Worse still, the bibliometrics can deceive. The STN shifted ten times as many copies of Dorat's nine-volume-collected works than Coxe's *voyage*. But, then, they *published* the Dorat collection, and simply resold Grasset's edition of Coxe. The numbers are thus uneven and treacherous. Nonetheless, by studying the bibliographical record and paying attention to temporal shifts in both the STN's developing business and trading conditions in the European francophone book market, significant patterns can be found, and sense can be made of years of archival toil. Having so thoroughly documented the trees, we must now attempt to make out the wood.

To begin, this chapter focuses upon the remarkable history of the STN. Following the spirit of Coxe's enquiries, it outlines the commercial and geopolitical importance of the location of Neuchâtel and the Swiss plateau. It discusses how and why printing and book wholesaling took hold there, and describes the story of the 1769 establishment of the Society under extraordinary political circumstances. It explains how the STN's business developed through fractious splits and strategic shifts. While it notes the remarkable size and pan-European reach that the publishing house attained at the height of its influence, it equally emphasizes the precariousness of the Neuchâtelois' trading model. This chapter has two purposes. First, it begins to provide the temporal and spatial context by which the bibliometric data in the FBTEE database might reasonably be interpreted. When evaluating the relative dissemination of texts by the likes of d'Holbach and Coxe, one has to constantly bear in mind the evolving size and market orientation of the STN's business. Likewise, a meaningful comparison of the Neuchâtelois' dealings with multiple clients, towns or regions across Europe depends upon a nuanced understanding of both the STN's constantly developing business relationships with their local rivals and allies, and the evolving position of the Romandy traders in the international market for French books. Second, it provides a potted history of the first decade of the STN's existence which, for all the Society's familiarity to specialists, is currently lacking, particularly in English. This new account recontextualizes previous scholarship using the spine of fresh data provided by the FBTEE database. It charts the remarkable rise of this printing shop across the French border during the 1770s.

It is not self-evident why small and isolated Neuchâtel should be an appropriate place from which to sell mail-order books in the late eighteenth century. To the south, the lake and Alps present horizon-wide barriers. Behind the town, to the north, brood the wooded mountains of the pre-Jura. Easterly passage might have appeared more inviting to contemporaries, but consumers of French books were largely limited to cosmopolitan elites in distant and disparate cities like Vienna, Berlin and Warsaw. To the west, the well-established Swiss book-trade towns of Yverdon, Lausanne and Geneva were all better placed to access Lyon, the de facto gateway to the French market. Neuchâtel, in short, was a world away from the upscale bookseller's boutiques of the Palais Royal in Paris, and slightly off the beaten track.

Nonetheless, Neuchâtel's location had certain advantages. Imagine two lines drawn on a map connecting London to Rome and Saint Petersburg to Cadiz. They would bisect somewhere over Lake Neuchâtel, giving the town a reasonable claim to European centrality. Moreover, by the eighteenth century the lake was navigable, and was connected via the rivers Thielle and Broye to the adjacent lakes of Bienne and Morat. From Morat, the small but bustling commercial town that shared its lake's name, Neuchâtelois merchandise could be forwarded by road in either direction across the Swiss plateau. The highway, which ran from Lyon to Basle via Geneva, Lausanne, Berne and Soleure, linked eastern France to the southern Germanic territories. From Lyon the river Rhône was navigable via Avignon to the Mediterranean. From Basle, the Rhine could be sailed through the Low Countries to the North Sea. As a consequence, this short and scenic track across the Swiss plateau was of international strategic and commercial significance as the only knot preventing goods from transecting the continent by cost-effective fluvial means. An ambitious project to connect the Swiss lakes by a series of canals began in the seventeenth century, although it never fully came to fruition.⁶

Centrality and connectedness ensured that Romandy printers could reach francophone reading publics which were genuinely scattered across the European map. Although late-eighteenth-century Europe played host to a number of strong vernacular printing traditions and public spheres – each exhibiting distinct characteristics – French remained the international language of the elites and French books were as necessary a part of a good library in the Swedish court as they were in an English country seat.⁷ It is somewhat paradoxical, then, that the Swiss Romand's additional market advantage lay in its *peripheral* location (see Figure 1.1), just beyond the borders of France. Taking advantage of relative freedoms to print, an arc of French-language print shops crowded France's eastern border, from the northern towns and cities of London, Amsterdam, Brussels and Bouillon through the Swiss heartlands of Lausanne, Geneva, Neuchâtel and Yverdon to the southern enclave of Avignon. These firms competed savagely and helped to sustain the literary culture of the French Enlightenment.⁸ The fortunes of individual houses rose and fell and, as we will see, turbulent times were coming for all, but at the time of the establishment of the STN Romandy printing was nonetheless extremely productive and competitive. A bibliographical sketch by Jean-Daniel Candaux suggests that ten foreign authors were printed in Switzerland in the first half of the eighteenth century, forty during the 1750s and 1760s, and seventy-eight during the 1770s and 1780s.⁹

Figure 1.1 The Swiss Romand.

This peculiarly Swiss fusion of centrality and marginality, as well as the fertility of the land and the relative political and religious freedom of its inhabitants, ensured that French-speaking Switzerland was a well-connected hive of commercial activity. The 1779 edition of Louis Dutens' popular guidebook for travellers listed nineteen staging posts between Lyon and Geneva and a further 26.5 to Basle. Visitors could reckon upon a suspiciously precise sixty-four hours twenty-four minutes to complete the journey.[10] En route, they would have passed through a string of richly diversified towns that played host to substantial professional classes. In total, 32 per cent (891 of 2,825) of the locatable businesses or individuals that either wrote to, or received letters from, the STN were based in territories bisected by the Basle–Lyon thoroughfare.[11] Of these correspondents, 214 were directly employed by the book trade; 208 worked in retail, commerce or manufacturing; 99 toiled in print-related trades; and 42 owed their livings to the postal, transportation or hospitality sectors.[12] In addition, 90 men of letters, 89 professionals, 72 officials and office holders, 65 clergymen and 26 military men exchanged correspondence with the Neuchâtelois.[13] These regional connections were among the STN's most engaged: together they penned 45 per cent (10,913 of 23,955) of the letters held in the archive.

A touch cut-off from the plenty of the plateau, the inhabitants of the principality of Neuchâtel had to find still more industrious occupations. Coxe's guidebook describes a regional landscape peppered with productive industries, from cannon powder manufactures in Champ-du-Moulin to stocking makers in Travers and paper producers in Serrières. The most lucrative activities were watchmaking, winemaking and lacemaking, the fruits of which made the region's economy export-driven and sufficiently wealthy for a significant service sector to develop.[14] By the 1750s, having built upon the successes of these industries, Neuchâtel was home to several key players in international commerce and banking – notably the families Pourtalès, Pury, Rougement and Perregaux.[15] Because these bourgeois men of business and letters dominated the region's politics, a virtuous circle of economic development was encouraged. With power and industry came leisure and enlightenment at every social level. Several salons, notably those of Alexandre Du Peyrou and Isabelle de Charrière emerged from the mid-century.[16] The sumptuous balls and *fêtes* of the Neuchâtel high society, complete with exquisite menus and beautiful girls, did not pass without comment from visitors.[17] And even the humble and courteous peasants of the towns, villages and hamlets of the Neuchâtelois mountains spent most of their free time reading, served by a network of circulating libraries.[18]

This, at least, is the story spun by the Neuchâtelois myth-makers. In reality, despite impressive proto-industrial development and steady demographic expansion, Neuchâtel's relative isolation ensured that the economies of both the town and its surroundings remained relatively limited.[19] A total of 335 STN correspondents, just 11.5 per cent of the total network, were based in the region. Digging much deeper into this part of the graph in search of comparators, however, would be unhelpful. The Society's local contacts were dominated by the individuals from commercial and manufacturing businesses, from grocers to tinsmiths, who supplied the print shop, occasionally bought a book or advertised in the *Nouveau Journal helvétique*. And most local interactions with the Society were, of course, conducted orally rather than by letter. Yet, hints of Neuchâtel's limitations are nonetheless to be found wherever one looks. The STN corresponded with only thirty professionals, eight postal-, transport- and hospitality-sector-workers and twenty-one book-trade employees (mainly their own workers and those related to the Fauche family) based in their own region. Anecdotal evidence also points towards lingering backwardness. The best way to get a message up to the Ponts-de-Martel on a Thursday, for example, was to pass it to the butter seller Susanne Jeanneret, who would deliver as she returned home from her day's trade.[20] Utopia-hunters like Coxe tended not to loiter in Neuchâtel, but instead headed for the mountains to marvel at Pierre Jaquet-Droz's extraordinary automata – including a pianist whose eyes followed her fingers as they danced across the keyboard of a custom built clavier striking out a tune. They were often surprised to find themselves forced to abandon their carriages by the lakeside to avoid damaging them along the region's rickety roads.

The history of printing in Neuchâtel also points towards this more modest reading. Between 1533 and 1535, the Frenchman Pierre de Vingle installed himself at the behest of Guillaume Farel, the regions' firebrand reformer. But this was an isolated affair, and it was not until the end of the seventeenth century, through Jean Pistorius (1664–1730) then later Jean David Griesser († after 1737), Moyse Gautier († after 1731), Abraham Boyve (1693–1767) and Samuel Fauche (1732–1803), that printing was established on a semi-permanent basis.[21] Several important texts, including the Bible and the biblical commentaries of Jean-Frédéric Ostervald, which were later reprinted and sold by the STN, and the first edition of Emer de Vattel's *Droit des gens* were printed in Neuchâtel prior to the establishment of the Society. A hint of controversies to come can also be located: the publication of the provocatively titled anonymous 1696 anti-Jesuit tract *L'art d'assasiner les rois, enseigné par les Jesuites à Louis XIV et Jacques II* led to the expulsion of its printer Jean-Jacques Schmid († after 1703) from the town.[22] However, the outputs of none of these pre-STN printers could be described as prolific. The bibliographical record suggests that they mainly survived through publishing religious and educational works for the local community, periodicals including the *Mercure Suisse* and *Feuille d'avis* from the 1730s, and more formal books only when the opportunity arose.

Such caution was born of the reality that establishing a successful printing shop *anywhere* in Europe was a difficult proposition. Admittedly, the set-up costs associated with printing – purchasing presses, associated equipment and renting suitable accommodation – were modest.[23] The real trick was managing liquidity. Printers needed to outlay substantial amounts of capital upfront each time they produced new editions. Paper and type was expensive (normally over 50% of the total costs of producing an edition), typographers' wages needed paying and type needed to be regularly renewed. Yet, problematically, they depended upon unpredictable revenue streams because demand for their wares was spastic. First, printers always struggled to spot the *gardes-magasins* – the warehouse-filling flops – from the bestsellers; such was the potential capriciousness of public opinion. Second, because copycat editions could be produced in a matter of days by distant and secretive competitors, the few guaranteed sensations that did appear always risked being over-produced. Third, buyers of most types of works were limited to the educated urban classes in France and dispersed francophone elites scattered throughout the rest of Europe. Locating demand was a time-consuming and costly undertaking. Fourth, even successful editions would take considerable time to realize a profit – not least because booksellers themselves tried to sell before they paid. In turn, all this uncertainty commanded still more capital, since the surest way to reduce risk was to publish several works simultaneously, on the presumption that some would be successful.[24] Fifth, despite all this, competition was fierce, as individuals were drawn to the publishing industry to satisfy political and cultural ambitions beyond mere profit. Printing, in other words, was an inherently unstable business – constantly dependent on a steady source of liquidity that could seldom be guaranteed.

One common way of mitigating against the liquidity trap was to encourage cash purchases. Physical shops and warehouse counters with restricted hours enabled printer–booksellers to exploit demand from within their local communities. Sizeable institutional buyers likely to furnish regular orders, such as literary societies and educational establishments, were equally highly sought after.[25] Of course, it helped to be located in Paris or Berlin: the operating costs of the biggest European firms were fuelled from their metropolitan stores. Another tactic was to carefully nurture multiple bilateral trading relationships. Because it was not standard industry practice to settle accounts immediately, or even annually, and since interest was rarely payable, these relationships could serve as valuable sources of cheap credit. Firms in temporary cashflow difficulties regularly let certain accounts drift into the red, safe in the knowledge that the system's inherent flexibility ensured that their shelves would remain stocked. Finally, once they could muster the necessary patronage, businesses quickly moved towards more stable types of printing. Newspapers, journals, lottery tickets, commercial receipts and official proclamations provided more predictable revenue streams than books. Innovators in large cities could diversify further. Friedrich Nicolai in Berlin produced miniature decorative peace books to be worn as watch fobs or pendants to mark the end of the Seven Years War.[26]

Put simply, size, contacts, privilege and monopoly all made life easier. For these reasons, early-modern printing and bookselling businesses were best inherited – preferably located in Paris with a healthy stock of books and several important certificates of *approbation et privilège*. Starting from scratch in the sticks and with just 9,000 *livres* combined capital to burn – the task beholden to the initial STN directors Jean-Elie Bertrand, Samuel Fauche and Frédéric-Samuel Ostervald – was never going to be easy.[27] Nonetheless, on 19 September 1769, as they swore a short printer's oath that bound them not to publish anything unexamined by local censors or likely to attract the rebuke of foreign powers, they must have appeared chosen to address the liquidity problem.

Fauche provided the necessary experience to wring out capital from local and international book markets. He began his career in November 1746 as a teenage apprentice to the bookseller Mussi in Morat, and then served as a bookbinder's assistant *chez* François Grasset in Lausanne. Around 1753, aged just twenty-one, he opened his own bookstore in Neuchâtel. Although he lacked presses, he published a handful of religious and educational works that he had printed elsewhere in the town or in nearby Bienne.[28] None of these books were remarkable, but Fauche harboured wider ambitions. His attempts to publish an edition of the works of Jean-Jacques Rousseau were foiled only by the scandal that erupted upon the publication of the Genevan's *Lettres écrites de la montagne* in October 1764. The following year, for reasons which remain unclear, his unassuming operation obtained a certain international credibility and notoriety when the final ten volumes of text of Diderot's *Encyclopédie* were published with the false name and address 'chez Samuel Faulche & Compagnie, Libraires & Imprimeurs à Neufchastel'.[29] Fauche was a true bookseller – as comfortable wining and dining authors as fighting dirty for every last sale. Regrettably for the STN, his involvement came with two considerable drawbacks. First, even after the establishment of the Society, he continued to trade in Neuchâtel and internationally on his own account, which he surely always intended to prioritize.[30] The STN thus neither profited from his stocks nor inherited his networks and order books. Second, his commercial instincts and risk-taking tendencies, as will soon become apparent, quickly dragged the Society towards the darker side of the print business.

Coxe's trusty guidebook, the *Description des montagnes ... de Neuchâtel et Valangin*, numbered among the titles published by Fauche during the 1760s. The work purported to have been printed from the original manuscript of two Polish noblemen who had enjoyed travelling in the region.[31] It would be rare tourists, however, who never once remarked the Neuchâtelois Jura's yellow stone beauty, but wrote authoritatively about microeconomic trends and historical climate statistics of each town and hamlet! In reality, the book sprang from the pen of Frédéric-Samuel Ostervald, the STN's second founding director, whose value to the organization was threefold. First, Ostervald enjoyed the knack of producing texts designed to appeal to local markets.[32] Second, he was a competent administrator: he led the day-to-day running of the Society and was their primary correspondent. Finally, perhaps most significantly, Ostervald's position of *banneret* – one of the most influential offices of the Neuchâtelois civil administration – ensured that he was well placed to attract printing commissions for ready cash from local businesses and authorities. As soon as the doors of its print shop opened in 1769, the STN began setting to type thousands of lottery tickets, posters, circulars, receipts and official edicts or regulations. The jobs which it fulfilled for the authorities ranged from publishing instructions for the cattle, wheat, wine and hospitality trades to printing lists of candidates for local elections.[33]

Jean-Elie Bertrand, the final initial STN director, was especially valuable because he possessed the intellectual capacities and editorial skills necessary to produce complex but lucrative periodical literature. Bertrand issued from a highly educated Dauphinois family which had fled France after the revocation of the edict of Nantes and eventually settled in Neuchâtel. His uncle, the famous naturalist Elie Bertrand, was a collaborator on the original *Encyclopédie* project and author of several books including the 1757 *Mémoires historiques et physiques sur les tremblemens de terre*. From 1759 Jean-Elie taught literature at the Collège de Neuchâtel, while from 1763 he commenced a parallel career as a Protestant minister. On 14 August 1770 he married Marie-Anne-Elizabeth, the daughter of his new business associate Frédéric-Samuel Ostervald, cementing the partnership that lay at the core of the STN.[34] Leaving the quotidian grind of the trade to his new father-in-law, Jean-Elie spent much of his time editing the *Feuille d'avis de Neuchâtel* and the *Nouveau Journal helvétique*. His talents also eased the STN's entry into the highly profitable market for subscription reference works. The *Descriptions des arts et métiers* and the *Encyclopédie* contributed significantly to both the STN's international reputation and bottom line.[35] The former was a particularly remarkable undertaking. Jean-Elie extended the text of the Parisian original by up to 40 per cent by translating articles from the augmented German edition and adding his own copious scholarly notes.³⁶ Alongside this work, he also published two volumes of sermons and saw many of the works of his more illustrious uncle into press.³⁷

The market prospects for the STN thus arose from the geographical and political advantages of Romandy and the complementary skillsets of three Neuchâtelois men of letters. A circular announcement of its establishment sent by the newly formed society to 187 European booksellers and printers in July 1769 gloried in the opportunity provided by this fortunate happenstance.³⁸ Nonetheless, Bertrand, Fauche and Ostervald had hardly fallen upon a get-rich-quick scheme, and nothing in their backgrounds, the history of Neuchâtelois printing or the way they operated the business during its early years suggests that they could have deceived themselves. The smart money in Neuchâtel was in making watches. We must thus search a little further in order to fully understand their motivation.

For starters, running a publishing house represented a credible route towards standing and influence in early modern communities. Print shops were prestigious and strategically important: they greased the wheels of commerce, communicated essential official information and could be used to promote home-grown agendas on wider stages.³⁹ Neuchâtel, a Prussian-governed principality eyed with equal measures of envy and disdain by both neighbouring France and the Swiss Confederation, acutely and constantly needed to declaim and reinforce its independence. Moreover, at the precise moment of the establishment of the STN, the standing of the Neuchâtelois bourgeoisie was under threat. Conflict had been brewing for two decades, ever since Frédéric II 'rationalized' the ancient Neuchâtelois method of collecting tax, which yielded inconsistent sums pegged closely to the annual grape and grain harvests. An impasse over the collection of 1766 led to open insurrection, the murder of the Prussian-installed advocate-general Claude Gaudot, the occupation of the town by Bernese and Swiss Confederation troops and, ultimately, the submission and pacification of the Neuchâtel bourgeoisie. The baron de Lentulus, commander of the Bernese troops, was henceforth installed as the governor of Neuchâtel to ensure continued loyalty.⁴⁰ The archives betray no evidence of a direct causal link between these events and the establishment of the STN yet, given the importance of printing to the independence of local communities, it would be amiss not to recognize that Bertrand, Fauche and Ostervald's move came at a welcome moment for the town's bourgeoisie.

All three also dreamt of horizons beyond the Col de la Tourne; they fancied participating in the transcontinental excitement of the francophone public sphere and the Enlightenment. The question of their commitment to the latter has been the subject of a lively debate between Elizabeth Eisenstein and Robert Darnton. Darnton has insisted that the STN directors' motivations were financial, citing their willingness to disseminate contradictory writings as supporting evidence; Eisenstein, by contrast, has focused rather upon their role as cultural ambassadors, emphasizing their commitment to printing important titles like the *Nouveau Journal helvétique*.⁴¹ Yet, it appears unlikely that Bertrand, Fauche and Ostervald would have recognized such a dichotomy between making money and spreading knowledge. The Enlightenment ran so deep in the Swiss literary culture of the 1770s and 1780s that scarcely a sheet traded by the Neuchâtelois was not influenced by its currents. Moreover, the Swiss printer's calling demanded both ideological neutrality and willingness to drive books into both cheaper and less well-serviced markets. The STN's chosen route towards money, in short, *was* selling Enlightenment. They stated as much in their 1769 missive: their purpose was to extend the diffusion of useful and enjoyable works with care, timeliness and economy.[42]

Of course, even the best laid plans of mice and men of letters occasionally go awry. The STN did sometimes stray from the honest values championed in its mission statement. These deviations from original intent are probably best explained by the reality that constant financial instability forced the Neuchâtelois into a series of pragmatic moves and dramatic tactical shifts. During their first twenty-six months, they partnered with experienced international houses and sold only their own printings; from late 1771, they abandoned this plan and switched to the 'classic' printer–bookseller's model operated by their regional rivals and allies; by the early 1780s they changed tack once more and took on risky job printings in order to crack important northern markets; from 1785, under administration, they looked to diversify and liquidate stocks; and, finally, from 1789, the business entered into a protracted winding-up period and was only notionally a going concern.[43] An analysis of the changing factors that motivated the STN directors to set specific works to type – itself a necessary first step towards a temporally aware interpretation of an FBTEE dataset dominated by Neuchâtelois editions – begins with these strategic shifts. Figure 1.2, a group-stacked bar chart showing STN shipments to France, Switzerland and the rest of Europe between 1769 and 1794, hints at their effects on the overall shape of the business. But to fully understand their force and importance, we must look into the stories that lay behind these peaks and troughs.

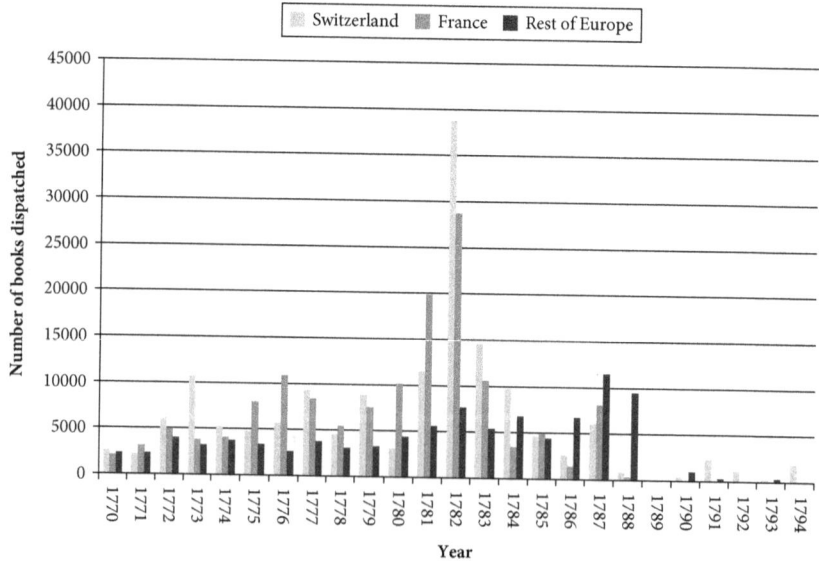

Figure 1.2 Group-Stacked Bar Chart displaying the annual repartition of STN sales for the geographic zones of Switzerland, France and the rest of Europe.

During their first two years of trading, the STN sold only sixteen distinct titles. The ambition of the summer of 1769 – which saw the resurrection of Fauche's plans for an edition of the works of Rousseau and projected printings of the *Descriptions des arts et métiers* and the *Encyclopédie* – quickly gave way to hard-headed pragmatism. Here was a classic chicken-and-egg bind: how could the Neuchâtelois build the requisite international networks to sell books without a substantial list of books to sell? Various responses to their 1769 communiqué suggested a three-pronged strategy: accept printing commissions; concentrate on local markets; and partner with experienced houses. As commissions, the STN produced 600 copies of two tracts concerning the Genevan 'affaire des natifs' for the Neuchâtelois clockmaker and political agitator Georges Auzière in March 1770, as well as 1,000 copies of the 'Tableau de la Monarchie française' for Louis-Valentin de Goëzman in Paris in May 1771.[44] For regional buyers, they published Ostervald's geographical textbooks, an edition of his father's catechisms, and a translation of a Swiss-German work concerning the abolition of monasteries in Catholic cantons.[45] The remainder of their output – nine works in total – was destined for international distribution in conjunction with partners in Berne, Brussels, Cleves, The Hague, Lyon and Paris.

The cooperative approach ensured that these early works were well chosen and widely and promptly disseminated. Take, for example, the 1770 edition of the *Lettres du comte Algarotti sur la Russie* by the Italian philosopher and essayist Francesco Algarotti.[46] This collection of observations about Russian economic might and *mores* in the wake of the Russo-Turkish War of 1735–9 had been first published in Italian nearly a decade previously to no evident international acclaim.[47] By 1768, however, tensions in Northern Europe were rising, and Algarotti's ready-made historical refresher appeared a good fit for the coffee-supping classes of Paris and Amsterdam who were anticipating a renewal of hostilities. The first French-language edition duly appeared towards the end of that year to instructive but consistently lukewarm notices.[48] By October 1770, as the Russians took the Moldavian capital of Jassy, the STN's *Nouveau Journal helvétique* insisted that the importance of Algarotti's work had been overlooked.[49] Before long, the Neuchâtelois had concluded the necessary deals to put to press a new edition, augmented with an essay specifically linking the text to the current conflict. Speed was of the essence in order to stay ahead of both the Russians and any potential competitors who might have stumbled upon the same idea. Between 6 and 15 February, the STN printed 995 copies. Out of these, 200 were dispatched immediately to the Société typographique de Berne (STB). Nine days later, 500 examples were sent to Pierre Gosse junior and Daniel Pinet in The Hague, and 150 more were forwarded to J.B. Henry and Company in Lille, on France's border with the Austrian Netherlands. From the STN's perspective, the edition had been printed and 85 per cent exhausted within three weeks, all before Catherine the Great's forces had awoken from their winter slumber.

This particular arrangement left the Neuchâtelois with a manageable 145 copies to sell directly; other printings left them with less or more. By the end of September 1771, the STN had sent out a total of 13,331 books, 7,977 of which had been commissioned or were to be distributed by partners. By examining how they dealt with the difference – the 5,354 works sold directly to booksellers based in thirty different towns – we can see the precise extent of the Society's networks by this moment. Certainly, some 3,000 sales (56%) achieved to traders located in fifteen towns dotted around French-speaking Switzerland suggest that their editions encountered relatively little resistance close to home. From the get-go, the STN sold works to Geneva, Lausanne, Le Locle, Morges, Vevey, Yverdon and – through Fauche's moonlighting – Neuchâtel itself. Beyond Switzerland, their sales were dominated by an arc of relatively nearby towns that stretched from Grenoble in south-eastern France to Manheim in the Rhineland, and took in the francophone book centres of Besançon, Lyon and Nancy. A total of 1,296 (24%) sales had been realized to this particular fertile crescent. Some inroads had also been made within the natural markets for Swiss traders of southern France and northern Italy. A total of 208 (4%) books had been sold to Montpellier and Nimes, while 528 (10%) works had been dispatched to Milan, Genoa and Florence. Only 218 (4%) books were directly shipped further afield. No consignments were sent to western and northern France, Great Britain, Ireland, Russia, Spain or to the majority of the German states and southern Italy.

In short, after two years of trading, the STN's direct distribution networks remained somewhat stunted and, as a consequence, the liquidity monster began to stalk the business for the first time. During 1771, having exhausted the 9,000 *livres* that Bertrand, Fauche and Ostervald had initially sunk into the business, the Society was forced to borrow 1,000 *livres* from the Chambre de Charité and another 2,000 *livres* from the Master-Bourgeois Jacques-Samuel Wavre.[50] At least the subtleties of their bind were starting to crystallize: long-distance clients tended to desire varied stocks by the crateful, primarily to economize on shipping costs; middle-distance traders, perhaps based in Lausanne or Lyon, regularly wanted to swap rather than buy books in order to shift their own printings; and because local retail buyers were so limited in number, the only way to increase counter revenues was to offer more choice and encourage repeat purchasing.

Of course, the STN's partners *were* supplying works from their *rue des Moulins* printing shop into each of these zones but, largely due to the discounts that they negotiated, this was barely to the Society's benefit. The STN's business model, in normal circumstances, was simple and common to the majority of their Swiss rivals. They priced books not according to expected demand or perceived literary worth, but by the number of printed sheets of which they consisted. The sale price that they sought to achieve was 1 *sol de France* (12 *deniers*) per sheet. Copies of the octavo 296-page *Lettres du comte Algarotti*, then, were made up of 18.5 printed sheets and would consequently sell, after a little advantageous rounding, for 19 *sols*. Should the Society achieve this price for each copy, they could expect to break even on direct printing costs after exhausting approximately 40 per cent of an edition.[51] After the fixed costs of running the business – from lighting the workshop to paying interest on borrowed capital – were taken into account, however, margins were much tighter and 'real terms' profits arrived only at a substantially higher threshold. Moreover, once the risks of slow-selling editions and the realities of non-paying customers were considered, it was clear to the STN directors that their long-term survival depended upon them not straying too far from the 1-*sol*-per-sheet golden rule. Keen to make a splash and build their networks during these early days, however, many of the bulk shipments dispatched by the Society were loss leaders. The widow Reguilliat in Lyon received her 500 copies of Voltaire's *Questions sur l'Encyclopédie* at 10 *deniers* per sheet; James Porter's *Observations sur la religion, les loix, le gouvernement et les mœurs des Turcs* was sold to the STB and J. B. Henry for 9 *deniers* per sheet; and the price negotiated by Gosse and Pinet for their 'Algerotti's' was just 1 Swiss creutzer, equivalent to 6 *deniers* or half a *sol*.[52] Only in exceptional cases, like the Brussels bookseller Jean-Louis de Boubers' commission for 500 copies of the baron d'Holbach's highly subversive 'atheists' Bible' the *Système de la nature*, did the STN manage to haggle the asking price that they required – and nary a *batz* more.[53]

This final job was particularly not worth the bother. The extraordinary illegality of d'Holbach's materialist *chef d'oeuvre* ensured that it could be retailed more dearly than standard editions, generally at a price approaching 2 *sols* per sheet.[54] Alert to the opportunity to make money, the STN printed 1,500 more copies than had been agreed with Boubers, the first 723 of which they sold surreptitiously on their own account between April and September 1771.[55] Unfortunately, by June this flurry of atheistic shipments had caught the attention of the Venerable Class of Neuchâtelois pastors, who angrily reported the STN to the Conseil d'Etat and the Quatre-Ministraux, Neuchâtel's legislative and executive bodies. The following month, an official complaint was made to Leurs Excellences de Berne, leaving Bertrand, Fauche and Ostervald at some personal risk. On 21 August, Voltaire wrote to Frederick II, King of Prussia and sovereign of Neuchâtel, pleading that he intervene against the persecution of his friend Ostervald at the hands of local priests who, he suggested, belonged in the thirteenth or fourteenth century.[56] As if to underline his point, the *Système de la nature* was officially condemned in Neuchâtel the following day and was subsequently burnt at the Croix-de-Marché, a stone's throw from the STN print shop, on 26 September.[57] Publicly humiliated, Ostervald was stripped of his position as *banneret* and Bertrand of his ministry.

The *Système de la nature* affair was not the only sign that the STN's partnering strategy was proving burdensome. First, the two pamphlets that the Neuchâtelois had printed for Georges Auzière were burnt by the Petit Conseil of Geneva on 22 February 1771.[58] Second, the mysterious 'Tableau de la Monarchie française', printed for the scandalmonger Louis-Valentin Goëzman, does not appear to have reached the public.[59] Third, while the Society's edition of Voltaire's *Questions sur l'encyclopédie* was set with the approval of its author and the Neuchâtelois authorities, it attracted the wrath of the Cramers in Geneva, who had expected their own printing to be exclusive.[60] Finally, after two years of troubles, the STN was forced by the arbitration courts to pay 420 *livres* to the printer Jean-Christophe Heilmann in Bienne for breaking their joint 1769 agreement to print the 'Oeuvres de Rousseau'.[61]

As the embers of the Croix-de-Marché auto-da-fé faded, therefore, a serious strategic rethink was in order. That week, the STN solicited two evaluation copies of the 'Londres, 1772' edition of Louis-Sébastien Mercier's subversive utopian fantasy *L'an deux mille quatre cent quarante*, from its publisher François Grasset in Lausanne. Within a fortnight, the Society had ordered and received 175 more; by the year's end a further 162; while the following August the Neuchâtelois secured an additional 400 copies of Grasset's second edition. Mercier's work was special – a sure-fire international bestseller and an exceptional business opportunity – but the STN's decision to sell a third-party edition represented a permanent revolution in their business model.[62] Having previously resisted the advances of regionally based printers, by the time that Grasset's second edition appeared they had accepted 2,558 copies of 60 different works.[63]

The Society took hundreds of copies of titles including Antoine-Léonard Thomas' *Essai sur le caractère, les moeurs et l'esprit des femmes*; dozens of examples of Jacob Vernes' anti-philosophical *Confidence philosophique*; and single copies of titles like Friedrich Samuel von Schmidt's *Recueil d'antiquités trouvées à Avenches*. The Neuchâtelois printed catalogues and went after new markets. They became wholesalers as well as printers.

Wholesaling warrants a moment's explanation, especially because its effects need to be understood to interpret the FBTEE dataset. As the STN's early history attests, the primary difficulty that early modern printers perennially encountered was that while production was generally fixed at a specific point, demand was normally dispersed and difficult to locate. It was as impractical for printers to sell directly to booksellers strewn across the map as it was for these booksellers to source every work from its point of origin. The need for some system for mediating supply and demand was thus paramount and universal. Over time, a number of different solutions emerged, each adapted to its particular market situation. Printers displaced themselves, sent out travelling salesmen or commissioned middlemen to handle their wares; great book fairs, notably those of Frankfurt and Leipzig, gathered vendors and purchasers at a single location and moment; and metropolises, especially Paris and London, served as hubs through which trade took place. The STN did use variations on each of these models to reach their customers, but none were ideal for the late-eighteenth-century trade in French-language books. The power of the Parisian booksellers' guild and questions of privilege and legality prevented the emergence of a centralized system revolving around Paris; single, expensive-to-reach, European fairs fell gradually out of fashion with the rise of vernacular printing and the low-cost models that accompanied the expansion of reading; and the consolidation of printing towards larger shops generally reduced mobility.

Instead, the primary wholesaling model that materialized depended upon printers swapping books directly among themselves within the confines of a cost-efficient regional nexus, before then separately attempting to sell their newly diversified stocks to retail booksellers further afield. Whenever a new work exited a press, then, it was immediately offered to fellow printers in the same region in exchange for their own new publications. Through such swaps most francophone printers could, at any given moment, offer more-or-less everything recently printed in their region. Their advantage was twofold: they reduced the risks associated with publishing failed editions by immediately divesting themselves of a substantial part of any run, while simultaneously diversifying their own holdings. For sure, houses still had to build large international networks but, freed from the responsibilities of locating all of the demand for a print run, they could concentrate upon soliciting substantial orders from a more restricted number of foreign booksellers. For these booksellers, the system was imperfect – none of these wholesalers were one-stop shops to rival the Leipzig fairs – but it was cost-effective and manageable. To offer all of Europe's *nouveautés*, they would have to order separately from each of its productive regions. But with three well placed letters to the Low Countries, Switzerland and Paris they could probably solicit most things, assuming offering such choice proved commercially desirable.

Starting with the Grasset deals, by the end of 1772 the STN had opened up exchange accounts with the STB; with Cailler, Gabriel Grasset and the partnership of Claude Philibert and Barthélemy Chirol in Geneva; with Jules-Henri Pott and Jean-Pierre Heubach in Lausanne; with Jean-Michel Barret in Lyon; with the Reycends brothers in

Turin; and with the newly disgraced and independent Samuel Fauche in Neuchâtel.[64] Early in the year, despite the disapproval of Bertrand and Ostervald, Fauche had purchased a large quantity of Charles Théveneau de Morande's outrageous anthology of anecdotes from the French court, *Le gazetier cuirassé*, to sell on his own account. After several months of successfully trading the volume, inevitably enough, he got sloppy. He slipped fifty copies, addressed to a third party, into an STN *ballot* destined for Pierre Duplain in Lyon. The shipment, which also contained 100 copies of the *Système de la nature*, was inspected by customs officials at the *chambre syndicale* of Lyon. The entire lot was seized and burnt and the matter was reported to the relevant authorities in Paris and Versailles. No armour-plated excuses could save Fauche this time; he was permanently ejected from the STN by his aggrieved partners. The separation was a lengthy and hostile affair, since Fauche pushed for considerable compensation for his three years of service. In May and October 1773, he settled for between 30 and 300 copies of each of the STN printings that remained in stock, as well as 800 Bibles and 1,000 catechisms – a total of 5,265 volumes.

The effects of the split are difficult to judge, although the fact that Fauche was already operating independently unquestionably lessened the shock to the Society.[65] In any case, free from his chaotic influence and settled upon a more realistic business model, the STN entered their heyday. Figure 1.3 shows the dissemination of STN-traded works across Europe between 1 October 1771 and 26 January 1780. Three points are especially noteworthy. First, the map demonstrates how successfully the Neuchâtelois managed to turn their early dependence upon the Parisian market into a genuinely diversified trade across France. The Society sent 55,235 books to seventy-five different towns throughout

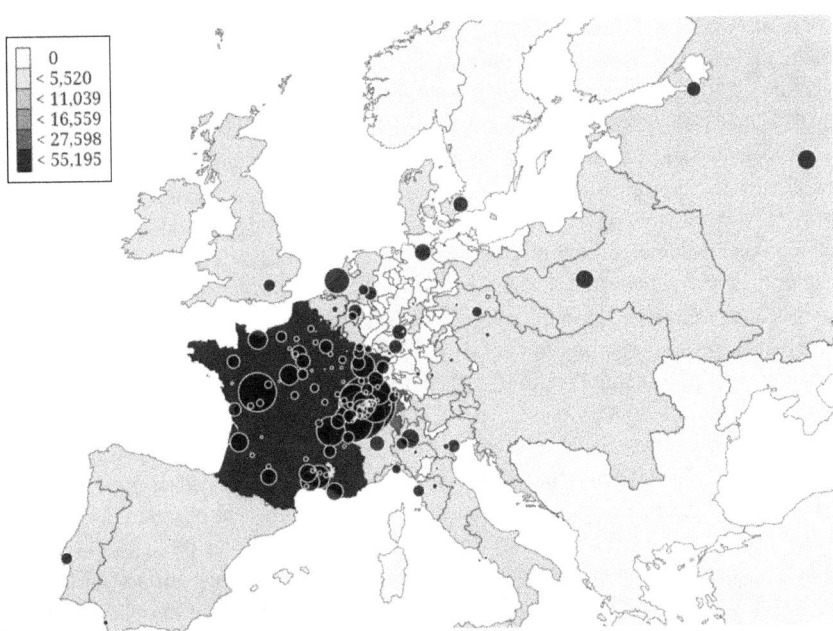

Figure 1.3 Map of STN envois 1 October 1771 to 26 January 1780.

the kingdom, enjoying extensive sales to regional centres including Bordeaux (1,910 sales), Montpellier (2,039), Nimes (2,895) and Orléans (2,176). Second, it illustrates how effective the STN became at establishing relationships with merchants based in Europe's more far-flung corners. For sure, only 21 per cent of their sales were made to customers located outside Switzerland or France. But the commerce of these metropolitan and court-based book sellers, which regularly consisted of significant orders for large volumes of difficult-to-shift catalogue stock, was valuable. Finally, it clarifies that the STN's local market – that elliptical splodge bridging Lyon and Basle – remained of primary importance to the proper functioning of the business. Shipments to this zone included extensive sales to towns dotted along the highway and just over the border, but were dominated by eleven key bilateral book-swapping partnerships that helped the Society diversify their stocks and embed themselves in the Swiss credit nexus.[66]

This impressive reach was accompanied by a similarly notable increase in shipping volumes. In total, by 26 January 1780, the Society had dispatched a little over 150,000 books. Without question, this upturn was aided by the STN's new ability to offer an ever-expanding catalogue of third-party-printed works to supplement its own offerings. In October 1771, the Neuchâtelois held ten different books (8,911 individual copies); by October 1774 stock levels had risen to 400 books (22,589 copies); by the end of November 1776 they offered 527 books (34,360); while in January 1779, 719 books with (34,899) unique titles were available to purchase from the STN. Yet, the Society's ballooning catalogues should not distort the reality that their own print shop continued to dominate the business. Of the approximately 150,000 copies shipped and the approximately 35,000 unbound examples remaining in their stockroom at the start of the 1780s, approximately only 63,000 – fractionally over a third – were not printed by the STN.[67] Indeed, if we compensate for the fact that the Society generally printed unusually long works – those complete works of Dorat ignored by Coxe, for example, ran to 2,696 octavo pages made up from 168 sheets – then the ratio falls closer to one in six. At the time of their January 1779 stocktake, the STN stocked 928,321 sheets of their own editions (valued at 29,010.0.6 *livres*) compared to just 185,359 ½ sheets of swapped books (5,792.9.6).

Alongside the trade in regular books, this prime period in the STN's history also witnessed the continuation of local job printing and the realization of prestigious projects first dreamt up in 1769. Alas, the quotidian trudge of printing ephemera, which was fundamental to both the mission and financial underpinnings of the STN, can only be treated anecdotally because its details were not systematically recorded in the Society's accounts. Upon the end of the War of the Bavarian Succession in 1779 – to give just one example among scores scattered throughout the ledgers – the STN printed 200 placards announcing the peace, 600 copies of the treaty, and hundreds of passports and certificates of military leave.[68] Yet Neuchâtel was not cosmopolitan London; the relative infrequency of such entries in the rich STN ledgers contrast sharply with the books of William Strahan, which show that approximately half of his output was jobbing for local businesses, corporations or individuals.[69] At the other end of the scale from these low-value jobs, a triumvirate of works – the infolio Bible, the nineteen-volume quarto *Descriptions des arts et métiers*, and the thirty-six-volume quarto third edition of Diderot and d'Alembert's famous *Encyclopédie* – were yet more important to the financial and reputational health of the STN. The January 1779 stocktake described

420,939 ½ sheets (with a value livres of 14,031.6.3 *livres de France*) of the *Descriptions des arts et métiers*; 90,130 sheets (8,423.0.6) of illustrations for that work; infolio Bibles totalling 25,254.13.0 *livres*; and a pile of volumes of the *Encyclopédie* worth 12,926.7.0 *livres*. Judged by value and printed sheets, these three works were more important to the STN's bottom line than the other 716 stocked works combined.[70] They were among the crown jewels of Swiss printing of the age, and they marked out the STN's print shop as something out of the ordinary.

Just how sizeable the Society became relative to other houses, however, is difficult to establish in the absence of comparable datasets. Certainly, those 719 unique titles that the Society had amassed by 1779 represented only modest holdings. Friedrich Nicolai found around 12,000 different books in stock when he inherited his father's Berlin business in 1752.[71] The Genevan booksellers Barde, Manget and Company's trade catalogue of 1789 offered 7,450 works.[72] Yet, holdings better indicate the age of a business than its size: the game was to sell books, not to collect them. Much of Nicolai's inheritance amounted to wallpaper – the same unappealing titles that his father was advertising without any luck back in 1737.[73] Client lists are perhaps a better indicator of scale. The STN corresponded with roughly three times as many individuals and businesses as Voltaire's Genevan publishers, the Cramer brothers, and about six times as many as their city-state compatriots Henri-Albert Gosse and Company.[74] Between 1759 and 1785 Gosse had 37 Italian clients, whereas between 1769 and 1787 the STN boasted 171 correspondents, with 50 of whom they traded books.[75] Otherwise we might look at the number of presses housed. Thierry Rigogne's work on the 1764 survey of French provincial printing has shown that the majority of the kingdom's 195 print shops harboured 2 or 3 presses, with only a trio of shops admitting to running more than 5.[76] In 1785, Heubach in Lausanne operated seven presses.[77] Within months of opening their doors, the STN had four presses churning out copy; by the time they began printing the *Encyclopédie* in 1777, they boasted twelve in simultaneous operation.[78] During these *Encyclopédie* days, few European printers could match their productive output, and none put them in the shade.

If these fragments of evidence are slightly unsatisfying, then they all at least point in the same direction: as the 1770s advanced, the STN became huge printers and substantial wholesalers, but remained more modest booksellers. That the Society's directors ran such an operation from a Swiss backwater testifies to their ambition, achievement and, perhaps, folly. Similarly sized printing outfits tended to be located in capitals and attached to larger, more diverse, and better connected businesses. The book-trade empire of the Trattner's in Vienna, for example, extended beyond their printing shop to a bindery, bookshop, reading room and type-foundry. It was built upon a cast-iron state-sponsored plan to pirate German bestsellers for the local market.[79] As the STN expanded, by contrast, weaknesses in their model became apparent. Yes, they were managing to diversify their stocks, but the fragmentation that this implied was difficult to manage without a large cosmopolitan book shop. Moreover, their 1771 abandonment of commission printing and partnering had come at the cost of their largest markets. During their initial phase, 53 per cent (7,217 of 13,531) of the STN's overall envois were dispatched to a golden quadrilateral located between, and encompassing, the cities of Amsterdam, Liège, London and Paris.[80] This northern European zone was the most densely populated, literate and affluent in Europe and was packed with booksellers and institutional buyers. After the restructuring, only 8 per cent (12,006 of 146,565) of their shipments were sent to this area. The Society's sales to Paris were particularly damaged, dropping from 22 per cent (2,969 of 13,531) of the total to just 2 per cent (2,780 of 146,565).

The liquidity to keep all these Neuchâtel presses running had to come, if not from the upscale boutiques of the Palais Royal or through extensive vertical integration, from closer to home. Several high-profile capital injections made by bourgeois Neuchâtelois have been unearthed by scholars of the archive.[81] In January 1777, Abram Bosset de Luze bought his way into the partnership as director for around 10,000 *livres* Neuchâtelois; in the following month a further 10,000 *livres* was invested by Anne-Marie Brun; while, in June 1781, 6,000 *livres* was received from the Quatre-Ministraux. These were significant sums – the Brun deposit alone the equivalent of 200,000 printed sheets. However, the true scale of the STN's borrowings and their punitive interest rates has passed unnoticed. By January 1779, the STN owed a remarkable 241,551.17.0 *livres de France* to its various creditors, including 11,714 *livres* to the Maison de Charité, 12,000 *livres* to the councillor Bertrand in Yverdon, 16,942.17.6 *livres* to the Chambre économique de Neuchâtel, and 36,000 *livres* to undisclosed investors.[82] They had also let their exchange accounts slip into the red. Balancing these debts were 72,361.2.0 *livres de France* that clients were yet to pay. Gosse and Pinet owed the Society 13,193.11.0 *livres*; the banker J. F. Perregaux in Paris sat on an outstanding bill of 5,216.3.0 *livres*; and the Loudun hawker Malherbe was in arrears by 1,267.4.0 *livres*. Nine alarming register pages listing more-or-less every client that the STN had done business with attested to the difficulties that they were encountering in getting customers to settle.[83] The sum of all these debts, every printed and unprinted sheet that filled the warehouse, and all the fixtures and fittings of the printing shop meant that the business was theoretically solvent. The books listed 262,904.12.1 *livres* of value.[84] But, if a study might be allowed one vulgar anachronism, the STN was leveraged to its eyeballs. Storm clouds gathered.

Later chapters explore the deluge. As the 1780s dawned, the STN's insatiable appetite for capital ultimately led them back to the high-stakes trade in commissioned editions, to tail-chasing imprudence and effective bankruptcy, and to their commis Victor Durand's remarkable four-year horseback swansong in search of new markets from the Mediterranean to the Baltic. For now, however, we might just accept that, however dubiously funded, the STN's rise was spectacular. After a little over a decade of trading, they had sold more than 150,000 books and had claimed a substantive place in the decentralized nexus of European printing. Bertrand, Bosset de Luze, Fauche and Ostervald had learnt the hard way: they had fallen for the tricks of the northern European booksellers; fallen into debt; fallen out of favour; and plain fallen out. But the principal lesson was clear. Success, for sure, was contingent upon grasping the subtle differences between their various markets and adapting to threats and opportunities as time advanced and events unfolded. But, most of all, it depended upon understanding their own business. Neuchâtel was a unique point on the map and the STN was comprised of a number of men with unique skillsets and competences. This should be at the forefront of our minds as we begin to analyse their shipments across space using the full power of the FBTEE database. After a brief methodological interlude, let us start this task closest to home, in Jean-Jacques' little utopia located in the heart of eighteenth-century Europe.

Bookkeeping Made Simple

A century after the demise of the STN, the historian and polymath Philippe Godet assumed that its archives had been pulped in the nearby Serrières paper mills.[85] During the 1930s, however, letters addressed to the Society bearing the signatures of several famous correspondents – notably Voltaire and Pierre Jaquet-Droz – began to appear for sale on the open market.[86] André Bovet, the inter-war director of Neuchâtel's library, acted swiftly. He followed the trail back through a Genevois collector to the proprietor of the Neuchâtel manor house 'La Grande Rochette' and, after some considerable effort, managed to secure the purchase of the archive in its entirety. Shortly afterwards, he recovered many of the letters that had already been hawked for their signatures. Bovet's actions were rewarded by the rediscovery of a remarkable series of documents: around 24,000 letters received by the STN, 11 substantial volumes of copies of letters that the Society sent, and an extraordinary set of account books and ancillary pieces. Together the papers record every detail of the running of the Neuchâtelois publishing house, from its directors' endless search for marketable copy to print, through their skilful shepherding of ink, paper, type and labour, to the final shipments of realized books across the continent. In a missive sent while trying to recover the archive, Bovet modestly described the collection as of great importance to Neuchâtel.

In fact, he had safeguarded a unique archive of considerable regional and international historical significance. For the study of the eighteenth-century Swiss francophone book trade, the STN papers are unrivalled. Nothing remains of the accounts of the majority of the Society's major allies and competitors, notably the Fauche family in Neuchâtel, the typographical societies of Berne and Yverdon and the various publishing houses of Lausanne and Geneva. For a period just before the Neuchâtelois began trading, between 1755 and 1766, a run of the 'Grand livre' of Voltaire's Genevan publishers, the Cramer brothers, has survived.[87] While these ledgers give some point of comparison to those of the STN, they contain only a summary overview of the firm's activities and divulge precious few details of specific book sales. Some 1,300 pages of the letter books of the fellow Genevan Henri-Albert Gosse, spanning the period 1759–91, are also extant, although they are not accompanied by accounts and are largely addressed to Italian clients.[88]

Indeed, surviving archives located *anywhere* in Europe that might be meaningfully compared to the Neuchâtel find are rare. Two particular sets of account books, which properly mined could yield datasets most comparable to those created during the FBTEE project, brim with potential and are relatively little known. First, it has recently come to light that several registers of the major Parisian publisher the widow Desaint, covering parts of the 1760s, 1770s and 1780s, have survived in the Bibliothèque historique de la ville de Paris (BHVP). The hoard consists of four day books covering over eight years of shipments sent and received, three lengthy volumes of exchanges with Parisian clients and competitor firms, and a magnificent set of mid-1770s client accounts.[89] Second, the accounts of the Luchtmans firm, booksellers in Leiden, held in Koninklijke Bibliotheek (KB) in Amsterdam and substantially available on microfiche elsewhere, are rarely employed or referenced.[90] The centrepiece of the collection is a seemingly complete and impeccably organized (although only partially catalogued) set of client accounts that run from 1697 to 1803. The firm's entire bookselling business begs reconstruction from these ledgers which, in many ways, surpass those of the STN. They cover a substantially lengthier period; they include works traded in German, Latin and French; and the Dutch-centric wholesale and retail networks that they reveal were arguably (and undoubtedly for the first half of the century) more active and influential than those of French-speaking Switzerland. Moreover, an unbroken series, they could be more straightforwardly mined than the STN source. Regrettably, however, the Luchtman's books are accompanied by few letters and a much poorer series of ancillary documents than those found in Neuchâtel.

Elsewhere, scattered accounting documents and significant collections of letters can also be found concerning various European publishers. The archives of Cambridge University Press and the papers of the London-based bookseller John Murray contain some accounts, although both collections are substantially stronger for the period following the demise of the STN.[91] The Boyers' accounts (1710–77) and those of the Ackers (1732–48) and Strahans (1738–1825) are equally invaluable for the study of the British trade.[92] Dutch studies have made use of accounting information relating to the business of La Mettrie's publisher Elie Luzac, Tijl of Zwolle and the Blussé family of Dordrecht.[93] In total, 2,000 pieces of the Amsterdam *philosophe* publisher Marc-Michel Rey's correspondence have survived in the KB, as have many of his catalogues and a collection of the advertisements that he placed.[94] A rich assortment of approximately 15,000 letters sent to the Berlin bookseller, publisher, author, editor and *Aufklärer* Friedrich Nicolai by his 2,500 correspondents, held in the Staatsbibliothek Preußischer Kulturbesitz in Berlin, has been admirably exploited by Pamela Selwyn.[95] Likewise, the work of Gilles Eboli has revealed the rich collections of materials relating to the David family's printing and bookselling business in Aix-en-Provence.[96] Finally, the 1784–9 cash book detailing Pierre-Augustin Caron de Beaumarchais' printing of the 'Kehl' edition of the complete works of Voltaire is also held in the BHVP, where it is accompanied by business correspondence detailing sales and various additional papers.[97]

Many more ledgers are entirely lost; others, surely, still to be found. Oh that the Amsterdam accounts of Arkstée and Merkus or the Parisian papers of Charles-Joseph Panckoucke might one day resurface in a dusty attic or forgotten strong room! Until then, the relative completeness of the STN archives assures that its unique importance to bibliophile *dix-huitièmistes* will remain. Yet the rarity of Bovet's find – our happenstance dependency upon a series of account books belonging to a firm that would otherwise be remembered by only the most committed bibliographers – might have better alerted a generation of scholars to questions of the Society's representativeness. Could the Neuchâtelois really have unknowingly chanced upon an exemplar, a fantastic shortcut towards understanding more stable and established houses and, by extension, the wider European book trade? Many case-study-based publications have implied this to be the case. Yet, this volume's close reading of the STN's rollercoaster fortunes, patchy dissemination patterns and skewed purchasing decisions paints a more sophisticated picture. We need to reassess how the archives of the STN – lost for nearly 150 years and in many respects unique – help us to understand the late-Enlightenment European trade in French books.

This task begins by returning to the ledgers. This chapter, alongside this volume's technical appendix 'Coding and Decoding the French Book Trade', documents key aspects of the FBTEE project's new methodological approach towards the STN archive. It explains how our data-centric reading of the Society's diverse accounting ledgers revealed a consistent stream of temporally and spatially located book dissemination information that yielded an unprecedentedly rich view of the STN's business. It describes the design and purpose of eighteenth-century accounting; demonstrates the extent to which the STN books conformed to standard practice; delineates the stream of information that could be dependably extracted throughout the STN's twenty-five-year trading existence; and evaluates the quality and usefulness of this information. In doing so, it is hoped that this method might, first, prove exemplary (to be accepted, extended, modified or rejected) for future research using comparable sources and, second, allow that the soundness of the statistically driven conclusions of the current volume be adequately assessed by the scholarly community.

Double-entry account books – even those accompanied by back-stories of survival against the odds – are hardly the most romantic of sources. Scholars often overlook them, intimidated perhaps by their ostensible impenetrability. Yet, early modern accounts are relatively easily understood. They were generally created for practical quotidian purposes, using a transparent and standardized system designed to clearly betray aspects of the business, to engender confidence in third parties, and to quickly settle disputes. First and foremost, accounts were employed by merchants to keep track of their credit dealings with the scores or hundreds of other traders whom they counted as clients. At a glance, the double-entry system allowed these men (and relatively frequently women) to appreciate to whom they were indebted, how much they owed and for which services. They could also, of course, keep tabs on their own debtors. Second, where debtors needed to be pursued through the courts, account books – especially those that were well kept, of the double-entry variety and belonged to respectable merchants – were often considered admissible evidence. Third, good bookkeeping was vital in the eventuality of the termination or sale of a business – whether caused by bankruptcy, death or as part of an orderly transition to a relative or partner. Fourth, faultless accounting was taken by other traders as a sign that confidence could be warranted; confidence, in turn, was the sole reliable route to credit, and was of pivotal importance to the success of any early modern business. Fifth, bookkeeping was employed as a form of control over the assets of a business and the workers that interacted with them on a daily basis. Theft, in short, was difficult to hide in double-entry books, particularly because access only to parts of the system could be granted to individual employees on a need-to-know basis. Finally, internally or externally arising error or misunderstanding could typically be exposed by a good set of double-entry account books.

Every reputable merchant understood the system and its importance to international trade. Thirteenth-century Italian in origin, double-entry bookkeeping spread, matured and standardized quickly. By the seventeenth and eighteenth centuries, it was codified in a series of practically identical popular manuals that could be followed by budding traders.[98] Mathieu de La Porte's *La science des négocians et teneurs de livres* – the title that the STN appear to have relied upon – was constantly available throughout the century of lights.⁹⁹ La Porte's guide led merchants through the basics of several single- and double-entry accounting systems, and offered practical advice concerning how to pen business letters of all types. It explained payment methods, insurance policies, weights and measures and other such contrivances of trading. La Porte left nothing to chance, detailing in which particular size of characters various pieces of information should be written, and exactly where functional dividing lines should be drawn on the manuscript page for each type of account. Helpfully, merchants tended to follow such rules remarkably closely, even copying formulaic conventions like opening new books with 'Au nom de Dieu' penned large across the first folio's header. Indeed, the international system became so standardized that traders even bought the blank manuscript books that they employed pre-prepared, ready to be filled in with the formulas espoused by La Porte and others. Upon its establishment in August 1769, the STN purchased a 'Grand livre', a 200-sheet 'Brouillard', a 'Journal', two 'Copies des lettres', a 'Carnet de poste' and a 'Carnet d'ouvriers' from Samuel Fauche and an unknown source in Lyon.¹⁰⁰

La Porte's work served as a fairly comprehensive overview, but it did not entirely negate the need for more specialist volumes dealing with specific aspects of record keeping and doing business. Pierre Giradeau's *La banque rendue facile aux principales nations de l'Europe* defied its title with a series of terrifyingly long-winded explanations of foreign exchange mechanisms. In addition, it served as an important source of trading information about various European towns, listing, for example, the privileges of corporate bodies in Lyon or the principal exports and imports of the port of Naples.¹⁰¹ Copies of this guide are often found bound with Giradeau's condensed accounting overview, 'L'art de tenir les livres en parties doubles', which offered a reasonable cut-price substitute for La Porte's lengthy work. François Barrême's *Livre de comptes-faits*, another work in constant production from the beginning of the eighteenth century, consisted almost exclusively of multiplication tables that allowed merchants to quickly calculate 10 or 150 copies of a stock item at a particular price without having to resort to an abacus.¹⁰² Invariably produced on poor paper, cheaply typeset and without any explanatory introduction, Barrême's work is a striking example of utilitarian publishing. At 17 *livres* 5 *sols* a piece, what would be the price of 35 pieces? Answer – 603 *livres* 15 *sols*. *Comte fait*; job done.¹⁰³

Taken together, these trade manuals can be used to unpick the secrets of the STN archives with considerable clarity. At its most fundamental level, the double-entry system employed by the Neuchâtelois allowed them to precisely reflect the duality of their trading transactions which, by definition, took place between a creditor and debtor. A single book sale transaction, then, had to reflect both the departure of stock from the Society's holdings and the arrival or, more usually, the promise of money, goods or services by way of exchange. According to La Porte's formula, seven elements needed to be recorded to fully capture the event: (1) *le date* (the date); (2) *le débiteur* (the debtor); (3) *le créancier* (the creditor, or crediting account); (4) *la somme* (the price per piece); (5) *la quantité et la qualité* (the quantity and quality of goods); (6) *l'action et comment payable* (the action and how it is payable); and (7) *le prix* (the total price of the transaction).¹⁰⁴ So, a typical STN book sale transaction entry – describing Jean-Pierre Heubach's 1776 purchase of 100 copies d'Holbach's *Système de la nature* – reads:

(1) 21.07.1776,
(2) Jean-Pierre Heubach, (6) current account, owes (7) 31.2.0 *livres de France*
To (3) *Système de la nature*, for (5) 100 copies of 6 sheets at (4) 1 *sol* per sheet,
(6, details) sent to him via J. Haberstock in Morat the 19.07.1776

Several clarifications are perhaps helpful. First, that the entry includes two different dates reflects the difficulty traders faced with pinpointing the precise moment that distance transactions took place. The process of soliciting, agreeing, shipping, confirming and settling book sales could take months, or years in rare cases, and the two parties rarely saw the same stage as a binding commitment to the deal. *La date* (1), then, here and generally in the FBTEE database represents simply the date when the STN first committed the transaction to their books. Habitually this took place within a day or so of the shipment or receipt of goods. Second, the entry's *débiteur* (2) is Jean-Pierre Heubach's eponymous Lausannois bookselling business Jean-Pierre Heubach and Company. External debtors would always be either individuals, institutions, societies or companies, who might each hold several accounts with the STN. In practice, multiple accounts were limited to two types: current accounts (as is the case in this example) or exchange accounts for swapping books. Stipulations regarding when payment should be made tended to be associated with these accounts rather than negotiated on a transaction by transaction basis. As a result, third, *L'action et comment payable* (6) is entirely implicit in account type and the direction of capital transfer. The fact that capital is being transferred from Heubach's current account indicates that he has bought the books. In this particular case, this reality is helpfully confirmed at the end of the transaction with a clarification that includes a trade route along which the merchandise was shipped. Fourth, the *créancier* (3) is not simply given as the STN, but instead their account for the work *Système de la nature*. To facilitate stock monitoring, each book that the STN sold was assigned its own account. Fifth, *la quantité* (5) of 100 copies, each comprised of six printed sheets, is stated. Because imperfect stocks were typically used as blotting paper rather than sold, and because the general product of Swiss printing was so standardized, issues of *qualité* tended to be confined to (admittedly somewhat frequent) grumbling by private letter. Commoditisation meant that such grousing rarely at this point extended to the genius or saleability of the actual text; the bookseller's art was to predict this in advance of any deal. Sixth, *la somme* (4) is here the industry standard price of 1 *sol de France* per sheet that applied to all but the STN's most exceptional transactions. And finally, *le prix* (7) should, of course, tally with the multiplication of *la somme* (4) and *la quantité* (5).

As daily trading activity unfolded, completed transactions were added first to the chronological stream that comprised the STN day books, the rough and good copies of which went by the various titles 'Journal', 'Main Courante' and, most appropriately, 'Brouillard' or fog. Their cloudiness stems from the fact that these ledgers list not only book sale transactions, but all sorts of quotidian and extraordinary financial occurrences from the humdrum purchase of candles to light the print shop to major new capital injections. Indeed, every financially consequent move made by the Society was first recorded in their day books, the entries of which served both as permanent records of activity, and as instructions to execute the consequences of that activity elsewhere in the double-entry system. Aftershocks quivered through a collection of auxiliary books – stock books, client account books and overview ledgers – in each of which information from the murky stream was selected or jettisoned according to purpose to give a clear view of a specific aspect of the business. Heubach's new debt, then, would have been immediately recorded in his individual client account, enabling the Society to efficiently monitor the state of that trading relationship. Simultaneously, an equivalent credit would have been registered in the STN's discreet account for the work *Système de la nature*, compensating for tremors already arrived from printing-cost transactions, and inching the edition slowly out of the red. The departure of 100 copies of d'Holbach's *chef d'oeuvre* would also have been recorded in the stock books, which, once they indicated the exhaustion of the entire edition, served as a reminder to close the account and transfer its balance, through a separate 'profit and loss' account, to be reinvested or extracted as dividend. The genius of the double-entry system meant that, while individual accounts might run up credit or debt, at any given moment the whole should balance and give a comprehensive view of the state of the business.

So, given a complete set of well-maintained account books, the entire trading history of the STN could have been relatively straightforwardly reconstructed, cross-referenced and double-checked. Alas, for all Bovet's diligence, together John Jeanprêtre's post-war cataloguing work and Jacques Rychner's important 1969 *Musée Neuchâtelois* article clarify that he recovered only the imperfect and lacunae ridden set illustrated in Figure 1.4.[105]

Substantially more than half of the STN ledgers are missing. Several series are entirely or substantively lost; others contain yawning gaps; and none bridge the entire period. Most alarmingly, nothing has survived of the STN's highest-level account books, the 'Grand Livre' or 'Livre de raison'. By selecting, reorganizing and summarizing important entries from the stew of the day books, the 'Grand Livre' presented the affairs of a business with such clarity that La Porte recommended it should be kept away from prying eyes and completed alone and without interruption.[106] Equally, no systematic and complete registers of STN client accounts have survived. The Luchtmans archive betrays the acuteness of this particular loss by exposing the clarity and simplicity with which these ledgers might otherwise have been used to reconstruct book shipments. More encouragingly, extant formal day books (Journals or Brouillards) cover 60 per cent of the period to July 1787; draft day books (Main Courante) cover 20 per cent; order books cover 60 per cent; and stock books cover 40 per cent. Assorted cash books, draft and irregular accounts and print shop and shipping records provide supplementary, if erratic, accounting information. Then there are the 24,000 letters received by the Neuchâtelois and 11 large ledgers of copies of letters sent, many of which harbour

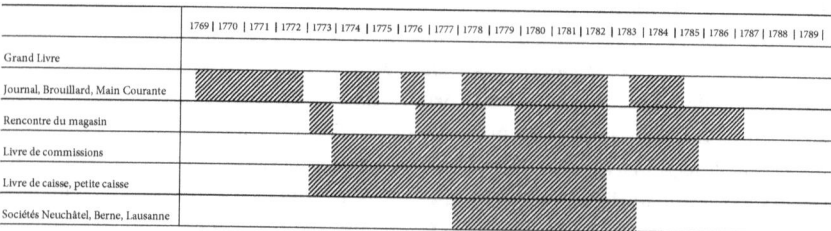

Figure 1.4 Surviving STN archive.

scattered formal and back-of-the-envelope accounts. Alas, most of these key extant sources, including the received letters, fall mysteriously silent from the summer of 1787.

Some knowledge of these lacunae, coupled with the perplexing reality that previous scholars of the archive had almost exclusively based their work upon the letter collections and order book series, meant that Simon Burrows and I arrived in Neuchâtel with modest expectations. The accounting material appeared rich but inconsistent and mysterious. Many shortened book titles seemed unfathomable; specialist terminology baffled; and a muddle of quotidian affairs and inscrutable accounting mechanisms clouded the bibliometrics. Yet as our pilot reached its eleventh-hour – with a chariot's worth of manuscripts cast across the BPUN's lake-view researcher's table – the miracles of double-entry accounting suddenly became clear. La Porte's aftershocks were so extensive, and so comprehensively implemented, that where transaction information was lost due to the lacunae in one series, it might confidently be recovered elsewhere. For the vast majority of the STN's trading history, the date (1); the debtor (2); the crediting account (of the book being traded) (3); the quantity and quality (5); and the action and how it is payable (6) of their transactions could be recovered. With this information stream – routine transactions defined by date, client, book and number of copies – we could reconstruct an unprecedented view of the STN's business. The task would be fantastically challenging, and it would not entirely unravel the secrets of the Society. Because financial information (La Porte's sum (4) and price (7)) did not pass into the stock books, the purpose of which was to count books rather than their value, it could not be holistically captured. It would also be risky. Taken alone, this barebones data stream of scruffy titles (sometimes one-work indications of the book like *réflexions* or *vérité*) linked to obscure client accounts (mainly indicated by a simple surname like 'Fougt' or 'Girardet'), however well spatially and temporally located, would hardly suffice. A massive bibliographical and biographical reconstructive effort, described in the technical appendix to this volume, would be necessary to make sense of our core transactions data stream. Yet the opportunity to peer into the early-modern international francophone book market like never before proved too tempting to ignore. Figure 1.5 shows the path through the account books that, four years of painstaking reconstruction later, ultimately materialized.

Our methodological approach assured that the STN day books, pristine and competently scribed folio *Journals* or *Brouillards* and their rougher *Main Courante* drafts, were the dominant source employed to recreate this core data stream. For chronological stretches where transaction information has survived in multiple places, the day books were preferred because they harbour the most trustworthy information. Theoretically, at least, their scribes had neither reason nor sufficient information to attempt their falsification; they recorded daily business as it unfolded in real time and independently of the financial or stock-keeping consequences of trading events. Critically, and in contrast to the stock books and client accounts, which are lightly spotted with suspicious redactions, the day books needed not balance. Over time, the value of the dependability of these books in the case of disputes, inheritances and liquidations became recognized in both conventions of good bookkeeping practice and by European lawmakers. In France, for example, a 1672 bookkeeping *Ordonnance* stipulated that day books were to be always filled in chronologically and with no blank

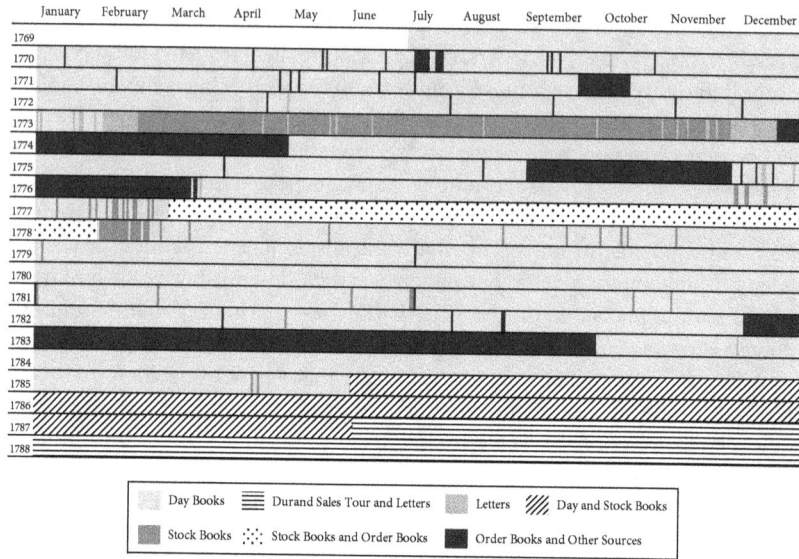

Figure 1.5 Sources used to construct the FBTEE 'core data stream'.

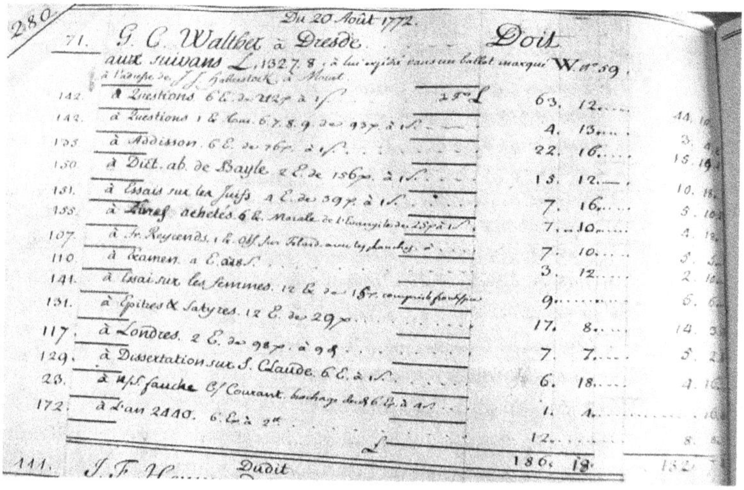

Figure 1.6 Typical day book entry.

spaces left between the transactions.[107] By fortunate coincidence, too, the STN day books happen to be the most substantively surviving series in the BPUN archives. Beginning on 27 July 1769 with the directors' initial injection of capital, and ending in the early 1790s with a peculiar series of books transfers between Louis Fauche-Borel and the Society, they are wholly extant for 80 per cent of the STN's chronological trading existence (Figure 1.6).[108]

A typical day book shipment entry, with La Porte's indicators again in brackets, reads,

[BPUN STN MS 1033 Brouillard A, f.] 280
(1) Du 20 Août 1772
(2) G. C. Walther à Dresde.................. (6) Doit
aux suivans l. 132.7.8, (6, detail) à lui expédie dans un ballot marqué W. n.59, à l'adresse de J. J. Haberstock à Morat
--

à (3)Questions (5)6 ex de 212f à [4]1s........ (7)63.12.0 [livres de France].....
...... 44.10.0[livres de Neuchâtel]
à (3)Questions (5)1 ex tom. 6, 7, 8, 9 de 93f à (4)1s........ (7)4.13.0........ 3.4.8
à (3)Addisson (5)6 ex de 76f à (4)1s........ (7)22.16.0...... 15.19.2
à (3)Dict. ab. de Bayle (5)2ex de 156f à (4)1s........ (7)15.12.0........ 10.18.0
à (3)Essais sur les Juifs (5)4ex de 38f à (4)1s........ (7)7.16.0....... 5.10.2
[etc. . .]

The example shows some real-world complexities that take us beyond La Porte's simplified formula. Books – priced by the sheet, described by the set and sometimes sold by the volume – prove challenging to satisfactorily quantify; abbreviated titles like 'Addisson' and 'Questions' make individual works (let alone editions) difficult to identify; and that Neuchâtel's currency differed from the international book-trade standard *livre de France* adds a further layer of calculation.[109] Yet, nonetheless, more than enough information necessary to create transaction entries in the FBTEE core data stream is here present. On 20 August 1772, a series of capital flows from the current account of G[eorge] C[onrad] Walther in Dresden were recorded to accounts representing individual STN-held works, given as shorthand versions of their titles.[110] By the first of these transactions, the account signified as 'Questions' was credited 3 *livres*, 4 *sols* and 8 *deniers de Neuchâtel* in compensation for 1 copy of volumes 6, 7, 8 and 9, totalling 93 printed sheets. By implication, and indeed in this case by brief description (see (6, detail)), these specific volumes had left the STN's storeroom and were working their way across patchwork central Europe to their Saxony destination.[111] This, then, is how book sales were recorded in the Society's day books. STN purchases look almost identical, but with the capital flows reversed. Free gifts, returns, swapped books and other such non-standard scenarios, too, were registered using this standard formula.[112]

For chronological stretches where the day books are lost, we turned in the first instance to the STN's extant *rencontre du magasin* or stock books, despite their dramatically different appearance, purpose, organizing principals and content.[113] Narrow, tightly bound and indexed for easy access, these ledgers were designed to be completed on the go while being carried around the stock room. They are now suitably dog-eared. Each stock book covers a stretch of time between two stock takes, which the STN conducted at irregular intervals varying between nine months and several years. Entries are organized by book title, usually alphabetically for the first part of the volume, but then more haphazardly as space ran short and new stock arrived.[114] Each title is normally followed by some minimal edition details, although the quality of this information varies wildly and is oftentimes (as in the below example) limited to a simple number of printed sheets. Below the title, filling blank space left when the book was first put into commission, every instance that stock of the edition arrived in, or exited from, the STN's store room is recorded, as well as the number of copies, the date and the client with which the transaction took place.[115]

A typical stock book entry, again with La Porte's indicators in curly brackets, thus reads,

[MS1000, Rencontre du magasin, f.] 115 (1)↓ 1773		(3)Sermons de Saurin (2)↓	387 ¼ f (5)↓
Fevrier	18	Il s'en trouve a cette date	7
Juin	26	(6)↓Reçu de J. H. Pott & Cie	1
« °		Plus	1
Août	26	Plus	10
1773		(6)↓**Vendu**	
Fevrier	27	à Des Bordes	1
« °		à Malherbe fils	5
Mai	4	à J. Chenoux	2
	25	à J. Gay	1
Juillet	14	à G. Rondy	1
Septembre	8	à Deinet	2
	15	à Dubois	1

The stock books proved a threefold nuisance. First, the absence of La Porte's sum (4) and price (7) from their listed transactions contributed towards our decision not to include financial data in our core dataset.[116] Second, unlike the day books, these ledgers never reveal whether STN stock transfers were the product of exchanges or capital transactions. As a consequence, we had to limit our definition of La Porte's 'action, and how payable' (6) to simple descriptors of stock movement (In, Out, Return and so forth). And finally, the stock books lack important contextual information and were difficult to process. Client data is limited to scribbled surnames; no trade routes, ballot numbers or special instructions are revealed; and single orders are scattered across as many pages of the ledger as they consisted of shipped books. Reconstructing the above 14 July 1773 Giuseppe Rondy order, for example, took us to thirty-six non-sequential ledger pages.[117] Larger commissions sprawl still more extensively. Yet, *commonality* between the stock books and the day books – that both unambiguously and holistically betray the date, client, titles and number of copies of STN's acquisitions and shipments for defined temporal stretches – was nonetheless the solid foundation upon which the FBTEE dataset was built. Much of the strength of the data, indeed, derives from the fact that the stock books could be used to extend and reinforce the perspective provided by the day books. By cross-checking orders between the two document types (where extant series exist of both), and by verifying predicted holdings based on day book transactions against actual contemporary stock take data, we could have total confidence not only in our methodological approach but also in the STN's bookkeeping standards.

Our third and final source of systematically recorded STN shipment information, the *livres de commissions* or order books, might be more familiar due to their exploitation by Robert Darnton and others.[118] Orders usually arrived at the Society via the post, sometimes buried deep within lengthy letters rich in background narrative, posturing and tedious confidence trickery. Few requests could be dealt with immediately, perhaps because of a lack of stock, but more usually because of practical packing and transportation considerations born of the fact that the Society liked to group orders that passed by common intermediary towns like Lyon or Basle to skimp on postage. Sometimes, too, the STN delayed shipment while they investigated the creditworthiness of the potential client, or waited for a winter waterway to thaw or a customs worry to pass. As such, so that never a potential sale went misremembered, orders were always written down on the left-hand page of the *livres de commissions* as soon as possible after their arrival.[119] Registered under a heading of the potential client's name and address, were the date of the order, any special shipping details and a note of the number of copies of each individual book requested. At a later date, assuming the order was realized, the book keeper would mark off successfully realized demands with a little marginal stroke of the pen and write details of the full works sent on the right-hand page.

A typical order book entry, once more with La Porte's indicators in brackets, reads,

139 Commission de (2) Charles Fontaine à Manheim par sa lettre du 20 Juin 1775	(6) Expedié le (1) 11 Juillet 1775 en un ballot C.F.
- 6 Le Jeune philosophe	- (3)6 (5)Le Jeune Philosophe
- 4 Millot	- (3)12 (5)Don Pédre
6 Recueil s ?	- (3)2 (5)Miroir d'or
12 Eloge de la raison	- (3)4 (5)Millot
12 D. Pédre	- (3)4 (5)Luciade ed de France
- 2 Miroir d'or	- (3)2 (5)Usong
1 Tom 2 Sébaltus	- (3)1 (5)Moliere
1 Tom 1, 2, 4, 5 questions	- (3)1 (5)Sacrifice de lamour
1 Tom 4 questions	- (3)1 (5)Nosologie de Sauvage
Y ajoutte 1 ex de tout que nous avons de nouveau	- (3)1 (5)Art d'accoucher
	- (3)1 (5)Onanisme n/ed
	- (3)1 (5)Viaud
	- (3)1 (5)Etat present du Portugal
	- (3)1 (5)de la musique et de la dance
	- (3)1 (5)histoire poétique
	- (3)1 (5)muses helvetiennes
	- (3)1 (5)Lart dobserver
	- (3)1 (5) (?)
	- (3)1 (5) Maximes de Rochefoucault
	- (3)2 (5) Rollin
	- (3)1 (5) Recherches sur les Americains
	- (3)1 (5) Recherches sur les Egyptians
	- (3)1 (5) Journal de Maupeou
	- (3)1 (5) Malheurs de l'Inconstance
	- (3)1 (5) Confidence
	- (3)1 (5) Voix du curé
	- Sagio

On the hunt for works sent, not simply ordered, we could safely ignore the left-hand-page commission information. Supply, as we see in this case, rarely mirrored demand.[120] While Charles Fontaine was sent his copies of 'jeune philosophe', 'Millot', 'Don Pédre' and 'miroir d'or', none among his 'recuil', 'Eloge de la raison, 'Questions' and 'Sébaltus' were dispatched. Moreover the STN rather enthusiastically responded to his request for 'nouveautés' by padding the order with copies of twenty-three additional works! The right-hand-page shipment information, however, contained all the information necessary – date, client, work and number of copies – to add dispatches to the FBTEE core data stream. As with the stock books, the information is somewhat minimal. Titles are given only as short indicators; no financial details are divulged; and no trade route information is recorded (although a ballot mark is generally noted). More problematically, the order books lack information about two types of transaction sets. First, naturally enough, they say nothing about STN purchases, printings, returned works and unsolicited envois (such as free gifts for distant censors). And second, they give no details about counter sales and immediately realized shipments to local clients.

After a thorough sweep through the day books, stock books and order books, we were still left with two types of gaps in the FBTEE core data stream. First, for the periods between 3 and 18 February 1773, 7 November and 22 December 1773 and 1 June 1787 and 31 May 1790, for which none of our three major source types survive, no data whatsoever had been recovered. And second, for those stretches where we had employed the *livres de commissions* – that is, between 22 December 1773 and 1 May 1774, 23 August and 27 November 1775, 3 January and 17 March 1776 and 1 January and 24 September 1783 – we lacked data relating to acquisitions and some local sales.

These gaps were plugged as best possible using isolated accounts scattered throughout a number of auxiliary ledgers and the STN's voluminous surviving correspondence. Early modern printers and booksellers, as we have seen above, obsessively cultivated client relations for reasons of confidence and credit. The STN kept tabs on their trade balances with each of their customers and patrons by copying relevant day book entries into ledgers of client accounts, which were organized alphabetically by client name and listed all acquisitions and purchases within a defined time frame. These books, regrettably, are lost. However, because the information that they harboured was to be shared with the client for billing purposes, and because scribes often produced rough copies before finalizing the figures, we find its echoes throughout the BPUN archive's ledgers and letters. By targeting our efforts towards the relatively short chronological stretches not covered elsewhere, and by using already gathered information to focus only on dossiers relating clients actively trading during those periods, it proved possible to at least partially bung our data stream holes using solid accounting information scatted throughout the archive. Following this methodological approach through to its logical conclusion, we worked through a variety of pay books, cash books and other auxiliary ledgers in a quest to also recover print runs, stock takes and counter sales wherever they were available.[121]

The problem of the 1 June 1787 to 31 May 1790 gap, however, was less obviously addressable. From the summer of 1787, for reasons discussed later in this volume, much of the archive falls silent. By this point, the Society had been under administrative measures for some time, and as a last throw-of-the-dice between 29 July 1787 and 19 November 1788 the travelling salesman Victor Durand was dispatched on a monumental tour of Europe to drum up business. Durand's letters sent back to Neuchâtel, which richly describe the trials and tribulations of a sometimes weary traveller and fully detail the transactions that he brokered, are our only significant means of understanding this key period. Nothing survives, regrettably, of the major account books, and few extant letters shed light on the Society's activities.[122] Until now, Durand's letters have always been considered problematic. The transaction details that they harbour were scribbled in a numeric shorthand code that rendered them undecipherable without, Jeffrey Freedman once suggested, a 'Rosetta Stone'. Durand's hieroglyphs, in fact, refer to the marginal references in fellow Neuchâtel bookseller Louis Fauche-Borel's printed catalogue of 1787.[123] Cracking this code and adding Durand's dealings to the core data stream allowed us to take our understanding of the Society further than previously thought possible. After Durand, between November 1788 and May 1790, alas, the trail goes cold. The STN was already as good as finished, and by the time the records resurface from May 1790, it was no longer a serious going concern.[124]

A total of 70,584 transactions detailing the 1769–94 acquisition, printing or shipment of 859,206 (445,496 in and 413,710 out) copies of 3,987 different books form our core data stream, which might be considered the backbone of the wider FBTEE dataset. Each entry was extracted directly from the STN ledgers and letters, and this was just the start of our travails. The most laborious and, perhaps, methodologically innovative work – turning this murky temporal stream of obscurely shortened book titles linked to anonymous business identifiers into a bibliographically rich reconstruction of the STN's business – will be described in the appendix essay to this volume 'Decoding and Coding the French Book Trade'. Through a complex process, by way of example, 'Addisson' from our above day book example was revealed to be the Genevan booksellers Philibert and Chirol's 1772 edition of Gabriel Seigneux de Correvon's translation of Joseph Addisson's *The Evidence of the Christian Religion* as *De la religion chrétienne* published in three volumes in octavo. 'J. Gay', from our order books example, was identified as the Lunéville bookseller Jean Gay who, among other operations, happened to run a sizeable reading room. Book by book, client by client, transaction by transaction, the secrets of the ledgers were gradually, methodically uncovered to the extent that we might make the following claim. Through the combination of the richness of the core data stream, this bibliographical and biographical work, and the analytical power of a structured database, we can now analyse aspects of the STN's business – sales by regions or genre, for example, or bestselling authors over time – more efficiently and accurately than could Bertrand, Bosset de Luze, Fauche or Ostervald.

This is a dangerous thought that needs to be carefully balanced with an acute understanding that our picture is only partial and, taken in isolation, can be misleading. First, our methodological approach artificially elevates books above other STN trading activities. The point must not be laboured: the Society's accounting system was overwhelmingly skewed towards the clear recording of book transactions, and ephemeral printing jobs were harder to come by in sleepy Neuchâtel than in larger centres. Nevertheless, regular day book entries usually registered under the catch-all rubric 'divers petits ouvrages' hint at, and occasionally detail, a host of modest commissions for printed hymn books, lottery tickets, official regulations, labels, invitations, passports and so forth that fell below our radar.[125] In 1774, to give just one example among many, the watchmaker Pierre Jaquet-Droz, with the help of his son Henri-Louis and several tradesmen, publicly demonstrated those remarkable clockwork automatons that were so flabbergasting tourists in the Neuchâtelois mountain town of La Chaux-de-Fonds. The first, a seated draftsman around 70 cm in height, could draw four separate designs, including the profile of Louis XV; the second, the young girl, played her custom-made harpsichord by striking its keys with her wooden fingers while her eyes appeared to follow the movement of her hands; the third, the most remarkable, housed a mechanism so sophisticated that it could be programmed to write any three lines of text. The Jaquet-Droz automates were among the artistic, technical and commercial crowning achievements of this golden age of Neuchâtelois proto-industrial activity. They attracted a constant stream of tourists. Towards the beginning of June 1774, the STN printed 2,000 copies (totalling 1,000 printed sheets) of what they described as a 'Description des méchanics', the pamphlet that served as a prospectus for the exhibition of these machines.[126] Alas, such job printings, because they were rarely accounted for individually, are absent from the FBTEE database. The dark matter of the print industry, the combination of archival lacunae and our chosen methodological approach leave us with no wholly satisfactory way of systematically gauging their importance to the Society over time.

Second, the FBTEE method also risks distorting our understanding of the successes and failures of the Society by considering books as single comparable units. Again, our approach only mirrors contemporary practice. Booksellers ordered books by title and number of copies, and the STN accounts are so organized. But, due to the 1-*sol*-per-sheet fixed price model that the Society operated, clients were effectively billed by the page. Sales of the ten-volume 387 ¼ sheet 'Sermons de Saurin' from our stock book case above were 387 ¼ times more valuable to the Society than Voltaire's single sheet pamphlet 'Dieu'. While the FBTEE database does give full bibliographical descriptions of traded works – volumes, pages numbers, printed sheets and so forth – the tools presently available in its web interface are built around the unit book. Thus, when this volume compares bestselling authors, or dissects sales to northern France, more often than not 'Dieu' and the 'Sermons de Saurin' count equally. Further, we might be minded that the analytic power and bibliographical detail of the database risk encouraging the analysis of certain features or categories of a unit 'book' over which the STN directors rarely lost sleep. In many cases, for example, they did not even enquire about the authorship of works that traded, whereas modern literary scholars and historians tend to obsess over bibliographic and paratextual detail. Unless the name might encourage sales (and there existed only a handful of such writers, Voltaire foremost among them), authorship often seemed of little consequence to Ostervald and his fellow directors.

And third, we know not the STN's precise business strategies. Practices that were typical of the time but now appear alien run through the accounts. The Society drew up their global balance sheets, for example, far too irregularly to suggest that they were using the bookkeeping process to effectively monitor their bottom line. Indeed, the directors often only tallied global profits, losses and stock holdings once the physical ledgers that they were using filled and balances needed transferring.[127] When they did so, further, they rarely wrote down assets in accordance with prevailing trading conditions. Their balance sheets, as such, were neither sufficiently nuanced nor regularly drafted to be tactically effective.[128] Likewise, although large sums of money were often owed on the balances of individual client accounts for several years, interest was rarely deemed payable. Booksellers could, and did, effectively use the STN as a source of cheap credit. Both of these accounting practices were common in early modern business, reflecting mentalities that cared more about cultivating long-term business relations than immediate profit. The trade in Swiss books was a profitable and stable one, the thinking went, so the Society needed only to grow to sufficient size and longevity to take advantage. Not charging interest suited everybody, providing a buffer for individual traders (who could let accounts fall into the red if necessary) that, in turn, protected the wider industry from demand troughs or a credit crunch. It also helped to keep bookkeeping simple. Yet, for us, the STN's willingness to ship books at real terms losses, added to our previous uncertainties about the political and literary motivations of its directors in establishing the business, make for choppy analytical waters. If we might hubristically claim greater diagnostic capability than Bertrand, Bosset de Luze, Fauche and Ostervald, then it must be of concern that they considered even the crudest of performance indicators wholly unnecessary.

After this methodological interlude, then, our literary road issuing onto the French Revolution appears still longer and more torturous. Layers of uncertainty need unpacking. Yet, thanks largely to good bookkeeping, the fluke survival of certain ledgers, Bovet's diligence and modern technology, the FBTEE project has at least been able to locate and exploit *an* authentic trail through the STN account books. Perhaps, indeed, given lingering ambiguities concerning the Society's financial goals, this stock-focused path is the most appropriate and valuable that might be extracted. The accounts suggest that the Neuchâtelois had two preoccupations: rapid growth and developing healthy and lasting client relations. To satisfy these concerns, they always tried to ship as many books to as many European wholesalers, booksellers and individuals as they deemed sustainable. Building the networks, in short, came first; a glimmer of future profit sufficed to render an opportunity worth pursuing. As such, we might proceed to the close study of the FBTEE dataset – with La Porte's action, date, client, title and quantity at its core – confident that the travails of one Swiss publishing house will teach us much about the European book trading nexus. So, to begin, we must right away get back to that little utopia in the heart of Europe.

2

The Myth of the Mountain Dwellers

The somewhat fortuitous survival of the STN papers has ensured that little Neuchâtel occupies a strangely prominent, yet curiously equitable, place in scholarly understanding of both the Enlightenment and the intellectual origins of the French Revolution. An intriguing number of key Revolutionary actors and agitators passed through the town and its surrounds in the decades that preceded 1789. Jean-Jacques Rousseau lived in the Val-de-Travers village of Môtiers between 1762 and 1765. He delighted in the gentle forest trails of the Jura, penned the *Projet de constitution pour la Corse*, advised village girls on the benefits of breastfeeding and, ultimately, was chased away by stone-throwing pastors.[1] Other writers were treated more generously by the Neuchâtelois. To celebrate the arrival of the Swiss naturalist Horace-Bénédict de Saussure, who was in town to measure the temperature of Lake Neuchâtel at various depths, Samuel Fauche organized a night-time boat trip accompanied by a troop of musicians.[2] The bestselling essayist Louis-Sébastien Mercier, future Girondin leader Jacques-Pierre Brissot de Warville, journalist and royalist Jacques Mallet du Pan, and the writer, diplomat and future revolutionary Gabriel-Honoré de Riquetti, comte de Mirabeau, all enjoyed agreeable sojourns in Neuchâtel during the 1780s. Isabelle de Charrière spent the last three decades of her life in Colombier, from where she hosted a literary salon and published her celebrated *Lettres neuchâtloises*.[3] Barely a mile away in Boudry, the much-vilified revolutionary publicist Jean-Paul Marat – stabbed by the royalist Charlotte Corday in his bathtub in 1793 and immortalized in the famous propaganda painting by Jacques-Louis David – was passing his formative years.

These elite political and literary ties extended across the Swiss Romand. From 1759 Voltaire lived in the French town of Ferney due, partially at least, to its proximity to the Genevan presses of Gabriel and Philibert Cramer and, perhaps, Gabriel Grasset.[4] Edward Gibbon wrote substantial parts of his monumental *The History of the Decline and Fall of the Roman Empire* in Lausanne. Jacques Necker, the French finance minister who played as significant a role as any individual in precipitating the Revolution, hailed from Geneva. Moreover, certain contemporary observers insisted that this marked literary culture penetrated deep into society. In 1789, on the trail of Rousseau's legend, Dugast de Bois Saint-Just insisted that he found in each house that he encountered a little library containing copies of the Bible and the *Encyclopédie*, the complete works of Rousseau and Voltaire and a collection of novels, histories and dictionaries.[5] Such dubious reveries have proven persistent and have begotten an historical legend – the 'myth of the mountain dwellers' (*le myth valorisant des montagnards*) – that has placed the educated Jura and wider-Romandy public at the heart of the Swiss Enlightenment. If true – if the Swiss plateau was dotted with as many readers as it was printers and sojourning intellectuals – then Neuchâtel would have been a great place from which to sell books.

Through a close examination of the STN's trade across French-speaking Switzerland, this chapter proposes two radical conclusions. First, it revises our understanding of the body of printed books that circulated throughout pre-Revolutionary Romandy and, by consequence, the utility of the STN archives. Rather than being able to source 'almost anything', as we have been led to understand, the printer–booksellers of the region traded almost exclusively in a single clearly differentiated product: locally published, of-the-moment, cheap editions destined for international markets. Their mutual desire to protect and promote the competitiveness of Swiss printing meant that they largely operated as a cartel. The archives of the STN and the FBTEE database, therefore, should be seen as representative primarily of the functioning and output of this league of traders and their unique productive zone. Second, it demonstrates the limitations of literary consumption in Neuchâtel and the Swiss Romand. For sure, books bounced around the region's wholesale networks as traders diversified their stocks and tried to satisfy international orders, but buyers were few and far between. It would take more than the myth of the mountain dwellers, this chapter suggests, to support a printing operation the size of that of the STN.

The fact that late-eighteenth-century Swiss printing had its own distinct identity will hardly surprise bibliographers and specialist librarians. Although sometimes produced under false addresses – most regularly 'Londres', but sometimes provocative fictions like 'Dans le pays de la liberté' or 'De l'Imprimerie du Louvre' – Swiss editions are generally identifiable by their physicality, content, typography and ornamentation.[6] Romandy printers usually employed paper sourced from neighbouring France, notably the Pays de Gex, Burgundy, Lyon and Besançon; they generally used type and (often baroque) typographical vignettes forged by Benoît Biollay or Marquet in Lyon, or by Guillaume Haas in Basle; they tended to include distinctive woodblock ornaments, such as the easily identifiable pastoral vignettes of Hieronymus von der Finck of Basle; they commissioned engravings by the likes of Abraham Girardet of Le Locle; they relied upon a pool of locally based translators and editors, notably Henri Rieu; and they set works to type according to a distinctive style.[7]

Historians, however, have tended to gloss over such typographical niceties, constructing the STN and their Swiss competitors as footloose businesses that might equally have been located anywhere just beyond France's eastern border from the Mediterranean to *La Manche*. Darnton's 'floating stock' thesis, remember, insists that the extensive swapping of books throughout a 'fertile crescent' that stretched from Avignon to Amsterdam left all European francophone printer–booksellers with more-or-less the same wares. The STN, he suggests, was a typical European publishing house capable of supplying its French clients with almost anything. As such, the Society's order books are considered sufficiently representative to permit the reconstruction of France's pre-Revolutionary clandestine 'bestsellers' with, it is claimed, as much accuracy as modern day lists.[8] Scores of case-study-based articles examining STN shipments to specific clients, towns or regions spread across the map have followed Darnton's lead. As their author's dissect bestselling genres in the Polish capital or the illegality of envois to Lorraine, few hesitate to ponder the sorts of books that were available to the Society.[9]

More caution might have been exercised since, by his own admission, Darnton was largely following his nose. Twenty-five summers spent poring over '50,000' letters had left him feeling convinced about the validity of the 'floating stock' thesis and the representativeness of the Neuchâtel archives.[10] Although he could forward little direct evidence, his hypothesis seemed particularly astute since it tallied with both scholarly understanding of the functioning of eighteenth-century intellectual networks and several facets of the bibliometric record. The francophone republic of letters was a dense communications nexus through which information – for example, scientific advances, cultural product or political news – travelled far and fast. The STN's participation in this web of knowledge screams from the dossiers; their directors constantly probed correspondents for information about new publications on the horizon or for news copy to publish in the *Nouveau Journal helvétique*. Moreover, they boasted correspondents throughout the border territories: forty-seven in the United Provinces; twenty-eight in the Austrian Netherlands; twenty in London; fourteen in Avignon; and scores more dotted throughout the Germanic lands. Books, too, appeared to have circulated with similar freedom. The Lausannois bookseller Jules-Henri Pott's 128-page 1772 catalogue, which is typical of many of the time, shows that he held and offered for sales scores of works printed in each of Europe's major publishing centres.[11] It displays no apparent bias towards Swiss editions. Auction catalogues of private library sales prove that individuals located anywhere in Europe, and indeed beyond, could amass remarkable collections of books sourced from far and wide.[12] Without question, then, booksellers *did* have sufficiently extensive networks to source most anything, and their books *did* invariably end up far from the nest.

Figure 2.1 – a map of the locations from which the STN obtained their books – represents perhaps the single most surprising discovery of the FBTEE project. It shows that the Society almost exclusively sourced works locally, exposes Darnton's malfunctioning *pifomètre* and punctures the 'floating stock' thesis. About two-thirds of the 445,496 copies the FBTEE database records as having been handled by the Neuchâtelois originated from their own presses. And two-thirds of the remainder (115,873 of 153,974 copies) were acquired from nearby Swiss towns including Lausanne (39,656 copies or 23%), Neuchâtel (32,067 or 19%), Geneva (26,544 or 15%) and Berne (10,927 or 6%). In total, well over 90 per cent of the STN's stocks were obtained from French-speaking Switzerland. Indeed, even this high proportion exaggerates the significance of foreign procurement to the Society; the majority of their extraterritorial purchases occurred during the exceptional trading conditions associated with their decline. During the comparatively stable 1770s, only 5 per cent of the STN's books were sourced from outside of Switzerland. Across their entire existence, a paltry 500 copies arrived from Paris – largely for benefit of the local literary society – and never was a single work brought in from either Amsterdam or London. Only the Lyonnais booksellers, who occupied a strategically vital position as gatekeepers to the French market, regularly provided substantial volumes of stocks.

This new evidence presents two possibilities. Either the STN's procurement activity was broadly typical of the Swiss printer–booksellers, suggesting the need to re-envisage a regionally variegated 'fertile crescent' where stock circulated less freely than previously thought; or, it was anomalous, intimating that we might preserve the 'floating stock' theory and assume that the Neuchâtelois acquired their more exotic works locally.

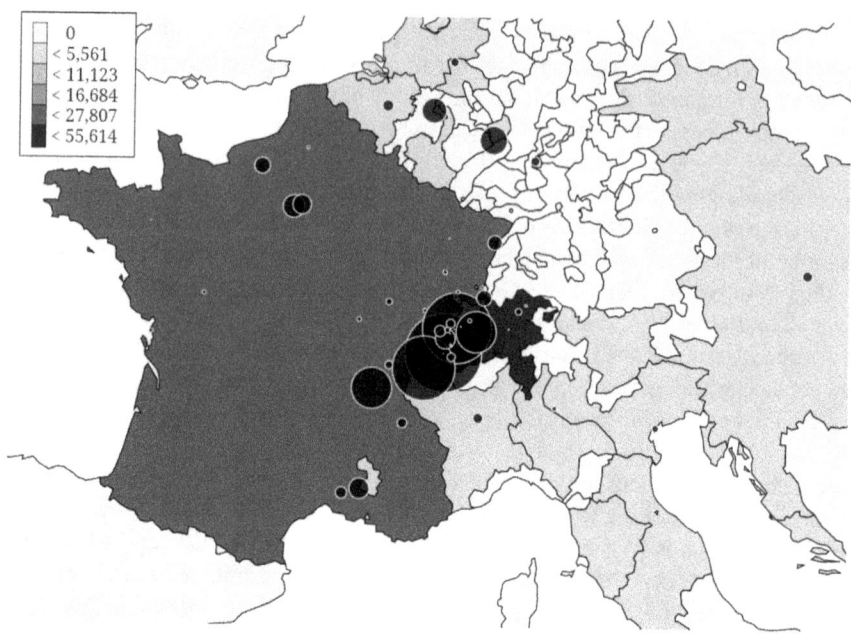

Figure 2.1 Books sourced by the STN, 1769–94 (including printings).

Perhaps, in the second case, the distribution system of the eastern border territories was not the decentralized nexus implied by Darnton, but rather a spoke-and-hub network where arterial routes running between Geneva and Amsterdam eliminated the need for secondary centres like Neuchâtel to deal directly with the northern booksellers. An analysis of the publication places of the works that the STN sourced from third parties, however, suggests the former scenario. Remarkably, it must be recognized, at least 185 different imprints passed through the hands of the Neuchâtelois, including books set in almost every major or minor European publishing centre from London to Cleves. However, few among these foreign editions trouble the FBTEE supply rankings. In total, 75 per cent of the 90,541 identified third-party copies were Swiss imprints.[13] Their Genevan and Lausannois rivals and allies largely supplied them with the new product of their own presses. Including Neuchâtel printed works, roughly 93 per cent of the copies that the STN handled were local.[14] The Swiss traders did not participate in some great pan-European wholesale network: they sold Swiss books.

The significant contrast between this reality and that suggested by the STN's own trade catalogues – seemingly cosmopolitan brochures which scan similarly to those of Jules-Henri Pott or any other from the time – helps to explain why historians have been led so far astray. The Society's catalogue of 1787 listed the 1,440 French-language titles that their travelling salesman Victor Durand was then touting around Europe on horseback, 1,258 of which were accompanied by a place of publication. Of this latter number, just 142 titles (11.3%) were given as published in Neuchâtel and its surrounds, with another 346 (27.5%) described as printed in other Swiss towns, most commonly Lausanne and Geneva. The remainder, just over 60 per cent of the titles, was stated as published in Paris (221 titles or 17.6% of the catalogue's total), London (113 or 9%), the Low Countries and its surrounds (239 or 19%) and an array of other towns from Lyon to Turin (197 or 15.7%).[15] Yet, the FBTEE database shows that the Society stocked just a copy or two of the majority of these foreign editions, compared with scores or hundreds of many published in Switzerland. The 450 'Parisian' editions that it harbours represent 15 per cent of the 2,984 titles that ended up in the Neuchâtel stock room, but just 1 per cent of the Society's total sales. The same lonely copies of unsalable foreign titles – *gardes-magasins* according the trade jargon – clogged up the stockrooms and catalogues year-after-year, combining to give an entirely exaggerated impression of their relevance.

The same bibliometric approach also significantly updates our understanding of the age of the editions that circulated throughout the Swiss zone. Because the Enlightenment is now largely recognized as having been a fast-paced movement, it will not surprise specialists that few old classics like Montesquieu's 1721 *Lettres persanes* inconvenienced Ostervald and his associates. Of the 1,324 titles listed with publication dates in the Society's 1787 catalogue, just 51 (3.9%) appeared before 1750, while 164 (12.4%) were published between 1750 and the establishment of the Society. The vast majority, then, were contemporary works, largely acquired around the time of their publication: 115 (8.7%) were printed between 1770 and 1774; 312 (23.6%) between 1775 and 1779; 426 (32.2%) between 1780 and 1784; while 256 (19.3%) appeared in the thirty months between January 1785 and the catalogue being produced. Similar trends have also been observed in German catalogues, which by the late eighteenth century featured fewer and fewer older titles.[16] Yet, the STN sales data reveals that even this picture vastly overestimates the length of time that books remained desirable in the wholesale trade. In total, 90 per cent of the works that the STN sold during the two-and-a-half years before the appearance of their 1787 catalogue were published during the 1780s. Just like foreign editions, old books proved difficult to shift.

As well as being locally produced and continually of the moment, a third and final characteristic defined the vast majority of the works that the STN and their Swiss compatriots sold: they were cheap. Replying to the Society's 1769 circular, the then aspiring Genevan bookseller Samuel Cailler applauded the initiative to undercut the extravagant prices charged by the Parisians that, he considered, 'everybody' found so revolting.[17] Their regular books would, and did, sell for 1 *sol* per sheet, regardless of their contents. A number of factors common to all of the Swiss printer–booksellers – including a plentiful and regular paper supply, developed infrastructure and European centrality – made the STN's business plan plausible. But, in truth, like their Genevan and Lausannois compatriots, the Society primarily opted for their cost-cutting model out of necessity. Romandy publishers lacked the diverse pool of intellectual talent and the proximity to structures of cultural and political power, privilege and patronage of their northern rivals. They were in no position to lead the industry. Instead, traders relied upon a two-pronged strategy to keep their market advantage: counterfeiting intellectual product and skimping on typographical extravagances. Occasionally, for sure, irresistible opportunities arose to purchase and publish original manuscripts from star authors including Voltaire, Rousseau and Mercier, whose popularity among readers allowed them to circumvent industry norms. But, generally, they gave short shrift to writers. In June 1777 Ostervald refused an undisclosed manuscript offered by the Besançon book dealer Lepagnez on the basis that the STN's golden rule of selling printed sheets at 1 *sol* a piece excluded the possibility of paying authors.[18] The same inflexibility explains why the Swiss printer–booksellers consistently employed mediocre paper.[19] Yes, quality Swiss-printed editions, including the STN's augmented *Descriptions des arts et métiers* and Fauche's richly illustrated first edition of Horace-Bénédict de Saussure's *Voyage dans les Alpes*, were occasionally set to type. But the rarity of these exceptions proves the rule. In March 1769, Rousseau's Neuchâtelois protector Pierre-Alexandre Du Peyrou sent the prospectus for the *Encyclopédie d'Yverdon* to the Amsterdam bookseller Marc-Michel Rey. In his accompanying letter, he doubted (wrongly it transpired) that the ambitious edition would ever be achieved since there simply was not the intellectual know-how in Yverdon – or, he opined, anywhere else in Switzerland for that matter.[20]

Du Peyrou underestimated the Yverdon printer Fortuné-Barthélemy de Félice's determination. But he understood this about the Swiss printer–booksellers: they were all cut from the same raggedy cloth. Their product – cheap, locally produced, contemporary editions – defined them and shaped the ways by which they did business. The razor-thin margins that inexpensive books commanded eliminated any possibility that they might drift aimlessly around France's borders before exiting the wholesale circuit; Swiss books needed to reach customers quickly and directly. Yet, as the STN found to its cost during those troublesome first months, no single establishment could satisfy international demand alone. As such, a geographically limited zone throughout which stocks could be swapped rapidly and economically developed along the Lyon to Basle thoroughfare.[21] Traders set up always-open bilateral exchange accounts that allowed them to asynchronously secure the fresh product of nearby presses against their own works as-and-when new editions appeared and without occurring onerous banking charges. Thousands of books per year zipped between Berne, Geneva, Lausanne, Neuchâtel, Yverdon and a number of other regional towns. The STN sourced 15,178 works from François Grasset and Company and supplied 5,433; acquired 3,485 books from Barthélemy Chirol in Geneva and dispatched 3,914; and received 14,596 from Samuel Fauche in exchange for 8,572.

The traders of this overwhelmingly Swiss stock-swapping zone effectively operated an informal and highly unstable cartel: they first banded together to ensure the international competitiveness of their common product against Dutch and Parisian rivals, before then struggling among themselves for hegemony within the market that their collaborative efforts commanded. For sure, because each firm had to fight for its slice of the Swiss-book pie with more-or-less the same stocks, they spent much of their time at loggerheads. A dispute over Mercier's *Tableau de Paris* in February 1782, for example, left Chirol so enraged with the Neuchâtelois bookseller Jérémie Witel that he insisted that he would extract satisfaction '*à la pointe de mon epée* (by the tip of my sword)'.[22] Competition for foreign buyers was unquestionably intense. Victor Durand was constantly frustrated to find Félice and members of the Fauche clan one step ahead of him as he toured France and Italy in search of demand.[23] But, the bigger picture – obfuscated among all the quotidian backbiting of the STN dossiers – is that businesses were fully aware that they owed their existence to one another.

The principal of collusion, indeed, was built deeply into the small-print of the exchange system operated by the Swiss publishers. Their particular market situation – a tight cluster of vertically integrated print-shop-to-book-store businesses all of which needed a diverse range of cut-price product to compete internationally – facilitated and favoured the operation of a not-for-profit wholesale model. Through mutual agreement, firms simultaneously satisfied their stock needs and bypassed the costly complexity of a third-party wholesale book exchange. The mechanism was simple: books were swapped sheet-for-sheet via exchange accounts, with a fixed value of 1 *sol* per sheet payable if one party fell seriously into arrears. Healthy margins were to be made before and after this intermediary stage: sheets consistently cost about 40 per cent of this amount to print, and publishers could use their discretion when pricing books at their own retail counters.[24] But there was no markup to be added in the middle of the chain. However many times a pile of sheets bounced around the wholesale circuit, its value remained unchanged. Further, the 1-*sol*-per-sheet stipulation – exactly the amount Swiss traders hoped to achieve selling their books abroad – prevented speculation from developing because it ensured that books could not be sold to a foreign retailer for further profit. When the STN sent Genevan-printed books to France, it was technically selling produce for which it had paid 1 *sol* per sheet for just 1 *sol* per sheet. Its margin had already been *made* upstream – on the difference between the printing costs and nominal price of the work that the Society had sent to Geneva in exchange – but was *realized* only at this point. Realizing the value of Romandy-printed books was, by this process, essential to the health of all of the Swiss international booksellers. The system bound the Swiss traders towards a common destiny, and ensured that it was in their mutual interest that only marketable works left the region's presses.[25]

This shared purpose naturally led, from time-to-time and especially when times were tough, to the formation of formal printing alliances. Roughly a tenth of the works that the STN shipped, indeed, were joint-editions published with the help of Romandy partners. In 1771, François Grasset of Lausanne approached the Neuchâtelois with plans to establish a coalition that never came to fruition.[26] Three years later, the Society produced *Histoire de Maurice, comte de Saxe* and *Relation des voyages entrepris par ordre de Sa Majesté Britannique* in collaboration with Jean-Pierre Heubach of the Société typographique de Lausanne (STL).[27] Both editions, despite their constituent volumes being printed at distance, were relatively typographically consistent and sold extremely well; print runs of 666 (*Histoire de Maurice*) and 1,008 (*Relation des voyages*) were almost entirely depleted within twelve months on the market. The great 'libraires associés' confederation formed by the STN, STL and STB, which published 25 editions of separate works comprising 50,000 individual volumes between 1778 and 1780, however, dwarfed this prototypical alliance in scale and ambition. The key to the alliance's unusual longevity and productive output appears to have been the strict conditions outlined by its founding convention. The three partners were duty-bound to keep two presses at the disposition of the collective; select works to print only by unanimity; consistently use high-quality paper and type; and to respect contracts of sales exclusivity concluded with partners. Most importantly, the proceeds of all confederation sales were to be annually redistributed for the common good, while each partner remained free to trade normally for their own account.[28]

The case of the Genevan polymath Jean-André Deluc's *Lettres physiques et morales sur les montagnes*, printed during the summer of 1778, demonstrates the association's value.[29] Deluc's work – a remarkable mix of cosmology, geology and biblical history intermixed with Rousseauian commentary on the pastoral virtues of the inhabitants of Switzerland – had months beforehand been published chez Detune in The Hague and, due to its local-interest content, appeared ripe for counterfeiting.[30] Nonetheless, the *Lettres physiques et morales sur les montagnes* was not the standard fare of the Swiss zone, and predicting precise levels of demand for such a sprawling and unusual thesis was difficult. The confederation agreed upon a relatively conservative 600-copy run, to be printed by the STL, of which the STN received their 200 copies during the middle of July. The Neuchâtelois respected their contract not to sell the work locally and immediately set about garnering international sales, beginning with shipments to Belfort and Colmar on 24 July. In August they sent copies to Chambéry and Lyon; in September to Caen, Montpellier, Soissons and Warsaw; in October to Lyon (again) and Orléans; and in November they dispatched the edition to Basle, Loudun, Naples, Ostend and Venice. Overall, Deluc's text proved a solid, if not spectacular, seller and by 1 May 1782 just nineteen examples remained in stock. Later in that month, the Society took twenty-eight further copies from the STL which, as was almost always the case, had been encountering a little more difficulty with the work. Just over a year later the STN had exhausted those final copies and switched to selling Detune's expanded 1779 edition. Together, the three societies had managed to shift the entire print run of 600 copies of a non-standard work that each among them might otherwise have avoided.

Other editions proved still better sellers. The confederation's 15 July 1780 joint balance sheet reveals Claude-Louis de Saint Germain's *Mémoires de M. le comte de Saint-Germain* to have been their most successful work as a trio.[31] The STN had sold 317 copies, the STB 444 and the STL an impressive 499.[32] Yet, this moment of financial reflection also reveals the development of serious cracks in the partnership. Heubach had proposed the 'libraires associés' alliance back in 1778 in order to increase Swiss production and capitalize upon the potential damage that new French regulations were expected to inflict upon the presses of provincial towns like Lyon.[33] However, despite his strong advocacy, and accepting his successes with Saint Germain's explosive memoirs, Heubach's STL had only managed to place between 20 and 111 copies of most of the confederation's editions. At their standard 1-*sol*-per-sheet accounting rate, the STN had sold 4,079.15.0 *livres de France* of books, the STB 2,807.0.0 and the STL just 1,971.7.0. For its formidable efforts, therefore, the STN was forced by the terms of the 1778 convention to pay the STB 145.14.0 *livres* and the seemingly disinterested STL an exasperating 981.7.0 *livres*.[34] Therein lay the problem – and the principal reason why such printing alliances seldom survived lengthy periods: partners eventually worked out who was doing the hoodwinking. Indeed, as Silvio Corsini has deftly demonstrated, after just a couple of years almost every one of the convention's clauses had been broken by more than one party.[35] After separating themselves from their Lausannois albatross, the STN and STB continued the association throughout 1781 and into the start of 1782 before, inevitably, reverting back to the standard book-swapping model.

Cooperation, then, tended to work more successfully when limited to the voluntary sharing of productive capacity, information and negotiating clout. Idle presses were habitually available for hire by third parties. Félice of Yverdon's two-volume *Causes amusantes et connues* of 1770 and 1771, for example, was begun by Veuve Droz in Neuchâtel, continued by the STN after its purchase of her presses and completed by Antoine Chapuis in Lausanne.[36] Once a Swiss printer decided against counterfeiting a book or publishing a new manuscript, they generally offered it among their rivals hoping, no doubt, that they might profit from at least part of the run. Chirol unsuccessfully suggested to the STN in 1775 that they should print a new edition of Beaux de Maguielle's response to atheism *Essai de philosophie elementaire sur le système de l'univers*. The Genevan attracted a more positive response four years later when he recommended the manuscript 'Considerations sur l'admission des navires neutres aux colonies françoises de l'amérique en tems de Guerre', for which the (now still unknown) author demanded only fifty free copies in lieu of payment. In this case, however, the STN was beaten to the chase by the Genevan printer Isaac Bardin, and had to make-do with the fifty copies they acquired through an exchange with Chriol.[37] Several years later, the STN offered Chriol a manuscript titled 'Observations sur la suisse occidentale', which appears to have never made print.[38] And finally, during the great francophone publishing crisis of the mid-1780s, as the French government closed the Swiss border to book imports, the Swiss showed their true mutually dependent colours by banding together to send an official delegation to lobby in Paris and Versailles for a return of the status quo.[39]

Admittedly, the Swiss printing brothers were a rag-tag band who, fatally reliant upon the tight margins of their singular product, encountered considerable difficulties developing collaborative organizational and intellectual infrastructure to match their northern rivals. The STN's travails with the *Nouveau Journal helvétique* serves as a case in point. Upon the Society's establishment in 1769, its directors purchased the rights to the *Mercure Suisse* (also known as the *Journal helvétique*) from the Droz family. The journal then boasted a respectable 401 subscribers, 333 of whom were divided among the Protestant Swiss cantons of Neuchâtel, Vaud, Geneva, Berne, Basle, Zurich and Schaffhausen. Because only thirty-seven of its customers were foreign, however, it hardly served as an effective tool for marketing Swiss books abroad.[40] Keen to change this situation, the STN focused upon the French market. It paid off François Lacombe, the proprietor of the *Journal des sçavans* and thus holder of the state-sponsored monopoly over literary and scientific news within the kingdom; it employed Parisian correspondents Barnabé Farmain de Rozoi, Daudé de Jossan and François-Thomas-Marie Baculard d'Arnaud to keep abreast of the City of Light's political and literary news; and it arranged preferential postal contracts to facilitate cost-effective distribution. Alas, buyers remained elusive. By 1772, indeed, subscribers to the journal had collapsed to a lowly 234, a mark from which they never substantially recovered. By comparison, over 2,500 copies of each issue of Friedrich Nicolai's *Allgemine deutsche Bibliotek* were published at the height of its influence in the mid-1770s.[41] Undeterred, the search for foreign clients continued apace; in February 1777, for example, the Society wrote to the Lyonnais booksellers the Claudet brothers agreeing to their offer to serve as an agent for the journal and to place an announcement in the local paper.[42] The following year, none the less, the vast majority of the journal's 237 buyers remained the same Swiss individuals the Neuchâtelois had inherited in 1769.[43] Further unsuccessful attempts to boost the journal's prominence and circulation followed the death of Jean-Elie Bertrand in 1779, including the erudite pastor Henri-David de Chaillet's brief reign as editor. During the early months of 1780, Ostervald and Bosset de Luze even travelled to Paris to try and persuade the great *philosophe* Jean le Rond d'Alembert to provide copy for the journal.[44] Their mission ended, predictably, in rejection.

The drawn-out failure of the *Nouveau Journal helvétique* appears, with hindsight, somewhat inevitable. Competition in the international French-language periodicals market had never been so fierce. The French *Almanach de la librairie* of 1781 reveals twenty-two nationally available periodicals that announced the appearance of new books, including established titles like the *Année littéraire*, *Catalogue hebdomadaire*, *Gazette de commerce*, *Journal ecclésiastique* and the *Mercure de France*. A further two-dozen news-sheet style '*Affiches*' served this function on a regional basis.[45] Further, the wider periodical trade was still more congested. Jack Censer's analysis suggests a market undergoing explosive growth: around twenty-one 'non-ephemeral' French-language periodicals were being published in 1750, fifty by 1770 and a remarkable eighty-two in 1785.[46] Privilege and patronage, and the isolation of Neuchâtel from centres of literary and political news production like Paris and London, further lengthened the odds of success for Bertrand's project. It hardly seems likely that Europe's erudite elites were gagging for the latest literary updates from the utopic foothills of the Jura.

Unless, of course, that news differed substantially from that available elsewhere – the upshot, perhaps, of an increasingly confident Swiss zone maturing beyond its counterfeiting roots towards international relevance. This was the STN's hope. In January 1777, Ostervald requested of M. Petitpierre, pastor of the French Church in Basle, that, because the principal purpose of the *Nouveau Journal helvétique* was to spread awareness of the productions of Swiss publishers, he be informed of everything that left the town's presses.[47] Throughout Romandy such information sharing happened as a matter of course, and issues of the journal were stuffed with reviews publicizing works from the shops of the Swiss zone.[48] As the *Nouveau Journal helvétique* flagged, the printers of Geneva, Lausanne and Yverdon all drew up plans for its functional replacement.[49] Their strategic approach was hardly untested: from the mid-seventeenth century, their Dutch rivals had been packing newspapers and journals with advertisements and reviews in order to promote their own product at home and abroad.[50] By throwing good money after bad for the better part of two decades on their ill-fated *Nouveau Journal helvétique* project, the STN revealed both its commitment towards, and dependence upon, the further establishment of Romandy as an important and independent centre of literary production. Swiss books, after all, were all that they sold.

While the Swiss productive zone was export focused – well over two-thirds of STN stocks shipped beyond Romandy – it was powered by domestic retail counters, which are the focus of the remainder of this chapter. Wherever located, we should remember, the printer's bind was maintaining liquidity: paper and type was expensive, but the marketability of books unpredictable; clients constantly sought new editions, yet they took an age to pay; and demand was scattered throughout a continent often ravished by war or capricious regulation, while margins remained frustratingly tight. Bert van Selm's discussion of Johannes Van Ravensteyn's business shows that while the Dutch Republic might have been the 'magasin de l'univers', it was the domestic book market that proved the most important source of ready cash to fill up the coffers for more speculative trading.[51] But French-speaking Switzerland was not the Dutch Republic. Neuchâtel was certainly not Amsterdam. And the STN was not even the only bookseller on the *rue des Moulins*. Given that the Society needed constant capital injections to stay afloat, then, did the myth of the mountain dwellers – the false hope of a robust homebook market that would serve as a platform to support an enormous printing operation – lie at the heart of its problems?

Skimming the FBTEE data, the STN's extra-Neuchâtelois Romandy trade at first appears to have been brisk. The Society managed to place its stocks with small booksellers dispersed widely across French-speaking Switzerland. Jean-Jacob Cramer in Orbe, for example, took 383 books – predominantly single copies of new STN printings and stacks of Bibles and catechisms – from their *fonds* in forty separate orders realized between June 1770 and September 1782. Perched on a Jura hill some 40 kilometres west of Neuchâtel, Cramer's business sat squarely in the natural catchment areas of the Yverdon and Lausannois dealers and thus the STN might readily have missed out upon his direct trade. But the proximity of Romandy's towns allowed the Society to thusly nibble away at the lunches of the region's larger traders. They sporadically dispatched small packets of books to businesses and private individuals like the bookseller Mme. Eggendorfer in Fribourg (828 sales), to the author (of a work on double-entry bookkeeping, no less) Jean-Jacques Imhoof (152), to the merchant Businat fils in Vevey (122), to the booksellers Schnell in Morges (367) and Daniel-Nicolas Tavel in Payernne (317) and to the doctor Chatelain (200) in La Neuveville. Such shipments, however, never accounted for more than a few hundred sales a year, and the Society never managed to make significant inroads into relatively large but better-served settlements like Rolle (218 sales) and Nyon (54).

No. The value in the French-speaking Swiss market came through trading with major publishing houses and independent booksellers located in larger settlements. The most important of these, naturally, were based in Geneva and Lausanne, historically successful twin publishing centres separated by just over fifty kilometres along the northern shoreline of Lake Geneva. A remarkable forty-three booksellers and printers corresponded with the STN from these two towns, sending a total of 2,741 letters. The STN sent 39,372 books to Geneva and received 26,544 in return; they dispatched 27,669 copies to Lausanne and received 39,656.[52] Exchanges were constant and uninterrupted throughout their normal trading history. Away from the shades of the Dents du Midi, the Bernese capital Berne (17,720 works shipped; 10,927 received) and its burgeoning spa-town sibling Yverdon (2,689; 2,707), also proved important outlets for STN works.[53]

The shipping totals were thus significant, but we must remember that most of this trade was *troc* – the swapping of printed sheets for the purpose of mutual risk reduction and diversification of stocks. These were not real sales. Take, for example, the STN's dealings with the major Lausannois printer–bookseller François Grasset. Between 4 April 1770 and 20 August 1790, a constant stream of books passed by boat and road between Neuchâtel and Lausanne. Of the 5,443 works that Grasset acquired from the Society, 4,878 (89.6%) have been positively identified as Neuchâtelois editions, and the majority of the remainder probably also issued from the STN or Fauche presses.[54] In turn, Grasset supplied the Neuchâtelois with 15,178 works, of which 9,735 (64.1%) have been positively identified as having been printed in Lausanne, Geneva or elsewhere in French-speaking Switzerland. Again, the majority of the remainder were surely also wider-Romandy books – the weaker bibliographical data simply precludes certainty.[55] The STN took cheap editions of everything from Mercier's *L'an deux mille quatre cent quarante*

(1,146 copies) to psalms, novels and the popular medical works of Simon-Auguste Tissot. Grasset reciprocated by relieving the Society of such products of their presses as Patrick Brydone's *Voyage en Sicile et à Malthe* (253 copies), Emer de Vattel's *Droit des gens* (177), Jean-Rodolphe Ostervald's *La nourriture de l'âme* (157) as well as numerous Bibles and catechisms. The pair parenthesized these transactions in accounting terms through the use of an exchange account that operated at a nominal 1/20th of the normal book value of the transactions. They tried to make sure that the number of sheets sent in either direction roughly balanced over time. Where they failed, 421 letters sent by Grasset richly detail how the deficit was usually on the side of the Neuchâtelois.[56] For as long as the balance of trade held firm, all told, both parties preserved roughly the same quantity and quality of stocks in their warehouses and nobody made a sou.

The *troc* trade was so much a part of doing business for Ostervald and his associates that it dictated *all* of the Society's major local relationships. For our purposes, alas, these baffling and extensive non-sales render the task of satisfactorily documenting the STN's true Swiss market impossible. Was Grasset sourcing works like the *Droit des gens* for local consumption, or to ship internationally? The STN ledgers are largely silent on this question, but other sources do allow us to suggest tentative answers. For starters, previous scholarly enquiry into the eighteenth-century Swiss bookseller–publishers has amply demonstrated their international orientation.[57] To set up shop in late-eighteenth-century Geneva, from before even the times of Calvin, *was* to seek distant readers. A second look at the best surviving Genevois bookselling sources, the 1755–67 Grand Livre of the Cramer brothers and various letter books of Albert-Henri Gosse's, supports these findings. During the first calendar year documented in the Cramer Grand Livre, which began on 9 August 1755, just 13.1 per cent of the general merchandise revenues came from Switzerland. The largest part of Cramer's stocks, in fact, were sold to France (32.8%) and the Iberian Peninsula (29.4%).[58] Likewise, when the Genevan bookseller Albert-Henri Gosse's business was in full bloom around 1760, only 30.1 per cent (26.2% of recipients) of the letters that he sent were to clients in Switzerland, although as things got tougher with the collapse of his Italian trade this rose to 51.6 per cent (39.2%) between 1777 and 1783, and then to 66.3 per cent (53%) between 1783 and 1791.[59] Added to anecdotal evidence of forward shipments – the Genevan bookseller Samuel Cailler, for example, sent numerous copies of the STN edition of Baculard d'Arnaud's *Epreuves du sentiment* to Naples – a case begins to emerge that many books sent by the STN to Romandy traders were probably far from their final destination.

The argument can be further strengthened by a brief examination of how the STN's Swiss sales evolved during a revealing period of stress. Politically and economically motivated policy changes issuing from Versailles, as we will discover in later chapters, led to the effective closure of the French market to Swiss book imports between the summer of 1783 and the spring of 1787.[60] Few shipments escaped the net, and the Swiss book industry fell into disarray. One immediate reaction to the changes was to cut internal orders already in progress. Barthélemy Chirol wrote to the STN on 24 June 1783 requesting that they halve his commission for copies of Mercier's *Tableau de Paris* and *Portraits des rois de France*. The French booksellers to whom he had intended to relay the works, he reported, had instructed him to suspend all envois.[61] Because everybody was in the same boat – that is, entirely dependent upon the French market and lacking sufficient local buyers to take up the slack – the STN's shipments across the Helvetic zone plummeted. From an already lowered 14,756 works sent in 1783, the Society's Swiss envois fell to 10,044 in 1784, and to 4,645 in 1785, before bottoming out at a pitiful 2,623 books dispatched during 1786. Trade with even solid and established clients like Isaac Bardin in Geneva entirely ground to a halt.[62] Not since 1771, when the Neuchâtelois stocked only about a dozen different titles, had dealings with their Romandy neighbours been so depressed. In 1787, as soon as a limited trading route to France via Lyon was re-established, and despite the devastation wreaked on the Swiss industry, orders from Lausanne and Geneva picked up to 6,089 works. For many the turnaround was too late. Shipments between the STN and Henri-Albert Gosse and Company ended late in 1784 as a torturous attempt to liquidate his stocks dragged on; the Society's ten-year relationship with Jean Abram Nouffer (another bookseller based in Geneva) came to an end in August 1785; and Chirol complained bitterly for years and eventually stopped trading with the Neuchâtelois in May 1786.[63] Their story is for telling later. For now we might simply note all of these wider-Romandy traders were dependent on shipping books on to international readers and that, without some sophisticated interpretation, the FBTEE database thus gives us a greatly distorted impression of the number of real sales that the Society could expect to achieve in the Swiss market.

The well-stocked stores of the *rue de la cité* in Geneva and the *place St. François* in Lausanne, however, were not at the heart of the STN's cash-flow problem. Closer to home, the Neuchâtelois complemented Romandy's thirstiest print shop with perhaps its least promising counter. Lacunae in the cash accounts, especially between 1778 and 1785, mean that the meagre 4,267 counter sales recorded in the FBTEE database somewhat underestimate the Society's true trade. Nonetheless, ample information confirms an unsatisfactory local market. Only two types of works – religious texts like J. F. Ostervald's *Abrégé de l'histoire sainte et du catéchisme* (345 sales), and school books including the *Cours de géographie élémentaire* (182) penned by his nephew, the STN director Frédéric-Samuel Ostervald – retailed substantially in Neuchâtel. Little else sold more than twenty copies. Not even locally published international bestsellers like *Le barbier de Séville* (22 sales), *La vie et les opinions de Tristram Shandy* (20), *Le miroir d'or* (9) stimulated more interest. A world away – from his plush central Berlin Brüderstraße shop replete with a bust of Homer beckoning potential customers from above the door – Friedrich Nicolai complained about being constantly interrupted by the public as he struggled to keep abreast of his correspondence, to direct his sister outlets in Stettin and Danzig, and to organize his offerings for the Leipzig fairs.[64] On a good day, Ostervald or one of his clerks might have had to momentarily suspend their activities once or twice to search out a catechism or perhaps some short novel.

The issue was not simply a matter of readers and means. Late-eighteenth-century Neuchâtel was in the throes of considerable demographic and economic expansion. The region's population increased from around 35,000 at the time of the establishment of the STN to more than 43,000 by 1790. Artisans and professionals in the town tended to earn between 300 and 1,000 *livres de France* per year (the head of the STN's workshop earned 936 *livres* in 1779), making small novels like Jean-Pierre Claris de Florian's seven-batz *Estelle* relatively inexpensive, and all but the most prestigious editions affordable luxuries.[65] Moreover, the town's surroundings were densely packed, by contemporary standards at least, boasting between forty-six and seventy-three inhabitants per square kilometre.[66] The issue, rather, was that it was very difficult to sell more than a couple of dozen copies of a text because few bourgeois individuals *needed* to buy books regularly.

Most problematically, Neuchâtel's subscription reading room and lending library sucked up demand.[67] Shortly after helping establish the STN, Samuel Fauche ceded his popular *cabinet littéraire* to his brother-in-law Jean-Pierre Convert, who kept it running until at least 1793. By then, the Girardet brothers and Abraham-Louis Fauche-Borel ran competing services in the town.[68] Little direct evidence of Convert's *cabinet* survives but, accepting heightened desires for news and distraction during the turbulent 1790s, the terms of the better-documented Fauche-Borel operation help us to understand the problem it posed to the STN. Customers paid monthly or annual subscriptions of 2 or 24 *livres de France*, for which they could use both the reading room and lending services. The *cabinet littéraire* was open daily, except on Sunday, between 8.00 am and 8.00 pm, and boasted ever-growing stocks of both new titles and popular classics. Members – including foreigners from beyond Neuchâtel's bounds – could borrow books on the condition that they accepted responsibility for postage and damage and returned in-demand new releases within two days. This was an unquestionably comprehensive service, although justifying the expenditure would have demanded serious investment in reading. A total of 24 *livres* equated to 11,520 duodecimo printed pages at the *1-sol*-per-sheet industry rate. After considering the disadvantages and restrictions of non-ownership, only clients that consumed perhaps double this amount would have felt entirely satisfied. Similar consumption *chez* Convert no doubt wiped out much of the STN's potential trade. They could little complain about the existence of such businesses, however, because a good proportion of their own business depended upon the presence of *cabinets littéraires* elsewhere in Europe.[69] The orders of Nicolas Gerlache in Metz, Choppin in Bar-le-Duc, Lair of Bois, Joseph Lex of Warsaw and Charles-Antoine Charmet of Besançon, and many more, betray the tell-tale signs of stocking-up their circulating libraries.[70] No, the STN's problem was rather that Neuchâtel's reading room and lending library was never under their stewardship.

Other forms of shared and subscription reading also lay largely beyond the Society's control. First, as was the fashion, it is probable that Neuchâtel's café Dardel made reading material available to customers.[71] Second, the STN account books evidence the popularity of shared subscriptions to the *Nouveau Journal helvétique* held by both private individuals and institutions. Third, the aristocratic *Société du jardin*, named after its summer meeting place in a garden on the easterly outskirts of the town, subscribed to a number of European journals through the STN.[72] And finally, for an annual fee of 5 *livres* 18 *sols de Neuchâtel*, individuals could also join the *Société littéraire*, established in 1759, the mission of which was to furnish the newest works for the recreational reading of its members. The Society's collection had no fixed home, but instead circulated among members normally located in Neuchâtel itself or in lakeside satellites including Colombier, Saint-Aubin and Vaumarcus. At the end of each year, its books were resold and added to incoming subscription dues to fund future purchases. Ostervald operated as the Society's chief 'librarian' from the early 1770s, although by the summer of 1784 Jean-Pierre Convert had taken the role. Schlup's assessment that it largely took novels, theatre pieces, travel-writing and histories is corroborated and extended by the FBTEE database.[73] Between 1771 and 1781 the *Société littéraire* took 243 books from the STN. Almost all of these Parisian editions were *nouveatés* that the

STN would normally neither stock nor provide to order. Members thus enjoyed the best of both worlds – the product of the Swiss presses and a direct literary link to the City of Light. And all for the price of an octavo Bible or a copy of Fanny Burney's *Cecilia*.

Worse, where the Neuchâtelois public did directly buy books, the STN faced fierce competition in both the town and mountains from more experienced booksellers who were fighting tooth and nail for their livelihoods. Samuel Fauche has generally been portrayed as a troublemaker, largely due to his expulsion from the STN and his subsequent printing of underground classics like Mirabeau's *Essai sur le despotisme* (1775) and the first edition of Mercier's *Tableau de Paris* (1782). Nonetheless, despite his risk taking, Fauche was an exceptionally gifted and powerfully backed publisher and bookseller of some standing in the community. His 1779–83 edition of the works of Charles Bonnet, one of the finer achievements of Swiss printing of the époque, was jointly financed by the notable Neuchâtelois Daniel and Henri de Meuron alongside Henry-Louis and François-Béat Borel.[74] Horace-Bénédict de Saussure wrote warmly of his hospitality.[75] The STN's trade with Fauche throughout the 1770s and 1780s attests to the continued vibrancy of his business; close to 20,000 books were exchanged between the two parties after their definitive 1772 settlement. The profile of these swap deals suggests that both businesses continued to offer similar works to the Neuchâtelois public, and Fauche's strength in religious and educational publishing would have been particularly damaging to his former partners.[76]

These problems, of course, were somewhat foreseeable since even during 1769 Samuel Fauche had failed to agree to amalgamate his business with the fledgling STN. As the next generation of his family emerged during the 1780s, indeed, the Society grew to lament the waning influence of the devil that they knew. Ostervald and his partners instead faced a hydra-like threat from various members of the Fauche family competing among themselves for dominance through a series of spectacular but short-lived ventures. The STN traded with Jonas-Samuel Fauche, Charles S. Favre and Company (14 December 1781–3 August 1784), Samuel Fauche, father and son (20 April 1782–31 May 1781), Jonas-Samuel Fauche (15 June 1784–18 August 1786), Fauche and Jérémie Witel (27 May 1784–11 August 1784), Charles Favre (13 June 1784–30 July 1792) and Louis Fauche-Borel (31 May 1790–28 October 1794).[77] Together, these businesses accounted for a significant increase in both book production and business activity in Neuchâtel that put further strain upon the STN's position in the local market.[78] Fauche, Favre and Company, for example, advertised copies of *L'esprit du citoyen*, *Discours sur cette question: 'Quels sont les moyens de perfectionner l'éducation des jeunes demoiselles?'*; *Mémoires pour servir à l'histoire du siège de Gibraltar* and *La Thébaïde de Stace* in the 30 October 1783 issue of Neuchâtel's *Feuille d'avis*.[79] A mixture of third-party editions and their own printings, all were works that the STN stocked at the time. Even more problematically, this rascal generation sowed seeds of disharmony within the Romandy zone and attracted the wrath of powerful foreign forces. As later chapters will reveal, the daring deals that the younger Fauche's cut with likes of Mirabeau and Mercier to ship thousands of illegal works directly to Paris helped bring Swiss printing to its knees.[80]

Finally, the entrenched presence of Samuel Girardet in Le Locle, stationed 20 kilometres north and half-a-kilometre above Neuchâtel in the Jura chain, meant that the true Neuchâtelois mountain dwellers had equally compelling alternatives to the STN's somewhat distant print shop counter. A bookbinder and bookseller since 1760, by the time of the establishment of the Society Girardet, offered an impressive range of wares.[81] His 1769 catalogue – one of the first products of the STN's newly commissioned presses – ran to forty octavo printed pages.[82] While Girardet's presence deprived the Society of precious retail margins, his lack of presses at least ensured that he paid his bills in ready cash rather than stocks. Indeed, his 167 orders totalling over 4,994 copies of 267 different works – an average of a little under 300 works per year – made him one of the STN's more reliable and valuable customers. The relationship was also close. Girardet's exceptionally talented 13-year-old son Abraham, who later made his name selling his remarkable scenes from the early years of the French Revolution in Paris, engraved the 466 vignettes found in the STN's 1779 edition of the Bible.[83] The tenderness of Osterwald's insistence of the talents of the younger Abraham-Louis, then ten-years-old and trying to emulate his brother, is just one among several affecting moments revealed in the Girardet dossier.[84]

All the good will in the world, however, cannot conceal the serious structural weaknesses with the STN's business that are implicit in Girardet's ordering patterns. The evidence shows that the Le Locle bookseller's commercial influence extended throughout the Neuchâtelois Jura. His reach meant that the STN barely traded with either the populous heart of the Neuchâtelois watch industry, La Chaux-de-Fonds or scores of smaller towns and hamlets across the region including Fleurier, Môtiers and Noiraigue in the Val-de-Travers and Chézard and Dombresson in the Val-de-Ruz. For the Society to only have achieved 1 per cent of their total sales to this extensive cash-paying local market was catastrophic; Girardet tended to take only a baker's dozen copies of things that he expected would sell well, and one or two copies of less promising titles to stock his *cabinet littéraire*. Once more, low demand and rampant competition dogged business. The remarkable survival of Girardet's shop shutters, painted in the early 1780s to advertise the availability of books including Raynal's controversial *Histoire philosophique des deux indes*, show that he was sourcing works from elsewhere.[85] Several promoted works – including the *La nourriture de l'âme* and the '*Sermons de Nardin*' – were stocked by the STN but never supplied to Girardet. The Le Locle bookseller had probably sourced them from the Fauche clan, or perhaps one of the larger Genevois and Lausannois houses. Perret's study of printing in Yverdon shows that he was certainly trading with J. J. Hellen and F. B de Félice.[86]

We might locate the myth of the mountain dwellers, then, somewhere between the assured symbolism of Samuel Girardet's shutters and the prosaic reality of his buying patterns. Without doubt, late-eighteenth-century French-speaking Switzerland was a remarkable zone of literary production, rich in industry and ambition. Romandy was a good place to produce books. The shared product of the region's presses – cheap, of-the-moment, locally produced editions – united and defined its traders. Regrettably, these individuals, partnerships and societies were hamstrung by a common problem: a relative lack of local buyers left them perpetually cash-poor. Neuchâtel's peripheral location coupled with its static, mediocre and well-catered-for population amplified this difficulty for the young typographical society. Selling Swiss books internationally – the subject of the following chapter – was, as a consequence, the STN's raison d'être. No matter, we might assume, as the opportunities of cosmopolitan, enlightened, francophone Europe could by exploited from Neuchâtel through the Society's extensive web of correspondents. Neither those networks nor 'Cosmopolis', alas, were anything like we have been led to believe.

The Triumph of Benevolence, or the History of Francis Wills

A set piece from a forgotten novel: en route from London to Nantwich in search of the fair Juliet, Francis Wills and his travelling companion Tom Lawson take pause at a strangely agreeable inn. Their young, beautiful hostess prepares a delightful supper and an impeccable room, while her husband joins the voyagers for a skinful of home-brewed beer. After their hearty meal, the quartet work their way through a large bowl of punch. Alas, the girl – no virtuous heroine of bygone times, readers are advised – gets ever more frisky and flirtatious; her innkeeper husband increasingly jealous and crotchety. He tries again and again to cut short the evening. Unaware, or at least unbowed, she serves up a second bowl laced with three-shillings-worth of liquor. But after some time in high spirits the travellers reach the bottom of the basin and, worse for wear, retire. Francis, impervious to the belle's amorous attentions, collapses and dreams of his beloved Juliet. When dawn breaks, he knows, he will be one step closer to her sweet face. How innocent and perfect is young love! Across the hallway, a domestic argument flares.

An hour passes before the hosting couple calm and bed down; but the husband, fearing that his wife will abscond in search of amorous adventure, determines to keep an eye-open. He drops-off. Zzz. He half-wakes, flustered and filled with a noxious mix of home-brew, punch and regret, and makes straight for the young men's pitch-black room, convinced that he is being cuckolded. He jumps onto the bed, mistakes Wills's beardless face for that of his wife, grabs a handful of the young man's unkempt hair and declaims his capture. Aha! Vile wench! Wills, suspecting a robber or an assassin, punches the innkeeper to the floor. Lawson stirs, and in an instant crushes the would-be assailant to the boards, cracking several of his ribs. And at that very moment the hostess enters the room with a candle, illuminating the scene. To cries of astonishment, our green-eyed monster is revealed. A domestic argument flares anew.[87]

Freshly pressed with every expense spared in the spring of 1774, the second French-language edition of the *Histoire de François Wills* began life as a stack of 1,542 copies of 33 printed sheets just like any other that the STN attempted to sell.[88] The commoditizing 1-*sol*-per-sheet industry standard price fixed the heap's value at a little over 2,500 *livres*. Only the text of *Wills* – the above scene included – and its paratextual formalities, distinguished it from thousands of competing Swiss books. But oh the extraordinary variety and agency of all those texts! Given the combined bibliographic and bibliometric potential of the FBTEE dataset, it would be amiss not to momentarily take pause to examine the magnificent belly and underbelly of pre-Revolutionary Europe's francophone literary marketplace as viewed from Neuchâtel. This chapter, for the first time, holistically evaluates the body of works outputted by an early-modern printing house weighed by sales. It reveals the titles, authors, editors, genres, discourses and translations that the STN most frequently shipped. In the process, a newly empirical picture of the richly intertextual and cross-culturally propagated francophone book market emerges. Further, this chapter extends our understanding of *how* these texts reached their publics. From describing the size of typical print runs to modelling their wholesale exhaustion, it sheds new light on the functioning of the early-modern print trade. Many numbers follow, so to root the FBTEE database's widescreen bibliometrics firmly in the texts that they describe, we will never stray too far from the story of a typical STN edition, the *Histoire de François Wills*.

I

A few pages into *Wills*, as the eponymous hero improbably buys a shoulder of mutton for a poor family of strangers threatened with eviction, readers find their feet. This is a typical second-rate didactic novel with lashings of sentimentality in the mould of Oliver Goldsmith, Samuel Richardson or perhaps Jean-Jacques Rousseau. The odd picaresque hangover amuses and an occasional wry observation charms. Little surprises. It is not very *good*, but no matter; it was the type of work that the STN's book-buying clients lapped up. The Society, indeed, quickly embraced the burgeoning reading public's hunger for such pieces from the 'belles-lettres', shipping 138,001 copies (33.6% of total envois) of 1,128 different titles during their trading existence. Only 'histoire' (111,823 or 27.70%), the other extensively literary high-level division of the Parisian bookseller's classification system, proved similarly popular. Sales of books numbering among the 'sciences et arts' (78,888 or 19.35%), and especially 'jurisprudence' (41,794 or 10.17%) and 'théologie' (36,095 or 8.27%), flagged by comparison.[89]

The FBTEE project team initially hoped to use this data to better understand what typical Frenchmen read before the French Revolution of 1789. A parade of great studies – expertly summarized in Darnton's 1971 essay 'Reading, Writing and Publishing' – had previously produced wildly different answers to this key historical question.[90] The polymath Jean-Jacques d'Ortous de Mairan's library was, Daniel Roche found, dominated by scientific tomes; numerous alternative private libraries, Daniel Mornet had previously shown, overflowed with historical books; the extant Parisian registers of official permissions to publish suggested to François Furet that the religious sector remained vibrant; while members of the *parlement*'s of Brittany and Paris, François Bluche and Jean Meyer revealed, were impressively roundly read. Differently limited approaches, in short, brought about no satisfactory consensus. Because the resulting datasets could be neither confidently trumpeted as representative nor dismissed as anomalous, the intellectual project had to be mothballed. Our group, then, hoped that by using modern database technology to capture the unprecedented volume and geographical reach of the data residing within the Neuchâtel account books, we might finally provide a breakthrough and, indeed, extend the scope of inquiry beyond France.

Alas, the previous chapter's revelation that the STN almost exclusively traded Swiss editions punctures this ambition. A somewhat unconvincing leap of faith – an avowal that Swiss books were substantially the same as those produced elsewhere – would be required before accepting the dataset's suitability for divining general reading tastes. For sure, the STN was a profit-driven operation at ease setting more-or-less anything – from the Bible to its atheist antithesis, d'Holbach's *Système de la nature* – to type. Relatively unencumbered by ideology, then, the Neuchâtelois had every commercial interest in closely shadowing general European market demand. And, indeed, some new FBTEE database evidence can be marshalled to bolster the view that Swiss books mirrored those produced elsewhere: the works that the Society printed or acquired locally were of the same broad make-up as those sourced in substantial numbers from further afield. To the casual observer, it would be logical to conclude that Swiss, Dutch and Parisian imprints were much alike.

Yet, upon closer reflection, the above statistics augur badly. That nearly two out of every three books handled by the Society were drawn from the 'belles-lettres' and 'histoire' is unpredicted by previous studies.[91] In reality, the STN specialized according to its particular market opportunity. It primarily produced forward-looking cheap octavo and duodecimo editions that were of broad appeal to burgeoning publics located beyond Europe's cosmopolitan capitals. Its directors (sometimes reluctantly) eschewed unrealistically highbrow products. Erudite legal texts, advanced scientific and medical tomes and sober theological treatises were all better published in metropolises where they might issue from confident cultural and intellectual institutions, find funding from extensive networks of power and patronage and be purchased by sophisticated local buyers. Counterfeiting such refined works from the sticks was a logistical nightmare and oftentimes the road to ruin. At the other end of the spectrum, while the Society could hope to quickly respond to a flash-in-the-pan local scandal with a quick pamphlet, they could hardly be sensitive to distant and abstruse literary or political flashpoints. Paris's secrets were best broken by Parisian printers. No, we should cast aside overly ambitious aims to determine a continent's past reading tastes using a single peripheral archive. The task, instead, must be to describe the nature of the Swiss books that circulated throughout pre-Revolutionary Europe and to show, when some solidity exists in the comparators, both areas where this corpus differed from those published elsewhere and where it reflected wider trends.

STN shipments by Parisian booksellers categorization, 1769–94

Belles-Lettres (137,713 or 35.6%)	bibliographie (275 or 0.1%)
	grammaires et dictionnaires (6,821 or 1.7%)
	philologie (136 or <0.1%)
	poétique (42,817 or 10.4%)
	polygraphes anciens et modernes (32,260 or 7.9%)
	rhétorique (2,057 or 0.5%)
	romans (53,346 or 13%)
Histoire (111,807 or 27.3%)	atlases (60 or <0.1%)
	cartes géographiques (370 or 0.1%)
	chronologie (272 or 0.1%)
	franc-maçonnerie (1,157 or 0.3%)
	géographie (16,785 or 4.1%)
	histoire asiatique (3,617 or 0.9%)
	histoire de France [regnès particulières] (15,467 or 3.8%)
	histoire ecclésiastique (8,653 or 2.1%)
	histoire European divers (23,310 or 5.6%)
	histoire Orientale (531 or 0.1%)
	histoire prophane (1,994 or 0.5%)
	histoire universelle et particulière (17,185 or 4.2%)
	voyages (22,405 or 5.5%)

Science et arts (78,545 or 19.15%)	art pyrotechnique, de la fonderie, de la verrerie &c. (19 or <0.1%) arts (7,797 or 1.9%) histoire naturelle (8,055 or 2%) mathématique (1,982 or 0.5%) métaphysique (7,202 or 1.8%) médecine, chirurgie (9,666 or 2.4%) philosophie (43,740 or 10.7%) physique (85 or <0.1%)
Jurisprudence (41,776 or 10.2%)	ancien droit des Grecs et des Romains (5 or <0.1%) droit canonique (4,530 or 1.1%) droit civil, droit de la nature et des gens, et droit public (8,873 or 2.2%) droit français (4,616 or 1.1%) œuvres héraldiques, généalogiques &c. (8 or <0.1%)
Théologie (36,095 or 8.8%)	catechétiques (8,768 or 2.1%) diverses ouvres théologiques (1,316 or 0.3%) La Sainte Bible et commentaires (13,139 or 3.2%) liturgies et conciles (3,280 or 0.8%) théologie hétérodoxe (994 or 0.2%) théologie parénétique, ou des sermons (6,129 or 1.5%) théologie polémique (2,457 or 0.6%) vies des saints (12 or <0.1%)

The rich FBTEE database Parisian-tree-system subcategory data, which allows users to look beyond catch-all arboreal boughs like 'sciences et arts' to their specific constituent branches and twigs, confirms suspicions that the Swiss printers specialized in dynamic, literary and popular publishing forms.[92] Where contemporary styles might be expected to merely flourish, they overwhelm. The STN's shipments of 'belles-lettres' were predominantly made up of an authorial triumvirate of novels (479 works or 53,346 sales), theatre pieces and other such works of 'poétique' (364 or 42,816) and sprawling polygraphic works (132 or 32,260) including Mercier's *Tableau de Paris* and the collected writings of Madame de Genlis, Rousseau and Voltaire. Sub-branches dedicated to dictionaries and grammar primers (80 works or 6,759 sales), 'rhétorique' – a largely academic form devoted to literary studies and criticism – (54 or 2,065), bibliography (4 or 275) and philology (6 or 136), withered by comparison. Indeed, even the Society's sales in these ostensibly sober and scholarly categories were largely dominated by popular and accessible pedagogical texts like Pierre Restaut's *Abrégé des principes de la grammaire françoise* (Neuchâtel, 1777) and Nicolas-Antoine Viard's *Les vrais principes de la lecture* ([Neuchâtel], 1775). Likewise, the STN's 'Histoire' sales were for the most part comprised of contemporary political works like Francesco Algarotti's *Lettres du comte Algarotti sur la Russie*, travelogues, geography primers and a battery of sensational page-turners like Mathieu-François Pidansat de Mairobert *L'espion anglois*. Most were designed to be consumed as much as studied.

More strikingly still, this dynamism and popularism extended to the tree's traditionally less literary-focused boughs. First, more than half of the works of 'science and arts' shipped by the STN (43,740 works or 78,545 sales) were not astronomical observations or architectural treatises, but 'philosophy'. This branch was itself largely comprised of lively works of contemporary political economy like Jacques Necker's famously fanciful 1781 *Mémoire*, which proclaimed the rude health of the French state's finances, provoking raised-eyebrow responses.[93] Of the remainder, formal works of *logique et morale* (logic and moral philosophy) were less of interest to the Swiss publishers than practical guides like Joseph-Aignan Sigaud de La Fond's moralizing *L'école du bonheur* (1,741 envois); heavy medical or surgical tomes were entirely eclipsed by controversial pamphlets like Jean-Emmanuel Gilibert's, *L'anarchie médicinale* (1,430), and especially Simon-Auguste Tissot's popular everyman medical vulgarizations; and although Jacques Christophe Valmont de Bomare's major reference work, the *Dictionnaire raisonné universel d'histoire naturelle* (1,119) was a top seller, it competed for attention with scores of condensations, pocket dictionaries and practical guides including the *Dictionnaire portatif de la campagne* (908), *Elémens d'oryctologie* (666), *L'art de faire le vin* (499) and *Le socrate rustique* (215). Second, despite the reality that Parisian publishers did a roaring trade in heavier anti-*philosophe* tomes by the likes of Nicolas-Sylvain Bergier, the STN's 'théologie' shipments were dominated by popular Protestant psalms, sermons and short catechisms. Finally, although substantial, the STN's 'jurisprudence' envois were almost entirely exceptional. The majority issued from the busy pens of just two authors: Rilliet de Saussure (*Planta gagnant sa vie en honnête home, Inceste avoué à un mari*), who was trying to clear his name after a messy divorce had led him to prison; and Brissot (*Théorie des lois criminelles, Un indépendant à l'ordre des avocats*), the grub-street archetype and future revolutionary leader who needs little introduction.[94] We will encounter both of these characters, who promised to pay for the entire print runs of their works themselves, in later chapters. For now, it is necessary only to note that if we set aside such vanity projects, the STN shipped only 8,521 copies of works of 'jurisprudence', less than 3 per cent of their total.

From whichever angle we probe the Parisian-tree-system data, the STN's shipments appear to have been dominated by dynamic and contemporary literary forms. Before declaring the Swiss printers as path-breaking harbingers of Enlightenment, however, we should remember that modern vehicles often carried old ideas. By the latter half of the eighteenth century, even the most anti-philosophical writers had warmed towards new publishing forms from novels to short-form dictionaries.[95] A healthy segment of the STN's readers – perhaps middling sorts convalescing in the baths of Lunéville or lesser nobles combating the ennui of a minor European court – lapped up socially and politically conservative writings. Many, of course, did not much care about *philosophe* controversies either way: they sought apolitical diversion, entertainment, knowledge or personal improvement. Timeless themes persisted. The top-ten thematic keywords recorded in the FBTEE database – France (21.3%), politics (17.5%), religion (16.9%), current affairs (14.4%), Christianity (13.9%), philosophy (12.2%), Switzerland (10%), Geneva (7.9%), economics (7.3%) and social mores (6.9%) – suggest that readers enjoyed a certain level of political engagement, but leave us far from effectively penetrating their mental worlds. More revealing nuggets hide further down the lists. Keywords that might be ascribed to radical constructions of the Enlightenment – for example, atheism (2.2%), despotism (1.1%), pornography (2%) and scandalous anecdotes (0.6%) – appear to have been comparatively niche interests. Evidence of a higher Enlightenment defined by commerce (2.5%), political theory (2.4%) and metaphysics (2.2%) is equally difficult to locate.

The case of *Histoire de François Wills*, moreover, further brings to the surface the dangers of reading too much into this thematic data. While these new statistics clearly help us to delineate the Swiss contribution towards a much-discussed eighteenth-century revolution in publishing forms, convincingly mapping the flood of novels and works of contemporary political commentary onto progressive social or political tendencies possessive of historical agency remains challenging. *Wills*, despite its modern form and blotto boudoir farce, was a conservative book. As well as providing some comic relief, frequent theatrical asides served to demonstrate the eponymous hero's incorruptibility faced with a chaotic and temptation-filled itinerant existence. The tragi-comic story of Wills's life, populated by a cast of good-guys and grotesques, unfurls through a seemingly endless series of such tests of moral fortitude. Never once is our hero's education and good nature found wanting. Benevolence triumphs. Further, somewhere along Wills's Quixotic route it becomes clear that, conservative or progressive, such works defy simple thematic categorization at every turn. Contemporary issues such as inheritance law (the orphan Wills is unjustly deprived of his due bequest by his avaricious grandfather) and summary justice (he apprehends and then frees a highwayman who later helps him find Juliet) punctuate the narrative. Yet these interspersions are too frequent, varied and fleeting to invite keyword tagging. *Histoire de François Wills*, in short, can only really be adequately described, as its brief and utilitarian FBTEE categorization record suggests, as a novel.

Having, then, learnt this much from the keywords – that the STN's books were modern and literary biased – we might be better turning back towards the safer paratextual shores of traditional bibliography to further our bibliometric differentiation of Swiss printing. The FBTEE 'sales by title' data betrays a first important truth: bestsellers mattered. *Histoire de François Wills*, which sold out its substantial print run of just over 1,500 copies, ranks in the database as only the STN's 49th most frequently dispatched book. The top-ten reads: T. Rilliet de Saussure, *Planta gagnant sa vie en honnête homme* (16,787 copies); L.-S. Mercier, *Tableau de Paris* (14,076); L.-S. Mercier, *La destruction de la ligue* (10,188); Anon., *Mémoire apologetique des Genevois* (8,428); J.-F. Ostervald, *Abrégé de l'histoire sainte et du catéchisme* (6,815); F.-S. Ostervald, *Géographie* (6,397)[96]; *La sainte Bible* (5,323); J. Le Scène-Desmaisons, *Contrat conjugal* (4,164); L.-S. Mercier, *Mon bonnet de nuit* (4,043) and Madame Riccoboni, *Collection complète des oeuvres de Madame Riccoboni* (3,843). Three types of works dominate: literary sensations, such as Mercier's trio, printed in truly extraordinary numbers; 'affair' books, including *Planta* and the *Mémoire apologetique*, where public interest burnt brightly but briefly; and 'drip–drip' catechisms and textbooks that rarely tumbled out of print. Taken together, these 'bestsellers' were critical to the business models operated by the Romandy printers: the top-ten works shipped 80,064 copies (19.5% of a total of 410,074 STN envois); the top twenty 109,118 (26.6%); and the top fifty 166,791 (40.7%). By stark contrast, a long tail of hard-to-shift stock haunted publishers: 2,443 works shipped less than 100 copies (81.9% of 2,984 titles); 2,195 less than 50 (73.6%); and 1,425 less than a dozen (47.8%). For sure, the upper echelons of these lists are populated entirely by Neuchâtel printings, but the Society's commitment to oversized editions none the less confirms that the pre-Revolutionary francophone book market was potted with highly anticipated bestsellers that stood out from the crowd as clearly as today's literary smashes.

This thirst for the next sensation naturally drew the Swiss printers towards an emergent bankable class of star-name authors. The difficulties that retailers encountered predicting marketable texts, the silent distances of the international trade, and the levelling 1-*sol*-per-sheet standard wholesale price combined to make paratextual material – concise snippets of supplementary information such as the author's name and a descriptive title or preface that could be circulated by private letter or in printer's catalogues – invaluable. For wholesalers like the STN, little was more effective than being able to push 'Voltaire's new masterpiece' or 'the latest Tissot'. Small wonder, then, that the system was susceptible to abuse. The title page of *Histoire de François Wills* screamed that the book was written by the author of the 'Ministre de Wakefied [sic]', Oliver Goldsmith. Few experts who have waded through its pedestrian prose agree.

The top-selling authors revealed by the FBTEE database map neither directly onto the Enlightenment as celebrated by the French Revolutionaries nor the roll of eighteenth century greats subsequently promoted by historians. Key figures, including Denis Diderot (314th place in the bestselling primary authors' tables) and Jean-Antoine-Nicolas de Caritat, marquis de Condorcet (235th), are absent. And contemporary book buyers were kinder to Elie Bertrand and Madame Riccoboni than has been posterity. More than anything, of course, the tables reflect the history of the STN. Yet they also illustrate some realities of the book business that were not specific to the Neuchâtel experience. First, the contemporaneousness of the wholesale trade is striking. Most authors whose major works were published before the 1770s – for example, Étienne Bonnot de Condillac (233rd), Julien Offray de La Mettrie (279th) and Montesquieu (157th) – appear to have entirely fallen from fashion. Quality was no guarantee of longevity and the slide towards wholesale irrelevance rarely took long. Only Mercier and the Holy Spirit, should one be inclined to attribute divine authorship to the Bible, appeared among the STN's 'top-ten' selling authors during both the 1770s and 1780s. Even the great Voltaire's sales spectacularly collapsed to about an eighth of their previous annual levels shortly after his death in 1778.[97] No doubt in libraries and reading rooms his works were still being read during the 1780s. And the second-hand trade kept many books more readily available in Europe's larger towns and cities. But texts dated quickly and it served the interests of everybody in the trade to ensure that *nouveautés* drove the continent's literary agenda.

Second, it is clear from the STN lists that the darlings of Swiss publishing, from Madame Riccoboni to Mercier, Madame de Genlis to Tissot, at times differed from their counterparts elsewhere in Europe. The publication of many Neuchâtel editions was prefigured by the physical presence of the author, if sometimes only fleetingly, in or around the canton. Frédéric-Samuel Ostervald was, of course, an STN director; Isabelle de Charrière and Jean-Jacques Rousseau were Neuchâtelois by residence; Tissot was a Vaudois; Rilliet de Saussure and Charles Bonnet issued from Geneva; the fellow Genevois Horace-Bénédict de Saussure sojourned with the Fauche family; Voltaire upped sticks to Ferney partially because of its proximity to the Swiss presses; and Brissot and Mercier travelled to Neuchâtel to strike their publishing deals. The intellectual honeypots of Geneva and Lausanne played host to the likes of James Boswell, William Godwin, Goethe, Moses Mendelssohn, John Moore, Adam Smith, Lazzaro Spallanzani, Laurence Sterne, Pietro Verri and Christoph Martin Wieland during our period.[98] Each of these figures had French-language editions of their works published locally during the 1760s, 1770s or 1780s. And copies of many of these books were traded by the STN. Unsurprisingly, Europe's competing printing centres also boasted their own resident authors and equally profited from itinerant stars. The theatre pieces and poems of Barthélemy Imbert, as well as the novels of Joseph-Marie Loaisel de Tréogate, for example, were in constant production in Paris and the Low Countries during the 1770s and 1780s. The original writings of Jean-Baptiste-Antoine Suard, such as his 1781 *Notice sur la personne et les écrits de La Bruyère*, were all printed in Paris. Because these men had few connections with French-speaking Switzerland their works barely register in the FBTEE database despite their popularity among francophone readers.[99]

This point concerning regionalism underlines a deeper truth about the functioning of the trade explored elsewhere in this volume. Of course the francophone book business was international in scope and without question many publishers found that editions of their most popular authors were counterfeited quickly across Europe. Within months of its first appearance, French booksellers had little need to write to Amsterdam in search of a copy of Rousseau's *Julie, ou la nouvelle Héloïse*. And many STN editions were indeed copies of works by a tranche of second-ranking authors from James Porter to Madame de Genlis first published far from Switzerland. The republic of letters *was* cosmopolitan. Yet it is important to recognize that few eighteenth-century authors generated sensational sales. According to the FBTEE database, only 96 authors achieved sales of more than 1,000 copies through the STN between 1769 and 1794. A further 269 writers could boast sales of between 101 and 999 units, while a substantial majority of 1,260 authors sold less than 100 individual books through the Society. And we must remember, too, that most editions were printed only once or twice, oftentimes by the same publishing house. The key determining factor that dictates the place of *any* author in these bestsellers lists, then, is whether their works were published in Neuchâtel, wider-Romandy or elsewhere in Europe. So while, yes, the upper echelons of the STN bestselling primary authors list might boast a certain resemblance to those of many European houses – Voltaire and The Holy Spirit *were* widely printed – the correlation can never entirely be seen to have transcended the influence of local factors and becomes still less clear-cut if one descends beyond the listings of Europe's literary elite. Swiss-printed authors and their books were generally most readily sourced from Switzerland, just like Paris-printed writers and their editions were most easily found in the City of Light.

Everyone, for sure, was looking north for inspiration. Despite Romandy's central European location bordering German- and Italian-speaking peoples and states, the current of literary translation consistently flowed thickest from English. The FBTEE 'translated authors' dataset is substantial: 11.4 per cent of STN-traded units (46,601 copies of 420 unique editions) were of works originally published in languages other than French.[100] Of these, 52.1 per cent (24,288 of 209) were translated from English originals, 33.8 per cent (15,762 of 91) from German, 7 per cent (3,283 of 46) from

Italian and 2.7 per cent (1,259 of 30) from Latin. The remaining 4.3 per cent (2,009 of 44) appeared first in Russian, Spanish, Swedish, Portuguese, Greek, Dutch and a mixture of ancient and oriental languages. The STN's taste for British works reflected the output of the region's presses. The Genevan bookseller J.-P. Bonnant's catalogues published between 1787 and 1789 boasted respectively fifteen (9% of total works), twenty-two (6%), forty-eight (9%) and fifty-two (14%) titles listed as translated from English.[101] Everyman novels by Fanny Burney and Henry Fielding, philosophical histories by David Hume and William Robertson and thrilling travelogues by Patrick Brydone and James Cook marked Swiss printing.[102]

Only a minority of these authors and their works, it must be noted, were translated *for* the Swiss. The lion's share of the STN's most-traded 'English' novels, histories and travelogues were simple counterfeits of successful translations first published in Paris, London or the Low Countries. Its printing of the *Histoire de François Wills*, for example, was copied directly from the edition produced by Daniel-Jean Changuion in Amsterdam in 1773.[103] By contrast, roughly half of the STN's bestselling translations from German originals *were* new products of the Romandy nexus. By the 1770s, German writing had shaken off much of the provincialism and pedantry of which Friedrich Nicolai had complained in 1755.[104] Yet while well over a thousand French works were being translated into German each decade by this point, it is generally accepted that the intellectual traffic that flowed in the opposite direction was so meagre that it left the French with precious little knowledge of German science and literature.[105] Switzerland's multilingual intellectual networks, and the specific talents of Jean-Elie Bertrand and translators including the Genevan Henri Rieu, left the STN and their partners well placed to provide an important cultural service by beginning to address this problem. And by directly translating popular German books including Nicolaus Ernst Kleemann's *Reisen von Wien über Belgrad bis Kilianova*, by expeditiously counterfeiting new translations like the Frankfurt printer Franz Varrentrapp's French-language edition of Christoph Martin Wieland's *Der goldne Spiegel oder Die Könige von Scheschian*, and by significantly augmenting the Neuchâtel edition of the *Descriptions des arts et métiers* with technical information lifted straight from the superior German version, its directors also hoped to leverage their locational advantage to turn a profit.[106] The majority of this work, it might be noted, was in the international Enlightenment tradition; the radicalism of Johann Wolfgang von Goethe, Johann Georg Hamann and the *Sturm und Drang*, alas, was a step too far for the STN's francophone public.[107] So too, for the most part, were books translated from other languages, aside for on the rare occasions – as we have seen was the case with Francesco Algarotti's *Lettres du comte Algarotti sur la Russie* – when specific events stimulated exceptional market demand.

The same internationalist and universalist spirit that led London's John Wilkie to proudly proclaim on his trade cards that he sold books in 'all Languages & Faculties', and that inspired Friedrich Nicolai to place that bust of Homer above his Berlin shop's door, ran through the stock holdings of the STN.[108] European literary networks and book markets were so interconnected, and print was so relatively inexpensive and abundant, that cultural transfer and intertextuality ensured that the overall product of Swiss printing substantially resembled that of other francophone publishing centres. Nonetheless, cosmopolitanism did not mean uniformity. Even when looking at the broadest indicators – the subject, genre and original language of STN-traded books – it becomes clear that Swiss printing had well defined characteristics. Physical and cultural geography, and especially the markets being targeted, encouraged the Romandy publishers towards novels and travelogues, Protestant works and translations. And at the level of individual authors and particular works Swiss printing was wildly distinctive. The secret to success was not to simply republish the most popular books being produced elsewhere. The supply of these books to francophone booksellers often already risked outstripping demand. Rather, the trick was to leverage any possible advantage – each personal and business connection and every scrap of information – to sniff out opportunities that rivals might have missed. In the world of the Swiss printers, Charles Bonnet's works sold like hot cakes while those of Carl Linnaeus were entirely ignored; Samuel-Auguste Tissot was nearly 100 times more popular than his great rival William Buchan, and the author of *Histoire de François Wills*, most probably Arthur Murphy, shifted far more copies than Oliver Goldsmith.[109]

II

If the themes, titles and intellectual provenance of Swiss books differed subtly but importantly from those produced elsewhere, so too did aspects of their production, advertisement and temporal exhaustion. Despite a busy schedule working on other projects, the STN pressmen 'Berthe', 'Fèry' and 'Foras' managed to print the entire edition of 1,542 copies of *Wills*, from A to Q according to its alphabetically ordered sheets, during February and March 1774.[110] This obscurely unrounded run signals a job well done. Charged with achieving 1,500 good copies, in addition to the requisite three *rames* of 500 sheets, the trio would have been given a further two or three 25-sheet *mains de passe* designed to cover process faults.[111] That they erred so little was impressive, since the job was large by STN standards. The FBTEE database, indeed, suggests that the Society's mean edition size was 1,148 copies.[112] For sure, this average conceals much variation: STN printings ranged from the 24 copies of Bertrand's *Sermons sur différens textes de l'Ecriture-Sainte* printed on 2 July 1773 to the 24,000 copies of Rilliet's *Planta gagnant sa vie en honnête homme* printed on 25 April 1783. Yet even if we discount such outliers – mainly vanity publications and 'affair' books – the average drops only modestly to 1,065.[113] Plotted as a graph, these print runs present an elegant bell curve following a standard distribution pattern that peaks at this average, although marked steps around 500, 1,000, 1,500 and 2,000 copies reflect some paper-delivery based decision making. There was no statistically significant correlation, finally, between number of sheets, pages or volumes that comprised a work, and the number of copies that the STN were prepared to commit to print.

These numbers suggest that STN print runs were broadly aligned with those of their European competitors. A register held in the *Archives de la Chambre syndicale de la Librairie et Imprimerie de Paris* and first analysed by Henri-Jean Martin lists the edition sizes of around 1,500 books published between 1777 and 1787 largely in Paris and the French provinces. French publishers, it suggests, most frequently committed to runs of between 1,000 and 2,000 copies, and about 10 per cent of their wares were printed in editions of more than 3,000 copies.[114] Because the register contains only works published by *permission simple*, however, its entries show some bias towards high-volume educational and devotional works and thus gives a modestly inflated view of French edition sizes. It lists, for example, 87,500 copies of 43 distinct editions of Jacques Coret's *Le nouvel ange conducteur*![115] Nonetheless, the evidence from this Parisian register chimes with surviving archival snapshots from publishing houses located elsewhere in Europe to suggest that STN edition sizes were entirely typical. In Berlin, Friedrich Nicolai's average print run was 1,400 before 1790.[116] And in London, between 1738 and 1785, William Strahan commissioned 175 editions of 500 copies, 139 editions of 1,000 copies, 77 editions of 750 copies and 43 editions of 1,500 copies.[117]

Regardless of whether the STN published 500 or 2,500 copies of any of their 1-*sol*-per-sheet regular books, they could be sure that print costs would amount to around 40 per cent of anticipated revenues. Because the workers' daybooks for the period when *Francis Wills* was pressed are lost, we might instead take the STN's part in the 1779 'Libraires associés' printing of Nicolas-Edmé Restif de la Bretonne's *Le nouvel Abeilard* as exemplar. The Society spent 770.1.0 *livres* printing 1,000 copies of 38 ¼ sheets of Restif's book. The wages of their compositors and pressmen (298.7.0 *livres* or 38% of total spend) and the paper employed (285.14.0 *livres* or 37%) comprised the lion's share of these costs, which were completed by wear and tear to printing characters (153.0.0 or 20%) and correction and finishing (33.0.0 *livres* or 5%). This outlay secured 38,000 printed sheets for the confederation, which its members trusted would be worth 1,900 *livres* when sold at the Swiss nexus's standard wholesale price, resulting in a gross profit margin of 59.5 per cent. Two books published by the confederation in almost identical circumstances, but with larger print runs of 1,500 copies, Claude-François-Xavier Millot's *Elémens de l'histoire d'Angleterre* and Pierre-Joseph Macquer's *Dictionnaire de chymie*, resulted respectively in margins of 58.6 per cent and 61.9 per cent.[118] Printing in fact offered no economies of scale. Any potential savings gained during the process of composition tended to be neutralized by the reality that pressing the same text over and over again exhausted sets of type unevenly and inefficiently.[119] Whenever the STN accounted for unsold stocks in their account books – whether printed or swapped in from their partners – they used a standard 'cost price' formula of 7.5 *deniers* or 37.5 per cent of the 1 *sol* per sheet that they hoped to achieve.

The consistency of these gross margins facilitated the Romandy book-swapping nexus by allowing transfers to be made on an uncomplicated sheet-for-sheet basis. And their size left traders sufficient leeway to absorb further business costs – shipping, storage and advertising expenses, for example – before still posting a healthy net return on sold-out editions. Finding buyers was the tricky part. In Neuchâtel, Samuel Ostervald's prominent position in local literary life and involvement with the local literary club, the *Société littéraire*, as well as the STN's ever-increasing economic ties to the town's relatively circumscribed elites, meant that little formal advertisement of new works was necessary. No posters, like the ones that the Society produced and sent to Pontarlier to advertise *L'école du bonheur* in French towns, adorned the yellow stone walls of the *place du marché*.[120] The Neuchâtelois did, however, briefly run an *ouvrage de la semaine* promotion from its print shop's modest retail counter and frequently used the *Feuille d'avis* to reinforce local knowledge of its *nouveautés*.[121] Since the earliest days of their establishment, indeed, the STN printed Neuchâtel's weekly news-sheet for around a 100, growing later to 132 in 1782, local subscribers.[122] The public-spirited *Feuille d'avis* carried announcements of new official regulations, advertisements for goods or services, offers for work, obituaries, the fixed prices of meats and bread, and so forth. We learn from the 10 February 1780 issue, for example, that M. Gioc of Hauterive, then a little village of perhaps 250 inhabitants beyond Neuchâtel's eastern wall, was on the lookout for the master of a little red-spotted and short-tailed hunting dog that he had found roaming the countryside. As M. Gioc begrudgingly cared for his new canine companion, another man announced that he had recently received several examples of *Le boulevard des chartreux*, an anonymous anti-monastic satirical poem by Pelleport, which he was looking to offload. The STN, for its part, announced the appearance of a new edition of Jeanne-Marie Leprince de Beaumont's *Magasin des enfans* at the back of the number.[123] Such 'house' advertisements were part of the privilege of running the news-sheet, and as such the STN often let them run for months. The 4 August 1785 edition of the *Feuille d'avis*, for example, was still carrying *nouveautés* notices for the Society's editions of Mercier's *Portrait de Philippe II* and the French naturalist and psychologist Justin Girod-Chantrans's *Voyage d'un Suisse dans différentes colonies d'Amérique*, despite their having been respectively printed on 24 March and 1 June.[124]

The principality of Neuchâtel was the only market where the STN could target potential readers with such precision, and this rarely yielded more than a few dozen truly local sales. The best way for the STN to spread the word to readers and industry insiders located beyond the wooded peaks of the Jura, Ostervald and his associates understood, would be by ensuring that its works were discussed at least in one prominent journal. From around 1750, as we have seen, the European periodical market had been expanding at breakneck pace.[125] Whether their main focus was literary or political, many of the new titles that appeared on the market carried book extracts or reviews that were oftentimes little more than thinly disguised advertisements for recent *nouveautés* published by, or available from, the journal's printer or its regional partners. Alas, the publishers of Lausanne and Geneva never managed to establish a credible mouthpiece for the region's presses, partially because the news was rarely forged in Romandy and partially because of the importance that non-French books still played in their businesses. So from the get-go in 1769, as we have seen, the STN tried to address this situation by taking over, rebranding and remodelling the flagging Neuchâtel-based *Journal helvétique*.[126] The Society's *Nouveau Journal helvétique* contained reviews of new Swiss works as well as those published elsewhere, diverse short poetic and scientific articles and European political news. It consistently pushed titles available from the STN and its regional partners; the *Histoire de François Wills*, for example, was covered in its April 1774 edition.[127] By aiming to cover Lausannois and Genevan editions as regularly as its own fare – 'il est principalement destiné à faire connoitre les productions littéraires de la Suisse', wrote Ostervald in 1777 – the STN hoped to avoid being seen as provincial, to advertise all of its diverse swapped stocks, and to make Neuchâtel essential to the good functioning of the Romandy nexus.[128] Unsurprisingly, then, the Society considered the *Nouveau Journal helvétique* as critical to its purpose and funnelled resources to the project through to its bitter end. The author Baculard d'Arnaud was briefly hired to provide news from Paris, for example, on a remarkable annual salary of 1,200 *livres de France*.[129] But, in truth, the economics of such moves never stacked up since subscribers to the journal remained few in number and were predominantly local. The failure of the *Nouveau Journal helvétique*, then, left the Swiss publishing industry without a viable voice on the international stage and ensured that Romandy's printers continued to find the stategy of counterfeiting works already known to Europe's readers their best option.[130] The STN no doubt chose to publish *Histoire de François Wills*, for their part, largely because of glowing reviews that periodicals like Fréron's wildly successful Paris-published *Année littéraire* had given to its first Dutch edition.[131]

Particularly lucrative publishing projects like the *Descriptions des arts et métiers* warranted the printing of a circular and its distribution to Europe's French-language booksellers. In September 1770, Voltaire went a stage further by having the STN press 2,200 copies of his short pamphlet *Dieu. Réponse de M. de Voltaire au système de la nature*. This spirited rejection of d'Holbach's 'atheists' bible', the single most talked about work of the moment, served largely as advance publicity for the patriarch of Ferney's forthcoming nine-volume *Questions sur l'Encyclopédie*.[132] Another advertisement technique was to conclude books with lists of other titles available from the publisher. And then there were trade catalogues. By standard industry practice, printers and booksellers periodically published catalogues of their wares. These lists tended to be compiled during the stocktaking process – the STN produced catalogues in 1777, 1779, 1781, 1785 and 1787 – and as a consequence were generally comprehensive.[133] The STN sent copies of their catalogues to both established and potential bookselling clients across Europe by the post or, when the timing was right, had them delivered personally by either a local contact or one of their travelling salesmen. In many ways, it should be noted, trade catalogues were better suited to retail booksellers and auctioneers than to wholesale-led businesses like the STN. Their alphabetical listings made *nouveautés* difficult to locate and they gave no indication of the number of available copies of any given work. The value of trade catalogues to the STN, rather, was twofold. First, advertising the availability of old stocks that might otherwise have been forgotten could prove important to a business that lacked its own significant retail presence. And second, most importantly, lengthy catalogues showed off the size of the Society's operation and, with luck, engendered confidence in potential clients. They were a good way to start a conversation.

Indeed, while it was only natural that publishers tried to harness the power of print to advertise their wares, more personal methods continued to prove preferable. New clients were won by writing speculative letters, by spreading the word with flyers and catalogues, by responding quickly to inquiries, and by dispatching travelling salesmen. And once a trusting relationship was built, the correspondence tended to flow thick and fast. The STN, for their part, rarely missed an opportunity to inform their clients which new works were about to issue from the region's presses and how many copies they might be able to supply. The tailored, up-to-the-minute information provided in such letters was many times more valuable than dated trade catalogues. After a few years of trading, indeed, the Neuchâtelois began to semi-formalize this process by producing regularly updated handwritten *aide-mémoire* catalogues of *nouveautés* that were to be copied out at the end of their outgoing letters. By always keeping several of these lists on the go, the Society streamlined and regularized their in-correspondence advertisement efforts while still retaining their ability to target clients differently according to their tastes.[134]

Ensuring that retail clients were always up-to-date with the region's *nouveautés* was critical because the STN understood that individual titles, the *Histoire de François Wills*, for example, could at best hope for a few years locked in the public's capricious gaze. It was in March 1773, as the snow melts once again swelled the river Seyon, that 'Berthe', 'Fèry' and 'Foras' printed their 1,542 copies of the new page-turner from 'l'auteur du Ministre de Wakefield'. The work raced towards profitability. By October 1774 only 791 of these copies remained available to buy, and on 30 November 1776 just 403 were still in stock. Around 75 per cent of the print run, then, had been sold in three and a half years. After the initial rush, however, stock declined at a much more leisurely pace as the Neuchâtelois lacked both the means to advertise old stocks internationally and the market to sell them locally. The 160 copies that still remained available to purchase on 31 December 1782, and that had been reduced down to a mere forty-seven copies by 1 June 1785, were not finally exhausted until 20 May 1794. Printing's long tail, although these copies represented only a relatively small proportion of the initial print run, looked positively serpentine from provincial Neuchâtel.

Given that the Society ultimately collapsed under a mountain of unsold stock and debt, it is perhaps surprising that a study of the exhaustion of nineteen more of their editions, published between 1773 and 1775, shows that the success of *Histoire de François Wills* was no exception.[135] On average, the STN dispatched 72 per cent of the copies of these editions within two years of publication. After five years stocks were 92 per cent sold, while after ten years rarely more than a handful of copies remained. The most rapidly depleting works – 1,008 copies of John Hawkesworths's *Relation des voyages entrepris par ordre de Sa Majesté* printed in collaboration with the STL in July 1774 and 676 copies of a second edition of Georg Jonathan von Holland's *Réflexions philosophiques sur le Système de la nature* pressed in August 1773 – took less than two years to sell out. And even the Society's least performant publication during this period – Elie Bertrand's *Elémens d'oryctologie*, 784 copies of which were printed on 20 March 1773 – effortlessly achieved net profitability, with 55 per cent of stock sold, during its first two years of availability. After ten years a hardly ruinous 170 copies remained available. We must remember, of course, that a substantial percentage of the early shipments of many STN editions were not regular sales, but page-for-page exchanges with Romandy partners for their own *nouveautés*. Most of these swapped copies had a further journey to make, unknowable from the STN evidence alone, before they reached their final retail destination. Yet the fact that the STN managed to exhaust its own swapped stocks *as quickly* as their own printings, suggests that we might have some confidence in the broad representativeness of these figures. They give us a reasonable understanding of just how quickly Romandy printers got shot of their *nouveautés*.

Some STN printings, for sure, fell short of expectations. The Society somewhat overestimated its ability to find homes for 2,500 copies of *Essai philosophique sur le plaisir*, a sentimental and philosophical Christian text written by Elie Bertrand, the uncle of its director Jean-Elie Bertrand. Printed on 26 October 1776, 1,535 copies of Bertrand's essay still remained in stock at the end of 1782. The Neuchâtelois later printed a new title page for the remaining copies, proclaiming a publication date of

1780 in hope that they might seem less ancient![136] The *Oeuvres complettes d'Alexis Piron*, too, were a hard sell to a francophone public obsessed with novelty, and David Hume's autobiographical *Vie de David Hume* sold rather slowly.[137] Despite being a first edition only available from the STN, Louis-Sébastien Mercier's play *Le mort de Louis XI* equally underwhelmed.[138] Although stocks of these works were exhausted at a more leisurely pace than page-turners like *Historie de François Wills*, it should nonetheless be recognized that they profoundly contributed towards the richness of the STN's offerings and were, eventually, individually profitable. Further, where the Society did end up fighting a battle to get rid of stock piles of any individual work, it could almost always blame its own mistaken judgement in printing too many copies. Sensibly chosen works printed in runs of 1,000 copies or less invariably all but sold out within 2–5 years.

There should be no doubt, then, that despite difficult local trading conditions and the failure of the *Nouveau Journal helvétique* project, the STN did a good job of selling its *nouveautés*. Like their rivals and allies in Lausanne and Geneva, the Neuchâtelois were justifiably terrified of what they termed *gardes magesins* – works likely to spend years gathering dust in their stockroom before finding buyers.[139] Healthy returns could be made from good books while they held the attention of industry buyers and the publics that they served. But the moment's bestsellers risked becoming the morrow's blotting paper. The STN managed risk well during its 1770s heyday. It generally avoided printing too many copies of its works and almost never committed to second editions. And of course, it largely stuck to cheap, small-format works of 'belles-lettres' and 'histoire' that could be confidently marketed. But even then, even when straw-lined crates of books like *Historie de François Wills* were daily being loaded on a boat to Morat, a serious issue with the Society's core business model was starting to crystallize. With each year that passed the Society's stock holdings were becoming ever more fragmented, largely due to the difficulty of selling the last 10 per cent of copies of both its own stocks and the already diverse selection of works that arrived as swaps from its regional partners. As the STN's directors completed a periodic stock taking exercise on 25 January 1779, they found that their business held more than 100 copies of only 64 of its 528 discrete editions being offered for sale. Those familiar with the industry would have found nothing unusual in this situation. Indeed, the vertically integrated 'printer–bookseller' hybrid model that so many publishing houses adopted worked precisely because it provided a way of storing and liquidating this long tail through a local retail shop. But for the STN to plough the same furrow as its rivals, mostly family-run conservative businesses based in Europe's larger towns and cities, it would have to accept the lay of the land. Much capital was guaranteed to be permanently tied up in expansive stock holdings and while profits were there to be made, they would not come quickly. Whatever the original intentions and ambitions of its founders, by the late 1770s, as we have seen, the STN depended upon speculative capital that would not wait. Change would have to come.

III

At the heart of Diderot's 1763 'Lettre sur le commerce des livres', an unapologetically elitist defence of the principal of *privilège en librairie*, sits the argument that many of the monopoly powers enjoyed by Paris's great publishing houses were in the wider public interest. Serious editions of mathematics, chemistry, natural history or law, Diderot insisted, were risky commercial ventures the stocks of which might take decades to exhaust. Great authors, indeed, oftentimes received the recognition that they deserved only posthumously. Francophone Europe's intellectual life, he concluded, would wither if left in the hands of purely commercial printers beholden to the lazy and superficial spirit of the day.[140] The bottom feeding printers and booksellers of the continent's *other* intellectual and commercial publishing centres – of Rouen and Lyon, of Amsterdam and Geneva – naturally saw things differently. They argued, rather, that Paris's privilege stymied innovation and was slowly asphyxiating the republic of letters. But, while the two sides differed as to how the tyranny of the market might best be combatted, they could at least agree that the landscape of Europe's publishing industry was uneven and dictated by slim margins. It was a cutthroat, breakneck-paced and unbalanced literary world, the type where any mediocre novel might easily be passed off as an Oliver Goldsmith, into which the STN was born. This reality dictated the Society's commercial fortunes, shaped its outputs and ultimately, we will see, hastened its demise.

Had Diderot's horse been any higher he might have wished it cast in bronze and hoisted atop a plinth on the Pont-Neuf. In the pay of the publisher André François Le Breton and the *syndic de la communauté des libraires parisiens*, and fearful for the future of his *Encyclopédie* project, the French *philosophe* did not pen the 'Lettre sur le commerce des livres' in the spirit of impartiality.[141] Nonetheless, his protectionist diatribe against the publishers of London, Amsterdam, Avignon and Geneva stands as a remarkable testimony to his failure to recognize the dynamism of the extraterritorial publishers and their role in forwarding the Enlightenment. Ostervald and his partners, like their counterparts elsewhere, operated at the cutting edge of the European francophone public sphere. These 'foreign' printers played a crucial role as cultural intermediaries in the chaotic commercial landscape of literary life beyond protected Paris, helping to shape the Enlightenment as it was experienced by ordinary Europeans through their hard-nosed decision making. And, despite Diderot's blanket dismissal, they were not all of a kind. Not only did the products of the extraterritorial presses differ radically from those situated in Paris but, a close reading of the STN data suggests, 'foreign' printing regions differed subtly from each other. Physical and cultural geographical, trade connections and logistics and legal frameworks combined with the pressures of razor-thin margins to ensure that all of these border traders grubbed around different parts of the literary pond.

The volumes hawked by French-speaking Switzerland's printers and booksellers, then, were subtly different to those offered from elsewhere. In a sense, we might have better understood this much from Michel Schmidt's meticulous bibliography of STN-printed editions, published in 2002 and described as precious by Daniel Roche, and from Silvio Corsini's valuable lists of books published in Lausanne during the eighteenth century.[142] Between these studies and the FBTEE database, and now armed with the knowledge that the Swiss almost exclusively traded their own wares, we finally have a satisfying appreciation of the goods that the Romandy traders offered to their international clientele. As such, the product understood, we can now more surefootedly advance to a closer examination of to where all these hundreds of thousands of novels and histories, dictionaries and devotional tracts were sold. All told, allowing for returns, the STN shipped 1,510 copies of their edition of *Histoire de François Wills*. 655 copies (43.6%) were dispatched to the Swiss partner houses and local booksellers, 430 (28.7%) to French clients in towns like Lyons (130, 8.7%) and Colmar (103, 6.9%), 208 (13.8%) were destined for the Frankfurt book fair and 84 (5.6%) were sent south to the Italian provinces. Intriguingly, tellingly, only three copies were sold to Paris. But the *Histoire de François Wills* is just one second-rate book that we might now jettison back towards literary obscurity. A more coherent look at what the STN sales data can tell us about the late-Enlightenment European trade in French books will require a more ambitious and systematic approach.

3

The Republic of Books

Of all the Swiss plateau's commercial modes of transport, from leisurely boats across the lakes to the speedy *coche de Berne*, the blind cankerous horse was surely the least practical.[1] The problem, as the STN commis David Mercier lamented as he entered the Lake Geneva town of Nyon at 6 o'clock in the evening on Saturday 19 June 1773, was that the beast had a terrible limp and struggled to walk in a straight line. Mercier's mount had been rented a few days previously in Neuchâtel from the wife of the master *voiturier* Frédrich Dotaux. How it had finished up in such a wretched condition, however, became the cause of some dispute. According to Mercier's testimony, upon entering Nyon he had immediately called the marshal, Aléxandre Levrat, who had registered the problem and examined the horse the following morning, declaring an infection resulting from an open wound on the mare's right front foot to have been the root cause of its troubles. The canker was dressed appropriately and Mercier continued his fact-finding journey on foot, writing to his Neuchâtelois masters three days later from Rolle to report his inconvenience. To the young man's disbelief, when the horse was eventually returned to Neuchâtel the *voiturier* Dotaux kicked-up an almighty stink and quickly took legal action. The beast represented a decent chunk of Dotaux's livelihood and, regrettably, its travelling days were over. Neuchâtel's magistrates heard the case on 5 August, taking evidence from both parties as well as the authorities in Nyon. Mercier insisted that the Society had no liability in the affair, claiming that he had noticed a limp and a lump upon leaving Neuchâtel; Dotaux countered that the unseeing nag had clearly been mistreated en route. The following day the magistrates found in favour of the *voiturier* and ordered the STN to pay unstated damages for his loss of revenue plus 14.6.0 *livres de Neuchâtel* for the judgement.

If a modest fact-finding trip to the *arc lémanique* could prove so irksome, selling books to Europe's four corners was an extraordinary challenge. Admittedly, over 300 years of transnational printing and bookselling across Europe had bequeathed sophisticated haulage and information transmission systems that contained risk and controlled costs with remarkable efficiency. Arterial roads and waterways were favoured; smaller packages from multiple sellers were joined together at nodal centres like Basle and Lyon before being shipped to their common destinations; traders helped each other source labour, expose bad debtors and market their wares; and printing houses looked to conduct as much of their reconnaissance and sales work in one go by sending travelling representatives on lengthy looping tours of the continent. But everything still cost and, directly or indirectly, expenses tended to accumulate by the kilometre. Regular haulage charges, of course, increased according to the weight of the goods, the distance covered, the route taken and the expediency sought. Insurance premiums, which officially covered eventualities such as water damage and theft but sometimes also extended to bribes to ensure the safe passage of merchandise through a border crossing or *chambre syndicale*, were usually calculated as a percentage of these haulage costs. And the danger of encountering some extraordinary situation – that war or extreme weather might entirely block a route, that a country's trade regulations might change overnight, that an edition or shipment might be targeted by foreign authorities – multiplied with the distance travelled and the number of jurisdictions traversed. A summer order to Saint Petersburg, for example, had to be sent promptly by lake to Morat, by road to Basle, and then by river to Amsterdam in order to make the Baltic crossing before the waters risked freezing over. There was a lot that might go awry, and so depending on the size and timing of the delivery such a treacherous journey could add between 20 per cent and 40 per cent to the cost of an order.[2] And what if the recipient never paid? Between May and October 1781, the STN shipped 545 works to the 'École typographique des Orphelins' in Homburg. This 'school' was in reality just a front dreamt up by the disreputable bookseller Karl de Grandmesnil, who quickly disappeared into the shadows after receiving his works only to resurface in Vienna years later with an entirely new identity.[3] Such hiccups could only realistically be limited through the gathering of solid information about potential clients from trusted sources, and the further that businesses traded from known territory the more costly it was to conduct such reconnaissance. Favarger's July to November 1778 information-gathering tour of France alone cost an eye-watering 1,289.2.6 *livres*.[4] And then, finally, there was competition. The Mannheim book dealer and STN correspondent Christian Friedrich Swann was hardly far wide of the mark when he described the international trade as a 'war of all against all'.[5] But if the combatants in this conflict were all ultimately fighting to save their own skins, they were nonetheless organized into armies, each of which formed alliances and dominated certain parts of the theatre of conflict. A Swiss printer attempting to ship books to Amsterdam, or Paris and its surrounds, could expect to encounter formidable resistance.

Given the regional nature of the alliances that formed, then, it is difficult to imagine what the likes of Ostervald would make of modern historical constructions of their trade as fundamentally 'cosmopolitan'. In *Grub Street Abroad: Aspects of the French Cosmopolitan Press from the Age of Louis XIV to the French Revolution*, Elizabeth Eisenstein evoked the term 'Cosmopolis', one of many false places of publication sometimes used by provocative Enlightenment printers, to designate the 'indeterminate, decentralised zone occupied by the dispersed citizens of the francophone Republic of Letters'.[6] Yet Ostervald's 'Cosmopolis' – the zone in which books and information really pinged about with the abandon described above – can be precisely pinpointed in space. It was bounded by the Jura and Alps to the north and south, the *Röstigraben* linguistic divide to the east and Geneva or, when the stars were particularly well aligned, Lyon to the west.[7] It was one thing to display the cosmopolitanism ideal on a title page or in a frontispiece, printers and booksellers understood, but quite another to free one's business from the logistical realities of shipping bulky and volumetrically inefficient products around Europe. This chapter extends our analysis to the STN's European sales beyond Romandopolis, with a particular focus on the period between 1771 and 1780 when the Society was at its most stable.[8] Painting a picture of regional variegation in the international francophone book trade which is largely absent in previous studies, it shows the extent to which fierce competition impacted upon the STN's ability to sell books to regions including the north of France, the Low Countries and protectionist Paris. Books, it suggests, never floated gracefully around Europe, they ground their way down highways and waterways haemorrhaging profitability and approaching fierce competition by the kilometre. In the process, this chapter highlights the difficulties that the STN's core bookselling business faced as it grew during the 1770s. Even in areas of the European map where the commercial opportunities were strong for the Romandy printers – eastern and southern France, Italy and a host of further flung pockets of francophone court culture including Saint Petersburg and Stockholm – it demonstrates that the STN struggled to establish regular, lucrative and long-lasting trading relationships with more than a handful of clients.

Shortly after the STN's 1769 establishment, remember, Ostervald and his new colleagues dispatched a circular that emphasized how Romandy's independence and neutrality ensured that its printers were particularly well positioned to supply books to a troubled continent. That the Neuchâtelois dreamt of drawing broad revenues from across the map was reflected in the far-flung locations of the missive's 187 recipients. The note was posted to booksellers in London, Paris, Amsterdam, Copenhagen, Edinburgh, Frankfurt, Dublin, Turin and Vienna.[9] And why not? Many Swiss suppliers of French and Latin books, including the frères Cramer and Albert-Henri Gosse, both of Geneva, had for decades enjoyed the luxury of extensive long-distance trade.[10] Alas, changed trading conditions from the outset of the 1770s, brought about primarily because the destruction of Jesuit centres of learning across Europe all but finished-off the Swiss export market for Latin books, immediately called such cosmopolitan ambitions into question. As their local rivals and allies struggled to liquidate piles of suddenly unsaleable Latin stocks, the STN altogether avoided the hitherto lucrative trade. Their customers would read French. And, for all that the European map was pocked with elite francophone communities – for all that the Society *hoped* to market French books in Dublin or Turin – this almost inevitably tied the success or failure of their fledgling business to the difficult task of cracking France. As the Marseille agent Jean Mossy acerbically pointed out to the Neuchâtelois in a December 1771 letter, yes he was fortunately located for access to the Mediterranean, but where did they expect that he might ship their far-from-universally-sought-after merchandise? To Italy? To Spain?[11] French books were not coffee or gold; not everybody could be expected to take an interest. Figure 3.1 shows the STN's sales during the relatively stable trading period enjoyed between 1 October 1771 and 26 January 1780 discussed above. The Society shipped 57,223 books to the Swiss nexus, 55,099 to France and 29,514 elsewhere in Europe. A total of 65 per cent of the 84,603 books that the STN dispatched beyond the Swiss zone, then, went to France. Many of the books that the Society sent to their Swiss wholesale partners in Lausanne and Geneva, oftentimes as wholesale swap deals, were, of course, also destined to be shipped on to Gallic clients. And so, overall, approximately half of the 141,836 books that the STN traded probably found their way to readers in France.

Neuchâtel's proximity to the mid-point of the kingdom's eastern border, at least, ensured that Ostervald and his partners were ideally positioned to supply their primary market. The Society's shipments to more-or-less anywhere in France were habitually dispatched across the Swiss plateau to Geneva, from where they joined the dependable flow of haulage traffic heading in a south-westerly direction towards Lyon. France's second city dominated the strategic confluence of the Saône and Rhône rivers and played home to a strong and independent-spirited book industry with historic ties to the Swiss printers. The thirty-five Lyonnais printers and booksellers and thirty-four business agents (*commissionaires* or *négociants*) with which the STN corresponded together boasted the contacts and know-how necessary to facilitate business in France. Further, the town's *ville d'entrée* status meant that the Lyonnais could discharge the import paperwork that accompanied the Society's shipments, freeing the *ballots* to be legitimately shipped to almost any of the kingdom's 506 retail booksellers, 207 printer–booksellers and 30 specialist printers.[12] Other routes into France existed – the 'smugglers' road through the Jura via Pontarlier, the route via Basle and across Alsace, the aquatic passage via the Rhine and North Sea to northern seaports like Calais – and they were occasionally used by the STN. But *only* the route via Lyon was sufficiently cost-effective and reliable to be suitable for quotidian business.

These distribution arrangements allowed the STN to sidestep the costs of dealing with whole sellers located in regional hubs like Limoges or Toulouse. And while selling directly to France's diverse and dispersed set of retail book dealers was never going to prove straightforward, the Society's directors understood that the unsatisfactory state of domestic French printing guaranteed demand for their product. Generations of risk-containing policy from the *direction de la Librairie* had enforced a marked contraction in the number of French publishing houses from 372 in 1701, to 247 in 1764, to just 237 in 1781.[13] Across the same period, by way of comparison, the kingdom's booksellers (retail booksellers and printer–booksellers) swelled from 634 to 713. France's consolidated provincial publishers were thus both few enough in number to be relatively straightforwardly monitored and, granted effective monopolies over an ever-expanding world of print, sufficiently wealthy and large that they saw little need to take on risk. Many contented themselves with churning out lottery tickets, business circulars, official proclamations and safe and lucrative editions unlikely to ruffle feathers: between 1777 and 1778 alone Voltaire's epic poem of 1723 *La Henriade* was reprinted four times in Rouen, four times in Lille and once in Lyon, Reims, Toulouse and Caen.[14] French booksellers, then, under pressure from customers for the most interesting and economical titles that Enlightenment Europe had to offer, *needed* links to the vibrant areas of printing located beyond the kingdom's borders. As Louis XV's state tried to find out more about functioning of trade in 1764, forty-five cities (31%) declared that their booksellers bought in foreign books, thirty claimed that only French books circulated, while seventy made no mention of foreign books.[15] In reality every bookseller worth their salt found ways to source imprints from abroad.

The difficulty faced by Ostervald and his collaborators, rather, lay in building and maintaining networks of book-ordering clients sufficiently strong as to ensure that it was the STN, and not their regional and international rivals, that profited from France's need. The richest pickings, naturally, were closest to home. The Society realized 40 per cent (43,498/108,644) of its total provincial French sales to the nearby regions of Besançon, Lyon, Strasburg, Nancy and Burgundy, despite their harbouring just 22 per cent (190/850) of the kingdom's booksellers.[16] These orders from eastern France came from 106 booksellers and individual clients located in 28 different towns. Lyon, whose traders took a total of 12,480 books, was a particular hotspot. And with 10,203 books dispatched, the highly literate and culturally rich university and *parlement* town of Besançon, capital of the Franche-Comté, also proved a vital market. Just 74 kilometres as the crow flies from Neuchâtel and accessible through the Val-de-Travers via Pontarlier, the increasing significance of Besançon to the Swiss book trade was recognized by the establishment of a *chambre syndicale* in 1777 and appointment of an inspector of the book trade in 1778.[17] A little more surprisingly perhaps, the booksellers of the modest Lorraine resort town of Lunéville – Marie Audéart, Augé, P. J. Bernard, Jean Chenoux, L'Entretien and Jean Gay – also filled their shops and reading rooms with an impressive 3,327 books supplied by the STN. Alone the Society did more trade there than with either Britain or the Iberian Peninsula. Beyond these easterly heartlands, the Society also sold disproportionately high numbers of books to south-eastern and western France including the regions of Montpellier (11,002 books dispatched), the Comtat Venaissin[18] (3,453), Provence (2,506), Toulouse (1,379), Grenoble (1,012) and Nice[19] (169). As the STN travelling salesmen Favarger reported back to base on his passage through these lands in 1778, he everywhere found bigotry, mediocrity and a lack of interest.[20] The conservative south was a difficult place for a progressive Protestant publishing house to call home territory. But over time the Society found just about enough diamonds in the rough – the great business of Rigaud, Pons and Company in Montpellier (2,369 sales in 42 orders over 14 years) being the standout example – to be relatively satisfied with its trade with the east and south of France.

A bout of scabies and the onset of winter forced Favarger to truncate his tour before he reached France's north. It was perhaps for the best, as these were territories into which the STN rarely made inroads. To the north-easterly regions of Amiens, Lille, Soissons and Valenciennes, rich reading territory sandwiched between Paris and the Austrian Netherlands that hosted 91 booksellers, the STN dispatched just 900 books across its entire existence. And the Society fared only a little better in the still-stronger book markets of Caen (2,746 sales), Châlons (2,116) Metz (1,484) and Rouen (1,377). Indeed, the relationship struck up with J. Manoury of the *rue St. Jean* in Caen, who took 2,448 books in 20 separate orders dispatched between October 1775 and October 1782, stands out as the only substantial, stable and long-lasting trading relationship that the Society enjoyed north of Paris. Manoury's orders regularly included specialist Swiss-produced Protestant liturgy and literature – works like Jacques Plantier's *Cours de religion* (Lausanne, 1772) and François-Jacques Durand's *Sermons nouveaux* (Lausanne, 1774) – that could only be sourced from the Swiss Romand and were never likely to be counterfeited elsewhere. A total of 56.8 per cent (750/1,320) of the books that the STN sent to Rouen, too, were Swiss Protestant Bibles, sermons or liturgies. This niche provided a helpful trickle of trade, but the grim truth was that even the North's French Protestant communities were much more accustomed to turning to Amsterdam or The Hague to satisfy their need for devotional texts. The account books of the Parisian book dealer the Veuve Desaint brim with lucrative deals with traders based in northern towns like Brest, Calais, Coutances, Dieppe, Le Mans, Provins and Senlis, to which the STN never made a single sale.[21] If such towns could not source works locally or from Paris, as the region's intendants reported in response to the 1764 survey, then they had them imported from the Low Countries.[22] The STN barely stood a chance.[23]

So what of Paris? Such was the ability of the Parisian bookseller's guild and the city's policing authorities to control imports that the STN generally found the City of Light to be still less receptive. Between 1 October 1771 and 26 January 1780 – the period that best allows for us to understand the state of its 'regular' trading – the STN dispatched a paltry 1,224 copies to France's capital.[24] The Neuchâtelois sent more French books to Bergamo in Italy, Warsaw in Poland and twenty-six other towns and cities. Shipments to Paris were dispatched only at infrequent and irregular intervals. Between January 1774 and June 1775 'De Longe', a resident chez Madame 'Lausane' on the *rue Saint-Honoré* managed to get an assortment of 349 Swiss-printed Protestant works through. On 22 July 1776 the journalist Simon-Nicolas-Henri Linguet had 200 copies of his STN-printed *Requête au Conseil du Roi, pour M Linguet* (n.p. [Neuchâtel], n.d. [1776]) sent to his home address in Paris. But the Parisian net was tight and broadly cast. The STN's only serious attempt to smuggle clandestine works into the city – a March 1777 order from the small-time chancer Jean-Baptiste Joseph Barré, of the *rue de Bassy (à la reine d'Espagne)*, that included Guillemain de Saint-Victor's *Adoption, ou la maçonnerie des femmes en trois gradés* and a host of other underground titles – was halted at Dijon and, with no obvious way to get past inspections that the Society described as frequent and thorough, the books were all returned to Neuchâtel.[25] In May 1777 the STN wrote to its Parisian agent Pyre of the *rue Saint Jacques (vis à vis le petit marché)* to confirm that they approved his new plan to seek the necessary permissions for their works, especially those exclusive Protestant sermons and liturgical works that were known to interest the city's dealers, to circulate freely in the capital. The letter noted that the Society had sent complimentary copies of Emir de Vattel's *Droit de Gens*, Elie Bertrand's *Essai philosophique et moral sur le plaisir* and *Le Thévenon, ou les journées de la montagne*, and Jean-Elie Bertrand's *La morale évangélique* to François-Claude-Michel-Benoît Le Camus de Néville, the director of the book trade, and asked Pyre to take all necessary actions to ensure that they were registered at the city's *chambre syndicale*. But nothing ultimately came of what turned into lengthy affair; the STN never managed to establish a stable and regular channel for selling its regular stocks to Paris.

A great part of the Society's problem in towns like Paris, Calais and Rouen stemmed from the reality that northern France's booksellers habitually sourced the majority of their foreign books from a region beyond France's north-eastern border that we might call The North. The North's core was to be found in the decentralized, Protestant and economically prosperous towns of the western provinces of the Dutch Republic, particularly The Hague, Rotterdam, Leiden, Utrecht and, most of all, Amsterdam.[26] The printers and booksellers of these towns dominated a vast sea of book-producing and book-buying centres that stretched from Bruges and Brussels in the Austrian Netherlands, through the Prince-Bishopric of Liège and secondary Dutch towns like Dordrecht and Delft, to the northern German cities of Cologne and Hamburg. The relatively weak governments of The North's core afforded its printers and booksellers the luxury, enjoyed also by their counterparts in French-speaking Switzerland, of loose regulatory environments and liberal censorship regimes. And while the towns of Holland lacked the immediate proximity to France's border enjoyed by their Swiss rivals, their logistical options for supplying the kingdom were more numerous. The North's books flowed most readily via the road that ran from Holland through Antwerp and Ghent to the French entry town of Lille. But road-bound crates could also be inspected at Amiens, Rheims or Paris while those placed on North-Sea boats could enter the kingdom via its northern and western ports including Calais, Rouen, Nantes and Bordeaux.[27] Many of the estimated 200,000 unique titles that left the Dutch presses during the eighteenth century, an extraordinary doubling of the mark achieved during the previous 100 years that defied the region's demographic stagnation, travelled these roads and waterways.[28] By the latter part of the century of lights, for sure, relatively high salaries, expensive ink and paper, and the growing conservatism of a certain section of the enriched bourgeoisie all contributed to a weakening of the status of the Dutch presses.[29] But if the flood of cheap print emanating from rival centres threatened The North's market share, it also quickly forced its publishing houses to integrate their operations more coherently and to offer more competitive products. From the 1750s the Dutch traders started to institutionalize their previously informal ties, fixing strict distribution deals and central lists of works published.[30] They developed modern and sophisticated systems of selling on consignment on a sale-or-return basis and 'main correspondent' specialist wholesaling which, although not always popular developments among publishers, ultimately ensured that books reached more potential readers.[31] They upped their game.

And they could always rely upon one key advantage: occupying the space between Paris, London and Berlin, the North's printers were based where the best part of Europe's news – economic, institutional and political – was made.[32] Newspapers and journals like the *Gazette d'Amsterdam*, Jean Luzac's *Gazette de Leyde*, the London-based *Courier de l'Europe* and the *Courier du Bas-Rhin* in Cleves symbolized the North's near-total domination of the periodical trade. The news was generally well read – the *Hamburg Correspondent* was sent to nearly 20,000 subscribers by 1789 and the most successful Dutch and London newspapers, including Luzac's, enjoyed between 4,000 and 6,000 paying individual and institutional clients during moments of high public interest.[33] And circulation allowed the North to set the literary agenda. Francophone Europe's thirst for a side dish of literary news to accompany the political main course led, from the early seventeenth century, to the establishment of specialist literary journals and, especially, the insertion of book 'reviews', extracts and advertisements into general titles.[34] With the lion's share of important newspapers, journals and periodicals controlled by the North's commercial publishers, the books presented to readers rarely came from south of Paris. The 'republic of letters' constructed in Europe's political and literary reviews, from Pierre Bayle's 1694 *Nouvelles de la République des Lettres* onwards, in short, *was* the North. Understanding the lay of the land, when the STN was appealing for subscriptions for the *Encyclopédie* it took out a half-page add in the *Gazette de Leyde* at the cost of 26 *livres* while, as we have seen, all the time taking steps to create a viable competitor that would give the Romandy presses a stronger voice.[35]

Given the region's power, it is not surprising that Ostervald and his associates always coveted a link-up with the North. The STN's initial circular letter of 1769 was sent to twenty Dutch booksellers, the vast majority of whom, alas, never even bothered to reply. Abraham Blussé of Dordrecht and Jacques Vetstein of Leiden responded only to scoff at the commercial prospects of such long-distance wholesale trading. The experienced and influential Amsterdam publisher of the *philosophes* Marc-Michel Rey was similarly unconvinced, insisting that the costs of transport and the risk of damage, especially water damage, rendered such commerce unfruitful.[36] In March 1777, with their business in better shape and their stockroom brimming with attractively priced Swiss books, the Society again tried its luck with a letter sent directly to fifteen booksellers and printers based in Rotterdam, Amsterdam, Dordrecht, Anvers, Leiden, Ypres, Ghent and Brussels, The Hague, Tournai and Bruges. A little wiser, Ostervald insisted that while swapping books was unrealistic, the quality and price of their editions was such that both the Society and any willing wholesaler could make a profit. While the STN did not stock *livres philosophiques* – books of dubious legality – his letter emphasized, it could readily procure them.[37] Determined to get the message across, later during the same week the Society instructed the Amsterdam-based agents Panchaud, Houlez and Schouw to forward the addresses of all of the region's booksellers so that they might make a similar offer.[38] Two years later, in August and September 1779, the Society's Abraham Bosset de Luze toured the booksellers of Holland only to find a saturated and protectionist market that largely dismissed the possibility of forging deeper commercial links.[39] The booksellers of the Swiss Romand had been hearing a similar story for decades and there was nothing sufficiently original and compelling about the STN's propositions to change the status quo.[40] Across its entire twenty-five-year trading existence, the STN sent sixty-eight works to the great European book trade city of Amsterdam, two books to Utrecht, one book to Leiden and not a single book to Rotterdam. The Society forged only four substantive relationships in The North.

Those associations were not inconsequential: the Society sent 6,098 copies to Pierre Gosse junior and Daniel Pinet in The Hague, 5,017 to Jean-Edmé Dufour and Philippe Roux in Maestricht, 2,577 to Delahaye & Co. in Brussels and 1,922 to Jean-Louis de Boubers, also in Brussels. Thanks to this quartet of clients, indeed, approximately 4 per cent of the STN's total shipments did go to The North. Yet all four relationships proved problematic and none provided anything approaching a reliable way of marketing STN works widely in their region. Before the autumn of 1771, when the STN made the strategic shift from selling only its own printed works to trading in the general product of the Swiss presses, 27 per cent of shipments were dispatched to the Dutch Republic and Austrian Netherlands.[41] In total, 500 copies of the baron d'Holbach's incendiary *Système de la nature* were printed for Boubers while 500 copies of Voltaire's seven-volume *Questions sur l'Encyclopédie* were sent, among other large shipments, to Gosse and Pinet. However, Boubers and Gosse and Pinet drove such hard bargains that this trade proved unsustainable.[42] The 242.16.3 *livres* that Gosse and Pinet paid for their 500 copies of Francesco Algarotti's 19.5 sheet *Lettres du comte Algarotti sur la Russie* in February 1770, for example, represented a 50 per cent discount of 1 crutz de Suisse per sheet that barely covered the STN's printing costs.[43] As soon as the STN's business model matured, Boubers altogether stopped trading with the Neuchâtelois, and Gosse and Pinet reduced their orders to perhaps 12, 25 or 50 copies of new works primarily for local, rather than regional, distribution.[44] In 1777 their relationship acrimoniously broke down.[45]

The modest hole left by the loss of the Gosse and Pinet account was immediately filled by Dufour and Roux, who proved reliable retail clients from December 1776 until the STN's demise. But the dream of a viable wholesale link-up with The North remained in suspense until it was mooted by Delahaye & Co. in April 1782. The Brussels booksellers wrote to the Neuchâtelois out of the blue to enquire if the Society, as they had heard locally, could supply all new works published in French-speaking Switzerland. Since they were well placed to supply new books printed in England, Holland and the Low Countries, they suggested, some reciprocal wholesale agreement could surely be reached.[46] By this time somewhat savvy operators, the STN dodged the idea of having to deal with northern editions and instead ultimately came to an agreement whereby Delahaye & Co. would print the atlas to their forthcoming edition of the abbé Guillaume-Thomas-François Raynal's *Histoire philosophique des deux Indes*.[47] Delahaye & Co. promised to advertise STN editions throughout The North and even hoped to ship a significant number to the 'three kingdoms of England'.[48] And while the *Bruxellois* initially sought a 25 per cent discount, threatening in the process to take their business elsewhere, a more mutually acceptable figure of 15 per cent was quickly agreed. Reality, alas, soon bit. On 6 July 1782, Delahaye & Co. ordered 108 copies of each of 3 about-to-be-published original plays by Louis-Sébastien Mercier – *Zoé*, *Les tombeaux de Vérone* and *L'habitant de la Guadeloupe*. By the terms of the order, the STN was forbidden from sending even a single additional copy of the plays to The North for at least a month, so that Delahaye & Co. could exhaust their stocks before either Boubers or Dufour and Roux inevitably produced counterfeit editions.[49] Once high transport costs had been taken into account, the Brussels booksellers insisted, there was no way that the STN original could compete with local knock-offs. The STN shipped Delahaye & Co.'s books on 18 July 1782, and while Ostervald and his partners respected the agreement not to send any more copies to The North, the following day they did send 500 copies of *Zoé* and the *L'habitant* and 375 of *Les tombeaux* to Quandet de Lachenal in Paris, and large volumes to clients based throughout Switzerland and the rest of Europe. To their horror, Delahaye & Co. almost immediately found Mercier's plays selling for eight sous in Brussels, practically half the fifteen sous price agreed with the Neuchâtelois, and demanded a further discount.[50] From this inglorious start the relationship quickly deteriorated further, as both parties realized that establishing a viable link was beyond their collective competence. A little over a year later, as a disastrous affair of concerning Delahaye's printing of the Raynal atlas headed towards litigation, all commercial links were severed.

The harsh reality was this: The North and Romandy were rival trading blocs built on commercial models that largely rejected extra-regional cooperation. And for the STN, the failure to substantively trade with the hostile North also hampered access to its hinterland markets of the British Isles and extra-European colonies. Customs records show that the dense network of booksellers located in Britain and Ireland imported wares primarily from Holland, followed by France, Flanders, Germany, Italy and Venice.[51] Negligible numbers of works were sourced directly from Romandy. In the capitals and learned centres of the British Isles, of course, demand for books in Enlightenment Europe's principal language was high. The London bookseller John Nourse took large shipments of French books from the Veuve Desaint in Paris with metronomic regularity.[52] Further, as Máire Kennedy's work on the Dublin Francophile Charles Praval and his publisher William Whitestone's short-lived 1777–8 *Magazin à la mode* had shown, provincial Britain and Ireland's dense networks of booksellers also bought surprising amounts of French books. From Dublin, Praval's periodical aimed at helping readers to improve their French was disseminated to, for example, grocers and innkeepers located in provincial towns like Derry and Belfast as well as travelling chapmen roaming the countryside.[53] The libraries of wealthy private individuals, too, confirm lasting demand for serious French titles in Ireland.[54] In total, the STN shipped just 1,155 works to London, 892 of which were sent to the specialist importer of French books Edward Lyde of The Strand between March 1778 and March 1779. Luke White of Dublin also took 1,034 books between March 1780 and April 1785. Sent via Basle, Brussels and Ostende (or sometimes Rotterdam), White's ordering pattern – he rarely asked for more than a dozen copies of any individual title – suggests that he was selling his STN works only locally.[55] In truth the Neuchâtelois were likely thankful to have landed even these meagre returns; nothing in the record books of their Genevois allies suggests that any of the landlocked Swiss printers and booksellers had much luck in the British Isles.[56]

The Swiss found ever-growing communities of European-language readers located beyond Europe's shores – on the high seas, in outposts and colonies and especially in North America – similarly difficult to exploit. The STN, indeed, neither corresponded with a single client nor directly sold a single work outside Europe. The orders that the London printer and bookseller John Murray regularly received from his naval contacts for their friends in India, as well as those that came from clients in the American colonies, Jamaica and China, by contrast, made a substantial contribution to the health of his business.[57] The 1784 catalogue of the Philadelphian booksellers Boinod and Gaillard reveals that the majority of their imports came from Paris, The Hague, Liège, Amsterdam, Leiden, Maastricht and London. Such was the prominence of editions from The North among Boinod and Gaillard's stocks, indeed, that even their copies of the Neuchâtelois pastor Jean-Rodolphe Ostervald's *La nourriture de l'âme* were printed in Rotterdam in 1768! Nonetheless, that this Philadelphian trade catalogue did contain some Neuchâtelois and wider-Romandy editions – the STN's editions of Pierre-Ambroise-François Choderlos de Laclos's *Les liaisons dangereuses* and the *Oeuvres complètes* of Alexis Piron among them – demonstrates that some Swiss books did cross the Atlantic.[58] Etienne Pestre of Geneva, in addition, admitted to having bought two copies of the STN's quarto *Encyclopédie* for customers based in Africa.[59] And the Cádiz booksellers Paul and Bertrand Caris once informed the Neuchâtelois that while negative experiences meant that he no longer sent items to 'Les Indes' at his own risk, he was willing to operate as a forwarding agent for any orders that the STN did receive.[60] One might reasonably wonder, by consequence, whether a proportion of the STN's sales to Atlantic ports like Cádiz (178 sales), Lisbon (2,186) or Bordeaux (2,180) ultimately reached more exotic climes. But the limited hard evidence suggests that The North dominated extra-European supply.

The shadow cast by the printers and booksellers of The North, then, was extensive and opaque. And in the sun-drenched states of Italy and the kingdoms of the Iberian Peninsula, where generations of Swiss printers had found constant demand for their works, the STN also faced adversity. Eighteenth-century Spanish and Portuguese printers and booksellers, unable to publish many popular works because of the censorship activities of Catholic Church and its Inquisition, lacked liquidity and became perpetual importers.[61] In 1763, the Parisian bookseller Antoine-Chrétien Boudet estimated that Spain annually accepted shipments of books to the value of 350,000 *livres* from Venice, 200,000 *livres* from Antwerp and 100,000 *livres* from each of Geneva, Lausanne, Lyon and Paris. Portugal, he suggested, imported 200,000 *livres*-worth of books from each of Anvers, Avignon, Italy and Switzerland.[62] Between 1755 and 1761, certainly, the Cramer family of Geneva traded bountifully with Barcelona, Alicante, Seville, Cádiz and Lisbon, from where their works were also forwarded to Coimbra, Salamanca and Valladolid. But the lion's share of the books that they shipped, of course, were in Latin.[63] The STN, due to their strategy of trading only in French editions, shipped a measly 2,186 books to Portugal and just 805 to Spain. The majority of those sales to Spain (578/805) were to Jacques Thévin, bookseller to the court in Madrid, who took three shipments via Marseille and Alicante between March and June 1783, and then never used the STN again. Having thoroughly sounded the market, the Society wrote off any ambitions to place serious numbers of copies of their quarto edition of Diderot and d'Alembert's *Encyclopédie* in the Iberian Peninsula as unrealistic.[64]

South of the Alps, by contrast, the STN's *Encyclopédie* sold fantastically well.[65] Enlightenment Italy's thirst for French literature was such that the trade catalogues of booksellers on the peninsula tended to list between 50 and 120 Genevan editions, as well as many more titles from the presses of Lausanne and Neuchâtel.[66] The STN sold a healthy 20,320 books to an unusually broad base of clients scattered across the map from Piedmont to Naples.[67] Together, these booksellers and individuals provided the Neuchâtelois with a steady, if never quite spectacular, stream of orders of between 500 and 1,500 books per year. Largely they sought a broad selection of works to fill their shelves and reading rooms; the Society, indeed, shipped a remarkable 1,648 different editions to Italy during the 1770s and 1780s. Packages were generally sent first to Geneva and then through the Valais and across the Alps to Turin or Genoa, from where they might be forwarded by boat to Rome or Naples if necessary. An alternative route via Lucerne, the Gotthard Pass and Milan was also sometimes employed for shipments to easterly towns like Venice. These routes, of course, allowed the Swiss to send books to the Italian Peninsula both more economically and expediently than many of their international rivals. And the shared border ensured that neither distant war nor foreign taxes could disrupt trade, as was so often the case when goods had to cross multiple major jurisdictions. The Dutch did, of course, enjoy a presence in the region.[68] But the stiffest competition that the Neuchâtelois faced in the land of Cesare Beccaria was from entrenched Swiss rivals like the Lausannois printer–booksellers Jean-Pierre Heubach and François Grasset.[69] Still closer to home, indeed, the important Yverdon printer and bookseller Fortuné-Barthélemy de Félice, born in Rome to a Neapolitan family and having settled at the western point of Lake Neuchâtel only in 1756, enjoyed deep and commercially lucrative ties with his homeland.[70] And competition from the likes of Félice was especially fierce because, with the Latin trade drying-up at a frightening pace, Romandy's traders were fighting for slices of a diminished pizza. The 121,300 *livres* of commerce that the Cramer family once enjoyed south of the Alps had become a distant dream by the 1770s.[71] Nonetheless, the STN was too young an institution to pine for times past, and its trade with the Italian Peninsula was at least as healthy as that enjoyed anywhere else on the continent. As the Society's travelling salesman Victor Durand quaffed his way around Italy in the spring of 1788, indeed, he had such a fruitful time that his paymasters in Neuchâtel eventually had to beg him to stop dragging his heels and move on![72]

When Durand did finally move on, he headed first to Vienna and then to Prague. These were the most accessible of an important group of major eastern European centres, completed by Moscow, Saint Petersburg, Stockholm and Warsaw, where the STN had enjoyed much success. Largely capitals and court cities, and all with substantial noble and bourgeois classes that looked towards the francophone world for their cultural fix, these eastern honeypots were sufficiently far flung not to be dominated by the Dutch and their allies. Between May 1775 and June 1791, the STN sent 7,139 books in just 24 shipments to the bookseller Christian Rüdiger in Moscow. Buying in bulk was the only way that Rüdiger could reduce the costs generated by the 4,000 kilometre passage to Russia's historic capital via Basle, Frankfurt, Lubeck and Saint Petersburg. And so the Muscovite packed his crates with titles drawn from across the range of the STN's stocks, although textbooks like Ostervald's *Géographie élémentaire* (277 sales) and Pierre Restaut's *Abrégé des principes de la grammaire françoise* (122) featured particularly prominently. Between June 1782 and October 1788, Antoine-Adolphe Fryberg, Elsa Fougt and Company and Charles G. Ulf, all booksellers in Stockholm, took 6,267 copies of 1,086 different books spread across 25 orders. Works of literature dominated the crates, which tended to be shipped via Basle and Frankfurt to begin their Baltic passage at Wismar. To Warsaw's booksellers, including Michel Gröll and Joseph Lex who timed their orders to coincide with the sessions of the Polish Diet, the STN sent 5,377 works, also drawn from a large variety of stocks.[73] The STN's shipments east of Germany, then, were generally of a type: infrequent, large and composed of just a few copies of scores or hundreds of different titles with a strong bias towards literature and educational works. So while francophone booksellers in these climes were few and far between, forming a relationship with one 'solid' enough to be trusted was a real prize.[74] The likes of Rüdiger and Ulf drained stocks that were difficult to ship in the faster-moving markets of Western Europe and were happy to settle their accounts for cash rather than attempt to make them balance through trade. The STN's impressive volume of shipments to this sextet of cities – 34,094 works were dispatched in total – represented an outstanding success.

Finally, then, there was Prussia and the Holy Roman Empire. The STN dispatched 17,220 books to patchwork geographic Germany which, through steady economic growth and Frederick the Great's enlightened influence, was reasserting its position as a major force in the international book trade during the second half of the eighteenth century.[75] A limited proportion of the 25,100 works that the Neuchâtelois sent to well-connected German-speaking Swiss clients in Berne, Basle and Zurich might also be assumed to have ultimately reached readers in the Germanic provinces.[76] This relatively modest yield – roughly 4 per cent of total shipments – was founded upon the relationships that the Society enjoyed with Jean-Guillaume Virchaux in Hamburg (4,262 sales between 1777 and 1784), the *Société typographique de Neuwied* (2,804 sales between 1782 and 1788), Charles Fontaine in Mannheim (1,204 sales between 1770 and 1783), George-Conrad Walther in Dresden (1,192 sales between 1771 and 1788) and Johann Conrad Deinet in Frankfurt (1,120 sales between 1773 and 1780). These men were, for sure, ideal clients that drew regularly from standard STN stocks and gave frequent and vivid updates about the state of the German market. But they were too few in number: the STN boasted just 22 German clients that took over 100 works in total, and just 8 (including the above quintet) that took more than 500. Considering Prussian dependency Neuchâtel's relative proximity and deep political ties to the region, which in 1781 boasted 261 booksellers distributed across 90 different cities, this represented a disappointing yield. Some of the STN's difficulties, certainly, can be attributed to the reality that so many of the region's booksellers sourced a substantial proportion of their foreign works not by mail, but through an annual pilgrimage to the Leipzig book fair. Even as its popularity waned, Leipzig was an extraordinary place: the Berlin bookseller Friedrich Nicolai's Leipzig operation consisted of six rooms, including two on the ground floor facing the street and, from 1782, an attic equipped with tables, chairs and benches that he used as an auditorium.[77] Alas, the supply of French books there was traditionally dominated by Dutch traders like Johann Schreuder of Amsterdam.[78] When back in Berlin, Nicolai's main international deals happened to the north and east and, crucially, he held both cash and exchange accounts with Pierre Gosse in The Hague.[79] As the wealth and importance of the Prussian heartlands grew, too, Paris's printers and booksellers drew ever closer. Nearly a third of the correspondents of Parisian booksellers of the early 1780s, by comparison, were based in Germany.[80] The Veuve Desaint's lucrative monthly shipments to Fontaine in Manheim put the STN's commerce in the shade.[81]

In total, for all their trials and tribulations in Germany and elsewhere, the reality that by the second half of the 1770s, the STN were consistently selling over 10,000 books per year to foreign clients *was* some achievement. This volume was realized, we must remember, through trading more-or-less the same products at roughly the same price points as more familiar rivals and allies from Geneva, Lausanne and Yverdon. Further, it was accomplished against the backdrop of fierce competition from the booksellers of Paris and The North *and* the devastation wreaked on the Swiss trade by the collapse of Latin sales to Southern Europe. Only by leaving no stone unturned in its relentless pursuit of growth did the STN manage to sell so many books so far and wide. The Society's failure – the reason that Ostervald and his associates found their business mired in financial difficulties by end of 1770s and in liquidation a decade later – was not, then, for want of effort or achievement. Rather, first, it was due to the STN's absurdly unrealistic ambitions. As, towards the end of the 1770s, 12 simultaneous presses clattered-out copies of the *Encyclopédie* and the Society's debts approached 250,000 *livres*, remember, the travelling salesman Favarger dismissed most of southern France's towns – Montélimar, Viviers, Orange and so forth – as pointless backwaters to which the Neuchâtelois could never hope to sell books. Where he did stumble across booksellers worth buttonholing, more often than not they barely glanced at his

STN catalogues before dismissing the possibility of trade out of hand.[82] The truth was that selling Swiss books on international markets was a grind totally out of step with Ostervald's dreams and financial planning. And second, the Society's relentless pursuit of sales volume oftentimes came at the expense of sustainability and profitability. Yes, the Neuchâtelois sold over 400,000 copies of roughly 4,000 distinct editions to 788 clients based in 226 cities, towns or villages over the course of their 25-year existence. But only thirty-five of those clients located outside Switzerland's borders regularly purchased significant numbers of books over time.[83] Most booksellers and individuals chanced their hand at an order or two and then declined further trade. The costs that the STN incurred in time, effort and hard cash establishing all these contacts – from writing letters and printing circulars to sending a man to Nyon on the back of a wounded blind horse – entirely nullified their benefits. Worse, many small account-holders never paid their dues, and small debts scattered across a continent were impossible to gainfully recover.[84] Much of the STN's foreign trade was effectively conducted at a loss.

More than two centuries later, we might be thankful for the ambition and naivety of the STN and its directors. If, ultimately, Ostervald and his associates failed to build the sizeable and stable international networks necessary to sustain a business, the restlessness and recklessness with which they explored opportunities shines a remarkable amount of light on the functioning of the European trade in French-language books. That the Neuchâtelois effectively never traded with Amsterdam, Leiden, Rotterdam and Utrecht, and only did so with Paris on extraordinarily limited terms, was not due to a lack of interest or effort. And the Society's inability to reach readers in Britain, the colonies and vast swathes of northern France cannot be explained by a lack of ambition or vision. No, these failures came because the commercial battlefield of the European francophone book space was highly mannered, with parts of the map dominated by sophisticated and organized trading blocks.[85] These alliances formed because it made sense for printers to swap their books in order to reduce risk and diversify stocks, and because transport costs ensured that they could only economically do so within a certain radius. Where dense concentrations of printers existed – notably in The North, Paris and Romandy – their combined product could run to several hundreds of new titles per year and could provide for most of the needs of the ordinary reading majority in a wider hinterland. There was little to stop the independent booksellers of Picardy or Flanders, of course, from writing directly to the STN or Lausanne to get books. And on occasion they did. But with any major international bestseller guaranteed to be copied locally, with the range of titles printed locally impressive, with the literary agenda largely set by the North's printers, and with transport costs making these editions more expensive, they rarely bothered. In the republic of books, it perhaps bears repeating, crates did not float gracefully around Europe, they ground their way down highways and waterways haemorrhaging profitability and approaching fierce competition by the kilometre.

If an ordinary eighteenth-century Frenchman, then, perhaps working his way around the Grand Tour, walked into a bookshop in London, and then later Amsterdam, then Paris, and then Geneva, he would have found dramatically different books stocking the shelves. But here is the question: Would the Enlightenment encountered in their pages have been different? Hold that thought, for before we come to addressing it, we must bring our story of one ill-fated Neuchâtelois printing house towards its wretched close.

4

The Storm Will Pass

A familiar sketch of characters in motion. For a long moment during the summer and autumn of 1784, as the wooded border that separates the little Neuchâtelois town of Les Verrières from Pontarlier in France baked green and then smouldered brilliant reds and oranges, seven crates of STN forbidden books destined for the Troyes peddler Bruzard de Mauvelain remained stuck Swiss-side atop a mountain. Fresh instructions from the French authorities in Paris and Versailles had heightened tensions at the crossing, and Mauvelain's commission was hot by any standards. His boxes contained scores of copies of illegal works including the baron d'Holbach's wicked *Histoire critique de Jésus-Christ*, Joseph-Michel-Antoine Servan's daring *Apologie de la Bastille* and Anne-Gédeon de Lafitte de Pelleport's scandalmongering *Le diable dans un benitier*.[1] They brimmed with irreligion, pornography, political criticism and libel. For the previous year, the Pontarlier-based *assureur* Faivre had been making hay from his Helvetic smuggling ring. His 16 August 1783 contract with the STN committed him to getting books across the border for 15 *livres* the hundredweight. Teams of supervised porters waited for nightfall, sought Dutch courage in the local tavern, strapped fifty-pound packs of paper to their backs, and then headed for France via torturous mountain trails. But a major bust targeting one of Faivre's competitors had, temporarily, changed the balance of power between cat and mouse. The French authorities had ordered more patrols and the men were getting twitchy. These Neuchâtel nights were a well-paid thrill, but it was they – not Mauvelain, Faivre or d'Holbach – who faced lives on the high seas as galley slaves if caught. Why only temporarily? Because wily *frontaliers* like Faivre always, one way or another, left the policy cats in Paris and Versailles pawing at shadows.

Robert Darnton's finely crafted history of the Les Verrières crates has helped to shape a generation's understanding of the practices of the pre-Revolutionary extraterritorial publishing industry.[2] Mauvelain got his books, Faivre his cut and France's body politic was administered a few more drips of literary poison through its hopelessly porous, unpolicable borders.[3] Soon enough, so the story goes, a revolution was precipitated.[4] Darnton, of course, is too great an historian to have erred in his depiction of the passage of Mauvelain's crates through Les Verrières. Every detail really did happen. And yet, it will be suggested in this chapter, a full telling of the story of the STN during the 1780s shows the smuggling of books through Jura passes in the autumn of 1784 not to represent a moment of triumph for the underdog Neuchâtelois, but the precise opposite: proof of the surprising power of *ancien régime* France's authorities' ability, when sufficiently motivated, to shut down debate coming from beyond its borders. The

STN, it will be contended, was driven to its strange Les Verrières dance by desperation born of economic failure. A toxic combination of limited and instable network growth, fragmented stock holdings, changes to the regulatory environment and persistant naivity led the Society to adopt a series of risk-laden strategic approaches from the early 1780s. Ostervald and his associates began working still more closely with their Swiss allies and competitors and, for the first time, sent large quantities of sometimes politically sensitive books directly to Versailles and Paris. Alarmed by the twin affront to the ideological foundations of the regime and the commercial interests of their native book industry, the French authorities responded by effectively closing the border. Mauvelain's crates, already in transit when the orders were affected, were sneaked through at considerable cost and risk. But there was no long-term future in such dealings, and the devastation wrecked upon the Swiss printing industry was total. The STN tried everything to avoid collapse. It took on commission printing for Paris, dispatched travelling salesmen across Europe, and attempted to reorient sales towards isolated francophone communities to the north and east. But the Neuchâtelois were trapped in a death-spiral from which they, like many of their Lausannois and Genevois counterparts, would never recover.

The road to Les Verrières was paved with forms of pride and greed that bibliography and bibliometrics alone fail to expose. Much of the STNs' early 1780s output, a quick look at the dissemination statistics suggests, built sensibly upon a decade's experience trading cheap octavo and duodecimo French-language editions that appealed to the provincial French market. Popular, uncontroversial travelogues like Nicolaus Ernst Kleemann's *Voyage de Vienne à Belgrade et à Kilianova* (1780), didactic works including Jeanne-Marie Leprince de Beaumont's *Magasin nouveau des jeunes demoiselles* (1780) and novels, such as Fanny Burney's passionate *Cecelia* (1782), continued to occupy the Society's presses. Their Romandy allies, too, continued to supply the STN with a potpourri of titles for international distribution. Isaac Bardin's edition of Henri Rieu's translation of John Moore's four-volume *Lettres d'un voyageur anglois sur la France, la Suisse et l'Allemagne* (Geneva, 1781) was particularly popular – the Society managed to place 285 copies as far afield as St. Petersburg and Turin. These titles were dispatched in gently increasing numbers to a modestly expanding network of clients. During the final three years of the 1770s, the STN dispatched 53,021 works of general stock to 109 different towns. In the first three years of the 1780s, they sent 60,238 such books to 122 towns.[5] Business ticked along satisfactorily.

Alas, neither the ambitions of the Society's directors nor the money-lust of its creditors could find satisfaction solely from the selling of such humdrum enlightenment. From the outset, Ostervald and his associates had embarked upon a series of grand publishing projects – most notably the *Descriptions des arts et métiers*, the quarto *Encyclopédie*, and the folio 'Ostervald' Bible – that elevated the status of their business and profoundly shaped its destiny. Far from vanity publications, the impact of these luxury editions upon the Society's finances can hardly be overstated. As workers totted-up stocks at the end of 1782, they found that 1.9 million printed sheets belonging to three long completed, half-depleted sets – the *Descriptions des arts et métiers*, folio Bible, and the complete works of the dramatist Alexis Piron – occupied almost exactly as much space as everything else combined. The 250,433 plates harbouring within the *Descriptions des arts et métiers*, further, made the former pile considerably more valuable.[6] Unsurprisingly, then, the STN directors tried to move heaven and earth to make these grand projects succeed. As well as fussing over the quality of their editorial and production, they negotiated with competitors, inked shady deals, charmed officials and advertised widely – as has been so skilfully documented elsewhere.[7]

The potential rewards offered by the STN's commitment towards upscale publishing help to explain why so much capital investment flowed into the business from the mid-1770s – the *Encyclopédie* project was at one point projected to net 430,218 *livres* for its cohort of investors.[8] And, with its modest local cash sales and tardily paying international customers, the Society constantly needed to borrow money to finance its immoderate ambitions. Convinced that the business was sound and that the answer to their cash-flow inconveniences lay in patience and greater scale, Ostervald and his associates offered attractive returns – sometimes as much as 7 per cent per annum – to local individuals and institutions willing to deposit capital. A kind of investment fever gripped Neuchâtel's tight-knit bourgeois elites. Twenty-nine distinct depositors, including the Quatre-Ministaux, the Rue des Halles Company and the Maison de Charité, sank 97,952 *livres* into the STN during the course of 1782 alone.[9] Those who got out during the late 1770s and early 1780s made tidy sums, and the Society's books always balanced on paper.[10] By December 1782, indeed, as the bubble swelled towards its maximum, the STN valued their stock holdings at 131,183.7.6 *livres*, their unprinted paper holdings at 14,236.7.0 *livres*, their fixtures and fittings at 18,325.9.3 *livres* and they held 13,696.6.0 *livres*-worth of banker's drafts to be cashed upon maturity. Their total asset value of 342,027.8.6 *livres* was completed by 164,585.18.9 *livres* owed by various creditors, largely international booksellers who had received goods during the previous five years but were yet to pay. By contrast, the Society's obligations amounted to 338,971.0.1 *livres* – 93,729.18.6 *livres*-worth of banker's drafts were held by suppliers, and the remaining 245,241.1.7 *livres* were owed to a host of creditors including those private and institutional investors.[11] The books, in short, still balanced, but the difficulty that the Society would have turning promises and paper piles into ready cash denoted – to the modern observer, at least – startlingly high leverage and a dangerous 'acid test' liquidity position.

The example of the dissemination of Kleemann's *Voyage de Vienne à Belgrade* – a typically inoffensive work that the STN produced as part of their collaboration with the STB and STL – might serve to demonstrate why regular trading was never going to extract the Neuchâtelois from this predicament.[12] The Society printed Kleemann's travelogue in the spring of 1780, and began distributing their 611 copies on 5 April 1780. Sales went well, but Ostervald and his associates had to wait for a third summer to arrive before the edition passed its theoretical break-even point, and by 31 December 1782, 244 copies still remained in stock. By this stage, when some liquid return on investment was at least a paper possibility, wholesale demand had been largely exhausted and copies trickled frustratingly slowly out of the storeroom. The pile numbered 154 examples in the summer of 1785, 135 two years later, and it was not until 31 May 1792 that Durand l'aîné took the final 68 copies off the Society's hands. During these later years, the STN failed to sell a single copy from the Neuchâtel counter. Demand, erratic and scattered across a continent, could not be harried. Understanding that even good payers took a year or more to stump up the cash, and that the STN counted precious few good payers among their clientele, a work like Kleemann's could take the better part of a decade to yield real returns. Oftentimes, they hardly seemed worth the effort. At 246 pages, or 1 printed sheets, Kleemann's *Voyage* sold for just a solitary *livre* the copy. After translation, printing, production and distribution costs were accounted for, there was barely 200 *livres* to be made on the whole affair. During the early 1780s, the paper profits that the STN made selling over 10,000 volumes like Kleemann's each year hardly covered the charges that they incurred servicing short-term debt.

The sobering 1776–83 letter books of Henri-Albert Gosse & Company of the *rue de la cité* in Geneva suggest that the STN's overreach could not have come at a worse moment. Before his death in 1755, Henri-Albert's moneyed father, Pierre Gosse, had established a small publishing empire with shops in London, The Hague and Geneva.[13] The Genevan branch enjoyed its best years under Henri-Albert's stewardship during the 1740s, 1750s and 1760s, selling Latin books to the Catholic Mediterranean and French books predominantly to the Swiss Romand, France and sometimes further afield.[14] Gosse's 1740-published catalogue of Latin works ran to 158 pages; and his French books catalogue of the same year numbered 141 pages. The collapse of the Swiss trade in Latin books during the 1770s, then, left the Genevan saddled with gargantuan holdings of unsalable books and perilously dependent upon the strength of the French market. On 24 May 1777, Gosse sent a letter to the Rouen book dealer Pierre Machuel pleading that he might take the Latin works. The Genevois suggested that Machuel should use his advantageous geographical position to ship the books directly to Spain and Portugal, in the process undermining the 'Brabant and German' traders who now monopolized the trade.[15] Machuel wisely declined the proposition. Upon Albert-Henri's death in 1780, his younger brother Jean took over the business and continued in vain to search for a resolution. In October 1782, with sales depressed and levels of business correspondence at just a quarter of their 1760s peak, Jean attempted to release liquidity by offering the business's stocks at an effective 40 per cent discount.[16] Alas, even at these prices, trading conditions were so difficult in French-speaking Switzerland that buyers were few and far between. A twenty-year squeeze finally killed off the Gosse family's Genevan bookselling business in 1789.

Ostervald and his associates were to blame for the STN financial straits: they wilfully let their ambitions slip out of sync with the realities of trading books from a little Swiss backwater. After a decade of successful dealing, their society boasted only a small number of bankable client relationships and had failed to break into the lucrative Parisian market. It had sold many *nouveautés*, but, in the process, had accumulated a ruinously fragmented pile of ageing books. Common sense demanded a focus on networks and liquidity. But instead, ruinously, the Neuchâtelois bet the future of the publishing house on inappropriate scale and a handful of highly ambitious and speculative ventures. Without excusing these strategic failings, however, we might also recognize that the STN's directors *were* unfortunate – just like the Gosse brothers – to have seen the growth potential of their regular business constrained by soft trading conditions. Four connected issues weighed upon the Swiss trade.[17] First, with the Latin market gone and Voltaire and Rousseau's High Enlightenment *belle époque* fading into memory, French-speaking Switzerland boasted too many publishers and booksellers.

Disruption was inevitable and some retrenchment through bankruptcies and mergers probably unavoidable. Second, French governmental efforts to control public discourse and promote home-grown industry, although only partially effective, contained the extraterritorial trade.[18] From the mid-point of the century a string of public writings – exemplified by Diderot's 1763 essay 'Lettre sur le commerce des livres' – suggested that balance of power between the Parisian, provincial and extraterritorial publishers might be usefully adjusted through state regulation. While the effectiveness of each of the hundreds of decrees that followed this debate cannot be satisfactorily gauged, the cumulative weight of legislation was significant.[19] Third, it has long been understood that late-*ancien régime* France was plagued by hypercycles of overproduction and falling prices, although it is unclear to what extent a number of specific economic difficulties became generalised before the pre-Revolutionary crisis.[20] The extent to which the book trade suffered is uncertain: if the book production statistics of Pierre Conlon, Robert Estivals and Joseph-Marie Quérard point towards long-term growth, they also describe enormous instability, especially during the 1780s.[21] But, even allowing an optimistic reading of the economic data, French economic growth was at best fragile and uneven and certainly insufficient to facilitate Ostervald's ambitions plans. And fourth, finally, shocks to the French banking system triggered first by the American War and then the precipitous fall of the *Caisse d'escompte* in November 1783 provoked a major European credit crunch. The beleaguered and credit-dependent book trade temporarily ground to a halt as businesses hoarded cash and delayed honouring debts.[22]

The instinctive reaction of the major Swiss publishing houses to the toughening outlook was to pool risk. From May 1779, the 'libraires associés' alliance between the STN, STB and STL, discussed above, began publishing the first of the nearly 50,000 copies of twenty-five works aimed at combating their French provincial rivals. Around the same time, the STN drew increasingly closer to their former partner Samuel Fauche's expanding bookselling and publishing business, increasing the number of works that they took from the Neuchâtelois from 659 in 1775 to 2,841 by 1784.[23] The new Neuchâtel printing ventures of Jonas Fauche, Jérémie Witel, Charles-Samuel Favre and Louis Fauche-Borel each also worked at times in collaboration with the STN. But while partnering and close cooperation reduced the risks associated with printing a *garde magesin* and potentially offered some efficiencies in the areas of information sharing, marketing and dissemination, the Swiss wholesale nexus was already so spectacularly well integrated that only marginal efficiencies could be found. Servicing the STN's debt mountain would require a more radical tactical turn.

The closest that the Society came to transformative action was offering its presses for hire to authors and patrons, and partnering with French-based booksellers and agents to improve distribution. Commission printing promised hassle-free profitability. Runs often in excess of 1,000 copies of books were sent straight to the customer at the STN's standard wholesale price of 1 *sol* per sheet to be paid within an agreed time frame.[24] Because clients were oftentimes based in Paris or Versailles, their commissions both offered the STN a viable entry into these lucrative markets and, however popular the editions proved, presented little risk of cannibalizing the regular offerings of the Swiss presses. The FTBEE database identifies 108,677 sales of fifty-eight commissioned works, 89 per cent of which (96,621 sales, fifty-one works) were published during the first half of the 1780s.[25] Almost the entirety of the dramatic increase in shipments that the STN enjoyed during these years, clearly visible in Figure 1.2, can be attributed to these books.[26] Indeed, the majority of this increased output issued from the pens of just three authors: 25,453 copies (26%) were written by Louis-Sébastien Mercier, 21,523 (22%) by Théodore Rilliet de Saussure and 12,683 (13%) by Jacques-Pierre Brissot de Warville. The trio's combined output represented between 15 per cent and 53 per cent of total STN unit shipments during every year between 1780 and 1785.[27]

Because most significant European towns boasted multiple presses, however, authors and their sponsors tended to resort to distance commission printing only when local publishers distrusted the commercial viability or legality or their works. On 31 August 1779, the young Brissot wrote the first of a series of letters addressed to Ostervald that outlined his plan to use a recent 4,000–5,000 *livre* inheritance to ease his entry into the world of letters.[28] The pair met in the Paris the following February, and soon afterwards Brissot embarked upon a campaign of eleven STN-printed reform-minded books that spanned legal reform, moral philosophy, literary criticism and contemporary politics.[29] During the years that Brissot's works were exiting their presses, the Neuchâtelois also took orders to print the subversive and explosive trial briefs of Honoré-Gabriel Riqueti comte de Mirabeau, who was defending himself in Pontarlier against accusations of 'seduction', and the Genevan economist Théodore Rilliet de Saussure.[30] Rilliet de Saussure, we will see in the following chapter, kept the Society's pressmen busy printing thousands of copies of a series of pamphlets that accused his wife of having previously and secretly borne an infant by her brother, the important Grisons nobleman baron Frédéric de Planta. Further, during these first years of the 1780s, the STN accepted a number of highly suspect individual commissions including the anonymous and libellous attack on the admiral who led France's navy during the American War *Extrait du journal d'un officier de la marine de l'escadre de M. le comte d'Estaing*.

The early Brissot commissions established the practicability of regularly sending 'joblot' editions of dubious texts printed in Neuchâtel straight to clients willing to handle their distribution. If the STN could find the right works and sufficiently connected partners, it followed, they might be able to adapt the model for some of their own publications. In February 1781, when the Swiss-born French finance minister Jacques Necker's *Compte rendu au roi* first exited the Parisian presses of the *imprimerie du Cabinet du Roi*, Ostervald sniffed an opportunity. Despite its official origins, Necker's work proved a sensational *libel*: by systematically exposing the royal finances it offered ordinary Frenchmen a tantalizing glimpse behind the curtain of state.[31] Within weeks the STN had sent 750 copies of their counterfeit edition of Necker's text to the bookseller Dominique Lepagnez on the *place St. Pierre* in Besançon for distribution throughout provincial France.[32] And during the spring and summer of 1781 the Society printed a further seven commentaries on the *Compte rendu*, the lion's share of which they shipped directly to the bookseller Charmet in Besançon and to their recently found agent-cum-fixer Quandet de Lachenal in Paris.[33] In July 1781 Jonas Fauche and Jérémie Witel (respectively, the son and son-in-law of Samuel Fauche) took the STN's strategy to its logical next step by purchasing the fresh manuscript of the augmented edition of Louis Sébastien Mercier's *Tableau de Paris* for 8,400 *livres*.[34] Mercier was a true literary star, and his work was a guaranteed smash worth the gargantuan price; but only if Europe's markets could be flooded with the Fauche and Witel edition before counterfeits appeared. Using the STN presses the pair thus published more than 9,000 copies of Mercier's four-volume work, a substantial number of which were sent from January 1782 onwards directly to Quandet de Lachenal, Claude Poinçot in Versailles, and the Parisian bookseller Robert-André Hardouin.[35] The commercial worth of the model proven, blitzkrieg editions of several other Mercier works as well as Mirabeau's still more daring *Les lettres de cachet*, *Errotika biblion* and *Le libertin de qualité* quickly exited the Neuchâtel presses.[36]

Where previously religious books and prose fiction dominated the output of the Neuchâtel presses, now works of politics and current affairs ruled.[37] And these new products were not standard-sized editions trickled through Jura passes to ambulant provincial *colporteurs*, but significant runs sent in bulky crates straight to France's political and cultural core. As we have seen, between 1 October 1771 and 26 January 1780, the STN shipped just 168 books to Versailles and 1,224 to Paris. Between 27 January 1780 and 7 June 1784, by contrast, the STN sent 17,595 works to the French court and 32,166 to the City of Light. Indeed, a staggering 68 per cent of the Society's sales to France (49,761/72,839) were suddenly being handled by the likes of Poinçot and Quandet de Lachenal in the twin cities. That the booksellers of Paris and Versailles could rely upon both in situ buyers and dense pan-European networks of clients encouraged the Neuchâtelois and their partners to commit to unfamiliarly sizeable print runs. The STN ran off 1,000 copies of most of Brissot's untested and specialized works; 2,000 of the *Extrait du journal d'un officier de la marine de l'escadre de M. le comte d'Estaing* and Mercier's three plays *Zoé*, *L'habitant de la Guadeloupe* and *Les tombeaux de Vérone*; and 4,100 of Jacques Le Scène-Desmaisons's commissioned work on conjugal law *Contrat conjugal*.[38] Fauche and Witel, flush with the success of their mammoth four-volume edition of the *Tableau de Paris*, printed 9,000 examples of the first volume of Mirabeau's *Les lettres de cachet*.[39]

Commission and displaced distribution printing, then, meaningfully changed Neuchâtel's publishing industry, providing new and sorely needed revenue streams from France's most lucrative markets. What is more, it was a thrill to have the likes of Mercier and Mirabeau in town and to finally *matter* to Europe's major publishing houses. But the price proved high. First, dealing directly with authors and their manuscripts was invariably infuriating. Some, including Brissot, overestimated the commercial potential of their projects and racked up large debts chasing success.[40] Others, such as Mercier, had an acute knowledge of the value of their manuscripts and played their hands skilfully. Distant booksellers and middlemen cared for little but their cut, and only in rare cases like the *Compte rendu* affair could publishing's trough nourish so many swine. Second, when 'job-lot' printing diverted capacity, energy and capital investment away from regular work, the quality of the general product of the Romandy publishers suffered. The STN did continue to publish regular editions, such as Henri Rieu's September 1783 translation of Fanny Burney's *Cecelia*, but Ostervald's focus was elsewhere and the importance of feeding the Swiss nexus slipped in his estimations. Worse, as we have seen, wet-behind-the-ears Fauche and Witel angered the region's established houses with their audacity and indiscretion.[41] And third, most significantly of course, it was only really a matter of time until shipping large quantities of works like Joseph de Servan de Gerbey's military-reform calling *Le soldat citoyen*, *ou Vues patriotiques sur la manière la plus avantageuse de pourvoir à la défense du royaume* – the title page of which crowed that it had been printed 'Dans le pays de la liberté' – to France's political heartlands triggered reprisals.

By blessing and, ultimately, curse the French foreign minister the Comte de Vergennes's early 1780s problems with the extraterritorial publishers extended far beyond Neuchâtel. From 1781, a small community of bookish crooks largely based in London threatened the publication of a series of *libels* that targeted the French state and some of its key actors and institutions.[42] At the head of the clique – responsible for '*Les Rois de France dégénérés par les princesses de la Maison d'Autriche*' and other such potential bombs – was Anne-Gédeon de La Fite de Pelleport, who had previously been living in Neuchâtel as a schoolmaster and occasional contributor to the *Nouveau Journal helvétique*, and had introduced Brissot to the STN back in 1779.[43] The French state initially paid suppression fees to keep these London rogues shtum, but as the American War drew to a close on 13 March 1783, the agent Receveur was sent on mission to observe and, hopefully, expose the group. Receveur's mission triggered a flurry of threatened and real pamphleteering, the publication of Pelleport's Paris-police-baiting *Le diable dans un bénitier* and, ultimately, the capture and imprisonment in the Bastille of Pelleport and Brissot on 11 and 12 July 1784 for their alleged literary offences.[44] Further, if London was the organizational brain of the early 1780s libel industry, the presses of the 'Dutch' zone remained its productive heart. Between October 1781 and September 1782, the Paris police went on mission to Amsterdam and Brussels to discover and detain the authors of a number of *libels* including *Les aventures de Mme de Polignac* and *Le Ministère de Vergennes*.[45] Throughout the winter of 1783–84, Vergennes and his diplomatic team discussed how best to pressurize the region's publishers and authorities following the publication of Pelleport's *La gazette noire* and Linguet's *Mémoires sur la Bastille*.[46]

Perhaps preoccupied and certainly confident in its ability to deal with errant publishers using tried and tested means, the French government's initial response to the Neuchâtel commission and displaced distribution editions was threefold.[47] First, they immediately exposed the supply-chain weaknesses of Ostervald's plan. Generally, the STN sent their 'job lot' editions in single shipments comprised of multiple crates straight to Lyon (or sometimes Dijon or Besançon), where a trade insider would remove the accompanying *acquit de caution* and have them repacked. From these eastern staging posts, the merchandise would be forwarded to a shipping agent like Mme La Noue, who operated a number of secret storerooms in Versailles. If deemed necessary the shipping agent would then have the boxes broken up into smaller packets that would be sneaked into the City of Light.[48] None of this was the least bit surprising to the Paris police, and a tip-off from one of their scores of spies could see the entire shipment intercepted at Lyon, Versailles, or upon arrival in Paris. Sometimes it proved even easier. In March 1781, when his 500 copies of *Théorie des lois criminelles* arrived at La Noue's stockrooms, Brissot forwarded them straight to Jean-Charles-Pierre Lenoir, the lieutenant general of the Paris Police between 1774 and 1785, in order to circumvent inspection by customs and booksellers guild inspection. Lenoir confiscated the works and had them sent back to Neuchâtel a year later.[49] Late in the summer of 1781, Lenoir's officers also seized and had pulped 470 copies of the STN's *Mémoire donné au roi par M. Necker en 1778*, 800 of the *Lettre du marquis de Caraccioli à M. d'Alembert*, and

1,000 of *Le philosophe du Port-au-bled*.⁵⁰ The raids were executed in Dijon and at the premises of the Society's Parisian agent Quandet de Lachenal.⁵¹ In March 1782 Fauche, Favre and Witel suffered the confiscation of at least a part of the set of 8,500 copies of Mercier's *La destruction de la ligue* that the STN had printed on their behalf.⁵² And then between April and August 1782, the STN published thousands of libellous pamphlets by Théodore Rilliet de Saussure, the entire Versailles *envoi* of which was seized from Quandet's warehouse shortly after its arrival.⁵³

Second, Lenoir, Vergennes and the director of the book trade Le Camus de Néville laid bare just how dependent Neuchâtel's publishing industry was upon French goodwill by overseeing the ruin of the *Descriptions des arts et métiers* and *Nouveau Journal helvétique*.⁵⁴ Back in 1779 the Parisian bookseller Nicolas-Léger Moutard of the fashionable *rue des Mathurins* had purchased the publishing rights to the still-incomplete original folio edition of the *Descriptions des arts et métiers* from Delatour and the *Académie des sciences*, as well as all unsold stocks and plates. In order to extract the most value from his acquisition, Moutard immediately increased lobbying efforts to see the Neuchâtel 'counterfeit' edition of the work outlawed.⁵⁵ The STN fought their corner by arguing, perfectly reasonably in many respects, that the expanded articles, extensive references and notes that Bertrand had added to their version ensured that it was no cheap copy.⁵⁶ And the Neuchâtel edition's quarto format, which Ostervald contrasted with the 'luxe inutile' of the Parisian folio edition, had been chosen to ensure that it would reach a different type of buyer. Nonetheless, on 24 July 1780, an order was sent to all of France's *chambres syndicales* insisting that the STN *Descriptions des arts et métiers* be confiscated upon discovery.⁵⁷ Néville's explanatory letter at least had the merit of being clear: the Neuchâtel publishing house's jewel in the crown was being suppressed as part of a wider crackdown on foreign counterfeits.⁵⁸ Early the following year, with subscribers losing their patience, the STN injudiciously dispatched a ballot of 65 copies of a new volume of their *Descriptions des arts et métiers* edition that was seized at Dijon. Work effectively stopped upon the project at this point, and despite years of further pleading remaining stocks were ultimately ceded to Moutard at three *livres* per volume in the summer of 1785.⁵⁹ Some years previously Ostervald had lamented that their great *Descriptions des arts et métiers* had been persecuted more thoroughly than any irreligious text.⁶⁰ Such were the risks of playing with fire. As for the *Nouveau Journal helvétique*, despite the introduction of political news from a local correspondent, the STN's perennially struggling periodical boasted just thirty-four Parisian subscribers (from a lowly European total of 220) in 1781. Hoping to increase the journal's audience, Ostervald instructed both Quandet de Lachenal and David-Alphonse de Sandoz-Rollin, the secretary to the Prussian ambassador in Paris, to investigate avenues that might lead to its being afforded an official privilège to circulate legitimately in the kingdom.⁶¹ Their numerous requests, alas, were ignored. When in August 1782 Mercier wrote to Ostervald concerning the confiscation of the Fauche and Witel edition of his *La destruction de la ligue*, he updated the sextagenarian about the quest to get official sanction for the *Nouveau Journal helvétique*: he could forget about it.⁶²

And third, the French government called upon its Swiss-based diplomats to observe and pressurize Neuchâtel's printers. From January 1781, following the Genevan bookseller Nouffer's interrogation on the basis of questions provided by Lenoir and

Vergennes, the Swiss nexus was closely watched.[63] The following year attention was focused specifically upon Neuchâtel. In July 1782, after the STN sent 1,800 copies of the *Extrait du journal d'un officier de la marine de l'escadre de M. le comte d'Estaing* to Poinçot in Versailles, Vergennes had the STN investigated by Bâcher, the *chargé d'affaires* in Solothurn.[64] And then in October, when word that Neuchâtel's publishers were printing substantial editions of Mirabeau's *L'éspion dévalisé* and *Des lettres de cachet et des prisons d'état* reached Versailles and Paris, the authorities further turned the screw.[65] Under pressure from both Prussian and French officials, Neuchâtel's *Conseil d'état* was obliged to find Jonas Fauche and Jérémie Witel guilty of breaking their printer's oath. The town was hardly going to further enrage its watch-buying and printed cotton-buying neighbours for the sake of a few piles of paper.[66] So the pair spent three nights in Neuchâtel's landmark prison tower and saw all remaining copies of *Des lettres de cachet* confiscated.[67] Panicked, Ostervald made a grab for the moral high ground by getting Sandoz-Rollin to explain the STN's independence from the Fauche family's operations and to protest the damage that unwarranted suspicion by association was causing to its reputation.[68] This was perhaps a little rich, especially considering that just days before the affair had blown up the Society had dispatched 108 copies of *l'éspion dévalisé* to Poinçot in Versailles.[69]

That Lenoir, Néville and Vergennes employed this standard-issue box of tricks to rein-in the naïve early 1780s excesses of the Neuchâtel publishers was entirely predictable.[70] But what followed shocked the entire European book trade. On 12 June 1783, the French state introduced new regulations that effectively outlawed the extraterritorial book trade by demanding that all foreign shipments be inspected in Paris before being forwarded to their final destinations.[71] Perhaps the trigger was the threats that issued from London's little clique of blackmailers during Receveur's mission. Perhaps official thinking was influenced by the frequency of events like the 8 June book-seizure that left the Lyonnais *commissionaire* Revol burning evidence and thankful for friends in high places.[72] Or perhaps the regulations are best read as a commercial sack on a foreign industry that the state no longer considered worth tolerating, which would benefit both the noisy Parisian bookseller's guild and its provincial rivals. In any case the STN knew immediately that the new rules could prove devastating. Legitimate shipments to nearby Besançon would pick up the unsustainable costs of a 550 kilometres round trip to France's capital. And they would take an age to be delivered.[73] Everyone in the know seemed in agreement: the 12 June 1783 regulations amounted to the granting of a monopoly to the Parisian booksellers that seriously risked destroying the entire European francophone book trade.[74]

Mercier, knowing that rules and realities can be very different things, advised the STN to sit tight and wait for the storm to pass.[75] Certainly the enforcement picture that emerged during the following year was patchy. While the Society's trade with many French towns fell dormant, by hook or by crook some routes remained viable, including those to Pontarlier and Marseille.[76] Where officials were no longer prepared to take bribes to turn a blind eye to foreign book imports, they could on occasion be bypassed. On 16 August 1783, indeed, the STN made that deal with the Pontarlier-based smuggler Faivre to see their books introduced to the kingdom through the Les Verrières-Frambourg crossing at the western extremity of the Val-de-Travers.[77] Alas, even before this agreement had been reached Fauche, Favre and Witel's travelling salesman Mallet – a thin black-haired man with poor diction, according to Ostervald – had been picked up in Paris for questioning. Mallet sold out his masters and explained to the French authorities how the Neuchâtel publishing houses did business.[78] Now better informed than ever, in August 1784, the French police arrested five porters carrying complete crates of Fauche and Witel's freshly printed edition of Mirabeau's *Le libertin de qualité* into the kingdom.[79] The crossing was immediately placed under the strictest surveillance and thanks once more to the infernal Fauches, as Ostervald explained to the booksellers Rigaud, Pons & Company in Montpellier in October 1784, the STN could hardly get anything through to its remaining French clients.[80]

We are now at that singular moment when the Pontarlier smuggler Faivre had seven STN crates hidden atop a mountain near Les Verrières as the autumn leaves burnt brilliant reds and oranges. The boxes, of course, were destined for the small-time illegal book peddler and literary adventurer Bruzard de Mauvelain, whom the STN had decided to continue supplying, despite the 12 June 1783 regulations, for three reasons. First, Mauvelain's extensive publishing plans appealed to the Society's new strategic approach and promised riches down the line. Second, Mauvelain seemed sufficiently knowledgeable and well connected to be worth cultivating. And third, vitally, Troyes appeared just about close enough to Neuchâtel – 259 kilometres as the crow flies – to be profitably reached through the Jura smuggling routes provided that orders contained high-value, high-margin illegal works. Indeed, the previous February the Society had successfully supplied Mauvelain's third book order, a modest assortment of seventy-five legal and illegal volumes. Mauvelain's Les Verrières crates, then, had been processed and dispatched by the STN on 26 July 1784 and were in busy Faivre's charge at the Swiss–French border when the *Le libertin de qualité* affair broke. Had the boxes still been in Neuchâtel, or had they contained regular stocks that could have been sold elsewhere, they would most likely never have been sent. Alas, this was not the case. Not only had the Les Verrières crates already been dispatched, but they consisted in large part of two commissioned editions – 200 copies of a biography of the seventeenth-century bishop of Châlons Pontus de Thyard, printed for its author the marquis de Thyard, and 400 copies of the prospectus for Mauvelain's own (and seemingly never realized) '*Histoire ancienne et moderne de Châlons-sur-Marne*'.[81] The STN's directors understood that the printing costs of these editions could only be recovered upon their successful delivery to Troyes. They thus instructed Mauvelain to hold tight until the storm calmed a little and, once the determination of the authorities became clear, decided to resort to expensive mountain trails never habitually used by smugglers of books.[82] Faivre's hardened porters initially protested and refused to carry the bulky crates of paper across difficult trails. But ultimately, once their wages were upped and some of their worst fears assuaged, the men did see that Mauvelain's books reached Troyes by the end of the year. Still, this was no way to do business. The 'insurance' costs that the books had picked up at the border, Mauvelain complained, made it impossible to price them competitively, and the insufferable delay had led to the loss of many clients.[83] After Les Verrières the STN never sent another book to Bruzard de Mauvelain.

The Mauvelain case reads, then, less as an object lesson in plucky resistance than as a stark reminder of the out-and-out hopelessness of the STN's situation. Much ink has been spilt foregrounding the gaping hole in France's system of *villes d'entrée* between Lyon and Lille and emphasizing the *possibility* of smuggling books through moonlit Jura passes.[84] Yet the reality of post-12 June 1783 life in the Swiss book nexus points towards a still more intriguing truth: the French authorities possessed the capacity to ruin the extraterritorial publishing industry.[85] For years after the regulatory changes the STN failed to send a single book to the vast majority of France's regions, including sizeable and important territories like Provence, Grenoble, Orléans and Burgundy. In November 1784, the Society informed Roland de la Platière in Villefranche-sur-Saône that its suspension of shipments to the kingdom was but a temporary measure put in place until the 'storm' passes.[86] But the following May, with no improvement to the situation in sight, the STN flatly refused a request to do business with the bookseller Delinani in nearby Chalon-sur-Saône – a town a mere 160 kilometres from Neuchâtel – for want of any reasonable way of sending books.[87] In August the Neuchâtelois informed the bookseller J. J. Garrigan in Avignon that there was quite simply no way of getting merchandise to him without it first passing by Paris.[88] Letter after letter betrays the same picture – the routes were closed and it was impossible to conduct trade in France.[89] There were only two exceptions. First, the smuggling route via Faivre in Pontarlier – although costly and hardly worth the bother – did allow for the odd commission to pass profitably to the nearby regions of Besançon, Nancy and Strasbourg.[90] And second, of course, the STN could send books via the Paris *chambre syndicale*, especially to Northern French towns that would be in any case served by a similar route. On the odd occasion where safe passage was assured in advance – notably the fifty copies of the Protestant Bible and 100 copies of Jean-Rodolphe Ostervald's *La nourriture de l'âme* sent to Jean Racine in Rouen via the bookseller Durand *neveu* of the *rue Galande* in Paris on 14 March 1786 – the Neuchâtelois did make use of this option. But the STN was under no illusions about the nature of the stitch-up: most of their stocks had no formal permission to circulate in the kingdom, and sending them directly to their Parisian rivals in the hope of even-handed and honest treatment was a laughable prospect.

The case of Ganges pastor Pommaret's *Le bon père* serves as another illustration of how even those few shipments that the STN did manage to spirit into France sometimes proved costly.[91] Back in 1778 and 1779 Pommaret (sometimes Pomaret) had used the STN presses to publish two self-penned books, *Le chrétien par conviction et par sentiment* and *Le catéchumène instruit sous une forme nouvelle*, for the instruction of his Protestant flock.[92] The works contained nothing that attacked Catholicism – indeed, the pastor rejected the idea of sending his potentially more controversial manuscript *Examen impartial de la réligion protestante* lest it might irk zealots – and were duly tolerated and shipped through Lyon's *chambre syndicale*. Pommaret proved an ideal client. He paid his bills promptly and even found buyers for a number of the STN's expensive folio Bibles. In May 1782 Pommaret saw first-hand the havoc being wrought throughout France's book trade as a local colporteur had 1,000 ecus' worth of stocks seized due to new orders from Versailles. But in the moment the sad plight of this lowly peddler hardly seemed related to his own special calling, and so the pastor pressed on with the publication of his new book, sending the manuscript to Ostervald on 9 April 1783. A total of 1,000 copies of *Le bon père*, then, were in press when the 12 June regulations dictating that all foreign books must pass through the Paris *chambre syndicale* before being shipped to their final destination were announced. Where a blind eye could have been turned in Lyon, inspection in Paris would see Pommaret's Protestant tract impounded for sure. Initially the pastor pondered chancing fifty copies through the City of Light, but then got cold feet. By December, with no obvious solution in sight, he wrote a letter explaining the loyalty of his flock to Louis XVI that he hoped the STN would forward to Le Camus de Néville, the director of the book trade.[93] And then in January Pommaret turned on his printers, insisting that the delay meant that the Neuchâtelois would have to take the books for their own account. If the STN could find a way of sneaking them through to Ganges, Pommaret promised that he would get updated '1785' title pages printed in Nîmes or Montpellier and sell them locally on the Society's behalf. The STN's directors grumbled and groused, but seeing as it was only on 1 June 1785 that their house managed to ship *Le bon père* – and then at the eye-watering 'assurance' cost of 105 *livres* – they ultimately had little choice but to acquiesce. Predictably enough, Pommaret never managed to sell many copies of *Le bon père*, and in 1787, amid complaints of disease and economic woes, he reported that he had temporarily stopped pushing the book for 'political' reasons. There the trail goes cold.[94]

From the moment that the de facto interdiction of the extraterritorial trade became clear, the STN's directors had initiated a frantic epistolary campaign to discover secret trade routes and, they hoped, save the business. In October 1784, the Society wrote to the bookseller Pavie in the Atlantic port of La Rochelle to enquire as to whether it might be viable to send books to him via the docks of Amsterdam or perhaps Rotterdam, thus avoiding French roads altogether. The Neuchâtelois estimated that shipments could be achieved for between 22 and 24 *livres* per hundred weight.[95] The following month, Blaizot in Versailles proposed a variation of the same idea – sending books via the Low Countries and then perhaps Le Havre – but his plan foundered on fears that France's northern ports were being watched with the same vigilance as the Swiss border.[96] In February 1785, the bookseller Bonthoux in Nancy informed the Society that he *had* managed to get some relatively small shipments through via Basle and Epinal.[97] And in July 1785, the La Rochelle bookseller Chauvet reported that he had found a way to unload *ballots* without them having to enter any office. The STN immediately tested the choppy Atlantic waters of Chauvet's new route by dispatching an assortment of eighty-four books, but it hardly proved economical and no regular shipments ensued.[98] More radical solutions to the Society's problems were also considered. In February 1785 the Neuchâtelois wrote to the Nantes-stationed Prussian diplomat Pelloutien to enquire as to whether he might be willing to help extend the Society's commercial horizons towards the Americas. Maybe he could include a well-chosen selection of Swiss books from the STN's catalogue with his frequent shipments of goods? Or perhaps the STN might follow the new peacetime trend set by some of its rivals and establish a new publishing house as a trans-Atlantic outpost. In that case Pelloutien might handle shipment, payment security and other such business services that would be impractical to arrange from Neuchâtel.[99] Nothing came of the plan.[100]

That the STN's rivals also longed for an American miracle speaks volumes: the new regulations of 12 June 1783, coupled with the strict enforcement realities of August 1784, devastated the already beleaguered Swiss book industry. Barthélemy Chirol wrote to the STN from Geneva on 21 February 1784 to outline just how dire the situation had become. When he had set up shop thirty-three years previously, Chirol fumed, booksellers were good men and corsairs (a term he had previously used to describe

Fauche and Witel, which would not have gone unnoticed) only existed at sea. Now, with the industry in such chaos he was receiving only *lettres de change* to be drawn fifteen, eighteen or even twenty-four months in the future. Without means to pay his bills he would be forced to shut up shop.[101] And so it proved. In December 1785, Chirol offered his stocks to his Genevan rival Jean François de Bassompière for 50,000 *livres*. The next month he accepted a bid of just 36,000 *livres* from the booksellers Barde, Manget and Company.[102] Perhaps Chirol took some comfort from the fact that his plight was far from unique. The once mighty Cramer, Gosse and de Tournes dynasties all exited the Genevan publishing scene during the early 1780s. Jean Abraham Nouffer's business went under in December 1783 with 70,192 *livres*-worth of unsold stocks.[103] Isaac Bardin moved his piles of printed sheets to a bedroom on the second floor of his family's shop in 1787, and eventually stopped trading in 1790.[104] And Bassompière sold his books to François Dufart in 1786. In Lausanne, between 1784 and 1787, Gabriel Décombaz fought a long and ultimately fruitless legal war to save his considerable stocks from being seized and liquidated due to his non-payment of debts.[105] The spectres of bankruptcy and consolidation loomed over every publishing house in the Romandy nexus.

The STN's own collapse was a protracted affair which began during the summer of 1784, before Mauvelain's crates had even been dispatched to Les Verrières. The commission and displaced distribution printing strategies pushed from the early 1780s had not only failed to ease the Society's financial troubles, but had made matters worse. Debts payable to the Society continued to mount – Brissot alone owed 12,301.9.0 *livres* in unpaid printing costs by October 1784.[106] And the risky practices of the Neuchâtel printers had directly influenced the policymaking behind the 12 June 1783 regulations, which wrecked France's extraterritorial publishing houses. Worse, panicked or opportunistic traders in France and beyond delayed payments until they better understood the situation, plunging the European book trade into a major credit crisis. The STN – highly leveraged and with no significant local market to fall back upon – never stood a chance, and collapsed under the weight of 75,000 *livres* of suddenly unserviceable debt. The 8 June 1784 'Acte de cautionnement pour la Société typographique de Neuchâtel' gave controlling power to 11 new partners who had stumped up 290,400 *livres* for the dubious privilege of liquidating the business and its considerable stocks. Although Ostervald remained involved with the running of the Society, the major strategic decisions were from this moment taken by Jean-Frédéric Bosset, J. H. de Chaillet d'Arnex and Jean J. de Luze.[107]

The Society's new administrators quickly found that winding down a publishing house was a devilish charge. They began by actively chasing outstanding French debts. Between 13 and 20 February 1785, the STN sent a series of polite invoices to clients in Nancy, Poligny, Lunéville, Paris, Orleans, Langres, Bourg-en-Bresse, Montpellier, Dijon, Melun and Toulouse.[108] And over the next months, the Society chased-up laggards with further reminders.[109] But because credit was the very lifeblood of the European book trade – debts outstanding for five years or more were entirely commonplace – few clients rushed to meet the STNs demands.[110] Indeed, it seems likely that many correctly interpreted this move as a sign of post-12 June 1783 weakness that augured still darker times to come for the STN. Why expediently settle a debt that might soon disappear? For the administrators, anyhow, this issue was of less consequence than the problem of the STN's mountainous piles of stocks, in which the majority of the real value of the business was locked. It would have taken the rest of the millennium to liquidate the Society's 1.8 million sheets through its insignificant Neuchâtel counter and, with the market depressed and all the Swiss booksellers holding more-or-less the same books, there was no hope of extracting a good price from rivals in Lausanne or Geneva. Gosse had learnt this lesson the hard way. No, value would have to be returned gradually through successful regional and international trade with the strategic aim of reducing holdings over time.

Little in either the prevailing trading conditions or the STN's previous fifteen years of experience in the international book trade suggested that success would come easily. And reveries of the Americas or new fluvial routes to France via the Rhine and the docks of La Rochelle proved time-consuming distractions. Nonetheless, in the wake of the 'Acte de cautionnement' the STN's new directors did take a number of prudent steps to rein-in previous excesses and reorient the business. First, although the structure of the STN's wholesaling model rendered the continued purchase of new stocks from the Romandy nexus unavoidable, they successfully contained its oversupply problem by publishing less.[111] From 1785 printing was limited to a trickle of short pamphlets like Mercier's *De Dieu* and the occasional reliable seller which could readily be swapped, including a new edition of their *Collection complète des oeuvres de Madame Riccoboni* in 1787.[112] Second, they courted new business opportunities in Paris. If the members of the Parisian guild had laid low their extraterritorial competitors without adding a single new press, then it followed they would soon struggle to cope with demand. With printing costs lower in Romandy due to the absence of any tax on paper (which ran at a rate of 20% in France), perhaps a Parisian partner could be found if the Society got its pitch right.[113] The most audacious of a number of such proposals was a 29 May 1785 missive to 'M. le Prince bibliothècaire du Roi', in which it was suggested that the STN had played no part in the recent Neuchâtelois typographical scandals and had never committed a single work of dubious morality or legality to print.[114] And third, the new directors focused upon maximizing shipments to distant clients, like the booksellers of Moscow and Vienna, whose businesses were unaffected by the new French regulations and who bought diverse stocks in bulk.

A six-legged spectre embodied this final strategic shift. In February 1786 the Vaudois travelling salesman Victor Durand *l'ainé* mounted his horse and headed off around Europe to conduct business on behalf of the STN. Durand, the courageous son of the Lausanne pastor and teacher, came to the Society by way of the collapse of Barthélemy Chirol's Genevan business, where he had been working until the previous December.[115] Chirol thought highly of the young man's abilities, and thus the STN had little hesitation sending him directly to Paris to gather information related to its various financial and political affairs. In April Durand left the City of Light and travelled through Frankfurt, Cassel and Leipzig before heading north to the Free Imperial City of Hamburg. Between June and October, the STN corresponded with its Vaudois traveller via a relay in Hamburg, although his actual route took him further north to Stockholm and Copenhagen. Durand was given considerable latitude by his Neuchâtelois masters to act in the best interests of the Society and his return home, negotiated from Berlin in January 1787, betrayed the importance that the traveller placed upon tapping neglected markets. From Frederick II's capital Durand headed east on a meandering diversion through Saxony, Bohemia, Austria and Bavaria taking in the towns and cities of Magdeburg, Dresden, Litoměřice, Prague, Vienna, Linz, Regensburg, Augsburg, Konstanz and Basle.[116]

When an exhausted Durand arrived back in Neuchâtel in the spring of 1787 he found the typographical community abuzz with the latest news from France: the *veuve* Barret had found a way of having crates shipped to her bookselling business in Lyon. The STN had first got wind of this possibility the previous December, and had immediately written to its Lyonnais connections Amable Le Roy, J. S. Grabit and Barret herself to enquire as to the possibility of a resumption of trading.[117] On 28 March 1787, the Society sent 516 books, including 200 copies of Johann-Christoph Gottsched's *Maître de la langue allemande* and 100 examples of Madame de Genlis' *Adèle et Théodore* to Le Roy via the *frères* Garnier in Geneva and the *veuve* Barret. The route proved secure and brought about a flurry of activity. In total the STN sent 4,578 books to Lyon during 1787, and received 4,307. During the previous sixteen years, by contrast, the Society had only dispatched 7,831 copies to the silk producing city, and received just 6,081. Further, using the *veuve* Barret route as a staging post allowed the STN to trade at thereto unprecedented levels with the booksellers of Avignon (2,324 books sent during 1787) and Nîmes (968).[118] This was, to be sure, an exclusively Rhône valley network that did not represent a normalization of trading relations with France, but it was a source of hope celebrated by Romandy's entire typographical community.

Victor Durand spent the spring of 1787 quaffing red wine and absinthe, which was rapidly spreading from the Val-de-Travers to become a popular regional delicacy, at the Neuchâtel inn 'le Faucon'. During the summer he looked after the STN's business interests from Berne, Lausanne and Geneva. And as the days began to shorten he saddled-up his horse and headed once again for the border. In September 1787, encouraged by the *veuve* Barret route, Durand visited Lyon, Avignon, Nîmes, Montpellier and finally Marseille. Whether the Vaudois might have discovered other new routes and opportunities had he travelled more extensively in France, and thus whether the situation in the Rhône valley was indicative of a general softening of enforcement of the 12 June 1783 regulations across the kingdom is, alas, impossible to know.[119] Instead, from Marseille he took a boat to northern Italy and was in Turin by the middle of November. The distaste that Durand expressed towards the Italians in several letters home failed to prevent him from organizing a mammoth tour of the peninsula that lasted until the last days of April 1788 and took in the towns Milan, Bergamo, Bologna, Florence, Livorno, Siena, Rome, Naples and Venice. Perhaps he protested too much, and his Neuchâtelois masters eventually resorted to reproach to usher their traveller east. From Venice Durand moved to Vienna, traced many of the steps of his previous adventure through central Europe in reverse, and ultimately returned home only in November 1788.[120]

While the road through the rolling plains of Bohemia and the brooding forests of the Holy Roman Empire was frequently arduous, at a trot and then a canter Durand successfully reoriented the STN's business away from France. During the Vaudois's travels the STN sold 46,509 books, 10,474 (22.1%) of which were dispatched to France, 9,429 (19.9%) to Switzerland, 7,401 (15.6%) to the Italian Peninsula, 4,846 (10.2%) to the Austro-Hungarian zone, 4,425 (9.3%) to the Germanic territories, 4,252 (9%) to Eastern Europe and 4,126 (8.7%) to Scandinavia.[121] The regional distribution of STN *envois* had never been so agreeably balanced: before Durand's first tour 284,703 of

351,985 sales (80.8%) had been made to Switzerland and France. And Durand could count several highly prestigious orders of several thousand books at a time from likes of Charles-Marie Toscanelli in Naples and Jean-Baptiste Mangot in Vienna among his successes.[122] Yet travelling was always costly – the bill for Durand's three-month stay in Neuchâtel alone came to 158 *livres* – and the STN's new clients numbered relatively few and were regularly offered considerable discounts.[123] Further, the reality that buyers were few and far between in Geneva, Lausanne and much of France was, ultimately, disastrous.[124] Durand's successes were thus tainted by the fact that he failed to steer the Society towards profitability. Worse, stock holdings barely budged throughout the period. On 1 June 1786, two years after Ostervald had lost control of the business and just a few months into Durand's first tour, the STN held 1.8 million unbound sheets in their warehouse. Towards the end of Durand's tour this number had fallen by less than 80,000 and, because the Vaudois had largely found buyers only for low-cost books, the total book value of the pile had in fact increased.[125] Perhaps the fact that the 'cursed' Fauche family always appeared in his footsteps was more damaging than Durand was prepared to admit.[126] In any case, by the time that Durand arrived back in Neuchâtel, the STN was no longer a going concern.

The opaque tale of Louis Fauche-Borel and the protracted winding up of the Society will be told in the epilogue to this volume. But with the important part of our potted history now complete, one key reality is worth underscoring: the STN was always a highly unstable and constantly changing business. Its initial decade of heady growth flattered only to deceive. Although these early years saw the realization of a number of exciting projects, the Society's networks remained fragile and its stock became ever more fragmented. It never came close to achieving sustainable underlying profitability. Debts, stocks and leverage were all allowed to steadily accumulate because the directors laboured under the historically rooted belief that growth would bring scale and that scale was a dependable guarantor of long-term viability. But Neuchâtel was not Geneva and the entire Swiss book industry was past its prime. And so, in the case of the STN, great scale led to monumental difficulties. And experimentation. Because the Society began trading with neither historic stock holdings nor clients networks, and because Neuchâtel's own market was too small to guide decision making, it was remarkably free to try out different models of publishing and bookselling. Driven initially by aspiration and later by desperation, the Society's directors tried everything. They shifted the business's focus from provincial France to Paris and then to francophone Europe's peripheries; they chanced their hand at prestige publishing and commissioned editions; they dabbled in the real underground; and they expanded and then all but closed the printing shop. In the process, the very essence of the Society evolved, both gradually as the realization that plans were going awry slowly dawned and more precipitously when external events like the 12 June 1783 forced immediate strategic realignment. Travelling Victor Durand's STN of 1787 hardly resembled the publishing house that had courted Brissot and Mercier five years previously. That troubled and Paris-focused 1782 business was a world apart from the hubristic society that simultaneously ran twelve presses to print the *Encyclopédie* half a decade beforehand. And those exciting 1777 days differed extravagantly from the early months of 1772, when the Neuchâtelois still stocked barely a dozen different books. There were many STNs, none of which ever quite cracked the art of selling enlightenment.

Procès Romanesque, offrant un sujet de comédie très riche et très heureux

Théodore Rilliet de Saussure had it coming. On 21 April 1783, when his lifeless cadaver was discovered washed up near his Cologny mansion on the shores of Lake Geneva, none of his friends or relatives mustered the least inclination to question the suspicious circumstances. Théodore had been stirring up trouble for years, had been stripped of his citizenship and served time, and his passing came as something of a relief to all concerned. But it did leave the STN in a bit of a fix. Just what exactly were they to do with the 28,000 copies of the disgraced Genevan's latest pamphlet that hung drying from their workshop's rafters? How might they dispose of Rilliet's remarkable accusations that his estranged wife, Ursule, had confessed upon their wedding night to having previously borne an incestuous love child fathered by her brother, the baron de Planta? It was, after all, dead Théodore's last earthly wish to see his poisonous brochure sold freely on the Pont-Neuf in the centre of Paris and sent to every bishop, knight and sergeant in France.

Such is our tendency to associate the STN with French literature's dark side that the idea that Ostervald and his associates once found themselves in such a spot is hardly surprising. As far back as 1846, when the Society's archives were still thought pulped, Charles-Godefroi de Tribolet used Neuchâtel's council-minute registers to reveal their involvement in the publication and dissemination of d'Holbach's *Système de la nature*.[127] Only a little later, as the same records yielded the details of the Mirabeau affair, James-Henri Bonhôte, Charles Berthoud, Alexandre Daguet and Louis Junod each moralistically criticized the STN, as well as Fauche and Witel, for their misadventures in publishing.[128] Thus, when Bovet made his remarkable discovery of the STN papers during the 1930s, certain preconceptions already existed among the town's literary intelligentsia. Charley Guyot, who was accorded special access to the archives during the 1930s, predictably dived into the dossiers of Louis-Sébastien Mercier, Brissot de Warville and Quandet de Lachenal, and examined the *Système de la nature* affair and the distribution of the *Encyclopédie*.[129] Only Jean Jeanprêtre, who archived the papers of the STN as well as those of Louis Bourguet and Isabelle de Charrière, might be said at this point to have had a real understanding that there was much more to the STN than dodgy books.

When Robert Darnton first arrived in Neuchâtel to research a planned biography of Jaques-Pierre Brissot, then, he found an underexploited and impeccably archived treasure trove known to be brimming with stories from the underground. This was 1965, the year that volume one of the François Furet directed *Livre et société dans la France du XVIIIe siècle* helped to fully co-opt book history approaches – newly invigorated by Lucien Febvre and Henri-Jean Martin's *L'apparition du livre* (Paris, 1958) – into the mainstream Annales tradition. The question of what Frenchmen were reading before 1789 – famously posed by Daniel Mornet in 1910 – was coming back into focus.[130] In a series of influential writings, most notably the 1968 and 1971 articles 'The Grub Street Style of Revolution: J.-P. Brissot, Police Spy' and 'The High Enlightenment and the Low-Life of Literature in Pre-Revolutionary France', the young American used the Neuchâtel papers to flesh out his extraordinary 'Grub Street' thesis. For Darnton, France's literary world during the 1770s and 1780s was marked by a number of radical writers like Jacques-Pierre Brissot and Charles Théveneau de Morande who lashed out against the twin evils of the Old Regime and the entrenched mediocrity of the post-Voltairean High Enlightenment.[131] While the gutters of Paris were this group's spiritual home, they generally employed publishers based in the relatively liberal regimes of a 'Protestant arc' of towns stretching from London to Avignon via Neuchâtel to print their works. These were the same houses, indeed, that had been responsible for publishing much of the Enlightenment. Despite some spirited patrols and the odd *auto-da-fé*, France's authorities could do little to stop wily smugglers shipping books through the kingdom's porous eastern border. And so the underground, with its impossibly colourful cast of hawkers and smugglers, flourished. The 1995-published statistical blunderbuss *The Corpus of Clandestine Literature in France, 1769-1789*, which accompanied the award-winning and highly influential *The Forbidden Best-Sellers of pre-Revolutionary France*, brought empirical vigour to Darnton's picture.[132] By listing 720 forbidden works, from *Candide* to *Venus dans le cloître*, which circulated during the 1770s and 1780s, it underlined the scale of France's illegal publishing problem on the eve of the French Revolution.

It is because of the remarkable influence of Darnton's reading of the STN papers that Rilliet's story hardly surprises.[133] The tale is nonetheless worth telling for its own sake; for the fact that the Genevan's attention-grabbing publishing plan was unprecedented and ingenious; since it underscores the precariousness of the STNs early 1780s business model; and because it points towards the dangers of employing FBTEE database evidence without a holistic understanding of its context. Especially, the Rilliet case deserves our attention because it serves to orient our thinking towards several problems with the standard interpretation of the clandestine publishing industry during the late Enlightenment. The previous chapter showed the beginning of the 1780s to have been a decisive moment in the history of Swiss publishing. A combination of factors – notably generational change and economic malaise – led the Romandy houses to publish a series of works that provoked an unprecedented and devastating reaction from Louis XVI's France. The kingdom's borders were closed. Here, it will be argued that the moment demands a new understanding of how censorship functioned and how 'illegality' was constructed across pre-Revolutionary francophone Europe's various states. Where previous studies have largely concentrated upon the size of the underground, often producing intimidating lists of titles to prove the point, here the focus will shift to its multiple layers and the extent to which its shallows were widely tolerated. Through a data-driven analysis of how the STN and other houses adjusted the advertising, shipping and pricing of books on an order-by-order basis, it will suggest that the 'real' underground was much more limited in size than has previously been recognized. Further, it will argue that the limits of the true underground were not simply imposed from above, but instead emerged through the actions of all book-trade actors from lowly forwarding agents to printers and authors.

Life might have gone better for Théodore Rilliet de Saussure. Born on 28 February 1729 into a prominent and financially secure Genevois family with deep ancestral roots, Théodore was as talented and studious as any of his peers. In 1751 he became a lawyer and set about following in the footsteps of his forefathers by gaining election to the Grand Council of Geneva. Yet, for reasons unknown – his biographer and descendent Jean Rilliet alleged atheism and social nonconformity – he failed to secure the necessary support in successive bids in 1758 and 1764. Worse, he was constantly plagued by poor health and a nervous disposition. And he never found love. His first marriage, to Lucrèce-Angélique de Normandie, was celebrated in a lavish ceremony at the Temple of Cologny in April 1760. It quickly descended into acrimony, and drawn-out divorce proceedings were only concluded in 1771. His second marriage, to the beautiful and impeccably mannered but fortuneless Ursule de Planta, the sister of the baron Frédéric de Planta, an important Grisons nobleman who served in the French army, was marked with a more modest fête in Coppet in November 1773. The union was a spectacular disaster and barely a year later, as Théodore was finally elected to the Grand Council, Ursule departed for her family home in the Grisons.

As the winter of 1774–75 bit, then, Théodore fretted that having two recent divorces attributed to his awful personal disposition might prove the death of a social and political life that was only just beginning to get going. Better, perhaps, to play victim than villain. So, for the chattering classes of Geneva and in a private letter to the pastor Chauvet, he spun the lie that his marital troubles stemmed from the fact that Ursule had confessed, on their wedding night, to having previously and secretly borne a child.[134] Chauvet replied quickly, warning Théodore to back down; with this accusation he was throwing himself into an abyss from which he might never be extracted.[135] And so the Genevan stepped back from the precipice and resolved to see this affair of separation as a long game.[136]

As Théodore patiently lined up his soldiers he kept himself occupied, steadily amassing a second fortune. In the wake of the Seven Years War (1756–63), and during the American War of Independence (1776–83), unsustainable French government spending forced a succession of careworn finance ministers (including Théodore's personal friend and fellow Genevan Jacques Necker) to find new ways of raising money. Fixed-income life annuities – whereby a lump sum investment was exchanged for a series of smaller annual payments until the death of a nominated individual – became particularly popular with investors in moneyed and money-lending Geneva. To overcome the one real problem with life annuities – the risk of the annuitant dropping dead – the city of Calvin's bankers came up with ingenious arrangements like the 'trente demoiselles' scheme. Policies taken out on the heads of low-death-risk individuals (often prepubescent Swiss girls from good family stock who had survived early childhood) were pooled together and then divided into shares for investment purposes.[137] Bold, prescient and capital-rich investors like Théodore, who was said to be worth 600,000 *livres*, could make a killing with such heavily securitized issues. Indeed, the only real danger was that they might end up bankrupting the French government! In 1779, in response to a royal edict of 27 November 1778 which he judged counterproductive, Théodore published his highly regarded (if now largely forgotten) *Lettres sur l'emprunt et l'impôt*.[138] The Genevan argued that a major financial crisis appeared unavoidable unless France enacted a considerable programme of reform. The problem, in a nutshell, was that the ever-escalating costs of global warfare obliged Louis XVI's state to borrow heavily. Yet the twin ills of feudal landownership and noble tax avoidance through privilege meant that this borrowing was not sufficiently underwritten. It was only a matter of time before jittery international money lenders (including himself) either lost their nerve, leaving the kingdom with unsubscribed issues and spiralling borrowing costs, or, in the case of a French default, lost out. Great Britain – whose national debt was underwritten by a parliament of landowners prepared to shoulder the burden of taxation – provided the model for France to copy.

That Théodore's *Lettres sur l'emprunt* were so thought provoking was remarkable considering the circumstances of their creation. Since 1775, the Genevan had dragged Ursule and her brother, Planta, into a series of increasingly bitter and personal epistolary exchanges. In one remarkable missive dispatched from Lyon on 14 May 1777, devious Théodore threatened that he would publicly reveal the second great secret that Ursula had supposedly confessed on their wedding night: that her brother, Planta, had fathered the bastard child. Planta's response suggested that the scheming cut both ways. Rather than exploding with rage, the baron gushed with *bonhomie* and suggested that the pair set aside their differences and meet in Paris to discuss a business venture concerning the royal lottery. Was Planta trying to draw Théodore to the City of Light for his assassination? A duel? A trial? Théodore could not work it out. Two things, however, were slowly becoming clear. First, Ursula and Planta were proving more difficult to blackmail than the Genevan had hoped. And second, because he dreamt of consolidating his status in Geneva by remarrying, time was no longer on his side. On 9 May 1778, then, Théodore wrote to Ursule to remind her of the threat of the Lyon letter and to request a divorce. When Ursule prevaricated – she was holding out for an annual pension of 3,000 *livres*, rather than the 2,200 *livres* that she was then receiving – Théodore responded in January with a letter (sent by the lawyer Naville) enquiring as to whether she had resolved unequivocally to stay in the Grisons. In March Ursule called Théodore's bluff: she would return. Outmanoeuvred once more and enraged, on 23 March 1779 Théodore threatened to publish his recent correspondence with Ursule and Planta, and thus to go public with his accusation of incest. And on 4 May 1779, the Genevan finally finished the final section of his wonderful *Lettres sur l'emprunt*.

So, as freshly printed copies of Théodore's little book worked their way down Europe's highways, the Genevan again stood on the brink. Throughout the summer of 1779 he pressed the authorities to grant his divorce on the grounds of desertion and was eventually accorded a hearing. On 18 September, before the tribunal, Théodore tried to seize the initiative by brandishing a sealed envelope bearing the words 'my secret' and demanding that Ursule be interrogated concerning its contents. This terrible coup de théâtre badly backfired and his divorce request was promptly refused. With the legal momentum now firmly behind her, on 1 December Ursule petitioned for formal separation from her husband with a pension of 3,000 *livres*. Her request would surely, it appeared, be granted. She would win. And so it came to pass that Théodore Rilliet de Saussure finally threw himself into the void. On 18 December 1779 the Genevan publically and formally accepted Ursule's request for separation, but offered a pension of just 300 *livres* on the basis of her sworn incest and infanticide. The news shook the city. Criminal proceedings were inevitable. On December 27, Ursule claimed defamation of character and demanded *la partie formelle* – the authorization to proceed towards a full-scale trial, which would be held in secret with both accused and accuser incarcerated throughout. Théodore agreed, but Geneva's authorities hesitated, wondering whether the matter might be settled more discreetly by its executive, the Petit Council. Before the question was resolved, however, it became an irrelevance. On 4 March 1780, the baron de Planta arrived in Geneva insisting that he too had been defamed. Théodore protested. A lawyer to his core, he argued that he had never accused Planta of *anything*. He had, rather, simply denounced Ursule for having *sworn* incest. But, with Planta's arrival, any chance of keeping a lid on the affair had passed. The trio were taken into custody to await trial.

Such was the volume of spurious evidence that Théodore had been gathering since 1775 – his dodgy dossier ran to thousands of pages – that the Rilliet-Planta case took five gruelling months to settle. The initial judicial interrogations of Planta, Théodore and Ursula took place during the last two weeks of March. They were followed by another series of interrogations, held between 27 April and 6 May and led by the *conseiller en charge des prisons*, the purpose of which was to confirm the evidence given in March. And finally the trio were interrogated in still more depth before the *Magnifique Conseil* between 15 May and 2 June. June saw the calling of witnesses – Planta summoned twelve – and their cross-examination. And the trial reached its denouement at the end of the month with five days of direct *confrontations* between Théodore and Planta. Because proving the decade-old murder of a fictive child borne of a non-existent incestuous affair was beyond even Théodore's talents, his defence centred upon painting Planta' and Ursule's post-1775 actions as conspiratorial. The pair's ostensibly benevolent actions, from Ursule's departure for the Grisons to Planta's response to the Lyon letter, were clearly motivated by shame and the fear that Théodore would reveal the truth and their moments of malevolence, like the letter in which Planta threatened Théodore 'sachez sur quel terrain vous marchez'? Well, they spoke for themselves. Théodore, with his lawyer Ami Lullin and his notaries Dunant and Mercier, picked through five years of bitter divorce correspondence and found the scent of incest lurking behind every phrase. For Planta's part, mounting a defence was terribly difficult. Silence risked leaving Théodore's unhinged assertions unchallenged, while engaging with the Genevan's fabulously detailed constructions risked lending them credibility. He muddled through, tried to keep cool, and placed his faith in the court.

And rightly so. The judgement of 24 August 1780, by seventeen votes to one, condemned Rilliet de Saussure to six months in prison, stripped him of his place in the Grand Council and his Genevan citizenship, forced him to pay 33,000 *livres* in damages to his brother-in-law and an annual pension of 5,000 *livres* to his wife.[139] The quinquagenarian insisted that he had not been given a fair trial, claiming that his accusations had not been properly investigated – the court had refused, for example, to physically examine Ursule – and that the testimony of his witnesses had been discounted. But he could hardly deny the total one-sided humiliation of the verdict. Théodore's pack of lies had been heard and exposed, and there was, alas, no higher court to which he could appeal.

Or perhaps just one: the court of public opinion. At 10 am on 12 September 1780, as Théodore contemplated his downfall from the confines of a sparse cell, a small crew comprised of his sister, the Veuve Revillod, her coachman and a domestic servant began distributing copies of a 360-page brochure entitled *Lettres, pièces et écrits concernant le procès civil en calomnie suspendu de Dame Ursule de Planta*.[140] Some copies were handed out on the streets of Geneva, others in the antechambers of the Grand Council. Planned in 1779 as blackmail and perfected during the trial, this collection of Théodore's correspondence with Chauvet, Ursule and Planta now served as redress.[141] Geneva's police swiftly banned the work and shut down the Veuve Revillod's operation. And they ignored her protests of Théodore's innocence and her demands to be taken immediately to see the censor. Instead, Inspector Bonnet searched the widow's house for remaining copies and for evidence that might lead them to the work's printer. Luckless, he instructed his lackey to conduct an impromptu tour of Geneva's printing shops. Monsieur Alric's first port of call was the *grande rue* shop of the printer–bookseller Jean François de Bassompière, who claimed no knowledge of the pamphlet and judged, on the basis of its paper and typography, that it was probably printed in Savoy. Next Alric headed to the print shop of Jaques Quiby and Joseph Boisselier on the *rue des belles filles*, where he learnt that the distinctive *Bâlois* characters employed to make the text suggested Swiss manufacture. And finally he visited Pellet fils on the same street, who told him that the *Lettres* were clearly printed in Geneva. Indeed, judging by the humidity of the paper comprising its final gatherings, Pellet fils told M. Alric, the work had been finished within the last few days. Despite the stories of the Genevois printers, the police never got to the bottom of the question of *who* printed the pamphlets, although another lead did at least guide them to the remaining stocks. The outstanding copies of Théodore's *Lettres* were recovered from the boutique of the master cobbler Nicolas Trim on the *rue du soleil levant*. Trim's apprentice, the shoemaker claimed, had taken receipt of the pile without his knowledge and would be suitably reprimanded.[142]

It is probable that on the evening of September 12 both sides were content with their day's work. The police had confiscated the *Lettres*, but not before Théodore's team had managed to press copies into the hands of many of Geneva's great and good.[143] Alas, for Théodore, no new support for his cause emerged in the days, weeks and months that followed, so upon his release from prison he bolted to Italy to plan his next move. If anything, the rigours of the road strengthened Théodore's resolve to clear his name. As he arrived back in Geneva during the autumn of 1781 he had 'several thousand' copies of Lullin's end-of-trial summing-up printed under the (somewhat misleading) title *Requête au Grand Conseil de la République de Genève en recours de la sentence criminelle rendue le 24 août 1780*.[144] Then he turned to the STN to further up the ante. Between April and August 1782, the Neuchâtelois printed: 3,061 copies of parts of Théodore's letter cache as *Correspondance, ou défense fondamentale de spectable Théodore Rilliet*; 4,762 copies of a rambling and unstructured summary of his defence entitled *Inceste avoué à un mari*; 10,000 copies of the trial's climactic *confrontations* under the title *Planta gagnant sa vie en honnête homme*; and 1,000 copies of a new edition of the *Requête au Grand conseil*.[145] In total over 20,000 copies of four distinct works that laid bare the details of Théodore's case and proclaimed his innocence exited the Swiss presses between the autumns of 1781 and 1782. For those who thought that was too much, Théodore packaged what he considered to be the essentials – *Planta gagnant sa vie* and *Inceste avoué* – together under the intriguing title *Procès romanesque, offrant un sujet de comédie très-riche & très-heureux*.

With this fit of publishing Théodore intended to turn his case into a European *cause célèbre* to rival famous miscarriages of justices like the Calas affair (whereby on

10 March 1762, the Protestant Jean Calas was broken on the wheel in Toulouse after having been falsely accused of murdering his son). The century of lights was not one, he insisted, to turn a blind eye to the judicial suppression of personal freedom wherever it occurred.[146] To be sure, even through the lens of his own telling, Théodore made for a fairly unlovable victim. Too privileged, too cunning and too clever. But his scheming, greedy and incestuous aristocratic villain perfectly suited the bill. Planta, after all, *had* threatened Théodore's life on more than one occasion; and his actions, especially his reaction to the notorious Lyon letter, *did* reek of double-dealing.[147] Set to type, the finely drawn detail that Théodore and Lullin had conjured up in the Genevan courtroom seemed to lend credibility to their fiction and nobility to their cause. At one telling moment in their courtroom showdown Théodore had reminded Planta of the precise route around Paris (from the *hôtel de Travers* to *Les Invalides* via the *rue Notre-Dame-des-Champs*) that their carriage had been driven as the pair had first spoken of Ursule's supposed wedding-night confession. Planta, always on the defensive, could only reply that he remembered not the route and that whether they were heading to *Les Invalides* or the *Les Incurables* was totally inconsequential.[148] In a sense, of course, the baron was proven right. To the wise eyes of Genevan justice, Théodore's baroque fiction appeared to be a frivolous and inconsequential subterfuge. But the print-driven international court of public opinion – 'Bienfaisante Typographie! ... réfuge de l'opprimé, la terreur des puissans' in Théodore's own formulation – held men to different standards.[149] It was all too possible that Théodore's passionate, lengthy, multilayered and compelling Romanesque might cause a sensation. In the autumn of 1782 Louis Mettra's Neuwied-based *Correspondence secrète, politique et littéraire* reviewed the details of the case and concluded that as long as the books remained unrefuted it would be natural to regard Théodore 'comme une victime de la prévention & de l'esprit de parti'.[150]

Théodore's deal with the STN was as follows. The ex-Genevan shouldered all of the project's printing costs and agreed to cede a percentage of his profits to the Neuchâtelois. In return the Society took the highly unusual step of disseminating his texts to its substantial network of major clients in key cities rapidly and on a sale-or-return basis. This distribution method, Théodore hoped, would get his works into the hands of the book industry's kingmakers – journalists, wholesalers and booksellers – who, amazed by their contents, would help stimulate demand. Paris, of course, was critical. On 19 July 1782, the STN sent 1,000 copies of the *Correspondance* and 1,050 copies each of *Planta gagnant sa vie* and *Inceste avoué* to Quandet de Lachenal in Versailles to service the City of Light.[151] At the same time, Théodore sent copies directly to Paris's newsmen. Northern Europe mattered too, not least because of its concentration of influential print journals. A total of 100 copies of the three titles were sent up the river Rhine to Pierre Gosse junior and Daniel Pinet in The Hague, while seventy-five of each were dispatched to Delahaye and Company in Brussels and J. G. Virchaux in Hamburg. Elsewhere the Neuchâtelois shipped thirty-five copies of the *Correspondance* and fifty copies of the *Procès romanesque* pairing to Lepagnez in Besancon, Jean-Baptiste Mailly in Dijon, Jean-Zacharie Logan in Saint Petersburg, Christin Rüdiger in Moscow, Jean-Jacques Flick in Basle, Louis Rosset in Lyon and Rigaud, Pons and Company in Montpellier. Théodore and the STN split the remaining stocks and, the pump suitably primed, awaited a flood of orders from Europe's four corners. And then nothing. The

STN's entire Versailles *envoi* was seized from Quandet's warehouse shortly after its arrival.[152] Théodore's shipments to his Parisian journalists were intercepted.[153] Rigaud, Pons and Company in Montpellier informed the STN that they would not be selling the works.[154] Disturbed by this development, Théodore wrote to all of the French booksellers that he knew held copies of his texts to monitor progress – only Mailly *fils* in Dijon had offered the items for sale, and he had sold only a single copy.[155] Louis Rosset in Lyon later confessed that he felt uncomfortable even to be holding Théodore's books in his stockroom.[156] Mettra's notice was the only sign of periodical-press interest in Théodore's writings. In Neuchâtel, the STN recorded a single counter sale of the *Correspondence* and of *Planta gagnant sa vie* and *Inceste avoué*, as well as two sales of the *Requête au Grand conseil*.[157] Distributing these works in the wider-Geneva area was, Théodore considered, out of the question.[158] In fact, only Gosse and Pinet in The Hague, who made 56.12.0 *livres*-worth of sales, reported even the slightest public interest in the Planta odyssey.[159]

Any reader expecting that at this point Théodore Rilliet de Saussure read the writing on the wall and beat a hasty retreat has yet to fully appreciate the man. In September 1782, upon receiving hints of his sales troubles and the solid news of his seized *ballots*, the still ex-Genevan struck a defiant and upbeat tone. The king of Prussia, Théodore insisted, had managed to endure greater defeats without losing courage because he understood that in all types of war the *final victory* was the only thing.[160] The following month he confessed to Ostervald that the affair was now his only passion.[161] He had fought against discouragement and persecution and had won many battles. (Regrettably, he failed to elaborate upon this questionable assertion.) Now he serenely awaited his final victory. There remained just one stumbling block: the cardinal de Rohan. Yes, Louis René Édouard de Rohan, bishop of Strasbourg and member of the *académie française*, to whom Planta served as major-domo.[162] The French booksellers' refusal to market his sure-fire blockbuster, Théodore reasoned, could only be explained by their fear of the protection that Planta enjoyed from the cardinal.[163] Why else would they fail to offer the public his guaranteed bestsellers? Clearly, Théodore would have to break this link. But this thought presented him with a real fix: the only way that Rohan would be likely to drop Planta was if the public exerted sufficient pressure regarding his incestuous activities, yet the public appeared destined to remain ignorant about these activities while Rohan's protection remained in place. Catch-22, *avant la lettre*.

This was a publishing problem to which Théodore decided there could be a publishing solution. He would cram a more succinct, pithier version of his story onto just three-fourths of a printed sheet by using specially ordered small characters.[164] The resultant pamphlet could be printed in huge numbers at relatively little expense. And it would be easier for Paris's colporteurs to handle *under the cloak*. In September, Théodore hesitated between having 18,000, 24,000 or even 30,000 copies printed.[165] By December, having stumbled across the idea that he might distribute the work for free, he wondered if a run of 100,000 copies would not be more appropriate.[166] And here was Théodore's coup de grâce: he would send a copy of his pamphlet by post to every bishop, knight and sergeant in the entire kingdom! With Planta's incestuous relations so plainly and universally known, Rohan's protection would fall in a heartbeat. And with Planta cut loose, the STN could make a killing selling Théodore's works. The pamphlet, he assured the Neuchâtelois, would sell as freely on the Pont-Neuf as the *palette*. If the price was kept low enough to discourage the inevitable wave of counterfeits, the Society could count on at least 30,000 sales.[167]

After some prevarication the STN, amazingly, resolved to participate in Théodore's insane plan. In December 1782, the Society ordered 418.7.0 *livres*-worth of specialized type and 52 ½ reams of cheap paper for the pamphlet, which Théodore decided to also title *Planta gagnant sa vie en honnête homme*.[168] The recent confiscations had left Théodore sufficiently paranoid that he sent his final manuscript directly to Ostervald on 27 December 1782.[169] But as more and more evidence accumulated that Europe's booksellers cared little for Théodore's fiction, and as it became clearer and clearer that the ex-Genevan cared little if there was any real financial profit in the enterprise, the STN got cold feet.[170] By 16 January 1783, the Society had decided that their being associated with the distribution of this new pamphlet was too risky, and that it would henceforth act only as Théodore's (undeclared) printers.[171]

Three months later, on 23 April 1783, as the STN's print-workers came to finish the not-inconsiderable task of pressing 24,000 copies of the new *Planta gagnant sa vie*, the news that Théodore Rilliet de Saussure had been found washed up on the shores of Lake Geneva reached Neuchâtel. A medical inquest conducted the previous day concluded accidental death – Théodore had apparently stormed down to the lake to bathe and suffered some kind of seizure brought on by the chilliness of the water.[172] Perhaps this was true. On 3 April Théodore had written of a 'maux des nerfs' that was horribly affecting his memory.[173] And he certainly was a man under considerable stress. Suicide is another possibility, although nothing in his final letters to the STN suggests that our anti-hero was ready to quietly exit the stage at the very moment that the curtain was about to rise for his final act.[174] Murder? Well, no direct evidence exists to support such a hypothesis, but if Planta was aware that his adversary was just days away from trying to further blacken his name in the most spectacular and damaging fashion, then the possibility has to be entertained. And the baron *had*, after all, threatened Théodore's life more than once. Perhaps, just perhaps, in death paranoid Théodore finally found his miscarriage of justice.

In any case, his pamphlet never found its public. On 26 April 1783 Jacques Rilliet-Plantamour, Théodore's inheritor, informed the STN that he had discovered printing samples among his disgraced relative's possessions and that all work on *Planta gagnant sa vie* should be suspended.[175] He was too late. According to their account books, at least, the Neuchâtelois finished printing 24,000 copies (18,000 sheets) of the pamphlet on April 25, packaged these on April 26, and delivered 9,000 of them to Théodore's agents, Pourtalès and Company, on April 28.[176] That day, the Society also requested that Rilliet-Plantamour settle Théodore's total outstanding balance of 5,549.19.3 *livres* (only 233.5.0 *livres* of which was for printing the final Planta pamphlet) from the proceeds of his substantial estate.[177] No doubt thinking of the damage that Théodore's Planta pamphlet might still do to the family name, Rilliet-Plantamour settled the debt without fuss. On 20 May 1783 he took receipt of the entire run of *Planta gagnant sa vie*, and apparently all of the thousands of copies of Théodore's other works that the STN still had in stock, in five substantial crates sent to his Genevan home via Nyon. He almost certainly destroyed the whole pile immediately.[178] In the space of little over eighteen months, Théodore had driven himself to the grave by commissioning the printing of around 45,000 copies of six successive imprints that, taken together, probably reached no more than a few dozen readers. Life, to repeat, might have gone better for Théodore Rilliet de Saussure.

The previous chapter showed how in October 1784, angered by the Fauche clan's attempt to smuggle Mirabeau's sulphurous *Libertin de qualité* through limestone Jura passes, the French government effectively closed the Swiss border to the importation of books. The Romandy traders, including the STN, searched high and low, but there was no way to get their volumes through; by the time the dust began to settle from the spring of 1787, many businesses had collapsed. In the process, the chapter questioned conventional wisdom by presenting France's censorship regime as determined and capable. It suggested that the classic liberal interpretation of pre-Revolutionary France's forbidden book markets – briefly, that there was little that hapless *ancien régime* authorities could do to stem rising Enlightenment tides – needs revisiting. The Rilliet case builds upon this revisionist picture by demonstrating how the French authorities, as well as those in Geneva, were equally capable of responding to specific literary threats with discreet, targeted interventions. Rilliet's works might have caused a sensation. The Genevan had the capital and determination to will them into print, while the STN had the know-how and networks to see that they were disseminated far and wide. Yet, due to effective surveillance and resolute action, the Planta affair barely made it beyond the courtroom. The Genevan police raided printing shops; Quandet's Versailles warehouse was turned over; Paris's wary journalists guarded their silence; the kingdom's booksellers never offered the works for sale; and, eventually, Théodore Rilliet de Saussure was found floating face down in a lake. The Planta saga could hardly have been suppressed more effectively.

Before we come to this chapter's principal argument – that a new appreciation of the efficacy of international censorship can significantly enhance our understanding of the role that extraterritorial publishers and their 'underground' literature played in the Enlightenment – it is worth considering what 'legality' meant to the STN. According to Neuchâtelois law, each book that the Society printed had to be submitted to the town's censor, Samuel de Petitpierre, before being released to the wholesale channel. In theory, at least, this complete pre-publication examination of texts, which was by no means standard across Europe, was as stringent a censorship regime as might be reasonably envisaged. Small towns with relatively circumscribed intellectual elites like Neuchâtel, however, habitually found it difficult to achieve sufficient distance between the printer and censor for such arrangements to function effectively. Ostervald and Petitpierre were close friends and a substantial and ever-increasing segment of Neuchâtel's bourgeoisie became stakeholders in the Society. In practice, then, from the early 1770s works like d'Holbach's *Système de la nature* and Voltaire's *Questions sur l'Encyclopédie* were passed with a wink and a nod, sometimes on the proviso that they would not be sold within the principality.[179] Neuchâtel's printers were also forced to swear an oath binding them not to publish anything that might attract the attention of foreign powers and bring the Quatre-Ministraux into disrepute.[180] The oath both allowed the STN to view 'illegality' as primarily a matter of avoiding external pressure from Versailles and Paris or Berlin, and ensured that it would be the Society's directors, rather than

Neuchâtel's authorities, who would be held responsible should complaints arise. The threat of foreign intervention was real. French diplomats like Pierre-Michel Hennin, who was stationed in Geneva between 1765 and 1777, monitored the products of the Swiss presses and regularly reported back to Versailles.[181] That the Quatre–Ministraux was sure to acquiesce to any request to suppress an edition and reprimand its printers served as a powerful incentive not to produce highly illegal books.

That none of this prevented the STN from making its presses available to an unhinged Genevan who intended to send copies of his libellous pamphlet by post to the greater part of France's aristocracy is clearly noteworthy. We must be equally mindful that the 'atheist's Bible', the *Système de la nature*, was among the most radical works of the late Enlightenment, and that the STN also published several works by Brissot and a substantial amount of Neckerana. Indeed, the Society printed twenty-five books that featured in Darnton's corpus of underground literature. Nonetheless, it is worth remembering the vast majority of the over 200 works that the Society printed were inoffensive, and that most of the STN 'forbidden' works in Darnton's list – titles like Mercier's *Jezennemours* (1,043 copies printed 24 September 1776) and Charles-Georges Fenouillot de Falbaire de Quingey's *Les Jammabos* (1,208 copies printed 11 January 1779) – appear to have been of little interest to the French authorities. The STN only really strayed into highly dangerous ventures during the early 1770s, as its directors learnt the trade and struggled to build a client base, and from the early 1780s, as collapse loomed. Further, the story of the involvement of Neuchâtel's printers in highly illegal publishing during the 1770s and 1780s reads primarily as farce. Ostervald lost his position as *banneret* for printing the *Système de la nature*; Samuel Fauche was ejected from the STN because of the *Gazetier cuirassé* affair; Fauche and Witel were locked up (albeit only for three nights) for printing Mirabeau's *Des lettres de cachet et des prisons d'état*; Rilliet's Planta crusade was the death of him; and, once a clear pattern emerged by the mid-1780s, the entire Swiss industry was devastated by external pressure. For the STN, at least, publishing highly illegal books was a last resort that rarely paid.

Such was the nature of book-trade censorship enforcement that the risks to the STN associated with wholesaling forbidden works that had been printed elsewhere were, by contrast, largely limited to any potential commercial losses that might stem from confiscations. As a result, as long as care was taken, the Society was prepared to supply buyers located all across Europe with more-or-less anything that it could source from Romandy. Seizures, of course, were best avoided. But judging illegality was difficult because it required an understanding of both the contents of thousands of available books and the constantly changing legal frameworks and enforcement realities of a vast and heterogeneous continent. A work that scandalized officials in Versailles might amuse their counterparts in London. Seemingly inoffensive novels, theatre pieces or histories might prove wolves in sheep's clothing. Worse, almost all of Europe's censorship regimes were deliberately vague and largely reactive. States realized that it was often simpler and more effective to proscribe 'immorality' and 'subversion' than to create clear lists of illegal books that risked legitimizing omissions, attracting accusations of despotism, and quickly becoming outmoded. The rules that did exist were constantly changing. In 1776 the Saxon and Prussian governments agreed to recognize each other's systems of *privilegia impressoria*.[182] In 1784, the notoriously strict Vienna censorship commission reduced their catalogue of illegal works from 5,000 books to just 900, in the process refocusing their efforts on the suppression of anticlericalism, atheism and pornography.[183] And enforcement priorities were, too, in a perpetual state of flux. Giraud and Giovine in Turin wrote to the STN in 1775 explaining that novels were not being allowed to circulate.[184] One year a book might pass through Lyon or Basle without any trouble, the next it might cause an affair. Viewed from little Neuchâtel, in short, the question of the 'legality' of their wholesale stocks was never straightforward.

The index of books banned within the Holy Roman Empire published in 1788, the *Catalogue des livres défendus par la commission impériale et royale, jusqu'à l'année 1786*, was an exceptional document that illustrates the rule. Drawn up during the hyper-rarefied atmosphere that prevailed in the European book industry in the wake of the French import ban, Joseph II's index listed over 1,000 forbidden Latin-, German- and French-language books, roughly 30 per cent (294/1006) of which had been published before 1750, 40 per cent (409/1006) between 1750 and 1779, and 30 per cent (303/1006) since 1780.[185] Yet even this extensive roll appeared incomplete and inconsistent. Of the 425 books flagged as by some measure illegal in the FBTEE database, only 108 appear in the Joseph register. Some works that scandalized the French court like *Le diable dans un bénitier* and *Le porte-feuille de Madame Goudan* were included, while other equally poisonous libels including *La vie privée de Louis XV* and *Apologie de la Bastille* were omitted. The baron d'Holbach's *Système de la nature* and *Le christianisme dévoilé* were on the list, while his equally subversive *Histoire critique de Jésus Christ* and *La politique naturelle* were absent. Most worryingly, a somewhat eclectic selection of forty-five especially odious or provocative books were marked with an asterisk to indicate to trade insiders that their sale should be prevented in all instances. Quite what this said about the other works on the list was a matter of some confusion.

To successfully navigate the French system, traders had to understand the spirit and implementation of the law as much as its letter. Vast and overlapping networks of guild representatives, customs officers, local office holders and *Intendants* were responsible for ensuring that a bewildering variety of privileges, tacit and explicit permissions, simple *tolerances* and outright interdictions were respected as books circulated throughout the kingdom.[186] *Ancien régime* to its core, the book trade was supervised by the *lieutenant général* of the Paris police (primarily Antoine de Sartine, Jean-Charles-Pierre Lenoir and Louis Thiroux de Crosne during the time of the STN) and the foreign minister (Louis Phélypeaux, duc de La Vrillère and Charles Gravier, comte de Vergennes). Their impossible job was to balance the commercial interests of hundreds of Parisian, provincial and extraterritorial publishing houses, while at the same time both to nurture the development of a nascent knowledge economy and to suppress, or at least marginalize, dissent. More often than not, the pressures of balancing these forces led to unproductive tinkering; 5,000 edicts concerning the book trade were passed during the eighteenth century, few of which appear to have made much difference to established practices.

These complex realities, of course, problematize attempts to quantify the amount of forbidden literature in circulation in pre-Revolutionary Europe. One productive method, employed most notably by Darnton in the French case, has been to create lists of works that were, at one moment or another and for a variety of reasons, confiscated or suppressed or otherwise earmarked as illegal. Darnton's list of 720 books indicates that, by this methodology, a *lot* of 'forbidden' literature circulated in France during the last decades of the Old Regime.[187] In a sense, the FBTEE database extends this work by highlighting its Swiss biases, shifting the focus to sales rather than orders, extending the scope of enquiry beyond France and providing granular detail and analytical tools commensurate with its digital form.[188] A total of 452 of the 2,984 (15%) titles that the STN sold, it reveals, issued from this broadly defined underground. Further, due to the extraordinary popularity of works like Mercier's *Tableau de Paris* (14,076 copies shipped, or 12% of 'illegal' sales) and Raynal's *Histoire des Deux Indes* (3,694/3%), these titles represented 117,031 of the 410,074 (29%) total copies that the STN shifted. Each of the literary tree's substantial boughs – Belles-Lettres (44,181 copies/37.8%), Science et Arts (23,976/20.5%), Histoire (23,459/20.1%), Jurisprudence (14,755/12.6%) and Théologie (10,648 9.1%) – were substantially represented among these 'illegal' *envois*. And French booksellers did indeed take a disproportionally high number of 'forbidden' books from the Neuchâtelois. Of the 116,208 STN-shipped 'underground' works whose final destination can be identified, the FBTEE database shows that 53,665 copies (46%) went to the kingdom. By comparison, only 96,915 of the STN's 290,518 legal sales (33%) were made to France. From this perspective, then, the STN was something of a clandestine publishing house across the French border.

The problem with this method is that it fails to meaningfully distinguish works like Rilliet's, which were actively sought by the French and Genevan authorities and were rejected by mainstream booksellers, from relatively uncontroversial texts that were once caught-up in some customs raid or bookshop inspection. It paints illegality's vast penumbra as black as its shady core. Three issues follow. First, the list technique exaggerates the true size of the underground by presenting a cumulative worst-case scenario. Did anybody in Louis XVI's Versailles really care, we must ask, if Montesquieu's *Lettres persanes* of 1721 sold freely in Montpellier? Was chasing Voltaire's literary ghost ever likely to have been considered a productive way to deploy limited state resources during the rollercoaster 1780s? Second, casting the net widely risks obscuring the true nature and shape of the highly illicit publishing industry. How might we hope to know which authors, genres and discourses were considered beyond the pale when they are so indiscriminately intermingled with those that were advertised openly and circulated more-or-less freely? And third, the method risks leading readers towards the conclusion that *ancien régime* book-trade policing was either comically inept or tragically corrupt. Almost all of the STN's significant shipments to France – sent in great crates directly down France's highways and through customs barriers with no special instructions – contained at least *some* works on Darnton's list. If the state were looking for these works, they really did have no idea.

Moving beyond this problematic method requires that we pay closer attention to how contemporary book-trade insiders understood their own underground. The contours of its deepest recesses are revealed in Louise Seaward's essential doctoral dissertation. Because Bourbon administrations employed diplomats stationed abroad to direct their efforts to deal with foreign-printed works, as Seaward shows, the vast correspondence archives of the French foreign ministry can be employed to systematically expose the books and pamphlets that most occupied government officials. Between 1770 and 1789, it was primarily works like Pierre Étienne Auguste Goupil's libellous *Guerlichon femelle* (apparently written in 1777, but suppressed before publication) and Linguet's venomous *Mémoires sur la Bastille* (London, 1783) – that is, works of contemporary politics (55 of 156 (35%) keyword instances), personal libel (48 (31%)) and scandal (26 (17%)) – that drew official attention.[189] Seaward also demonstrates that, generally, these diplomatic efforts were pragmatic and productive. Weighing each case on its merits, French officials raided foreign print shops, seized editions, paid off authors and exerted pressure to ensure that publishers were admonished or imprisoned. Where they found little evidence of real damage, they even learnt to walk away.[190] Mostly they combatted threats issuing from London, the Dutch Republic and Holy Roman Empire towns like Mannheim and Brussels, where political and intellectual networks were dense and authors hoped they might enjoy some protection from their governments. And while occasionally, especially during the desperate 1780s, the Swiss printers did plumb the underground's darkest depths, none among Romandy's bestselling 'illegal' classics particularly preoccupied the French foreign ministry.

When the STN used the phrase *livres philosophiques* as a shorthand code to denote unlawful texts, then, it generally evoked a class of works one stage removed from the underground's darkest recesses. Few booksellers wished to touch of-the-moment weapon-books like Rilliet's which, largely thanks to the efforts of the French diplomatic service, were anyhow in exceedingly short supply. No, the underground's dominant tier was largely comprised of tracts of keen anticlericalism or outright irreligion like d'Holbach's *Histoire critique de Jésus Christ*, libertine classics such as Antoine Bret's *La belle Allemande, ou les Galanteries de Thérèse*, and sometimes the latest sorties of more mainstream authors like Mercier's *L'an deux mille quatre cent quarante* and Voltaire's *Questions sur l'Encylopédie*.[191] None of these works had the potential to cause an immediate crisis of state. But their offensiveness was such that they were considered best marginalized lest they scandalize French society and damage the reputation of the book trade. Inspectors duly disrupted shipments, confiscated copies and admonished agents and sellers with sufficient frequency as to ensure that the trade remained underground. For foreign-based wholesalers like the STN, there was little political risk associated with handling these works, so long as conservative elements within their local communities remained uninformed. But the danger of confiscation was a sufficient commercial threat that these books had to be treated differently to regular stocks. *Livres philosophiques* were generally not included in printed stock catalogues; instead their availability was advertised to established and potential customers by private letter. Rather than keeping such works in their stockroom, 'respectable' traders like the STN sourced to order from smaller and less risk-averse traders based in Geneva, Lausanne and Neuchâtel.[192] And instead of shipping these works to their destination alongside normal stocks, traders organized separate shipments with individually negotiated arrangements designed to minimize the risk of confiscation.[193]

Because shipping *livres philosophiques* only became especially risky and thus expensive once they left Switzerland, wholesale prices within the Romandy nexus generally hovered only a little higher than regular stock. One example that illustrates this point is the case of the Genevan clandestine book specialist Jean-Samuel Cailler's exchange-account invoice to the STN of 19 December 1774. The twelve copies of d'Holbach's *Le militaire philosophe* and *Le bon sens* that the Neuchâtelois had taken from Cailler made for a pile of 240 printed sheets which, because it stank of the underground, was valued as equivalent to 360 regular printed sheets. This two-for-the-price-of-three formula was roughly repeated for many illegal works: Cailler billed Du Laurens's *Etrennes aux gens d'église, ou La chandelle d'Arras* at 7 for 10; the *Recueil des comédies et de quelques chansons gaillardes* at 8 for 12 and the erotic classic *Le parnasse libertin* at 13 for 19.[194] In February 1777 the STN charged Madame Eggendorffer in Fribourg 20 *sols* for Pidansat de Mairobert's seventeen-sheet *Anecdotes sur Mme la Comtesse du Barry* on the basis that it was a *livre philosophique*.[195] The 3-*sol* premium over any other regular work of the same length stocked by the STN was typically modest. Prices charged to foreign clients, by contrast, were substantially higher due to the risk, as Ostervald explained to the bookseller Caldesaigues of the *rue Saint-Ferréol* in Marseille the same month, that a single *ballot* lost to capricious foreign authorities might wipe out any profits accrued during several successful shipments.[196] The answer, although it led to many a grumble from penny-pinching clients, was to charge a considerable premium for *livres philosophiques* and to use the margin to bribe officials, ship via less profitable channels and insure against inevitable losses.[197] Two *sols* per sheet – double the standard rate for regular Swiss-printed books – was typical, although sometimes the Society charged more if it deemed that a work was highly sought after.[198] The 59 1/4 sheet *Système de la nature*, for example, was advertised for a whopping 8 *livres* in the STN's printed catalogue of illegal works of 1781.[199]

We get a much clearer sense of how trade insiders delineated the underground, then, from an examination of how the STN held, advertised, priced and distributed books. Further, because, each 'illegal' shipment was organized by individual negotiation with the client, the Neuchâtel archives allow for a more spatially and temporally sensitive view of clandestine publishing than has hitherto been achieved. Take, for example, the case of technically illegal Protestant works sent to France before the *édit de tolérance* of 1787. Protestant works including Jean-Elie Bertrand's *La morale évangélique* and Georg Jonathan von Holland's *Réflexions philosophiques sur le Système de la nature* appear so frequently on lists of works confiscated that they account for 7 per cent (8,031/117,031) of the STN-traded 'illegal' copies recorded in the FBTEE database. Yet, by the mid-1770s, the Neuchâtelois seldom worried about dispatching such works to France and duly priced them as regular stocks. In 1777 Ostervald outlined the situation in a letter to the Ganges author-pastor Pommaret as he agreed to print his *Le chrétien par conviction et par sentiment*.[200] As long as Pommaret's text contained nothing pertaining to religious controversies or attacking Catholicism, Ostervald explained, the STN's contacts could see it pass through the *chambre syndicale* in Lyon without issue, as they habitually did for Protestant Bibles, psalms and devotional texts.[201] By the time that the STN released their 1779 folio Bible, only the *chambre syndicale* of Toulouse preserved a rigid interpretation of the law.[202] Toleration was the order of the day, and Protestant devotional tracts were no longer things of the underground.

Nor were most of the books of the Enlightenment. On the cover of the Lausanne bookseller Jules-Henri Pott's 1783 trade catalogue, a printed sun sets over some nameless European port where several securely packed crates of books have just been offloaded outside a neoclassical warehouse. The words *prudentia et probitate* hang over the scene.[203] Pott's publishing house, he hoped buyers would deduce, was respectable, established and dependable and could supply books anywhere. The Lausannois did actually sell *livres philosophiques* – in July 1781 the STN used Pott to supply two copies of Voltaire's *La pucelle d'Orléans* and d'Holbach's *Système de la nature*, and three copies of each of *Thérèse philosophe*, Nicolas Chorier's *L'académie des dames* and *La nouvelle académie des dames* – but they were not to be found in this trade catalogue. Instead the booklet contained a typical selection of regular fare from across Romany and beyond, including much dross and many of the great intellectual and literary achievements of the age: d'Argens's *Lettres chinoises* and *Timée de Locres*; Diderot's *Histoire générale des dogmes et opinions philosophiques* and *Lettre sur les sourds et muets*; Helvétius's *De L'Esprit*; d'Holbach's *La politique naturelle*; Mably's *De la législation, ou Principes des loix*; Marmontel's *Bélisaire*; Mercier's *L'an deux mille quatre cent quarante*; Mirabeau's *Lettres sur la législation*; De Pauw's *Recherches philosophiques sur les Américains* and *Recherches philosophiques sur les Egyptiens et les Chinois*; Morellet's translation of Cesare Beccaria's *Traité des délits et des peines*; Raynal's *Histoire philosophique et politique des établissements et du commerce des Européens dans les deux Indes* and *Recherches sur l'origine de l'esclavage religieux*; Retif de la Bretonne's *La fille naturelle*; Robinet's *De la nature*; Rousseau's *Les confessions* and *Rousseau juge de Jean-Jacques*; and many, many works by Voltaire, including *Candide*, *Commentaire sur le livre des Délits et des peines*, *Commentaire sur l'esprit des lois de Montesquieu*, *L'homme aux quarante écus* and *Les singularités de la nature*. The catalogue's 212 pages, in short, harboured many of the age's most forward-thinking texts. Also present were a number of ageing works of contemporary politics that no longer especially troubled officials including François-Antoine Chevrier's *Le point d'appui entre les principales puissances de l'Europe*, Pidansat de Mairobert's *Journal historique de la révolution opérée dans la constitution de la monarchie française, par M. de Maupeou*, Barthélemy-François-Joseph Moufle d'Angerville's *Vie privée de Louis XV* and Antoine, sieur Le Roy's *Le momus français*.[204] And Pott saw no good reason to conceal his freemasonry stocks – Karl-Friedrich Koeppen's *Essai sur les mystères et le véritable objet de la confrérie des Francs-Maçons* and *Les plus secrets mystères des hauts grades de la maçonnerie dévoilés* included – from potential buyers. In total, Pott's 1783 catalogue and its supplements list 135 of the 720 supposedly 'forbidden' works listed in Darnton's *Corpus of Clandestine Literature*.

Because each Romandy dealer advertised according to their stock holdings and individual understanding of legality, no two catalogues are alike. Yet most point towards the same reality: works that most modern historians describe as 'clandestine' were openly advertised and circulated relatively freely towards the end of the Old Regime.[205] An examination of the trade patterns recorded in the FBTEE suggests the same conclusion. The STN, of course, generally tried to avoid sending *livres philosophiques* to clients in the same shipments as large quantities of regular stocks. It made no commercial sense to risk hundreds or thousands of *livres*-worth of guaranteed revenue for the sake of a handful of dodgy books. Yet thousands of volumes indicated as illegal according to the lists of Darnton and Robert Dawson *were* shipped by the STN in exactly this fashion. Take, for example, the trade of the Perisse frères in Lyon. On 26 September 1776, the brothers' first STN shipment contained a total of 123 copies of forty different works, including, for example, twelve examples of Jean Bertrand's *Elémens d'agriculture fondés sur les faits et les raisonnemens*, twelve of Dorat's *Les sacrifices de l'amour*, and two of the multi-authored *Lectures pour les enfans*. Also in the shipment were the following potentially clandestine titles: one copy of Gustaf III (king of Sweden) and Voltaire's *Discours du roi de Suède*, six of Louis Guidi's *Dialogue entre un évêque et un curé sur les mariages protestans*, six of Simon-Nicolas-Henri Linguet's *Essai philosophique sur le monachisme*, six of Jean-Pierre-Louis de La Roche du Marin, marquis de Luchet's *Histoire de Messieurs Paris*, and six of Voltaire's *Histoire du Parlement de Paris*. All of these 'illegal' works were shipped at the STN's standard per-sheet prices in the same crate as the regular stocks. The box was marked F.P. n.225 and sent via Jean-François Pion in Pontarlier with no special instructions. Later *envois* to the Perisse frères included examples of Voltaire's *Candide* (six copies, 23 December 1776), Charles Palissot de Montenoy's *La Dunciade* (three copies, 23 December 1776), Nicolas-Edmé Restif de la Bretonne's *La fille naturelle* (six copies, 23 December 1776), *L'albert moderne* (twelve copies, 23 December 1776), James Rutledge's *Le bureau d'esprit* (six copies, 20 June 1777), Mercier's *Jezennemours* (six copies, 20 June 1777), the *Oeuvres complettes d'Alexis Piron* (one copy, 5 May 1778), Guillemain de Saint-Victor's *Adoption, ou la maçonnerie des femmes en trois gradés* (three copies, 17 April 1779), *Les bigarrures d'un citoyen de Genève* (one copy, 1 April 1780) and Pidansat de Mairobert's *L'espion anglois* (four copies, 12 January 1783). Although they always tried to steer clear of actively sought works of pornography, atheism or slander, a total of 213 of the 1,831 copies that the Perisses took from the STN are denoted as illegal in the lists of Darnton and Dawson. But their calculation was clear: these titles were not likely to be confiscated.

Scenarios like this are repeated with such abandon across the FBTEE dataset that the limits of the *livres philosophiques* category can be seen at every level of statistical analysis. Generally, works of pornography or atheism sold not to the STN's largest French markets – towns like Lyon and Marseille – but to places like Caen, Orléans, Loudon and Toulouse where the STN had established contacts with a number of colporteurs and smaller dealers looking to make a fast buck. The respectable traders of Lyon took 118 copies of the widely circulating *L'an deux mille quatre cent quarante*, but never touched *Le parnasse libertin*, *Etrennes aux gens d'église, ou la chandelle d'Arras* and *Venus dans la cloître*. The established booksellers of Montpellier accepted 127 copies of the uncontroversial *La fille naturelle*, but avoided *La fille de joye*, Pietro Aretino's *Histoire et vie de l'Arrétin* or Michel Milot's *L'école des filles*. And Rhiems's well-to-do dealers bought seventy-six copies of the rarely proscribed *Le monarque accompli*, but shied away from Jean-Baptiste-Louis Coquereau's *Mémoires de l'abbé Terray*, Mirabeau's *L'espion dévalisé* and *Thérése philosophe*.[206] *Livres philosophiques* were best avoided. And because they were few in number and only of marginal public interest, they were easy to avoid.

Although the perceived limits of legality differed radically according to bookseller, moment and geographical location, nowhere in Europe did the real underground match its theoretical composition. This, at least, is the impression that Victor Durand gave as he wrote to the STN with instructions to execute shipments that he negotiated during his European tour of 1787 and 1788. When the orders that Durand forwarded contained highly illegal books, they were unswervingly accompanied by instructions as to how these editions should be handled. Joseph Stahel in Vienna, for example, wished for the *livres philosophiques* among his order to be divvied up into three small packets to be sent to separate addresses – Johann Michael Weingand in Pest, Johann Doll and Schweizer in Pressburg and Antoine Gerle in Prague – from where they would be forwarded to the Austrian capital. As Durand relayed the exact works to be sent to each client in his numeric code that corresponded to entries in the Louis Fauche-Borel catalogue of 1787, he underlined works that were to be treated as clandestine. Many of these, of course, were not included in the Fauche-Borel catalogue because of their illegality; so in such cases he wrote the titles out longhand. The Naples bookseller Merande's 9 March 1788 commission contained forty-two books denoted by Durand as worthy of special treatment, most of which were works of libertinism and atheism like *L'académie des dames*, *La fille de joie*, and d'Holbach's *David*. Free to be sent by the normal channels, by contrast, were the *Les devoirs, statuts ou règlements généraux des F.* [rancs] *M.* [açons], *Secrets merveilleux de la magie naturelle et cabalistique du petit Albert*, d'Holbach's *La morale universelle*, Mairobert's *Anecdotes sur Mme la Comtesse du Barry* and *Journal historique de la révolution opérée dans la constitution de la monarchie française, par M. de Maupeou*, Rousseau's *Emile* and *Julie*, Mercier's *L'homme sauvage*, Voltaire's *Discours de l'empereur Julien, contre les chrétiens* and *Prix de la justice et de l'humanité*, and many other such titles. Some clients, such as Weingand and Johann Georg Köpff in Pest, reported that the authorities did not censor books; others, like Giovani Antoine Curti in Venice, indicated that only a small core of highly illegal works might attract attention; while a minority, notably Stahel in Vienna and Charles-Marie Toscanelli in Turin, lamented the rigidity of their town's censure and sent lengthier lists or forbidden texts. Everywhere, books that we might expect to have been proscribed circulated freely.

'A regime that classified its most advanced philosophy with its most debased pornography', insisted Darnton in his 'Grub Street' examination of *ancien régime* France's underground, 'was a regime that sapped itself'.[207] No such regime existed. Although trade insiders often found French censorship baffling, capricious and arbitrary at the level of individual shipments, they generally understood the larger picture as workable. Books or pamphlets (and publications in the periodical press, not our concern here) that slandered the powerful or that openly attacked the government or its policies were not free to circulate. These literary bombs were ruthlessly suppressed by the highest levels of state and, as Rilliet de Saussure found to his chagrin, were rejected by French booksellers. Generally, works of atheism, strident anticlericalism and 'debased' pornography, as well as texts of potentially damaging political heterodoxy and other seriously subversive works, were confined to the underground. Perhaps because they found the works objectionable or tedious, or maybe because they saw no need to chase such a small section of the market, and surely because they feared reputational damage, many prominent booksellers avoided this trade. The underground was a peripheral space located far from the main public sphere; participation, for the most part, ensured marginality. Between the underground and the legitimate publishing world of approbations and permissions, however, lay a vast no-man's-land of print that, despite suffering some losses to officious customs officers and guild-controlled inspections, generally circulated rather freely. It is within this space that we might best locate pre-Revolutionary France's most advanced philosophy.

In one persistently influential telling of the origins of the French Revolution, the *ancien régime* and its censorship regime is tragically cast as an unknowing Cnut, powerless to hold back liberal, secular and democratic tides. The story goes that the intellectual undoing of the Old Regime took place outside of, and in opposition to, establishment modes and practices. Darnton's 'Grub Street' thesis, although it iconoclastically substituted one set of establishment-kicking literary heroes for another, never seriously questioned this central dynamic. Indeed, by fusing romantic stories of wily smugglers outwitting hapless border guards with long lists of their illegal works that made no fundamental distinction between *Candide* and *Le diable dans un bénitier*, Darnton's 1995 twinned *chef d'oeuvre* deepened the construction of a regime slipping ever more out of step with its leading literary lights. Yet the evidence presented here, taken alongside a wider body of recent scholarly work, suggests that France's censorship regime functioned rather effectively.[208] Marshalling limited resources over vast distances, book-trade officials managed to all but eliminate the most highly subversive texts and marginalize swathes of morally unpalatable and politically and religiously heterodox books. At the same time, by broadly tolerating the majority of their age's more interesting literary and scientific works, they oversaw an unprecedented space of intellectual innovation that was of real economic benefit to the kingdom. In at least one sense, furthermore, the principles that underpinned late-*ancien régime* censorship were ruthlessly modern: broad surveillance backed up with limited but energetic interventions were deemed more effective than unenforceable blanket interdictions. Public debate was monitored and extreme discourses were pushed to the periphery. The system, of course, failed to please everybody. From the perspective of the assembly of the Clergy, the censorship regime was a disaster. With clockwork regularity France's assembled bishops lamented that too little was being done to stop irreligious works from circulating throughout the kingdom.[209] The rising tide of irreligion was a matter, they rarely failed to point out, which should have been of paramount concern to Louis XV and Louis XVI. Dark days might lay ahead, they suggested, should the new spirit of *philosophisme* be allowed to break society's most fundamental bonds. But such doom-laden prophecies rarely swayed those who wielded influence. France's ambiguous and unswervingly politically focused censorship regime was too ingrained, too necessary, and too effective to be changed.

It would be quite wrong, however, to focus too much of our attention on the state. With the official rules of the game set purposefully abstruse, the constantly shifting limits of the real underground emerged as negotiation between all stakeholders in the publishing industry – authors, middlemen, publishers, readers, protestors and authorities. The better part of this dialogue took place not behind closed doors but through active participation in the millions of small decisions that comprised quotidian trade practice. The archives teem with traces – from Rilliet's attempts to see his Planta saga reach French bookstores, to the selectivity of Pott's trade catalogue, to the STN's fluid pricing of books, to Durand's town-by-town instructions concerning which books to ship separately – of this process of mediation in action. Everybody participated, oftentimes unknowingly. Adventurous readers played their part by seeking out clandestine books, or by helping to normalize texts and discourses through public and private discussion. Others fed back their outrage to the industry and its overseers, drawing the battle lines from below. Publishers and booksellers made tricky decisions regarding which books needed to be excluded from their regular channels of advertisement and distribution. Mindful of public opinion and recent state interventions, on a shipment-by-shipment, month-by-month, year-by-year basis they constantly redrew the limits of the underground. Authors, in turn, learnt to understand where their thoughts might be situated in the spectrum of available opinion and tailored their texts to suit or subvert public mores. Most preferred to stay at least in the half-light of the semi-legitimized part of the trade from where their majority of readers could still be reached. The real greats – certainly Voltaire and Rousseau in their day and Mercier in our later period – flirted with the limits of the underground without ever falling into its murky depths. Au fil des années, through catalogue listings and confiscations and book shop conversations, the underground's limits slowly developed. Once vilified writers became literary heroes, underground 'classics' started to be referenced in respectable periodicals and books; and the politics of yesteryear – the Jesuit question, the Maupeou affair, or Louis XV's private life, for example – all passed from the shifting sands of the underground to firmer terrain as interest waned.

An undue emphasis on the 'Tom and Jerry' aspects of the French state's relationship with the Enlightenment book trade thus distracts from a bigger picture of tolerance and symbiosis. With this thought, admittedly, we have come rather far from our point of departure: the wretched Théodore Rilliet de Saussure's suspicious death in the shallows of Lake Geneva. If nothing else, two things are clear. First, the Rilliet case illustrates the problems that accompanied the STN's early 1780s strategic turn towards commission printing. The Planta tracts were weapons which should never have found a publisher, nothing more. Perhaps Ostervald fell momentarily under Rilliet's spell and believed in his cause. More likely the STN lost sight of its moral compass as the demands of servicing spiralling debts beholden to local notables and institutions mounted. And second, Rilliet's adventures in publishing underscore the central challenge of placing bibliometric approaches at the heart of literary enquiry. From the accountant's perspective, the 24,000 copies shipped to Rilliet-Plantamour on 20 May 1783 made Théodore's second *Planta gagnant sa vie* the STN's highest selling book. Yet one cannot but help but wonder whether sales realized to a dead author's estate to be immediately destroyed really count. Few books are created equal. And few authors would wish to be judged on sales alone. It is time, then, to take stock of the lessons gleaned from this bibliometric adventure through the STN archives, and ask what we have really learnt about the process of selling Enlightenment.

5

Conclusion: Selling Enlightenment

In October 1785 the tireless English traveller William Coxe once again passed through Neuchâtel.[1] This time he approached from Pontarlier in France, slipping through the mountain passes where, for a few months during the previous autumn, the smuggler Faivre had hidden and later hauled Mauvelain's book crates. Coxe delighted in the dramatic precipices and grottos and asphalt mines that shaped these forested highlands; he marvelled at how France's border with the Prussian dependency Neuchâtel was marked only by a stone; and he drank in the opportunity to visit the late Jean-Jacques Rousseau's untouched bedroom in the Val-de-Travers town of Môtiers. As he skirted La Tourne, remarking the quality of its meandering yellow stone road, glimpses across Lake Neuchâtel and much of the Swiss plateau began to appear through clearings in the trees. Time, commerce and enlightenment, Coxe's account of his travels revealed, were slowly leaving their ineffaceable marks upon this enchanting landscape. And as the Englishman descended into the town of Neuchâtel, he must have sensed that these same forces of progress had really done a number on the STN. The ambition and excitement that characterized the Society's establishment in 1769 had been thoroughly crushed by the cutthroat realities of the international trade in books. The great *Descriptions des arts et métiers* project was dead, smothered by vested interests in Paris. The French border was closed to book imports. Only an agonizing and largely futile attempt to liquidate their great stock pile of nearly two million printed sheets lay ahead. Watches were still being made in Neuchâtel's mountain workshops and *Indiennes* were still being dried in the Areuse delta. But the finest and most improbable episode in the town's literary history was as dead as poor Jean-Jacques.

Our story, too, is all but done. The FBTEE database has to this point largely been employed to develop scholarly knowledge of the history of the STN and the European trade in French books during the eighteenth century. And so one substantial question remains: Can it be used to extend our understanding of the Enlightenment? Attentive readers might find the prospect fanciful, for the preceding pages have shown that the archives of the STN are clearly not quite as 'representative' of the wider Enlightenment book trade as previously envisaged. Ostervald and his partners could not effortlessly pluck Dutch or Parisian editions from some 'floating' soup of European print product. Their society sold Swiss books. And Swiss books differed substantively from those produced in Lyon, or the Low Countries or indeed anywhere else. Further, certain areas of Europe did not trade freely with the Swiss. The STN never sold its regular stocks to Paris and barely traded *anything* with the cities of the Low Countries and their vast hinterlands. And further still, the Society never became a fully established, stable and 'normally' functioning business. During two rollercoaster decades of trading, the Neuchâtelois made an endless series of strategic tacks in their ill-fated quest to turn spectacular growth into sustainable profitability. But nothing really worked.

Based upon the account books of a single unstable business selling Swiss books only to parts of the continent, then, the FBTEE data set contains systematic biases and significant blind spots. And, while the data is invaluable for many purposes, it is too patchy and ultimately insubstantial to be straightforwardly marshalled in support of broad conclusions about regional bestsellers or comparative reading tastes across the vastness of European space.[2] It is not surprising, of course, that the STN never enjoyed any dealings with a majority of the continent's booksellers. And it is perhaps only marginally noteworthy that when the Society did make contact with foreign *libraires* – by circular, personal letter or through one of their travelling salesmen – its advances were more often than not rebuffed. Such is business, and these snubs failed to prevent the STN, at its peak, from shipping roughly 10,000 non-commissioned copies per year to foreign booksellers. But 10,000 books were only a drop in the vast ocean of the Enlightenment's francophone book trade. Even to France, its principal foreign market, the STN sold just one book per year for every 4,000 inhabitants or 90 square kilometres of land. The Society failed to do *any* business in thirty-seven of the country's ninety-six present-day *départements*. It very rarely traded with more than a handful of booksellers in any European regions or cities. Further, the STN *never* managed to simultaneously maintain more than a handful of truly stable, high-volume foreign client relationships. Its foreign clients came and went with remarkable regularity. Some ordered in dribs and drabs over long periods, others tested the waters with one or two substantive orders before taking their business elsewhere. But almost none depended upon the Neuchâtelois to regularly stock their shelves.[3]

Some of the shortcomings of the data set can, thankfully, be partially addressed. The FTBEE database's information structures were designed in such a way as to enable complex enquiries limited in time and space, according to the types of editions and genres of works being shipped, the nature of the clients being served and so forth. The years when the STN operated under unusual trading conditions, or the different business models and printing strategies that the Society attempted, then, can be examined in isolation. These database tools are invaluable when conducting targeted enquiries and help to surface meaning from a seemingly endless sea of information. But, used indiscriminately or for purposes that stretch the realistic scope of what can be gleaned from the Neuchâtel archives, they can introduce distortions into a data set that's principal strength is its integrity. Removing outlying works like those authored by Rilliet (which were, remember, sent almost exclusively to his inheritors to be pulped before reaching market), or dismissing years where the French border was effectively closed to imports from the STN, is tempting because it makes the data set appear less problematic. But, in the process, events key to understanding both the Society and the wider book trade, are hidden from view.

Further, these tools do nothing to address the data's fundamental slightness. To tackle that issue, of course, we might be tempted to add data from beyond the Neuchâtel archives, using sources including those that have been employed in the current volume. Certainly the prospect of triangulating the STN data set with, for example, information extracted from the archives of the Luchtmans of Leiden and the Paris-based printer–bookseller, the Veuve Desaint is tantalizing. Tantalizing and problematic, for adding even a single piece of data drawn from outside the STN archive risks destroying the database's precious coherence. This book has shown how contextual factors – for example, the size and tactical leanings of the STN's business at the time sales were made, or the way that stock-swap agreements functioned within the Swiss productive zone – provide the essential foundations for understanding every bit of information contained within the FBTEE data set. That the Luchtmans of Leiden sold, say, 100 copies Mercier's *Tableau de Paris* to Northern France in any given period, while the STN sold eighty and the Veuve Desaint sixty would prove, on its own, largely meaningless. Future compatible data sets, then, would have to be adequately embedded within a framework of explanatory infrastructure – perhaps books and articles, perhaps electronic resources – to sufficiently facilitate their comprehension. They would need, too, to be wholly self-contained and isolated from one another to facilitate proper analysis. And, finally, by consequence, adequately interpreting the composite whole would require such an intellectual investment and level of specialized knowledge that the results would have to be presented to the wider community of Enlightenment scholars through mediated forms. More books, more articles and more electronic resources. The approach certainly has the potential to provide a more detailed picture of the trade in Enlightenment books, but it will not be for the faint of heart!

What the STN data set does currently and straightforwardly provide is a faithful and meticulous rendition of a small fragment of the *fabric* of the Enlightenment – of the 'matrix in which ideas, actions and events acquired new meaning' according to Dan Edelstein's formulation.[4] This book has concentrated on what the FBTEE database reveals about the European francophone book trade, rather than the literary contents of the boxes exiting Neuchâtel, in the conviction that focusing upon this fabric represents the surest route that the STN data provides to deepening our understanding of the Enlightenment. This chapter contends that three consistent trends in the numbers are telling. First, the STN data gives a precious insight into the slenderness of the window of time in which Enlightenment authors, books, discourses and ideas could hope to hold public attention. The fact that the sales of Voltaire collapsed so dramatically after his death, it will be suggested, should have bearing on how we view the *grands hommes* of the Enlightenment and, by extension, the intellectual origins of the French Revolution. Second, the data shows that the fabric of the Enlightenment varied subtly across Europe from city to city, region to region and country to country. If an ordinary eighteenth-century Frenchman walked into a bookshop in London, and then later Amsterdam, then Paris and then Geneva, the conclusion to the third chapter of this study asserted, he would have found significantly different books on the shelves. Here it will be argued that these variations were not merely bibliographical. They left different communities exposed to significantly different debates, arguments and literary forms. And third, the consistent presence of spikes and troughs in the Neuchâtel numbers reminds us that the size, structure and nature of the eighteenth-century book trade meant that influencing public debate was not beyond the capabilities of state actors and private individuals. When Louis XVI's state finally flexed its muscles in the mid-1780s, it brought the entire Swiss publishing industry to its knees. Rilliet, Brissot and others bought their way to the top of the STN's 'best sellers' lists. Whatever the Enlightenment was, it was *not* free from the grubby hands of money and power.

Before anything else, it must be recognized that our piece of the fabric of the Enlightenment – our slice of Edelstein's matrix – is a mere fragment and there are limits to what we might hope to learn from putting it under the microscope. The FBTEE database systematically reveals the journey of hundreds of thousands of physical books from the Romandy print shops in which their type was set, via a series of trade middlemen, through to the retail destination across Europe where they were first sold. But there the trail generally falls cold, leaving us with only scattered evidence and speculation to complete the full story of where, when and by whom these books were consumed. Which individuals or institutions bought the books? Did they pass through the hands of members of the purchaser's family or friendship circles? How did those individuals react to the contents of the text? Were the books resold after their useful life or left to gather dust? We know, systematically at least, little of these things. And the FBTEE database only really concerns books, which were but a small part of the greater Enlightenment cloth. It tells us neither of the STN's experiments with newspapers and periodicals, nor of smaller print jobs such as pamphlets that the Society, lumped together under the impenetrable accounting rubric '*divers petits ouvrages*'. Still more importantly, it sheds no direct light on the vast tapestry of sites and spaces and forms and forums that comprised the eighteenth-century public sphere. What was said in Europe's academies and salons and courts and churches, or was discussed in her coffee houses and pubs, or was scribbled on manuscript, or was performed on stages and streets mattered enormously and is entirely absent from our view.

Nonetheless, while it would clearly be wrong to see our scrap of the Enlightenment's fabric as representative of the whole, the book trade was so intimately interwoven with all other contemporary forms and forums of intellectual exchange that its study does reveal much about the functioning of the wider public sphere. The multiple roles played by many authors, printers, agents, speakers, readers and their publics helped to root this complex and interconnected web of competing and complementary forms of media and sites of exchange in common intellectual and operational infrastructure. And ideas, discourses and whole chunks of text were sufficiently free from the bondage of form as to bounce around the 'communication circuit' with abandon. Thoughts that became fixed in print under the name of an author may have emerged from collective discussions in a salon or coffee house; many published books had their origins in their authors' responses to academy-sponsored essay competitions or, as with the Rilliet case, in legal proceedings or trial briefs; the contents of sermons and panegyrics were often printed; and gossip, rumour and hearsay found its way into scandalous novels. As such, the public conversations advanced in similar ways, and at something approaching the same pace, across all of the different media and forums of the public sphere. The books that the FBTEE database harbours occasionally helped to kick start new chapters in the permanently unravelling intellectual conversation that was the Enlightenment. They oftentimes echoed, amplified and enriched debates already well underway in Europe's coffee houses, academies and salons. And they sometimes provided an eloquent last word to a discussion that had well run its course. But when they failed to engage in some way with the rich conversations that were unfolding elsewhere, they risked becoming Ostervald's worst fear, unsaleable *gardes magesins*.

The pace at which those public sphere exchanges developed, the analysis of the FBTEE database presented in these pages suggests, was startlingly fast. On average, the STN dispatched 72 per cent of the print runs of its own editions within the first two years of availability. After five years, generally, its printings were more than 90 per cent exhausted. And then? Well, then, in the majority of cases, the dozens or scores of copies that remained in its Neuchâtel store room depleted only slowly. Almost no work, however well received and popular it proved during its initial sales phase, was immune to becoming part of publishing's long tail. It took the STN just 18 months to sell the first 1,000 examples of its 1,542-copy 1774 print run of *Histoire de François Wills*. And yet, through the good times and bad that followed, the Society never managed to entirely shift the remainder.[5] After a flood of initial sales of their 2,000-copy 1771 edition of d'Holbach's 'atheists Bible' *Système de la nature* turned into a stream and then a trickle, the STN had just 26 examples left in stock at the start of 1779. When Victor Durand worked his way around Europe on horseback nearly a decade later, towards the tail end of 1787 and through 1788, a dozen copies of the baron's masterpiece still remained unsold. Perhaps the publishing phenomenon of the previous decade – a work that provoked public burnings, condemnations and scores of refutations across Europe – went everywhere unwanted.

Not even Europe's most powerful printers – those that owned or published important literary journals and had friends in influential places – could do much to steer the public's fickle gaze towards their dated stocks. And anyhow, because their broad commercial interests were almost always served by the reality that even the greatest works quickly became obsolete, they were little inclined to try. The whole Swiss printing and bookselling industry, indeed, was set up to serve the orgy of consumption of *nouveautés*. When new books were published in Romandy, remember, they tended to be rapidly swapped among the region's publishers and booksellers who each tried to shift their batch as expediently as possible. The arrangement worked for the Swiss suppliers because it allowed them to diversify risk and ensured the rapid and profitable distribution of their wares. And it worked for *nouveautés* hungry client booksellers around Europe because it allowed them to regularly source a range of new works from a single source. The system, of course, depended on the free flow of information concerning which works were exiting the Swiss presses. Travelling salesmen visited Europe's booksellers in person and a never-ending flow of letters, usually written in a conversational style but sometimes containing formal handwritten lists of *nouveautés*, criss-crossed the continent.[6] Where the fog of commercial war left booksellers unclear as to the situation, they often preferred to give their Swiss suppliers carte blanche to send a few copies of everything fresh off the presses than to miss out. And where printers feared that their original new works might be quickly counterfeited in the Low Countries or elsewhere, they were more likely to double a print run than to cut it in half. Without an effective copyright protection to fall back on, instant and total market saturation – as the Fauche's attempted with their gigantean runs of works by Mercier and others in the mid-1780s – was often the only sure way of fully profiting from being the original publisher of a manuscript.

Publishing's restless pursuit of the new suggests two things about the fabric of the Enlightenment. First, the STN data implies that the leading edge of public sphere discussion had little time for outmoded authors and their books, irrespective of genius or reputation. Of course, since the great French historian Daniel Mornet found a sole copy of Rousseau's *Contrat social* in his 1910 study of pre-Revolutionary auction sale catalogues and private libraries, the idea that Enlightenment France was not awash with the 'classics' is well accepted.[7] Given the contemporaneousness of the STN's trade, it thus comes as little surprise that stars of the early Enlightenment – Baruch Spinoza (1632–77), John Locke (1632–1704), Pierre Bayle (1647–1706) and Isaac Newton (1643–1727) among them – are barely present in the Neuchâtel data.[8] And it is perhaps to be expected, too, that many of the key works of the eighteenth-century *philosophes*, including Montesquieu's 1721 *Lettres persanes*, Diderot's 1746 *Pensées philosophiques* and, indeed, Rousseau's 1762 *Contrat social* hardly appear in the STN ledgers. But the fact that the STN data suggests that the bestselling authors and books of the 1770s were radically different from those of the 1780s is new and revealing. Despite shifting nearly 2,000 copies of Voltaire's popular nine-volume *Questions sur l'Encyclopédie* during the early 1770s, to give one final example to add to those above, the STN never managed to exhaust the ten sets that remained in their care when they checked their stocks in January 1781. Indeed, as the 1780s progressed, the Society rarely sold more than a handful of copies of each of the works that counted as its bestsellers early in the previous decade. For Enlightenment authors, then, the only way to guarantee a continued place on the Society's 'bestsellers' list was to continue feeding the machine with new works. The sales of the STN's most consistently bankable author of the 1770s, Voltaire, for example, collapsed to around 10 per cent of previous values almost immediately after his death in 1778. And like the patriarch of Ferney, the *philosophes* had all either passed or were no longer productive by the 1780s. Not only were key theoretical works like the *Contrat social* difficult to come across on the eve of the French Revolution, we might suppose, but the entirety of the High Enlightenment was yesterday's news.

But rather than arriving too hastily at this conclusion, our view of the fabric of the contemporary publishing industry suggests, it would be perhaps better to take a fresh look at the importance and influence of the *grands hommes* of the Enlightenment and their key works. For sure, a handful of star names – some, like Voltaire, now much vaunted, and others, such as Madame Riccoboni, now largely forgotten – stand out in the STN account books as having had enough 'pull' to attract multiple publishers and guarantee some visibility for each of their new works. But even the biggest-selling texts proved to be next year's blotting paper, and having penned one huge commercial hit rarely guaranteed an author another. D'Holbach's much sought-after *Système de la nature*, for example, was followed by a string of similarly themed books that were received with only tepid interest.[9] And the middle reaches of the FBTEE's bestselling authors tables are populated by strings of authors like Patrick Brydone, Jean-Emmanuel Gilbert and Georg Jonathan von Holland that contributed only a single successful edition to the world of publishing. It is notable, indeed, that the only works that the STN sold which enjoyed some commercial resistance to the ravages of time – school books, religious texts and so forth – were precisely those that made little or no attempt to engage with the Enlightenment Zeitgeist. Aside from these texts, then, continuity across time in the STN books is primarily found not at the level of authors and titles but rather among ideas, discourses, genres and modes of thinking.

If the challenge of plotting a sure course through the windstorms of public debate was common to all of Europe's printers and booksellers, no doubt businesses located in some towns and cities felt better sheltered then others. For, as we have seen throughout this volume and especially in Chapter 3, the commercial battlefield of the European francophone book trade was distinctly regionally variegated and highly mannered. Transport costs, demography, national and regional trade rivalries and the uneven distribution of centres of political and intellectual power all ensured that books did not flow evenly around the continent. Sophisticated and organized trading blocs – tied together primarily by the fact that printers needed to swap books to diversify risks and could only cost-effectively do so locally – dominated the map. For the STN and its Swiss allies, it was effectively impossible to sell regular stocks directly to important markets like Amsterdam and Paris. The FBTEE database provides systematic proof, then, that Robert Darnton's 'floating stock' thesis – the idea that European booksellers all ended up with similar wares because they swapped books so extensively – holds no water. And, in the process, it confirms the more complex picture of how books flowed unevenly through European space suggested by a number of contained case studies. Silvio Corsini's study of links between Lausannois and Dutch booksellers between 1725 and 1775 suggested that collaboration was limited and rare.[10] Raymond Birn showed that the 1754 trade catalogue of the Amsterdam-based bookseller and printer of the *philosophes* Marc-Michel Rey contained many editions published in Paris and The North and precious few printed in Romandy.[11] And George Bonnant's work on the auction sales and booksellers' catalogues of Dutch, German and London-based francophone booksellers suggests that only a meagre amount of Genevan editions, perhaps 1 per cent in total, made up their listed stocks.[12] Books, then, one last time, did not gracefully float around Europe, they ground their way down highways and waterways haemorrhaging profitability and approaching fierce competition by the kilometre. And so, as was concluded previously, it seems perfectly clear that if an ordinary eighteenth-century Frenchman walked into a bookshop in London, and then later Amsterdam, then Paris and then Geneva, he would have found different books on the shelves.

The question that remains, then, is whether or not those differences really amounted to anything? Where our lonesome traveller came across different shelves of physical books, did he also encounter different ideas, discourses and modes of thinking? Could he sense the fabric of the Enlightenment subtly beginning to shift underfoot as he left the cobbled streets of Paris and worked his way across the muddy roads of Picardy? The great capacity of the printing press to faithfully replicate texts, of course, leaves open the possibility that counterfeiting was so commonplace that the printers of Europe's different productive zones could trade in more-or-less the same texts without ever having to collaborate. Certainly, the moment's most in-demand works – Mercier's *Tableau de Paris* during a spell in the early 1780s, for example – were widely printed and could be found anywhere. And many travelogues, histories, novels and other popular genres were worthy of a second edition in a different zone if they could be obtained at the right moment and expeditiously printed. Nonetheless, it is clear from the bibliographic record that the majority of Europe's French-language books were printed only once or twice, usually by a single publishing house. And while the titles of these books no longer trip off the tongue, together they nonetheless formed the majority of all *nouveautés*, thus ensuring that the works in circulation in Europe's different zones of production differed wildly. Where the FBTEE database contains 129 books traded by the STN known to have been published in 1784, Pierre Conlon's extraordinary chronological bibliography of eighteenth-century French editions, *Le siècle des lumières*, shows that least 1,930 different new titles were actually published in the French language during the course of that year.[13] Some of the works that never made it to Neuchâtel were ephemeral pamphlets like the six-page *Voyage autour de la terre avec le globe aérostatqiue*, locally focused religious or educational texts including *Heures à l'usage du collège de Cahors*, or works of esoteric interest like the *Abrégé de l'antiphonaire à l'usage de la province de Vienne*.[14] But many more – Jean-Benjamin de La Borde's *Voyage pittoresque de la France* (1780–86), to give one example among hundreds – would have complimented and strengthened the Society's offerings.[15] Without richer and more comparable data, it is impossible to say what percentage of Europe's French-language books would have been available to booksellers who primarily depended upon the Swiss suppliers to stock their shelves. But all the evidence suggests that they would have found hundreds and perhaps thousands of works a year in short supply.

They would have certainly struggled to get hold of works of serious science and progressive literature. When the colourful STN client and literary agent Mauvelain of Troyes attempted to foist a manuscript of his friend the medical doctor Etienne-Jean Pierre Housset on the Society, he was rebuffed on the basis that serious scientific works were not commercially viable to printers without ready access to the Parisian market, where they principally sold.[16] The science considered palatable in the markets to which the STN traded was of the popular sort. In mathematics, the Society sold school books like De Pelt's *Eléméns de mathématiques*, alongside accountancy aids for business owners, rather than the sophisticated writings of d'Alembert. In chemistry, the Neuchâtelois never sold a single work by Antoine Lavoisier, and only ever traded a single rogue volume of Joseph Priestley's *Expériences et observations sur différentes espèces d'air*. Only seventeen copies of any works by the era's most influential francophone economist, François Quesnay – all the Dupont de Nemours's Yverdon edition of *Physiocratie, ou Constitution naturelle du gouvernement le plus avantageux au genre humain*, printed in 1768 and 1769 – passed through the Society's books.[17] And while scores of editions of Linnaeus's dozens of contributions to the perfection and popularization of botany exited the northern European presses throughout the 1770s and 1780s, the STN shipped only a solitary Latin example of the *Systema naturae*.[18] In the field of literature, little trace resides in the FBTEE database of the fierce innovation and popularity of the German *Sturm und Drang* movement headed by Johann Wolfgang von Goethe, Johann-Gottfried von Herder and Friedrich Schiller.[19] And only a disappointing two-dozen copies of the French translation of Edward Gibbon's remarkable *The History of the Decline and Fall of the Roman Empire*, which was partially written in Lausanne, were sold by the STN. Their readers preferred Madame Riccoboni and imitations of Oliver Goldsmith!

The extent to which the works offered by the Swiss publishers differed from those available elsewhere can also be observed in the illegal volumes that the STN traded. The Neuchâtelois did, without question, sell a lot of nominally forbidden books: 29 per cent of shipped works had been by some authority at some moment in time proscribed. The majority of these books however, as we have seen, were titles like Mercier's *Tableau de Paris* (14,076 sales) and Voltaire's *Questions sur l'Encyclopédie* (2,525), which failed to really excite the interest of hard-pressed central authorities. Many of the moment's most dangerous works, by contrast, are nowhere to be found in the STN accounts. Of the 457 titles listed in Darnton's *A Corpus of Clandestine Literature in France* as ordered from the STN, indeed, 144 were never traded by the Neuchâtelois.[20] Prevalent among the absentee editions – works that we know Frenchmen ordered but the Neuchâtelois were unable to supply because they did not circulate in volume in the Swiss zone – were politically charged and often libellous weapon-books like François-Marie Mayeur de Saint-Paul's *Le désoeuvré, ou l'espion du boulevard du Temple* (Londres, 1781). Such books were generally dreamt up, produced and sold in Paris and The North. Their at-once plausible and fanciful attacks on influential court figures emerged from those with proximity to power. They were usually printed in Paris, London, Amsterdam, Brussels, Liège and various places in the Rhineland.[21] And they were consumed; it appears from all the available evidence, almost exclusively in Paris and its hinterlands, Versailles and across the Northern Zone canvas.[22] Readers reliant on the Swiss presses would have been largely oblivious to their contents.

So, of course, wherever our lonesome traveller wandered he would have found stacks of novels and travelogues and histories and works of popular science of such a fundamentally intertextual composition that it might have hardly mattered whether the authors and titles on the title pages always matched. If he couldn't find Goldsmith, he could perhaps get the gist from the *Histoire de François Wills*! And when our voyageur craved familiarity, he could find solace in the fact that the moment's bestsellers – new works penned by the likes of Mercier and Voltaire that had their original printers flooding markets and counterfeiters everywhere poised to satisfy any residual demand – were almost everywhere available. Many of the places he travelled, too, naturally, would source books diligently from printers based in more than one productive zone. Cities like Lyon with considerably literary independence and no real geographical, political or historical reasons not to source from Paris, The North and Romandy in equal measure proved extraordinary bibliographic melting pots. The spheres of influence of Europe's zones of literary production shaded into each other with such subtlety that the available evidence allows radical differences to be clearly located only close to their respective centres. Each of these things is clear. And yet, if we accept that what the great mass of francophone Europeans were reading during the Enlightenment is of real interest, then the presence of measurable and considerable variation in the availability of books across the landscape is important. The average consumer walking into bookshops in Amsterdam, Geneva and Paris found different books, bibliographically and thematically, on the shelves. And because the commercial book trade was so thoroughly connected to the wider public sphere and did a decent job of reflecting the concerns of its readers, these differences tell us something of the differences of the conversations happening in these places as well as, perhaps, the mental worlds of their inhabitants. The Enlightenment read and enacted on the streets of Geneva was not the same as that consumed and lived in the taverns and cafes of Marseille. And subversive literature enjoyed in the baths of Lunéville was not the same as that which shook the court of Versailles.

The fabric of the Enlightenment book trade was, then, in a constant state of rejuvenation and varied in texture and tone across space. It was also, the analysis of the FBTEE debase presented in this volume has suggested, consistently marked by deep and significant tears and irregularities, fissures in the predictable market-oriented functioning of the trade borne of the complexities of the human experience that it both shaped and was shaped by. It was initially tempting, of course, to view many of the spikes and holes and apparent anomalies in the FBTEE data set – notably Rilliet's brief spell as a 'best-seller' who never reached his audience – as deficiencies that needed to be removed or corrected so that a clear view of the 'normal' fabric of the Enlightenment book trade might emerge. How else might one view the 'sales' of thousands of volumes of libellous ramblings to the estate of the work's expired lunatic author, the sole purpose of which was to ensure that the copy could be pulped and the family spared further public embarrassment? But to have taken this path would have represented a failure to take advantage of the extraordinary capability of the FBTEE database to preserve minute detail in its original context while still providing a coherent window onto the bigger picture. It has been the contention of this volume that the ability of the likes of Rilliet to employ the publishing apparatus of the Enlightenment while entirely circumnavigating the need for 'bottom up' demand for their works is telling. Rilliet's watery ghost reminds us that the search for literary importance is neither simply a question of locating originality or genius *nor* of merely discerning which titles and authors, given a level playing field, were most demanded by readers. The literary marketplace was regularly and significantly shaped by the actions of states and their institutions as well as key individuals, including authors and businessmen. Public discourse was everywhere open to manipulation by the powerful and the wealthy.

Rilliet's unbalanced scribblings were, then, only in one sense exceptional. The nature of the francophone Enlightenment book trade, particularly the daily struggle for commercial survival in a highly competitive international marketplace and everybody's obsession with *nouveautés*, ensured that publishers invariably found vanity publishing commissions too attractive to ignore. Over a quarter of the STN's total sales came from fifty-eight commissioned editions, works like Brissot's *Théorie des lois criminelles* (Neuchâtel, 1781) that the Society would never have committed to print without the expectation that their authors would stump up the publication costs in full.[23] These commercial pressures, further, helped to fuel still more dramatic spikes in the regular flow of books, as publishers dramatically sought to fan the flames of public affairs for private gain. Even for a business based in little and out-of-the-way Neuchâtel, explosive controversies – the *Système de la nature* affair, the *affaire des Natifs*, the Necker moment – could prove remarkably profitable. In 1781, the STN managed to sell 13,851 copies of fourteen different books associated with the French finance minister Jacques Necker's unprecedented glimpse into the state of Louis XVI's finances, the *Compte rendu au roi*. Across Europe, well over 100,000 copies of Necker's work were sold, and, judging by the STN evidence at least, demand for printed explanations of and commentaries upon the minister's voodoo accounting was many times larger.[24] Still more remarkably, by the end of the year, for the STN at least, the affair was entirely over, with just a few hundred copies of the Necker corpus sold thereafter. The strong temptation, then, to see such dramatic spikes in the data as anomalous must be avoided. The actions of profit-seeking publishers like the STN significantly contributed to the fact that the 'affair' was an important part of the regular functioning of the public sphere on the eve of the French Revolution.

And if egotistical authors and commercially motivated publishers helped to shape the Enlightenment's fabric in ways that can be clearly seen in the FBTEE data set, so too, of course, could states. The remarkable sales drought that the STN experienced during 1785 and 1786 was due in large part to the decision made by Louis XVI's France to close the Swiss border to book imports. Darnton's study of the passage of Mauvelain's crates – where wily smugglers strapped weighty packs of books to their backs and took to moonlit mountain paths to beat the border guards – seemed to perfectly capture the notion that the late-*ancien régime* French state's attempts to halt or alter the flow information, to interfere with the rise of the freewheeling international francophone public sphere, was doomed. But the context of the wider FBTEE data set shows the true meaning of the events of the autumn of 1784 to have been almost the exact opposite: the French border was in reality so well sealed as to force the STN into the hopeless situation of trying to ship its low-value, bulky products by foot and by night through mountain passes to its distant and unreliable customers. The entire Swiss industry faced ruin at the hands of the French state. The effectiveness of the minister Vergennes's actions here, then – coupled with its differently focused but similarly successful campaigns against the counterfeiters of Avignon and the blackmailers of the North – suggests that where the will existed, the shaping of the fabric of the Enlightenment through focused regulation and direct action was not, in limited circumstances at least, beyond France's capabilities.

So with this digital enquiry into the STN, the eighteenth-century European book trade and the fabric of the Enlightenment coming to a close what, if anything, have we learnt? Well, certainly that the establishment in 1769 of a typographical society in little and off-the-beaten-track Neuchâtel was a courageous and joyous experiment undone by hubris and poor timing. Under the bold and flexible direction of Ostervald and his partners, the STN enjoyed such remarkable growth that it quickly rivalled, as the third edition of the *Encyclopédie* was clattering off new presses during the last years of the 1770s, Europe's most significant publishing houses. From start to finish, the Society satisfied demand across the European map with some quite wonderful editions that, for better and sometimes worse, covered the Enlightenment in almost all of its forms. But even at its peak, the STN was never a profitable or sustainable business. The collapse of the trade in Latin books had left the Romandy book industry fighting a losing battle for survival from the moment that the STN was conceived. And Neuchâtel, a small town that lacked the luxury of a decent retail bookshop where old books could be liquidated, was no place from which to make a stand. And so, little over a decade after its establishment, as stocks of difficult-to-shift older printings mounted and questions concerning the creditworthiness of some clients surfaced, doubts began to emerge about the future of the STN. The Society's directors tried everything to steady the ship. They solicited investment, entered formal partnership with allies in Berne and Lausanne, struck deals with Parisian rivals, and took punts on risky agreements with the likes of Brissot, Mercier and Rilliet. But nothing that they attempted had any real impact on the overall picture. Administration with a view to liquidation followed. And the French government's mid-1780s assault on the Swiss traders ensured that even this was a desperate affair. In other circumstances, perhaps the fact that the partial reopening of the Swiss–French border to book imports in 1787 coincided with the explosion of print of the pre-Revolutionary crisis in France might have provided occasion for nimble and opportunistic printers to plot a return to the good old days. But by this point the whole industry, the STN included, was in dire straits.

The colourfulness of the STN's short history, of course, has made this volume's attempts to use the Neuchâtel data to draw broad conclusions about the European book trade challenging. And yet, by providing such a rich view of the entire life cycle of an early-modern publishing house, the FBTEE data set has proven in many ways more revealing than we might ever have hoped. First and foremost, it exposes the functioning of the Swiss zone of francophone literary production. Those competitor printers and booksellers in Lausanne and Geneva: they were not foes, they were partners in the dance. The Romandy printers and booksellers, rich in industry, ambition and experience, essentially operated as an informal cartel. They specialized in a common product – cheap, of-the-moment, locally printed editions produced primarily for foreign markets. They shared information with each other about which books might best be printed; they each worked hard to market *nouveautés* that exited all of the region's presses; and they swapped books extensively among themselves so to ensure the competitiveness of their offerings. Then they fought tooth and nail with each other to place their diversified Swiss stocks to their overlapping networks of international clients. The system worked well save for one uncomfortable issue. Romandy's publishers had traditionally relied upon income from the sales of Latin works that all but entirely dried up around the time that the STN was established. For everybody to have survived, production of French books would have had to be ramped up and market share would have had to be wrestled from competitors in Lyon, Paris, Amsterdam and elsewhere. But located a long way from the centre of literary power and patronage, with relatively 'soft' domestic markets and no effective literary journals to promote their books, the industry was not sufficiently competitive. Consolidation came first. And then followed collapse.

The model operated by the Romandy publishers before their devastating fall was, of course, not replicated in carbon copy across the European map. We are unlikely to satisfactorily understand the subtleties of how the book trade functioned in Paris, The North, the French provinces and elsewhere, without further serious study that channels the focus and technical prowess, if not necessarily the exact approach, of the FBTEE project. Nonetheless, by placing the data that we currently have in conversation with existing scholarly treatments of the specific regions and cities and a fresh look at other book-trade archives, the current volume has been able to indicate something important about the functioning of the wider European trade in books. The forces that underpinned the Swiss publishing model – most notably the common need of all printers to diversify their stocks of *nouveautés* so as to spread risk and offer a compelling product, coupled with the impossibility of cost-effectively doing this beyond a limited geographic radius – it has suggested, were relevant everywhere. The Veuve Desaint swapped on an almost daily basis with her Parisian counterparts, and the Luchtmans of Leiden thrived in precisely the areas that STN struggled to make any penetration. Because books were material objects printed at specific moments and particular locations, the European francophone book trade naturally organized into competing trading blocs, each of which held sway over different parts of the map. For consumers the net result was simple: they found different French books on the shelves of bookshops in Geneva, Paris, Amsterdam and London.

Whether they found more texts written by Voltaire than by Rousseau, or sensed that theology was slowly being eviscerated by the scientific method, has not been our concern in this volume. Issues stemming from the contents of the Neuchâtel books are the focus of its twin, written by Simon Burrows. Here, our interest has rather been what the FBTEE project's unique perspective on the structure of the European book trade reveals about the underlying fabric of the Enlightenment. First, it has been suggested, the breakneck speed at which the late-eighteenth-century information circuit turned ensured that public interest was always focused upon *nouveautés*. New books, of course, did not always carry new ideas, and the cult of the moment certainly encouraged mediocre imitators that produced more heat than light. Nonetheless, *nouveautés* at once satisfied the commercial appetite of Europe's printers and booksellers and, by leaving little room for reputation-worship or the fetishizing of the past, kept Enlightenment debate dynamic and relevant. Second, we have seen that the French Enlightenment's fabric showed subtle variations in tone and texture across the European map. The economics of the book trade ensured that, while traders like Rey in Amsterdam were more than happy, when the occasion arose, to break bread with the Swiss and revel in their shared progressive values, they steadfastly refused to do serious business. Different books, as a result, filled the shelves of the French-language bookshops in different European regions. And these differences amounted to something. The Swiss Romand's version of the Enlightenment – that of William Cox and Louis-Sébastien Mercier and Madame Riccoboni – was popular, intertextual and different enough to that read and spoken in Paris, Marseille, London or Amsterdam to alter the way that people viewed the world. And third, we have noted that the Enlightenment's tissue was sufficiently fragile to be subject to manipulation by those with capital or influence, and was prone to sudden and significant rupture. From the *Système de la nature* scandal to the Necker affair, the public sphere regularly amplified certain ideas, discourses or works to cacophonous levels, with unpredictable consequences. And from Rilliet to Brissot, authors of little real merit but many means – financial or temperamental resources not shared by their contemporaries – could buy or bargain their way towards disproportionate influence. The fundamental economic realities that underpinned the Enlightenment book trade were never likely to produce even-handed and meritocratic debate.

As the 1780s drew to a close, of course, as if to prove this point to anybody still convinced that they might be living in the fairest of all possible media worlds, the mother of all public sphere shitstorms broke out. Given the obsession with *nouveautés* displayed by the French public and their information providers and the structural volatility of the public sphere, any attempt to better understand the link between ideas and the French Revolution must surely begin with a renewed focus on the national and regional publishing orgy of the pre-Revolutionary crisis of 1787–9. Despite the prominence of the abbé Sieyes's *Qu'est que le tiers état* in serious explanations of the origins of the Revolution, we understand relatively little about the overall size, geographical variegation and fundamental nature of this explosion of publishing. One clear thing, alas, is that role played by the Swiss publishers – usually so quick to profit from foreign turmoil but in such disarray at this moment that the presses had all but ground to a halt – was only minor. And so the FBTEE database's contribution to our understanding of the link between ideas and the events of 1789, then, is somewhat less direct than might be wished. The data suggests, first, that any enquiry into the authors and works that most shaped serious public conversation as the pre-Revolutionary crisis broke must look significantly beyond the High Enlightenment canon. Yes, the tone and content of works like the *Lettres persanes* and *Contrat social* were so etched into the collective consciousness of pre-Revolutionary Europeans that their influence was pervasive. But philosophy was only one part of the equation, and by the 1780s even the 'philosophical' baton had been passed. Highbrow readers were then in the thralls of the likes of Brissot and Mercier who inhabited and projected significantly different mental worlds to their predecessors. Second, the database provides a basis for understanding at least some small part of the great geographic rifts – intellectual, social and cultural – evident in French public life from 1789. Demographic, economic and political factors, for sure, created these fissures. But the great disconnects between the publishing worlds of Paris, France's provinces and the extraterritorial presses, both before and during the Revolution, helped to ensure their widening. And third, by extension, it should come as no surprise that when the elected deputies, political agitators and pressmen that poured into Paris from all over francophone Europe in 1789 tried to form some kind of shared intellectual identity and philosophical programme to rally behind, it was not our fractured and *nouveautés*-obsessed public sphere of the 1780s that provided a common grounding. Instead, the revolutionaries looked into common factors in their educational backgrounds and vocational practices and dreamt up a hybrid version of the classical past and the High Enlightenment as their inspiration that would have been wholly surprising to the average bookshop browser just a few years previously. The revolutionaries' ritualistic and symbolic transferral of Voltaire's remains to the Pantheon in July 1791, viewed from this perspective, marked the moment that the Enlightenment enjoyed by ordinary readers of the 1770s and 1780s was truly dead.

With these final thoughts we have, perhaps, moved too away far what can be definitively read into the data and have strayed some distance from our initial brief! The challenge set at the beginning of the book was to facilitate the scholarly exploitation of the FBTEE database by providing the contextual information necessary for its data to make sense. With this survey of the STN's history and its place in the European book trade now complete, specialists better placed to understand the STN sales and purchase records for certain authors, books, genres or fields might now proceed, one hopes, without falling foul of the data's many potential pitfalls. And with the sales of hundreds of thousands of books to pore over, many of which are unknown even to the most hardened bibliophiles, there is much data left to exploit. Perhaps that is enough. But a further challenge was set, too, towards the beginning of these pages: to push forward our knowledge of the eighteenth-century European book trade in a way that could not have been possible without a digital approach. Aspects of each of this volume's principal conclusions – which have concerned, at the broadest level, time, space and the importance of specific space-time events – can certainly be found in scores of inspirational articles and books previously written about the STN and the wider Enlightenment book trade. Yet the systematic way in which facts repeat in the FBTEE data has allowed the current volume, one hopes, to give a clearer direction to debates that have struggled to move beyond their reliance on anecdotal and fragmentary evidence. That Bosset sat down to dinner with the Amsterdam publishing legend Marc-Michel Rey in 1779 and had his dreams of establishing a trading relationship with the STN unceremoniously dashed is intriguing. That the Neuchâtelois made just 68 sales to Amsterdam in twenty-five years, despite selling 410,006 works elsewhere, is conclusive. And if the sheer weight of the FBTEE data has provided some clarity, its structure and detail has, on occasion, delivered real illumination. Previous and predigital attempts to approach the STN archives systematically – Robert Darnton's *The Forbidden Best-Sellers of pre-Revolutionary France* and its companion volume being the most prominent example – had to rely upon sometimes unwieldy containers, like 'France' and '1769–95' as singular entities, to manage the scale of the available data. The FBTEE database's ability to keep time and space simultaneously in the picture, and to preserve all data in its original context while still allowing broad conclusions to be drawn, has enabled the current volume to break apart these methodologically imposed containers with unexpected results. The database, then, despite the unquestionable veracity of Matthew Kirschenbaum's Washington criticism, has proven a somewhat handy tool!

Epilogue – The End of the STN

Of all the species of birds indigenous to the wooded peaks of the *arc jurassien*, only the common starling, capable of 'gaping', or forcibly opening its beak under some pressure to reveal insects that might be hidden in, say, the base of a clump of frozen grass, was sufficiently hardy to weather the severe European winter of 1788–9.[1] With rivers frozen over and roads blocked by snowfall, European commerce temporarily ground to a halt. In France, the cold quickened the march towards revolution. In Neuchâtel, the chill focused the minds of the STN's liquidators and marked the beginning of the end for a once admired typographical society. Early in 1789, three of the STN's presses were bought for 8,000 *livres* by Louis Fauche-Borel, who also acquired the services of the *prote* Jean-Barthélemy Spineux and the rights to print Neuchâtel's *Feuille d'avis*.[2] On 1 April 1789, the STN wrote to their former travelling salesman Victor Durand, who had set up shop in Lausanne with the support of Jean-Pierre Heubach, hoping that he might make an offer for their remaining 1,277,506 ¼ sheets, which boasted a catalogue value of 99,932.13.0 *livres*.[3] Over the coming months, the Society tried to run down its stocks by fire sale, offering discounts of between 30 per cent and 50 per cent to booksellers based all around Europe, were they willing to place large orders and pay promptly. These, however, were tough times to find buyers: the round of consolidations and liquidations taking place throughout the Swiss zone and elsewhere left the market oversupplied with aging books at precisely the moment that political events in France left readers more focused upon news and *nouveautés* than ever. So, as discontent in the kingdom of Louis XVI turned to revolt, and revolt to revolution, the STN kept trading as normally as circumstances allowed.

Neuchâtel's once mighty *banneret* Frédéric-Samuel Ostervald was on the verge of ruin and, following two legal pleadings printed in 1791 that have hitherto passed unnoticed, bitter.[4] By 1790, the administrators had succeeded in liquidating two-thirds of the STN's stocks for a gain of 165,358.17.3 *livres*. In the process, alas, they had incurred costs amounting to a staggering 158,940.2.7 *livres*. With creditors still to pay, it appeared increasingly likely that by the time that the STN's last remaining books were traded, the process of liquidation was going to result in a shortfall of over 40,000 *livres*, for which Ostervald and his associates would be responsible. The former *banneret* judged, not unreasonably, that he had been stitched up. Given that the stated goal of the 'Acte de cautionnement pour la Société typographique de Neuchâtel' of 8 June 1784 had been to recover just 7 *deniers* per sheet (a little over a third of the 1-*sol*-per-sheet catalogue value), he insisted, the whole affair of liquidation could and should have been concluded in months. But expediency, he suggested, had never been the goal of this particular operation. With each year that had passed since the August 1784 act, the STN's new boss, despite having no experience in the book trade, had pocketed a salary of 120 *louis d'or*, or 2,880 *livres*, as well as expenses that totalled nearly 2,000 *livres*. Further, the interest due on the bail-out money that had been stumped up in 1784 netted its recipients 13,960.17.0 *livres* per year. And so the administrators, Ostervald alleged, had created a smokescreen of secrecy and obtuse, illegal, bookkeeping to deliberately slow the process of liquidation for their own private gain. While he had continued to help the STN with its day-to-day affairs, reduced to the status of a simple 'commis' he had been shut out of all decision making, accused of slander if he complained, and left to watch the administrators grow fat on what part of his former fortune might have been recoverable.

There appears little doubt that capital and its stooges ruthlessly gorged on the carcass of the STN. This was an awful world. For Ostervald, the administrators' dealings with the Orléans bookseller Jean-Baptiste Létourmy, who had bought nearly 2,000 volumes from the STN between 1774 and 1779, summed up the wretched situation. For many years Létourmy had owed the Society 348.14.0 *livres*, the payment of which was again demanded in a letter dated 28 June 1787. The Loire Valley bookseller responded to this missive in a mocking tone and suggested that he might forward 92 *livres* to settle his account definitively. When the STN's administrators meekly acquiesced, Létourmy immediately withdrew his offer. Showing a complete lack of stomach for a fight, the Neuchâtelois proposed that Létourmy might send some wallpaper, another of his specialities, in lieu of payment. And when Létourmy failed to reply to this suggestion, the STN's administrators abandoned the chase. Time had been spent, costs had been incurred, and thus everybody had profited from the exchange except for poor Frédéric-Samuel, whose money was on the line. The only glimmer of hope that the former *banneret* saw was that, according to several conditions and presumptions of the 1784 act, this great swindle was supposed to end definitively after six years. And so, casting his plight as an unparalleled horror of concern to all those interested in human freedom – this dramatic faux-Enlightenment rhetoric, he might have remembered, had done little to help the cause of Théodore Rilliet de Saussure – during the course of 1791, he tried to wrest back control of the STN's remaining stocks before Neuchâtel's tribunal. If the direction of the STN were ceded to himself and Mme. Bertrand (the legal heir of his former associate Elie Bertrand), Ostervald assured the judges, its former administrators would receive all the capital and interest demanded by the 1784 agreement. And, with a third of the Society's stock pile still to be liquidated, Ostervald's trade expertise and sound judgement would ensure that enough money could be raised to prevent the STN's former directors from financial ruin and the traumatic inevitability of having to expatriate their children.[5]

Ostervald's version of events glossed over some uncomfortable truths. He had played fast and loose with other people's money for a long time, and his comeuppance was greeted in society with indifference. If he had a point that the STN's liquidation was not being managed equitably, it was quite another matter to suggest that *he* – as responsible as anybody or any event for the STN's woes – might be trusted to take over from the appointed administrator. Further, few of his specific claims sit well with the history of the final years of the STN as revealed by the Society's account books. His suggestion that the STN had not printed anything during the three years that passed between the 'Acte de cautionnement' of 8 June 1784 and the middle of 1787, for example, was an outright lie.⁶ By extension, his gripe that the administrators had not immediately sold the Society's idle presses upon taking office may be dismissed. (The suggestion also, of course, ignores the reality that the French crackdown meant that no Romandy printers were in the market for additional presses during the summer of 1784, or for several years afterwards.) Further, the extent of Ostervald's involvement in the reorientation of the STN's trading profile between 1784 and 1787, which is clear from the epistolary record, gives lie to his protestations of ignorance of the strategic and tactical manoeuvring that had taken place. And so, somewhat inevitably, the former banneret lost the case and died a ruined man in 1795, the year after the administrators had finally all but stripped the carcass of his beloved print business.⁷

By this point another vulture in the form of Louis Fauche-Borel, the son of Samuel Fauche who by the late 1780s had emerged best placed to continue his father's printing and bookselling legacy, had been circling for a decade. The extent and timing of Fauche-Borel's involvement in the STN's liquidation is a real mystery. According to his 1829-published memoirs, Ostervald and a 'M. Vaucher' (who figures among the signatures of the 8 June 1784 'Acte de cautionnement', having invested 12,000 *livres* in the Society) helped Fauche-Borel to acquire the STN's stocks and print-shop equipment.⁸ Fauche-Borel placed this acquisition early in his narrative, before his receiving the *brevet d'imprimeur de Roi* in 1786 and his subsequent 1787 trip to meet Mirabeau in Paris to discuss the potential publication of *De la monarchie prussienne, sous Frédéric le Grand*. Further, Fauche-Borel claimed to have made considerable profits from the STN's edition of the *Descriptions des arts et métiers*, the last copies of which, as discussed above, were ceded to the Parisian rights-holder Moutard in August 1785.⁹ Memoirs, of course, must be treated with some suspicion, and the evidence of the STN archive – that the Society traded with Fauche-Borel normally during the late 1780s, that he is not mentioned in Ostervald's 1791 complaint, and so forth – does not corroborate these recollections.¹⁰ But when Victor Durand toured Europe in 1787 and 1788 gathering orders on behalf of the STN, he did so with a printed catalogue precisely recording the STN's stocks that bore the title 'Catalogue des livres de Louis Fauche-Borel, imprimeur du Roi, à Neuchâtel en Suisse, 1787'.¹¹ The possibility of some significant connection between the businesses of Fauche-Borel and the STN prior to 1789, then, must be seriously entertained.

If the timeline is mysterious, then it is at least clear that, ultimately, Louis Fauche-Borel restored the Fauche family to the centre of Neuchâtelois printing using the STNs formal and informal privileges, networks, some of its presses and many of its stocks. One of the first books to leave the new Fauche-Borel print shop was a discourse on the subject of genius by Henri-David de Chaillet, the newly promoted pastor of Neuchâtel, who had edited the STN's *Nouveau Journal helvétique* between 1779 and 1782.¹² Before long, many more titles that might previously have been published by the STN – from new editions of works by Isabelle de Charrière and Jean-Jacques Rousseau to a series of locally focused ordinances, religious titles and textbooks including Ostervald's *Cours de géographie élémentaire* – appeared.¹³ From 1791, Fauche-Borel also secretly puts his presses at the service of the stream of *emigrés* that were fleeing revolutionary turmoil in France, publishing more than forty counter-revolutionary works before 1798. Enthused by the royalist cause, in 1795, Louis embarked upon a new career as a counter-revolutionary agent, which quickly drew him away from Neuchâtel on a permanent basis.[14] By 1798 he had handed control of the print shop to his wife, Marianne Fauche-Borel, who, after many years of distinguished service, sold the business to Chrétien-Henri Wolfrath in 1814.

The unmistakable presence of many still-unsold former STN items in the 1806 trade catalogue of Marianne Fauche-Borel shows that, although technically liquidated, a good part of that extraordinary stock pile – those stacks of printed sheets that, laid end to end, could have been used to pave a literary path to Paris and Amsterdam and back – failed to reach contemporary readers.[15] With each year that passed the world that these old books described was fast becoming unrecognizable. And while the STN had helped to put Neuchâtelois printing on a permanent footing, it was watches, not written words, that would dominate the town's story henceforth. And so, as stocks of kites and swifts recovered in the wooded Jura mountains, the remarkable account books and letter collections of the STN remained forgotten and thought pulped in 'La Grande Rochette'.[16]

Appendix Essay – Decoding and Coding the French Book Trade

Folded inside many of the letters that Victor Durand sent back to Neuchâtel from his European sales tour of 1787 and 1788 were thin strips of paper filled with columns of sequentially rising numbers. Durand was not keeping tabs on his whist debts, but rather sending coded instructions to his Neuchâtel paymasters to forward specific books to various clients. While these orders were initially unfathomable, once the source of Durand's cipher had been located in the form of Louis Fauche Borel's trade catalogue of 1787, they actually proved the most precise in the entire archive. '112' meant the abbé Coyer's *Bagatelles morales* (Paris, 1769), '457' signified Tissot's *Essais sur les moyens de perfectionner les études de médecine* (Lausanne, 1785) and so forth. Every other instruction recorded during the STN's long history, by contrast, came wrapped in the softer codes of contemporary language and quotidian practice for which no crib sheets exist. Adrien-Marie-François de Verdy Du Vernois's *Essais de géographie, de politique et d'histoire, sur les possessions de l'empereur des Turcs en Europe*, for example, appears variously in the Society's accounts as 'Essai de géographie', 'Essai de géographie sur les Turcs' and 'Essais sur les Turcs' (as well as simply '443' when Durand was on his travels). In 1778 the STN referred to the first edition of Claude-Louis-Michel de Sacy's *Histoire générale de Hongrie* (Paris, 1778), logically enough, as 'Histoire de Hongrie'. A decade later 'Histoire de Hongrie' meant, equally naturally to those working in the print shop at the time, François Claude Le Roy de Lozembrune's *Histoire de la guerre de Hongrie*, published in Vienna in 1788.[1]

The 'Bookkeeping Made Simple' section described how the FBTEE project managed to solve the BPUN archive's greatest puzzle by locating a methodological pathway through the STN ledgers. By focusing upon core information common to many of the Society's surviving runs of account book – those dates and debtors and crediting accounts from the contemporary double-entry accounting system as described by La Porte – the essence of almost every book transaction made throughout the STNs history was recovered. But alone that torrent of 70,584 transactions linking oftentimes obscure client names like 'Mailly' to short book titles such as 'Anecdotes théâtrales' had limited value. For the data stream to facilitate arguments such as those that have been presented in this book, each client and book had to be identified and described in detail in the FBTEE database. 'Mailly' had to become Jean-Baptise Mailly, the bookseller that operated from the place *Saint Fiacre* in Dijon (DD: 47.320464, 5.040902), who corresponded with the STN between 1 June 1780 and 30 August 1783 (sending sixteen letters to the STN and receiving ten). And 'Anecdotes théâtrales' needed to be revealed as the single-volume octavo edition of Jean-Nicolas Servandoni's *Observations sur l'art du comédien*, published in Paris in 1775 by Costard and La Veuve Duchesne. This short methodological essay gives an overview of how that biographical and bibliographical work was achieved.

The process of identifying the larger part of the STN's business associations was relatively straightforward due to Jean Jeanprêtre's careful cataloguing of the archive.[2] During the late 1940s the retired Neuchâtelois chemist organized over 24,000 letters received by the STN into 2,387 separate dossiers. Each of the Society's contacts was given a unique dossier, within which his or her missives were arranged chronologically. On the cover of each dossier Jeanprêtre listed the correspondent's name, their life dates (where available), location, profession, the dates of their first and last letters to the STN, the total number of extant letters, whether those letters bore wax seals, and any further relevant information. The extraction and verification of all this information was a remarkable achievement for which the Neuchâtelois has rarely been given sufficient credit. To facilitate the enquiries of researchers, Jeanprêtre created a summary card index of these records, organized alphabetically by correspondent name, which still serves today as the primary public interface to the archive. At a later date, the BPUN produced MS1000a, a pared-down typed list of STN correspondents based upon Jeanprêtre's card index but (helpfully for certain researches) organized by correspondent location rather than name.[3]

The FBTEE project's own efforts to understand with whom the STN traded, then, began with the creation of a client database section sufficiently flexible to capture the details of both Jeanprêtre's card index and MS1000a. These two sources yielded rich information related to 2,387 STN correspondents, all of whom (whether booksellers or printers or candle makers) we considered *potential* suppliers or recipients of STN books. But because not everybody with whom the STN traded sent letters (or at least sent letters that have survived), new client details also had to be added to these tables as the FBTEE project developed. First, before the core task of working through the STN's transactions began, the indexes to the 'copie de lettres' series – ignored by Jeanprêtre – were plundered for information regarding all clients to which the STN wrote without ever receiving (surviving) responses.[4] This approach yielded 408 new individuals and businesses. And second, as the long process of adding the STNs transactions to the FBTEE database was carried out, the names, locations and supporting biographical details of any clients not already found in the database were added. During this stage, 172 clients were added to the data tables. Further, after this trawl through the STN's transactions was complete, the client data was analysed for potential duplications and anomalous cases. Over the course of the 1770s and 1780s, for example, several individuals migrated between different businesses, and a number of booksellers changed location, or operated from multiple places. The flexibility of the relational database designed in collaboration with Sarah Kattau allowed us to deal with such cases in sophisticated ways unavailable to Jeanprêtre and the compiler of MS1000a.[5]

Where the STN manuscripts give tens of thousands of transactions involving oftentimes obscure or ambiguous third parties like 'Manoury, Caen' or 'Fauche, fils aîné', then, the FBTEE database, wherever possible, identifies and locates these actual individuals and their businesses. Indeed, it does much more, for after the process of entering data from the archives was complete, the client records were significantly enhanced. To facilitate electronic mapping and geographic analysis, the precise locations of the towns, villages and hamlets that each individual or business called home were geolocated. The database records the latitude and longitude coordinates of 'Chalon-sur-Saône', for example, as DD: 46.784216, 4.852947. Each place was also located within regional and national boundaries, both contemporary and modern. So the town of Ferney is recognized in the data tables as being a constituent part of not only the modern department of Ain and eighteenth-century Burgundy, but also modern and ancient France. In addition, Jeanprêtre's professions data – which is riddled with ambiguous and context-dependent descriptions like 'secrétaire' or 'ministre' – was grouped into coherent trades (from beekeepers to publishers) and organized by economic sectors (such as 'agriculture' or 'print-related trades'). The resultant FBTEE client tables combine to form an important business database in their own right which can significantly extend the work of Inderwildi and others concerning the trade networks of STN.[6] Further, they offer a new gateway to the studying the Society's letters that is significantly more complete and flexible than either the BPUN's card index or MS1000a. And, most importantly for our purposes, they help the FBTEE database turn a bewildering stream of transactions into data sufficiently nuanced to allow us to better understand the functioning of the eighteenth-century European book trade.

This last point is only true, of course, because the thousands of obscure book titles revealed in the STN's transactions data stream have been treated with as much care and attention as the client names. When the Society recorded a transaction in its ledgers, the only element that was consistently given to indicate the book concerned was a version of its title. Other paratextual details like the name of the work's authors, its format, the number of printed sheets of which it comprised, and its price *sometimes* accompanied this title, but never with enough consistency to be relied upon. Alas, to save time and effort, almost all of the over 70,000 titles that the STN recorded were in shortened form, sometimes to the extent of obfuscation. So, as transactions were recorded in a hurry, the *Essai contre l'abus du pouvoir des souverains* became 'Essai sur l'abus' or 'Essai sur l'abus d'autorité', and Frédéric-Samuel Ostervald's *Cours abrégé de géographie historique* turned into 'géographie d'Ostervald' or simply 'géographie'. Elsewhere the STN described works variously by either their proper titles or subtitles, so d'Holbach's *Système social, ou Principes naturels de la morale et de la politique* was referred to variously throughout the ledgers as either 'Système social' or 'Principes de morale'. In many cases, indeed, even if we ignore frequent spelling errors and variations, the same edition of a book appears under five, six or more different titles. Gioacchino Bonaventura Argentero Brezé's *Observations historiques et critiques sur les commentaires de Folard et sur la cavalerie* is recorded throughout the STN manuscripts under its full title, as 'Brézé, ou observations sur Folard', as 'Brézé observations sur la cavalerie', as 'Brèze sur la cavalerie', as 'Essai sur la cavalerie de Folard', as 'Observations de Follard', as 'Observations sur la cavalerie', as '964', and, finally, as 'Brézé'.

The task of turning each entry from this torrent of dirty data into a full bibliographic expression of a specific edition of a particular book, then, was not straightforward. To begin, the database was seeded with the edition details of the works that the STN was known or suspected to have printed itself, using Michael Schmidt's bibliography as well as Jeanprêtre's manuscript notes and the RBNJ library catalogue.[7] Together these sources at least tentatively identify the significant majority of the STN's own titles (including those published in partnership with the STB and STL), which, of course, generated around two-thirds of the Society's total sales (although only 5% of the individual editions traded). At an early stage the details of about 2,000 further works traded, but not published, by the STN that were listed either in its surviving stock ledgers or published trade catalogues (which were in fact drawn up directly from their stock ledgers) were also added to the database. Although these sources fall short of modern bibliographical standards and could not always entirely be relied upon – the names of authors and publishers were almost never given, for example, and the STN only rarely attempted to look behind false places and dates of publication – they proved ample to provide the basis for records that could be clarified and enhanced later.

As each of the STN's 70,584 transactions were added to the FBTEE database, Sarah Kattau's custom designed data-entry software allowed for every manuscript 'short-title' to be associated with, where a clear match was assured, a known STN-traded edition. For each transaction a 'superbook' record containing only the core information of author and title – 'Voltaire, *Candide*' for example – was also added to the transactions data tables, to allow all STN-traded editions of particular books to be easily grouped together. Where a transaction entry in the manuscript gave a short-title that was sufficiently clear to allow a book to be identified, but not necessarily a specific edition, the 'superbook' information alone was entered. And where manuscript short titles were too ambiguous to allow for even basic identification, they were simply entered in the form that they appeared on the page. Any further information that could not immediately help identify an edition, but that none the less appeared relevant – perhaps the number of printed sheets that made up the book, or its octavo format – was also recorded on a transaction by transaction basis.

This phase of data entry, then, left the project with a stream of transactions associated with bibliographic records of disappointingly varied quality. But at the same time, by unveiling the source from where each traded work arrived in the STN's stock rooms, and by grouping together clues from across the archive, it provided the basis for a massive post-archival push to significantly enhance almost all of these records. Around a dozen new STN editions, as well as thirty books that Schmidt had only considered *possible* STN editions – including our *Histoire de François Wills* – were identified as having exited the Society's presses on the basis of the printing and dissemination data. The arrival of lots of perhaps 1,000 or 1,500 copies of these works into the STNs stocks from its printing shop's account, followed by their rapid dispatch to the Society's Swiss and extraterritorial networks, was a sure tell. It was also possible to extend Silvio Corsini's work on the editions that the STN published in collaboration with regional partners by tracing the dispatch or arrival of each individual volume of books like Mathieu-François Pidansat de Mairobert's *L'espion anglois* (Londres [Berne and Neuchâtel]: John Adamson [Société typographique de Berne and Société typographique de Neuchâtel], 1782–1783) as they left their respective presses. Further, the bibliographical details of most of those nearly 2,000 editions with which the database was seeded due to their presence in the STN stock or trade catalogues were fleshed out with the help of modern library catalogues (especially RBNJ and RERO) and resources like Corsini's Biblos 18. Here the task was largely confined to confirming and correcting false places and dates of publication, and adding missing information concerning authors, editors, publishers and so forth. Where the STN stock books give 'Imitation de Jésus Christ, 12. Lausanne, 1771' the FBTEE database now clarifies 'Thomas à Kempis, *L'imitation de Jésus Christ, ou le Kempis approprié à toutes les communions chrétiennes* (Lausanne: J. P. Heubach, 1771) trad. Pierre Poiret [original title – *The Imitation of Christ*; original language – English] 1 volume, in-12°, [2], 406pp'. and links to an full example of the edition available online.

Little about this work was out of the ordinary. But the extent to which it proved possible to group together and identify the vast majority of the thousands of complicated cases that still remained in the database – those transactions that gave nothing more than an obscure short title – *was* quite remarkable. By this stage in the process it was clear that successfully identified editions were generally accompanied by a coherent set of printing, purchase and sales datapoints. The purchase or printing of a certain number of copies of a particular edition was followed in the data tables by an equivalent series of dispatches, with predicted holdings usually corroborated by the STN's periodic stock take figures. Unexpected discrepancies in the transactions data associated with any given bibliographical entity, then, were key signs that the record perhaps needed to be merged with another. Little by little, by working through the records chronologically, and by focusing upon possible short title matches like 'Observations de Follard' and 'Brézé', our long list of unidentified short titles was forged into a coherent set of identified books traded by the STN. Further, the process of piecing together these records often revealed clues as to the actual edition being traded. Buying and restocking patterns strongly suggested that the STN were purchasing certain editions from their place of origin at the time of their publication (a fact that could be checked in the Society's correspondence); the number of transaction notes associated with each bibliographic entity dramatically increased as records were fused together; and even the short titles by which the STN referred to its book sometimes gave reason to suspect one particular edition rather than another. Once the edition was identified and corroborated it often proved possible, as had been the case with the STN's better-documented holdings, to flesh out the edition details using modern OPACs and scholarly bibliographies.

The project might, indeed, have gone still further with this bibliographical work were it not for the risk of creating a circular argument. Many of the major findings presented in the current volume – from the contemporaneousness of STN's trade to the reality that the Society largely traded Swiss books – are rooted firmly in our work identifying editions on the basis of the current bibliographical record. The statistical case offered in support of these conclusions is robust, I believe, because it was erected with enormous caution. Where any doubt existed, books were only identified as being from a particular place or publisher if direct manuscript evidence could be located. And yet, had the project attributed editions on the basis of the clear purchase patterns that emerged from the STN transactions – most notably of the Society's buying of works directly from their publishers in the year of their publication – still more records could have been enhanced. The database is packed with scores of 'London' editions, for example, that, following the logic of STN's purchasing habits were clearly printed in Romandy. For example, after both the STN manuscripts and modern bibliographical sources, the FBTEE database describes Mirabeau's *Essai sur le despotisme* (London, 1776) and Antoine-Marie Cerisier's *Le destin de l'Amerique* (London, 1780) as 'foreign editions'. The STN sales record and the physical and typographical attributes of the actual volumes, however, suggest otherwise. That labour, however, is for another day, for it would be inappropriate and confusing to here argue both that the bibliographic record suggests that the STN almost exclusively sold Swiss editions, *and* that the fact that the STN almost exclusively sold Swiss editions suggests that the bibliographic record is in need of substantial alteration.

What is clear, one hopes, is that even with these shortcomings the bibliographic tables of the FBTEE database are a marvel. Their 3,987 records represent the maximum known bibliographical information concerning every book or edition that appears in the STNs transaction records across the Society's entire trading history. Where the data proved possible to reconstruct, they record: edition type (e.g. STN-published edition), author(s), secondary author(s), editor(s), full book title, short (manuscript) book title(s), translated title, translated language, language, stated publisher, actual publisher, stated publication place, actual publication place, stated publication year, actual publication year, format, number of volumes, number of pages, number of printed sheets and notes. Ninety-four per cent of the distinct books that the STN traded have been identified by the project, 60 per cent to the highest levels of bibliographical detail. Because the missing works are invariably those that the STN seldom traded – those 'grammaire anglaise' and 'Mélanges du poésie' that appear once or twice in the records with no additional information – over 99 per cent of the STN transactions recorded in the FBTEE database are associated with a known book (and usually edition). In addition, each book has been tagged according to its presence in several contemporary and modern lists of illegal works, and categorized according to both eighteenth-century and modern taxonomic systems. Simon Burrows will discuss this particular labour of love further in this volume's twin.

In a sense, then, the FBTEE project gives its users not one database, but three. The first is a set of client tables that provide an unprecedented view of the STN's pan-European business networks. The second is a bibliographical databank that offers every last detail that we might hope to recover from the archive concerning each book that the STN traded. And the third, the heart of the FBTEE database, is a set of book transaction records that connect these rich information sets together. Every time the STN recorded a transaction it linked some French-reading client located somewhere in *ancien régime* Europe to a book that came from somewhere else. The FBTEE records 70,584 such transactions, representing the movement of 445,496 books. Alone, each of the database's three sections is of considerable scholarly value; together the three create a view of the history of the STN and its experiences trading French-language books on the eve of the French Revolution that should excite scholars for years to come.

Notes

Preface

1   BPUN STN MS 1009, Inventaire de la Société typographique en juin 1786 et juin 1787, à Neuchâtel et à l'étranger, 81.

Introduction

1   At the time of publication, the online database with its web-based user interface is hosted by the University of Western Sydney Digital Humanities Research Group at http://fbtee.uws.edu.au/main/. A customizable MySQL version of the database can be downloaded at http://fbtee.uws.edu.au/main/download-database/. Scholars should cite academic use of the FBTEE database as follows: Simon Burrows and Mark Curran, *The French Book Trade in Enlightenment Europe Database, 1769-1794* (http://fbtee.uws.edu.au/stn/interface/..., date accessed). Further citation instructions are available at http://fbtee.uws.edu.au/main/eula/#cites. The current volume makes such extensive use of the FBTEE database that query results are not cited individually.
2   The Leeds Electronic Text Centre (LETC) was a path-breaking digital humanities centre led by Peter Millican at the University of Leeds. It is hard to imagine how the FBTEE project might have got off the ground without the specialist support that the centre provided. The centre was, alas, disbanded in 2011 due to a lack of institutional backing.
3   For a detailed explanation of what is understood here by FBTEE project terms – clients, transactions, books, editions and so forth – see the online documentation that accompanies the FBTEE database interface, as well as the appendix to the current volume 'Decoding and Coding the French Book Trade'.
4   Between its launch on 25 June 2012 and 4 March 2015 the FTBEE database's online interface welcomed 10,000 unique visitors, who collectively clocked up 70,000 page impressions. A number of reviewers generously praised the database upon its appearance, including Jeremy Caradonna who considered it 'one of the best and most cutting-edge digital tools that historians of early modernity now possess'. See Jeremy L. Caradonna, 'The French Book Trade in Enlightenment Europe, 1769–1794', *French History* 27, no. 2 (2013): 286–7. The database won the British Society for Eighteenth-Century Studies Digital Prize in 2017.
5   Feedback from scholars that organized and attended the following conferences, at which the current author spoke, was essential to the development of the FBTEE project: The Society for the Study of French History Annual Conference (SSFH), June 2010, University of Newcastle; Material Cultures 2010: 'Technology, Textual-

ity, and Transmission', July 2010, University of Edinburgh; Society for the History of Authorship, Reading and Publishing Annual Conference (SHARP) 'Book History From Below', August 2010, University of Helsinki; Click on Knowledge Conference, May 2011, University of Copenhagen; The Library of Congress Public Lecture Series, July 2011, Library of Congress, Washington, DC; SHARP 'The Book in Art and Science', July 2011, Washington, DC; Intellectual Geography Conference, September 2011, University of Oxford; 'Books Beyond Boundaries', November 2011, Trinity College, Cambridge; Oxford Enlightenment Seminar Series, January 2012, University of Oxford; Cambridge Bibliographical Society Seminar Series, May 2012, Cambridge University Library; and SHARP 'The Battle for Books', June 2012, Trinity College Dublin.

6 See the current author's contribution to George Williams' blog post in the Chronicle of Higher Education ProfHacker blog, entitled 'Social History and Book History' http://chronicle.com/blogs/profhacker/social-media-and-book-history-sharp11-and-twitter/35009

7 See Matthew G. Kirschenbaum, *Mechanisms: New Media and the Forensic Imagination* (Cambridge, MA: MIT Press, 2008).

8 The major findings of the FBTEE project are revealed in this study and its companion volume, Simon Burrows, *Enlightenment Best-Sellers: The French Book Trade in Enlightenment Europe, Volume 2* (London: Bloomsbury, 2018).

9 See, especially, Robert Darnton, *The Forbidden Best-Sellers of pre-Revolutionary France* (New York and London: HarperCollins, 1995), xvii–xxiii; Robert Darnton, 'Trade in the Taboo: The Life of a Clandestine Book Dealer in Pre-revolutionary France', in *The Widening Circle: Essays on the Circulation of Literature in Eighteenth-century Europe*, ed. Paul J. Korshin (Philadelphia: University of Pennsylvania Press, 1976), 11–83 at 30–41.

10 Robert Darnton, 'The High Enlightenment and the Low-Life of Literature in Pre-Revolutionary France', *Past and Present* 51 (1971): 81–115; Robert Darnton, *The Business of Enlightenment: A Publishing History of the 'Encyclopédie', 1775-1800* (Cambridge, MA and London: Belknap Press, 1979).

11 See, especially, Jacques Rychner, 'Le travail de l'atelier', in *Histoire de l'édition française, t.ii: Le livre triomphant*, ed. Henri-Jean Martin, Roger Chartier and Jean-Pierre Vivet (Paris: Promodis, 1984), 42–61; Michel Schlup, 'La Société typographique de Neuchâtel et ses auteurs: rapports de force et affaires de dupes', in *Le rayonnement d'une maison d'édition dans l'Europe des Lumières: la Société typographique de Neuchâtel 1769-1789*, ed. Robert Darnton and Michel Schlup (Hauverive: Editions Gilles Attinger, 2005), 139–60; Frédéric Inderwildi, 'Acteurs et réseaux commerciaux dans la librairie d'Ancien Régime: la Société typographique de Neuchâtel, 1769-1789', unpublished PhD thesis, Université de Neuchâtel, 2010; and Louise Seaward, 'The French Government and the Policing of the Extra-Territorial Print Trade, 1770-1789', unpublished PhD thesis, University of Leeds, 2013.

12 See, particularly, the various contributions towards Michel Schlup, ed., *L'édition neuchâteloise au siècle des Lumières: la Société typographique de Neuchâtel (1769-1789)* (Neuchâtel: Bibliothèque publique et universitaire de Neuchâtel, 2002); Jeffrey Freedman, *Books Without Borders in Enlightenment Europe: French Cosmopolitanism and German Literary Markets* (Philadelphia: University of Pennsylvania Press, 2012). For many more such articles and book chapters, see the bibliography to the current volume.

13 See Michael Schmidt, 'Liste des impressions et éditions de la Société typographique de Neuchâtel', in *L'édition neuchâtelois au siècle des Lumières: la Société typographique*

de Neuchâtel (1769-1789), ed. Michel Schlup (Neuchâtel: Bibliothèque publique et universitaire de Neuchâtel, 2002), 233–85. Schmidt's bibliography of STN editions, an exceptional piece of scholarship, can be modestly clarified and extended using FBTEE project data.

14 See Darnton, *The Business of Enlightenment*; Alain Cernuschi, '"Notre grande entreprise des arts": aspects encyclopédiques de l'édition Neuchâteloise de la Description des arts et métiers', in *Le rayonnement d'une maison d'édition dans l'Europe des Lumières: la Société typographique de Neuchâtel 1769-1789*, ed. Michel Schlup and Robert Darnton (Hauterive: Editions Gilles Attinger, 2005), 185–218. The 'Geneva and Neuchâtel' *Encyclopédie* quartos were published between 1777 and 1779 by Joseph Duplain in Lyon, Charles-Joseph Pancoucke in Paris, the Société typographique de Neuchâtel, Clément Plomteux in Liège, Gabriel Regnault in Lyon and other partners.

15 The most notable exception to this rule, of course, is the use of the STN order books in Robert Darnton, *The Corpus of Clandestine Literature in France, 1769-1789* (New York and London: Norton, 1995). On Darnton's use of these books see below, and Mark Curran, 'Beyond the Forbidden Best-Sellers of pre-Revolutionary France', *Historical Journal* 56, no. 1 (2013): 89–112.

16 The archive also contains around 15,000 copies of letters sent by the STN to its clients around Europe, but these have seldom been exploited because they are neither listed in the BPUN card index nor BPUN STN MS 1000a, Société typographique [de Neuchâtel], correspondants, répertoire géographique. An index of these 'out' letters is now available for the first time in the FBTEE database.

17 On the history of the STN see Michel Schlup, 'La Société typographique de Neuchâtel (1769-1789): Points de repère', in *L'édition neuchâteloise au siècle des Lumières: la Société typographique de Neuchâtel (1769-1789)*, ed. Michel Schlup (Neuchâtel: Bibliothèque publique et universitaire de Neuchâtel, 2002), 61–105; Jean Jeanprêtre, 'Histoire de la Société typographique de Neuchâtel, 1769-1798', *Musée neuchâtelois* 1949: 70–9, 115–20, 48–53. Schlup's study is an updated and extended version of Jeanprêtre's account. While extremely valuable both, as overviews, are short and uneven in their coverage of events.

18 Lucien Febvre and Henri-Jean Martin, *L'apparition du livre* (Paris: A. Michel, 1958–9); Bertrum H. MacDonald and Fiona A. Black, 'Using GIS for Spatial and Temporal Analyses in Print Culture Studies: Some Opportunities and Challenges', *Social Science History* 24, no. 3 (2000): 505–36. On historical geography and GIS see also David J. Bodenhamer, John Corrigan and Trevor M. Harris, eds., *Deep Maps and Spatial Narratives* (Bloomington: Indiana University Press, 2015); Ian N. Gregory and A. Geddes, *Toward Spatial Humanities: Historical GIS and Spatial History* (Bloomington: Indiana University Press, 2014); Miles Ogborn and Charles W. J. Withers, *Geographies of the Book* (Farnham: Ashgate, 2010); Innes M. Keighren, *Bringing Geography to Book: Ellen Semple and the Reception of Geographical Knowledge* (London: I. B. Tauris, 2010); and Owen Gingerich, *The Book Nobody Read: Chasing the Revolutions of Nicolaus Copernicus* (New York: Walker, 2004).

19 Many of the techniques that McDonald and Black's article discusses were pioneered by the excellent University of Toronto based *History of the Book in Canada/Histoire du livre et de l'imprimé au Canada* project. For further relevant reading on the quantification of early modern trade networks see also Elizabeth L. Eisenstein, *The Printing Revolution in Early Modern Europe* (Cambridge: Cambridge University Press, 2005), 14; Harold Adams Innis, *The Bias of Communication* (Toronto: University of Toronto

Press, 1951); Edmund Snow Carpenter and Marshall McLuhan, eds., *Explorations in Communication: An Anthology* (Boston: Beacon Press, 1960); and Alexis Weedon, 'The Uses of Quantification', in *A Companion to the History of the Book*, ed. Simon Eliot and Jonathan Rose (London: Wiley-Blackwell, 2009), 33–49.

20 Thierry Rigogne, *Between State and Market: Printing and Bookselling in Eighteenth-century France* (Oxford: Voltaire Foundation, 2007).

21 If the work of Rigogne and others gives a good overall impression of the shape of France's printing and bookselling networks, it is nonetheless regrettable that equivalents of neither the British Book Trade Index (BBTI) nor the English Short Title Catalogue (ESTC) exist to cover eighteenth-century France. On printing and bookselling in late-*ancien régime* France see Gilles Eboli, *Livres et lecteurs en Provence au XVIIIe siècle: autour des David, imprimeurs-libraires à Aix* (Méolans-Revel: Atelier Perrousseaux, 2008); Jean Quéniart, *L'imprimerie et la librairie à Rouen au XVIIIe siècle* (Paris: C. Klincksieck, 1969); Suzanne Tucoo-Chala, *Charles-Joseph Panckoucke et la librairie française, 1736-1798* (Pau: Marrimpouey jeune, 1977); Brigitte Bacconnier, 'Cent ans de librairie au siècle des Lumières: les Duplain', Unpublished PhD thesis, Université Lumière Lyon, 2007; Frédéric Barbier, *Lumières du Nord: imprimeurs, libraires et 'gens du livre' dans le Nord au XVIIIe siècle (1701-1789): dictionnaire prosopographique* (Geneva: Droz, 2002); René Moulinas, *L'imprimerie, la librairie et la presse à Avignon au XVIIIe siècle* (Grenoble: Presses Universitaires de Grenoble, 1974); Robert Estivals, *La statistique bibliographique de la France sous la monarchie, au XVIIIe siècle* (Paris: Editions de l'EHESS, 1965); and François Furet, 'La « librairie » du royaume de France au 18e siècle', in *Livre et société dans la France du XVIIIe siècle*, ed. François Furet, vol. 1 (Paris: Mouton et Cie, 1965), 3–32.

22 No comprehensive history of either Swiss or Dutch printing in this period yet exists. On Dutch publishing see, especially, Arianne Baggerman, *Publishing Policies and Family Strategies: The Fortunes of a Dutch Publishing House in the 18th and early 19th Centuries* (Leiden and Boston: Brill, 2013); C. Berkvens-Stevelinck, Hans Bots, P.G. Hoftijzer and O.S. Lankhorst, eds., *Le magasin de l'univers: The Dutch Republic as the centre of the European book trade* (Leiden and New York: Brill, 1992); Lotte Hellinga, *The Bookshop of the World: The Role of the Low Countries in the Book-trade, 1473-1941* (Goy-Houten: Hes & De Graaf, 2001); Elizabeth L. Eisenstein, *Grub Street Abroad: Aspects of the French Cosmopolitan Press from the Age of Louis XIV to the French Revolution* (Oxford: Clarendon Press, 1992); Graham C. Gibbs, 'The Role of the Dutch Republic as the Intellectual Entrepôt of Europe in the Seventeenth and Eighteenth Centuries', *Bijdragen en Mededelingen betreffende de Geschiedenis der Nederlanden* 86 (1971): 323–49; and Jonathan I. Israel, *The Dutch Republic: Its Rise, Greatness and Fall, 1477-1806* (Oxford: Clarendon Press, 1995). For the Swiss case see, especially, Inderwildi, 'Acteurs et réseaux commerciaux dans la librairie d'Ancien Régime'; Silvio Corsini, *Le livre à Lausanne, cinq siècles d'édition et d'imprimerie, 1493-1993* (Lausanne: Payot, 1993); Georges Bonnant, *Le livre genevois sous l'ancien régime* (Geneva: Droz, 1999); Giles Barber, 'The Cramers of Geneva and their Trade in Europe between 1755 and 1766', *SVEC* XXX (1964): 377–413; and Jean-Pierre Perret, *Les imprimeries d'Yverdon au XVIIe et au XVIIIe siècle* (Lausanne: F. Roth, 1945). For further reading, see the bibliography that accompanies this volume.

23 See Giles Barber, 'French Royal Decrees Concerning the Book-Trade, 1700-1789', *Australian Journal of French Studies* 3 (1966): 312–30; Furet, 'La « librairie » du royaume de France au 18e siècle'; Raymond Birn, *La censure royale des livres dans la France*

des lumières (Paris: Odile Jacob, 2007); Robert L. Dawson, *Confiscations at Customs: Banned Books and the French Booktrade During the Last Years of the Ancien Régime* (Oxford: SVEC, 2006).

24 In its focus upon how books flowed around networks, the FBTEE project shares something in common with Stanford University's 'Mapping the Republic of Letters' project, led by Nicole Coleman, Dan Edelstein and Paula Findlen. Ball State University's pioneering and exceptional 'What Middleton Read' database, which documents books borrowed by the patrons of the Muncie (Indiana) Public Library between 1891 and 1902, also describes flows of books, albeit on a local scale.

25 For definitions of terms and further explanations of these figures, see the materials that accompany the online FBTEE database interface and the appendix 'Decoding and Coding the French Book Trade'.

26 See Darnton, *Forbidden Best-Sellers*, 52–7.

27 On the circulation of information outside of books see, especially, Arlette Farge, *Dire et mal dire. L'opinion publique au XVIIIe siècle* (Paris: Le Seuil, 1992); Sarah C. Maza, *Private Lives and Public Affairs: The Causes Célèbres of Prerevolutionary France* (Berkeley and London: University of California Press, 1993); Jeremy L. Caradonna, *The Enlightenment in Practice: Academic Prize Contests and Intellectual Culture in France, 1670-1794* (Ithaca: Cornell University Press, 2012); and Jack R. Censer, *The French Press in the Age of Enlightenment* (London: Routledge, 1994). On attempts to define book history and place the discipline in this wider world of information culture, see Robert Darnton, 'What is the History of Books?' *Daedalus* 11, no. 3 (1982): 65–83; Robert Darnton, '"What is the History of Books?" Revisited', *Modern Intellectual History* 4, no. 3 (2007): 495–508; G. Thomas Tanselle, *Literature and Artifacts* (Charlottesville: Bibliographical Society of the University of Virginia, 1998), 41–55; and John P. Feather, 'The Book in History and the History of the Book', in *The History of Books and Libraries: Two Views*, ed. John P. Feather and David McKitterick (Washington: Library of Congress, 1986), 1–16.

28 This quote is attributed to the Mannheim bookseller Christian Friedrich Schwan. See Pamela E. Selwyn, *Everyday Life in the German Book Trade: Friedrich Nicolai as Bookseller and Publisher in the Age of Enlightenment, 1750-1810* (University Park: Pennsylvania State University Press, 2000), 15.

29 See Simon Burrows, *Blackmail, Scandal, and Revolution: London's French libellistes, 1758-92* (Manchester: Manchester University Press, 2006); Robert Darnton, *The Devil in the Holy Water, or the Art of Slander from Louis XIV to Napoleon* (Philadelphia: University of Pennsylvania Press, 2010).

30 The current volume owes a great debt to frameworks of understanding provided by a number of important works of book history not specifically or exclusively focused on France and/or the Enlightenment period, most notably James Raven, *The Business of Books: Booksellers and the English Book Trade, 1450-1850* (New Haven and London: Yale University Press, 2007); Adrian Johns, *The Nature of the Book: Print and Knowledge in the Making* (Chicago: University of Chicago Press, 1998); David McKitterick, *Print, Manuscript, and the Search for Order, 1450-1830* (Cambridge: Cambridge University Press, 2003); Elizabeth L. Eisenstein, *The Printing Press as an Agent of Change: Communications and Cultural Transformations in Early-modern Europe* (Cambridge: Cambridge University Press, 1979); Fredson Bowers, *Principles of Bibliographical Description* (Princeton: Princeton University Press, 1949); and Philip Gaskell, *A New Introduction to Bibliography* (Oxford: Clarendon Press, 1972).

Chapter 1

1 William Coxe, *Sketches of the State of Swisserland* (London: J. Dodsley, 1779), 273–7. Neuchâtel was governed by Prussia between 1707 and 1848.
2 See Jonathan Lamb, 'Fantasies of Paradise', in *The Enlightenment World*, ed. Martin Fitzpatrick, Peter Jones, Christa Knellwolf and Iain McCalman (London and New York: Pickering & Chatto, 2007), 521–35.
3 Frédéric-Samuel Ostervald, *Description des montagnes et des vallées qui font partie de la principauté de Neuchâtel et Valangin* (Neuchâtel: Samuel Fauche, 1766), 94–5.
4 The FTBEE database shows that by 9 September 1776 the STN had dispatched 93,860 books; the Society's 30 November 1776 stocktake recorded 33,978 copies of 527 different works present in the stock room. Although every care has been taken to ensure their accuracy, partial volume sales, lacunae in the sources and particularities of the FBTEE project's methodological approach combine to ensure that all statistics given in this volume are subject to slight margins of error. For further information, see Chapter 2, 'Bookkeeping made Simple' and the appendix essay 'Decoding and Coding the French Book Trade', as well as the documents and materials that accompany the online database interface.
5 William Coxe, *Essai sur l'état présent, naturel, civil et politique de la Suisse: ou lettres adressées à Guillaume Melmoth, écuyer* ([Lausanne]: François Grasset, 1781).
6 See Paul Louis Pelet, *Le Canal d'Entreroches, histoire d'une idée* (Lausanne: F. Rouge, 1946).
7 Further, Robert Estivals' statistical work on book production in France suggests that from around 1770 the overall market for French books entered a phase of rapid expansion that continued until the end of the nineteenth century. See Estivals, *La statistique bibliographique*, 410.
8 On this point, see especially, Eisenstein, *Grub Street Abroad*.
9 Jean-Daniel Candaux, 'Imprimeurs et libraires dans la Suisse des Lumières', in *Le rayonnement d'une maison d'édition dans l'Europe des Lumières: la Société typographique de Neuchâtel 1769–1789*, ed. Michel Schlup and Robert Darnton (Hauterive: Editions Gilles Attinger, 2005), 51–68 at 64–66.
10 Louis Dutens, *Itinéraire des routes les plus fréquentées, ou journal d'un voyage aux villes principales de l'Europe, en 1768, 1769, 1770, 1771, & 1777* (London: William Faden, 1779), 160–1.
11 This calculation is based upon the FBTEE database 'lower territories' of Basle (including the Bishopric of Basle), Berne, Burgundy, Fribourg, Geneva and Lyon.
12 When the letters of the STN archive were first catalogued, the profession of each correspondent was determined. See the chapter 'Bookkeeping Made Simple' and the appendix essay 'Coding and Decoding the French Book Trade'. The FBTEE project has grouped these professions into 'economic sectors'. 'Book trade professionals' includes printers, booksellers and engravers employed directly by the industry; 'retail commerce and manufacturing' includes all types of merchants and shopkeepers; 'print-related trades' includes ink makers, paper makers and book binders; 'Post, transport and hospitality' includes innkeepers, postal clerks and coachmen. For a complete list of constituent terms of each 'economic sector', see the FBTEE database online interface.
13 'Men of letters' are here defined as those that generally described themselves by their literary or academic interest (astronomers, mathematicians and writers, for example); 'professionals' includes doctors, magistrates and tutors; 'office holders' range from councillors to ambassadors to princes.

14 Ostervald, *Description des montagnes*, 12, 15, 16.
15 Phillipe Henry, 'Le pays de Neuchâtel à l'époque de la naissance de la STN', in *Le rayonnement d'une maison d'édition dans l'Europe des Lumières: la Société typographique de Neuchâtel 1769–1789*, ed. Robert Darnton and Michel Schlup (Hauterive: Editions Gilles Attinger, 2005), 33–49 at 43.
16 Henry, 'Le pays de Neuchâtel à l'époque de la naissance de la STN', 46.
17 Michel Schlup, ed., *Le mangeur Neuchâtelois et quelques voisins au temps des Lumières (1730–1800)* (Neuchâtel: Bibliothèque publique et universitaire de Neuchâtel, 2003), 119–25.
18 William Coxe, *Travels in Switzerland: In a Series of Letters to William Melmoth*, vol. 1 (London: T. Cadell, 1789), 467.
19 The population of Neuchâtel expanded only negligibly during the first half of the eighteenth century, and then increased from 32,000 in 1760 to 46,000 in 1806. See Henry, 'Le pays de Neuchâtel à l'époque de la naissance de la STN', 41.
20 André Bandelier, 'La clientèle Neuchâteloise et Jurassienne de la STN', in *Le rayonnement d'une maison d'édition dans l'Europe des Lumières: la Société typographique de Neuchâtel 1769–1789*, ed. Robert Darnton and Michel Schlup (Hauterive: Editions Gilles Attinger, 2005), 317–40 at 323.
21 Michel Schlup, 'Aperçu de l'imprimerie et de l'édition Neuchâteloise avant 1769', in *L'édition neuchâteloise au siècle des Lumières: la Société typographique de Neuchâtel (1769–1789)*, ed. Michel Schlup (Neuchâtel: Bibliothèque publique et universitaire de Neuchâtel, 2002), 29–37.
22 Schlup, 'Aperçu de l'imprimerie et de l'édition Neuchâteloise avant 1769', 55.
23 The STN began trading with three printing presses, bought from the Veuve Droz in August 1769 for 3,700.0.0 *livres* de France. Its initial premises were a crowded and inexpensive second-floor suite of small rooms off the *rue des Moulins*, the medieval street that ran parallel to the river Seyon through the centre of Neuchâtel. See Inderwildi, 'Acteurs et réseaux commerciaux', 343.
24 Lucien Paul Victor Febvre and Henri-Jean Martin, *The Coming of the Book: The Impact of Printing, 1450–1800*, trans. David E. Gerard, ed. David Wootton and Geoffrey Nowell-Smith (London: N.L.B., 2010), 115.
25 The few surviving eighteenth-century scraps of the archives of Cambridge University Press, for example, demonstrate the financial importance of large orders of prayer books from the university's various colleges. See CUL, Archives of Cambridge University Press, GBR/0265/Pr.
26 Selwyn, *Everyday Life in the German Book Trade*, 32.
27 A fourth director, Jonas-Pierre Berthoud, also initially injected capital into the STN. Berthoud, however, pulled out of the Society on 12 March 1770, when he was credited 420.0.0 *livres* for his troubles and saw his initial investment refunded. See BPUN STN MS 1033, Brouillard A du 27 juillet 1769 au 3 février 1773, 21; Jeanprêtre, 'Histoire de la Société typographique de Neuchâtel', 72.
28 These included *Les rudimens, ou Les premiers principes de la langue latine* (Neuchâtel: Samuel Fauche, 1763); Jean Alphonse Turrettini, *Abrégé de l'histoire ecclésiastique depuis la naissance de Jésus-Christ jusqu'à l'an MDCC* (Neuchâtel: Samuel Fauche, 1765); and Jean-Frédéric Ostervald, *Abrégé de l'histoire sainte et du catéchisme* (Neuchâtel: Samuel Fauche, 1760).
29 Schlup, 'Points de repère', 69–70.
30 Fauche continued to trade for his own account, although some of his stocks appear to have been ceded around 1770 to his brother-in-law Jean-Pierre Convert, who established a *cabinet littéraire* in Neuchâtel.

31 Ostervald, *Description des montagnes*, 3–6.
32 Alongside his history of the region, Ostervald also produced: Frédéric-Samuel Ostervald, *Cours de géographie élémentaire* (Neuchâtel: Société typographique de Neuchâtel, 1770); Frédéric-Samuel Ostervald, *Cours abrégé de géographie historique* (Neuchâtel: Société typographique de Neuchâtel, 1770); and Frédéric-Samuel Ostervald, *Les loix, us et coutumes de la souveraineté de Neuchâtel et Valangin* (Neuchâtel: Samuel Fauche père & fils, 1785). Under his stewardship, the STN also published editions of the internationally popular biblical commentaries of his uncle, Jean-Frédéric Ostervald.
33 See, for example, BPUN STN MS 1050, Carnet pour les ouvriers (Banque des ouvriers), 9 août 1769 à février 1774, 4, 7, 90–1. As time progressed, the STN tended to group all such printing jobs together and account for them simply under the rubric 'divers petites ouvrages', without giving further details of their nature. They cannot, as such, be studied systematically aside from, where the STN daybooks survive, by their combined price. See the chapter 'Bookkeeping Made Simple'.
34 Schlup, 'Points de repère', 68–9.
35 Darnton, *The Business of Enlightenment*, 376–81; Cernuschi, 'Notre grande entreprise des arts'.
36 Cernuschi, 'Notre grande entreprise des arts', 186–91.
37 Elie and Jean-Elie Bertrand are, still today, often confused in the bibliographical record. For correct attributions, see Charles Berthoud, 'Les deux Bertrand', *Musée neuchâtelois* 7 (1870); Schmidt, 'Liste des impressions'. The STN's 'Bertrand' works included Elie Bertrand, *Elémens d'oryctologie, ou Distribution méthodique des fossiles* (Neuchâtel: Société typographique de Neuchâtel, 1773); Elie Bertrand, *La morale évangélique, ou Discours sur le sermon de Jésus-Christ sur la montagne* (Neuchâtel: Société typographique de Neuchâtel, 1775); Elie Bertrand, *Essai philosophique et moral sur le plaisir* (Neuchâtel: Société typographique de Neuchâtel, 1777); Elie Bertrand, *Le Thévenon, ou Les journées de la montagne* (Neuchâtel: Société typographique de Neuchâtel, 1777); and Jean-Elie Bertrand, *Sermons sur différens textes de l'Ecriture-Sainte* (Neuchâtel: Société typographique de Neuchâtel, 1779).
38 BPUN STN MS 1095, Copies de Lettres A, 8. See also Inderwildi, 'Acteurs et réseaux commerciaux', 6.
39 The *subdélégues* that responded to a state survey of France's book trade conducted in 1764, admittedly fearful that the axe might fall in their patch, consistently stressed how indispensable printing was to local life. See Rigogne, *Between State and Market*, 186–7.
40 Jean-Pierre Jelmini, 'Politique intérieure et extérieure de Neuchâtel, de 1707 à la veille de la Révolution française', in *Histoire du Pays de Neuchâtel: De la Reforme à 1815* (Hauterive: Attinger, 1991), 91–105 at 100–3. On the affair, see also Olivier Petitpierre, ed., *Histoire abrégée des troubles de Neuchâtel pendant les années 1766, 1767, et 1768, suivie de divers autres documens historiques* (Neuchâtel: Petitpierre et Prince, 1832).
41 Robert Darnton, 'Two Paths Through the Social History of Ideas', in *The Darnton Debate*, ed. H. T. Mason (Oxford: Voltaire Foundation, 1998), 251–94; Darnton, *The Business of Enlightenment*, 40; and Eisenstein, *Grub Street Abroad*.
42 BPUN STN MS 1095, 8.
43 The dates used throughout this volume to define the trading periods illustrated in Figure 1.2, for reasons explained in detail in this chapter and in Chapter 4, 'The Storm Will Pass', are: 1 July 1769 (the establishment of the STN) to 30 September

1771; 1 October 1771 (the decision to sell third-party works) – 26 January 1780; 27 January 1780 (the beginning of the period of displaced distribution printing) – 7 July 1784; 8 July 1784 (the date of the 'Acte de cautionnement' that dictated the terms of the STN's liquidation) to 19 November 1788; and 20 November 1788 (the end of Victor Durand's tour of Europe) to 28 October 1794.

44 See BPUN STN MS 1033, 70, 80, 97.
45 Jean-Frédéric Ostervald, *Abrégé de l'histoire sainte et du catéchisme* (Neuchâtel: Socété typographique de Neuchâtel, 1771); Heinrich Heidegger, *Reflexions d'un Suisse sur cette question: seroit-il avantageux aux cantons catholiques d'abolir les ordres réguliers, ou tout au moins de les diminuer?* (Neuchâtel: Société typographique de Neuchâtel, 1769).
46 Francesco Algarotti, *Lettres du comte Algarotti sur la Russie* (Neuchâtel: Société typographique de Neuchâtel, 1770).
47 Francesco Algarotti, *Saggio di lettere sopra la Russia* (Paris: G. Briasson, 1760).
48 *Année littéraire* 1768, VIII, 169–80; *Mercure de France*, January 1769, 65–69; *Journal des Beaux Arts*, June 1769, 478–87; *Journal de Sçavans*, December 1769, 812–4.
49 *Nouveau Journal helvétique*, October, 428–40; November, 775–582.
50 Inderwildi, 'Acteurs et réseaux commerciaux', 343.
51 See the chapter 'The Triumph of Benevolence' below.
52 BPUN STN MS 1033, 19, 27, 38, 39, 63, 71, 86.
53 Ibid., 86, 94.
54 Ibid. Boubers took his 500 copies of *Système de la nature* from the STN for 1 *sol* per sheet, or 2.17.6 *livres* for each two-volume set comprising of 57.5 sheets. Generally the STN thereafter sold the work for four *livres* although the highest achieved price was six *livres* each for five copies sent to the hatter Renaud in Besançon on 25 June 1771.
55 On the dissemination of the STN's edition of *Système de la nature* see, Mark Curran, 'Mettons toujours Londres: Enlightened Christianity and the Public in Pre-revolutionary Francophone Europe', *French History* 24, no. 1 (2010): 40–59. On the wider affair, see Charly Guyot, 'Imprimeurs et pasteurs neuchâtelois: l'affair du Système de la nature 1771', *Musée nuechâtelois* 1946: 74–81, 108–16; Schlup, 'Points de repère', 70–7; Robert Darnton, 'The Life-Cycle of a Book: A Publishing History of d'Holbach's Système de la nature', in *Publishing and Readership in Revolutionary France and America*, ed. Carol Armbruster (Westport, CT: Greenwood Press, 1993), 15–43.
56 Voltaire, 'Letter to Frederick II, king of Prussia, 21 August 1771' in Robert McNamee, et al. (eds.) *Electronic Enlightenment* Vers. 2.3. (Oxford: University of Oxford, 2011), at http://www.e-enlightenment.com/item/voltfrVF1220057b_1key001cor/
57 Schlup, 'Points de repère', 74.
58 BPUN STN MS 1033, 80. See also BPUN STN MS 1103, Copies des Lettres F, 305.
59 The STN shipped 1,000 copies of a 'discours préliminaire' to the 'Tableau de la Monarchie française' to Louis-Valentin Goëzman on 20 January 1771 followed by the entire 1,000 copy print run of the work itself on 7 May 1771.
60 Schlup, 'Points de repère', 70–2.
61 BPUN STN MS 1033, 114.
62 Part of the text of this exceptional work is reproduced and discussed at length in Darnton, *Forbidden Best-Sellers*, 115–36, 300–36.
63 Barthélemy Chirol in Geneva, for example, offered the STN an extensive list of works in a letter dated 13 June 1770, but the Society declined to establish a trading relationship. See BPUN STN MS 1135, Dossier Barthelemy Chirol, 221 (Chriol to

STN, 13 June 1770). Throughout 1771 Chirol continued to offer dozens of titles to the STN, but it was not until the spring of 1772 that the Society began trading books with the Genevan and his then partner Claude Philibert.

64 BPUN STN MS 1033, 205, 19, 45, 68, 78, 81, 82, 88, 95.
65 Samuel Fauche quickly strengthened his own bookselling business, and published at least twenty-five books between his expulsion from the STN and the end of the 1770s. Many of his editions, most notably the *Oeuvres d'histoire naturelle et de philosophie de Charles Bonnet* (Neuchâtel: Samuel Fauche, 1779–83) were highly accomplished. See, Michel Schlup, 'Etude d'un processus éditorial et typographique: l'impression des œuvres de Charles Bonnet par Samuel Fauche, 1777–1783', in *Aspects du livre neuchâtelois*, ed. Jacques Rychner and Michel Schlup (Neuchâtel: Bibliothèque publique et universitaire de Neuchâtel, 1983), 271–335. During the 1780s, as several of Fauche's sons entered the bookselling and publishing business, the output of the Fauche family rivalled and eventually surpassed that of the STN in terms of both volume and quality.
66 The following eleven clients exchanged large numbers of works with the STN during this period. Neuchâtel – Samuel Fauche; Lausanne – Gabriel Décombaz, François Grasset, Jean-Pierre Heubach, Jules-Henri Pott and Company, Société typographique de Lausanne; Berne – Société typographique de Berne; Geneva – Isaac Bardin, Jean-Samuel Cailler, Jean Abram Nouffer (including his various partnerships), Claude Philibert and Barthélemy Chirol.
67 On average, between 1772 and 1780 the STN brought in 7,736 books each year while it sold 17,285.
68 BPUN STN MS 1025, Copie de comptes C, 20.
69 Patricia Hernlund, 'William Strahan's Ledgers: Standard Charges for Printing, 1738–1785', *Studies in Bibliography* 20 (1967): 89–111 at 95.
70 BPUN STN MS 1034, Brouillard B, 328–48. For accounting purposes, the STN valued its own printed sheets at their 7 ½ *deniers* per sheet cost value, rather than the 1 *sol* per sheet that they hoped to achieve when selling. The illustrated prints of the *Descriptions des arts et métiers* were valued at 1 *sol* 7 ½ *deniers* apiece.
71 Selwyn, *Everyday Life in the German Book Trade*, 8.
72 *Catalogue général des livres qui se trouvent chez Barde, Manget & comp. imprimeurs-libraires à Genève* (Geneva: Barde, Manget & company, 1789).
73 *Catalogus von Alten und Neuen Büchen welche vor beygesetztem billigen Preiß zu haben sind bey Christoph Gottlieb Nicolai Buchhändlern in Berlin* (1737).
74 Inderwildi, 'Acteurs et réseaux commerciaux', 216.
75 Bonnant, *Le livre genevois*, 112. Bonnant's use of the word 'clients' is ambiguous, making a direct comparison here difficult.
76 Rigogne, *Between State and Market*, 132.
77 Darnton, *The Business of Enlightenment*, 137.
78 Inderwildi, 'Acteurs et réseaux commerciaux', 117–8.
79 Selwyn, *Everyday Life in the German Book Trade*, 159, 85.
80 The statistics given here were calculated by combining the FBTEE database French 'lower territories' of Rouen, Amiens, Lille, Paris, Soissons and Valenciennes; the Austrian Netherlands; the United Provinces; Liège; Cleves; and London, the only English town with which the STN corresponded or traded.
81 See especially, Inderwildi, 'Acteurs et réseaux commerciaux', 119–20.
82 BPUN STN MS 1034, 363–5.
83 Ibid., 354–62.
84 Ibid., 366.

85 Philippe Godet, ed., *Histoire littéraire de la Suisse française* (Neuchâtel and Paris: Delachaux et Niestlé: Fischbacher, 1890), 364.
86 On the rediscovery of the STN archives, see Michel Schlup, 'L'achat mouvementé des papiers de la Société typographique de Neuchâtel (1931-1932)', in *L'édition neuchâtelois au siècle des Lumières: la Société typographique de Neuchâtel (1769-1789)*, ed. Michel Schlup (Neuchâtel: Bibliothèque publique et universitaire de Neuchâtel, 2002), 171-7.
87 Archives d'État de Genève (AEG), Commerce F57, Grand livre de Gabriel et Philibert Cramer, 1755-67.
88 AEG, Commerce F61-63, Copie de lettres H.A. Gosse & Cie. See Giles Barber, *Studies in the Booktrade of the European Enlightenment* (London: Pindar Press, 1994), 176. Gosse's surviving letters are largely addressed to Italian clients, although the collection does include missives sent to individuals based in Switzerland, France, Portugal, Holland and Germany.
89 BHVP MS Na 490 (1-8). The eight volumes are as follows: 1. 'Journal de Province' (day book) 2 January 1765-7 February 1766, 200ff.; 2. 'Journal de Province' 20 January 1768-23 December 1768, 252ff.; 3. 'Journal de Province 8 June 1776-5 November 1778', 245ff.; 4. 'Extrait de Province' (client accounts) 1 January 1773-c. 12 May 1778, 299ff.; 5. 'Journal de Province' 5 April 1783-29 December 1786, 235ff.; 6. 'Journal de Paris' (local day book) 27 April 1771-27 October 1773, 204ff.; 7. 'Journal de Paris' 29 October 1773-7 August 1776, 224ff.; and 8. 'Journal de Paris' 3 June 1780-2 July 1787, 212ff.
90 The archive is available in two separate microfiche series as 'International Book Trade in the 18th Century: The Luchtmans Archive, 1697-1845'. Part I, Booksellers' Accounts (346 microfiches) and Part II, Private Accounts and other documents (473 microfiches) (Lisse: MMF Publications, Leiden, 1993). The microfiches are accompanied by a modern index of clients that runs until 1760, but was thereafter abandoned. Although the archive is used comparatively in this study, it is still to be mined systematically.
91 CUL, Archives of Cambridge University Press, GBR/0265/Pr. For a history of the press during the long eighteenth century, see David McKitterick, *A History of Cambridge University Press. Volume 2, Scholarship and Commerce 1698-1872* (Cambridge: Cambridge University Press, 1998). The John Murray Archive, held at the National Library of Scotland, includes continuous letter books of outgoing correspondence that run contemporaneously with the STN. See NLS, The John Murray Archive, MS.41896 – MS.41906 (11 October 1765-3 August 1769; 6 March 1769-21 February 1771; 26 February 1771-19 April 1773; 19 April 1773-22 November 1774; 5 December 1774-22 December 1775; 23 December 1775-26 November 1777; 27 November 1777-23 June 1779; 29 June 1779-15 June 1782; 20 June 1782-16 January 1786; 21 January 1786-16 May 1791; 24 May 1791-27 January 1802). On the Murray archive, see William Zachs, *The First John Murray and the Late Eighteenth-Century London Book Trade* (Oxford: Oxford University Press, 1998).
92 See Raven, *The Business of Books*, 297-8. The four surviving Bowyer legers and associated papers are available in an edited hardcover and microfiche edition as Keith Maslen and John Lancaster (eds.) *The Bowyer Ledgers: The Printing Accounts of William Bowyer, Father and Son* (London and New York: The Bibliographical Society and The Bibliographical Society of America, 1991). On the Ackers firm, see F. McKenzie and J. C. Ross, eds., *A Ledger of Charles Ackers, Printer of the London Magazine* (Oxford: Oxford Bibliographical Society, 1968). Twelve volumes of Strahan's business records – which include day books, cashbooks and inventories and form an unbroken series of transactions between 1738 and 1790 – are extant in the British Library

and the American Philosophical Society Library in Philadelphia. See Hernlund, 'William Strahan's Ledgers', 89–111.
93 Arianne Baggerman, *Een lot uit de loterij: het wel en wee van een uitgeversfamilie in de achttiende eeuw* (Den Haag: Sdu, 2001); Han Brouwer, *Lezen en schrijven in de provincie; de boeken van Zwolse boekverkopers, 1777-1849* (Leiden: Primavera Pers, 1995); and Hannie van Goinga, *Alom te bekomen: veranderingen in de boekdistributie in de Republiek 1720-1800* (Amsterdam: Buitenkant, 1999). I am grateful to Simon Burrows for passing on an email from Erik Jacobs on this subject.
94 Raymond Birn, 'Michel Rey's Enlightenment', in *Le magasin de l'univers*, ed. C. Berkvens-Stevelinck, Hans Bots, P.G. Hoftijzer and O.S. Lankhorst (Leiden and New York: Brill, 1992), 23–48 at 24. Part of this collection is available on microfiche as 'The Correspondence of Marc-Michel Rey, 1747–1778, Publisher of the Enlightenment' (Leiden, Lisse: MMF Publ. [u.a.], 1998).
95 Selwyn, *Everyday Life in the German Book Trade*, xiii–ix.
96 For full details of the archives, which are divided between the Bibliothèque de l'Arsenal in Paris and the Bibliothèque Méjanes in Aix-en-Provence, see Eboli, *Livres et lecteurs en Provence au XVIIIe siècle*, 295–304. The combined collections are rich, including a 'livre de comptes' (1734–84) and various journals, collections of correspondence and catalogues. Other studies with a regional focus, of course, also draw upon contemporary accounting information and bookseller's letters. See, for example, Quéniart, *L'imprimerie et la librairie à Rouen*, 259–67.
97 Barber, *Studies in the Booktrade of the European Enlightenment*, 328.
98 Hugh Grant, 'Bookkeeping in the Eighteenth Century: The Grand Journal and Grand Ledger of the Hudson's Bay Company', *Archivaria* 43 (1997): 143–57 at 144; Basil Yamey, 'Scientific Bookkeeping and the Rise of Capitalism', *The Economic History Review* 1, no. 2/3 (1949): 99–113.
99 La Porte's work survives in the following French-language eighteenth-century pre-Revolutionary editions: Paris, 1704; Paris, 1714; Paris, 1715; Paris, 1732; Paris, 1741; Paris, 1748; Paris, 1753; Paris, 1769; Amsterdam, 1770; Amsterdam, 1781; Rouen, 1782; Amsterdam, 1783; Rouen, 1785; and Amsterdam, 1787.
100 BPUN STN MS 1033, 2.
101 Pierre Giradeau, *La banque rendue facile aux principales nations de l'Europe* (Paris: Saillant & Nyon, 1769), 137, 248.
102 Extant editions of Barrême's *Comptes-faits* are too numerous to list here, with several often being produced in a single year. During the STNs pre-Revolutionary trading existence, the following editions have survived: Avignon, 1769; Paris, 1771; Paris, 1774; Avignon, 1775; Paris, 1777; Rouen, 1782; Limoges, 1783; Lyon, 1787; and Paris, 1789. Others are surely lost. On Barrême, see Simon Burrows, 'Forgotten Best-Sellers of Pre-Revolutionary France', in ed. Julie Kalman, *French History and Civilisation: Papers from the George Rudé Seminar*, 7 (2017).
103 François Barrême, *Comptes-faits, ou Tarif général des monnoies, avec lequel on peut faire toutes sortes de comptes* (Avignon: Jean Aubert, 1790), non-paginated.
104 Mathieu La Porte, *La science des négocians et teneurs de livres, ou Instruction générale pour tout ce qui se pratique dans les comptoirs des négocians, tant pour les affaires de banque, que pour les marchandises, & chez les financiers pour les comptes* (Paris: Libraires associés, 1769), 79.
105 Jacques Rychner, 'Les archives de la Société typographique de Neuchâtel', *Musée neuchâtelois* 1969: 99–122.
106 Mathieu La Porte, *La science des négocians et teneurs de livres, ou Instruction générale pour tout ce qui se pratique dans les comptoirs des négocians, tant pour les affaires de*

banque, que pour les marchandises, et chez les financiers pour les comptes (Amsterdam: Aux dépens de la Compagnie, 1783), 121. On the STN 'Grand Livre', see Jacques Rychner, 'Le travail de l'atelier', in *Le rayonnement d'une maison d'édition dans l'Europe des Lumières: la Société typographique de Neuchâtel 1769–1789*, ed. Michel Schlup and Robert Darnton (Hauterive: Editions Gilles Attinger, 2005), 257–96 at 291.

107 Pierre Gervais, 'A Merchant or a French Atlantic? Eighteenth-century Account Books as Narratives of a Transnational Merchant Political Economy', *French History* 25, no. 1 (2011): 28–47 at 33.

108 BPUN STN MS 1033, 1; BPUN STN MS 1043, Caisse du 4 Octobre 1793 à 31 Mai 1797, 106. The Society legally existed for several years after 1790, but it did not conduct normal trading. See Chapter 4, 'The Storm Will Pass' and 'Epilogue: The End of the STN'. The lacunae in the day book series are: 27 November to 22 December 1773; 22 December 1773 to 1 May 1774; 23 August to 27 September 1775; 28 September to 27 November 1775; 3 January to 17 March 1776; and 1 January to 24 September 1783.

109 The *livre de Neuchâtel* was worth about 1.41 *livres* de France. 12 *deniers* made 1 *sol*, and 20 *sols* made 1 *livre*. All the works in this example are charged at 1 sol per sheet, with the number of sheet given followed by the price, first in *livres de France* then *livres de Neuchâtel*. The STN also conducted much of its local business in *batz*, each of which was worth 2 *sols*.

110 This particular order actually contained twelve transactions, but has been cut short here for the sake of simplicity. Current account deals, as in this case, are indicated in the day books by simple client business name; swap deals went through a separate account designated by the client business name and 'compte d'échange'. Only a small group of local clients operated book-swapping accounts, although the volume of works exchanged was often substantial.

111 In this case the given trade route is disappointingly short – Morat is just a nineteen kilometre boat trip from Neuchâtel, across two adjoined lakes – but others orders betray more detailed and interesting routes.

112 Free gifts, for example, were registered as a capital flow from a profit and loss account to the book's account; in the case of returns, the capital was transferred (back) from the book's account to the client account; swapped books were dealt with through 'exchange accounts' with a nominal financial value.

113 The word 'rencontre', meaning 'verification', appears to be peculiarly Neuchâtelois. See Jacques Rychner, 'Les archives de la Société typographique de Neuchâtel', in *L'édition neuchâteloise au siècle des Lumières: la Société typographique de Neuchâtel (1769–1789)*, ed. Michel Schlup (Neuchâtel: Bibliothèque publique et universitaire de Neuchâtel, 2002), 179–209 at 192.

114 Sometimes these books are sub-divided according to the umbrella accounting headers used to organize stocks 'nos éditions [our editions]', 'livres troqués [swapped books]', livres en commission [books sold by commission]' and 'marchandises générales [general merchandise]'. These categories were important to the society for the purposes of monitoring its business.

115 Where the STN scribe foresaw extensive transaction activity, he allotted the left-hand page of a spread for purchases, and the right-hand page for sales. Otherwise sales and purchases were listed in-line on a single page.

116 On this decision, see the appendix essay 'Coding and Decoding the French Book Trade'. The fact that, in normal times, the STN sold all of their regular stocks at the price of 1 *sol* per sheet made the omission of price data much more palatable than it might otherwise have been.

117 BPUN STN MS 1000, Rencontre (inventaire) du magasin, févriér 1773, 1, 12, 21, 22, 42, 78, 79, 80, 82, 87, 95, 103, 115, 125, 126, 127, 128, 131, 146, 148, 149, 167, 189, 194, 195, 196, 199, 200, 202, 204, 206, 208, 209, 210, 212, 213.

118 See especially Darnton, *The Corpus of Clandestine Literature in France*; Freedman, *Books Without Borders*.

119 For the sake of completeness, it should be mentioned here that the STN archives contain another form of order book, the 'Livre des défets', which record orders made by clients for replacement sheets that were either missing in the original envoi or had been damaged en route.

120 For a more systematic treatment of the gap between supply and demand, see Curran, 'Beyond the Forbidden Best-Sellers', 94–105.

121 Various print-shop ledgers, where extant, name the compositors and press workers that worked on each STN edition, and reveal precious detail about print runs, costs and the nature of small printing jobs that are lost in the higher-level account books. To give just one example, on 14 July 1770 the compositor Brand and press workers Mayer and Vogl printed 500 copies of an Italian poem for M. Sylvett in Berne and were respectively paid 1 *livre* 10 *sols* and (together) 1 *livre* for their toils. See BPUN STN MS 1050, 29.

122 It is clear that most of the letters received by the STN during this period are missing because copies of letters sent by the Society consistently refer to exchanges that are absent in the dossiers. See, for example, BPUN STN MS 1112, Copies des Lettres M, 657 (STN to Orlando Orlandini in Trieste, 8 January 1789); ibid., 724 (STN to Graff in Bollingen, 26 March 1789).

123 The complicated relationship between the STN and the Fauche family, especially Louis Fauche-Borel, during the 1780s is discussed in Chapter 4, 'The Storm Will Pass', and in the epilogue, 'The End of the STN'. Suspicions that the STN were using this numbered catalogue first arose due to out-of-sequence commissions in the Bratislavan bookseller Antoine Loewe's July 1788 missive. From the run of books '... 514, 567, 637, 919, 958, 955, 1608, 977, 1037, 1300', it was noticed that numbers 955 and 1,608 in the 1787 Fauche-Borel catalogue were both editions of François-Thomas-Marie de Baculard's *Nouvelles historiques*. See BPUN STN MS 1145, Dossier Durand l'aîné, 325 (Durand to STN, 18 July 1788). Further proofs confirmed the Fauche-Borel catalogue as the source of Durand's numeric code. Illegal works singled out for special attention by underlining tallied with dubious titles in the Fauche-Borel catalogue. Among those underlined in the Viennois bookseller Joseph Stahel's 22 June 1788 commission, for example, are 1,002 (*Œuvres de Grécourt*), 1,012 (*Œuvres de La Mettrie*), 1,067 (*La philosophie du bon-sens*), 1,149 (*Recherches philosophiques sur les preuves du christianisme*), 1,225 (*Les admirables secrets d'Albert le Grand*), and 1,551 (*Essai sur les prêtres*). See ibid., 321 (Durand to STN, 22 June 1788). Orders for incomplete sets, such as the Venice bookseller Antoine Foglierini's request for '1 ex 272 avec le tome 10', match up with multivolume works. In this case, number 272 in the Fauche-Borel catalogue is volumes 7–9 of d'Arnaud's *Délassemens de l'homme sensible*. See ibid., 309 (Durand to STN, 11 May 1788). Finally, once the principle had been established, it was possible to further confirm against snippets of accounting information in two surviving letters. The STN's description of works in bills sent to Amable Le Roy on the *quai St. Clair* in Lyon (relating to his 1 October 1787 order) and the Lausannois printer-bookseller Jean-Pierre Heubach (27 August 1787) matched those predicted using the Durand dossier orders and the Fauche-Borel catalogue. See BPUN STN MS 1175, Dossier Amable Le Roy, 100; BPUN STN MS 1145, 206.

124 See Chapter 4, 'The Storm Will Pass'.

125 The STN's business in ephemera is difficult to trace using the major ledger series because transactions were all funnelled through a single account nominated as 'divers petits ouvrages'. However, the surviving auxiliary books often provide more detail. MS 1022, the 'Livre de comptes des menus débiteurs', for example, is rich in mentions of small printing jobs such as the 500 'Lettres circulaires' printed for 'Deluze père, fils & Cie' (f.2) and the 'impression des plans et billets de lotterie' run-off for the Môtiers merchant Durand (f.74). MS1053 'Livre de Banque 1773-1775' details the sale of 500 'passe port, pour M. M. les quatre minstraux' (ledger not paginated, at 29 May 1773), 1,100 'Lettres de voiture, Morat et Neuchâtel' (15 January 1774), and 100 'affiches pour le lait' (21 May 1774). Schmidt also used a range of sources, notably the printshop accounts, to reconstruct the STN's longer-form ephemera including the 'Pièces justificatives concernant la déclaration des sentimens faussement attribués à M. de Ripert de Monclar, procureur-général au Parlement de Provence' (1773) and the 'Statuts et règlemens généraux & particuliers de la vénérable Chambre de charité de la ville de Neuchâtel' (1775). See Schmidt, 'Liste des impressions'. Samuel Fauche, and later Jérémie Witel and Louis Fauche-Borel, also undertook job printing for institutional and private clients, squeezing the STN's potential market.

126 BPUN STN MS 1030, Main Courante, 33 (6 June 1774); BPUN STN MS 1053, Livre de banque (4 June 1774).

127 STN stock takes took place on 8 October 1771, 18 February 1773, 18 October 1774, 30 November 1776, 15 February 1778, 25 January 1779, 2 January 1781, 31 December 1782, 1 June 1785, 1 June 1786 and 1 June 1787.

128 On the widespread nature of this phenomenon, see Yamey, 'Scientific Bookkeeping and the Rise of Capitalism'.

Chapter 2

1 Maurice Cranston, *The Solitary Self: Jean-Jacques Rousseau in Exile and Adversity* (Chicago: University of Chicago Press, 1997), 129.

2 Horace-Bénédict de Saussure, *Voyages dans les Alpes: précédés d'un essai sur l'histoire naturelle des environs de Genève* (Neuchâtel: 1779), 318–19.

3 C. P. Courtney, *Isabelle de Charrière (Belle de Zuylen): A Biography* (Oxford: Voltaire Foundation, 1993).

4 Andrew Brown, 'Gabriel Grasset éditeur de Voltaire', in *Voltaire et le livre*, ed. François Bessire and Françoise Tilkin (Ferney-Voltaire: Centre international d'étude du XVIIIe siècle, 2009), 67–105.

5 See Pierre-Yves Tissot, 'Les débuts de l'imprimerie dans les montagnes neuchâteloises, des origines à 1848', in *Aspects du livre neuchâtelois*, ed. Jacques Rychner and Michel Schlup (Neuchâtel: Bibliothèque publique et universitaire de Neuchâtel, 1986), 453–72 at 453.

6 On Swiss typography during this period see Silvio Corsini, *La preuve par les fleurons? Analyse comparée du matériel ornemental des imprimeurs suisses romands 1775–1785* (Ferney-Voltaire: Centre international d'étude du XVIIIe siècle, 1999); Perret, *Les imprimeries d'Yverdon*, 101–5. On their use of 'Londres' as a false address, see Curran, 'Mettons toujours Londres'. See also the articles and books of Giles Barber, Georges Bonnant, Jean-Daniel Candaux, Silvio Corsini, Robert Darnton, Charly Guyot, Jean Jeanprêtre, John R. Kleinschmidt, Jacques Rychner, Michel Schlup and Michael Schmidt in the bibliography to the current volume.

7 As a result, it is generally possible to identify clandestine editions as having been produced in the Swiss Romand quickly and with perhaps 90 per cent certainty. The problem for historians of the book, rather, is that this common 'Romandy' identity obfuscates the precise place of publication or printer of any given work: identical (or at least indistinguishable) sets of type and ornaments, sometimes made in the same workshop using the same punches, were in concurrent use across the print shops of Geneva, Lausanne, Neuchâtel and Yverdon throughout our period. Contemporary insiders insisted that it was impossible to be sure of the precise place of publication of some editions, and despite the remarkable efforts of Corsini and others, this remains the case. Further, to be 90 per cent certain an edition was published in Romandy is to be *uncertain*: all of the materials and techniques used by the Swiss publishers were also employed, at times, in print shops located elsewhere in Europe.

8 This hypothesis underpinned the substantive statistical work presented in Darnton's award-winning 1995 twin volumes *The Corpus of Clandestine Literature in France* and *The Forbidden Best-Sellers of pre-Revolutionary France*. See, specifically, Darnton, *Forbidden Best-Sellers*, 52–7, 60.

9 On articles and books based upon evidence from the STN archive see, 'Introduction: The French Book Trade in Enlightenment Europe', as well as the bibliography to this volume.

10 Darnton, *Forbidden Best-Sellers*, 57.

11 Jules-Henri Pott, *Catalogue des livres françois de Jules Henri Pott et Comp.* (Lausanne: 1772).

12 To give just one example, the 1789 public auction of the Paris-based atheist and *philosophe* the baron d'Holbach's modest collection contained 2,777 French-language works published across Europe from Amsterdam to Vienna. See *Catalogue des livres de la bilbliothèque de feu M. le baron d'Holbach* (Paris: 1789).

13 In total, the STN received (through purchase or swapping) 172,572 copies during its trading existence. The FBTEE database records the place of publication of 83,021 of these copies as being unknown, 67,942 as of Swiss origin and 22,599 as foreign. The database, therefore, shows 75 per cent (67,942 of 90,541) of identified incoming works as having been printed in Switzerland. When preparing the FBTEE database, every attention was taken to pinpoint the proper publication place of editions in the light of the new STN data. Nonetheless, the project was still heavily dependent upon a bibliographic record that is, given the number of false editions produced in the Swiss Romand during our period, problematic. Almost all of the 2,569 'London' editions currently recorded in the database, for example, were clearly produced in Lausanne, Geneva and Neuchâtel. It is probable, therefore, that closer to 80–85% of currently identified incoming editions in the database were actually printed in Switzerland.

14 For further thoughts on this issue, see Burrows, *Enlightenment Best-Sellers*.

15 *Catalogue des livres de Louis Fauche-Borel, imprimeur du Roi* (Neuchâtel: 1787). For a (partial) explanation of why this catalogue of STN stocks was printed under the name Louis Fauche-Borel, see 'Chapter 4: The Storm Will Pass' and 'Epilogue: The End of the STN' below. The catalogue gives the false places of publication for counterfeit editions, 'Lyon sous Londres' for example, although by no means in all cases.

16 Ernst Weber, 'Sortimentskataloge des 18. Jahrhunderts als literatur- und buchhandelsgeschichtliche Quellen' in *Bücherkataloge als buchgeschichtliche Quellen in der frühen Neuzeit*, ed. Reinhard Wittmann (Wiesbaden: O. Harrassowitz, 1984), 209–57 at 223; Selwyn, *Everyday Life in the German Book Trade*, 138.

17 BPUN STN MS 1131, Dossier Jean-Samuel Cailler, 26 (Jean-Samuel Cailler to Samuel Fauche, 28 September 1769).

18 BPUN STN MS 1103, 335 (STN to L'Epagnez in Besançon, 8 June 1777).
19 Ibid., 140 (STN to Méliere near Blamont, 24 March 1777).
20 Pierre-Alexandre Du Peyrou, 'Letter to Marc Michel Rey, 6 March 1769', in McNamee, et al. (eds.) *Electronic Enlightenment*, at http://www.eenlightenment.com/item/rousjeVF0370063b_1key001cor/
21 Latin books were, during the sixteenth and seventeenth centuries, exchanged over longer distances. See Henri-Jean Martin, 'La librairie française en 1777–1778', *Dix-huitième siècle* 11, no. 1 (1979): 87–112 at 103. But the fragmentation of the book market on linguistic and national lines, the proliferation of cheap editions and more aggressive competition all caused a radically altered system of wholesale book distribution to emerge during the eighteenth century.
22 BPUN STN MS 1135, 425 (Chirol to STN, 27 February 1782).
23 BPUN STN MS 1145, 212 (Durand in Lyon to STN, 11 September 1787); ibid., 298 (Durand in Bologne to STN, 21 April 1788).
24 On STN production costs, see 'The Triumph of Benevolence, or The History of Francis Wills'.
25 On cooperation in the English book trade, see Raven, *The Business of Books*, 227. For the Dutch case, see Baggerman, *Publishing Policies and Family Strategies*, 227–54.
26 Silvio Corsini, 'Un pour tous … et chacun pour soi? Petite histoire d'une alliance entre les Sociétés typographiques de Lausanne, Berne et Neuchâtel', in *Le rayonnement d'une maison d'édition dans l'Europe des Lumières: la Société typographique de Neuchâtel 1769–1889*, ed. Michel Schlup and Robert Darnton (Hauterive: Editions Gilles Attinger, 2005), 115–37 at 116.
27 Jean-Baptiste-Joseph Damarzit de Sahuguet d'Espagnac, *Histoire de Maurice, comte de Saxe* (Lausanne and Neuchâtel: Société typographique de Lausanne and Société typographique de Neuchâtel, 1774); John Hawkesworth, *Relation des voyages entrepris par ordre de Sa Majesté Britannique* (Lausanne and Neuchâtel: Société typographique de Lausanne and Société typographique de Neuchâtel, 1774).
28 Corsini, 'Un pour tous … et chacun pour soi?', 118.
29 Jean-André Deluc, *Lettres physiques et morales sur les montagnes et sur l'histoire de la terre et de l'homme, adressées à la reine de la Grande-Bretagne par J. A. de Luc* (En Suisse [Lausanne]: Libraires associés [J. P. Heubach; Société typographique de Lausanne], 1778).
30 Jean-André Deluc, *Lettres physiques et morales, sur les montagnes et sur l'histoire de la terre et de l'homme* (La Haye: De Tune, 1778).
31 Claude-Louis [comte de] St. Germain, *Mémoires de M. le comte de Saint-Germain, ministre et secrétaire d'état de la guerre, lieutenant-général des armées de France* (En Suisse [Berne]: Libraires associés [Société typographique de Berne], 1779).
32 BPUN STN MS 1025, 179–80.
33 On these regulations see Robert L. Dawson, *The French Booktrade and the 'Permission Simple' of 1777* (Oxford: Voltaire Foundation, 1992).
34 BPUN STN MS 1025, 180.
35 Corsini, 'Un pour tous … et chacun pour soi?', 122–9.
36 BPUN STN MS 1033, 8.
37 BPUN STN MS 1135, 227 (Chirol to STN, 18 July 1775 [Essai]); ibid., 328 (Chirol to STN, 14 July 1779); ibid., 335 (Chirol to STN, 13 October 1779 [Considerations]).
38 Ibid., 321 (Chriol to STN, 1 June 1779).
39 See Seaward, 'The French Government and the Policing of the Extra-Territorial Print Trade', 131–85.
40 Michel Schlup, 'Le rêve impossible de la STN: un Journal helvétique et "parisien"!' in *L'édition neuchâteloise au siècle de Lumières: la Société typographique de Neuchâtel,*

1769–1789, ed. Robert Darnton and Michel Schlup (Hauterive: Editions Gilles Attinger, 2005), 143–55 at 143.
41 Selwyn, *Everyday Life in the German Book Trade*, 34, 73.
42 BPUN STN MS 1103, 68 (STN to Claudet frères & fils in Lyon, 6 February 1777).
43 Schlup, 'Le rêve impossible de la STN', 149.
44 See Robert Darnton, 'The Life of a "Poor Devil" in the Republic of Letters', in *Essays on the Age of Enlightenment in Honor of Ira O. Wade*, ed. Jean Macary (Geneva: Droz, 1977), 39–92 at 42.
45 Antoine Perrin, *Almanach de la librairie* (Paris: Moutard, 1781), 16–18.
46 Censer, *The French Press*, 7. Non-ephemeral titles were taken by Censer to be those that survived for more than three years.
47 BPUN STN MS 1103, 52 (STN to Petitpierre in Basle, 30 January 1777).
48 See 'The Triumph of Benevolence, or The History of Francis Wills'.
49 Séverine Huguenin and Timothée Léchot, 'Introduction à l'histoire du Journal helvétique', in *Lectures du 'Journal helvétique', 1732–1782: actes du colloque de Neuchâtel 6-8 mars 2014*, ed. Séverine Huguenin and Timothée Léchot (Geneva: Slatkine, 2016), 23–82 at 63–4.
50 See 'Chapter 3: The Republic of Books'.
51 B. Van Selm, 'Johannes Van Ravesteyn, "Libraire Européen" or Local Trader?', in *Le magasin de l'univers: The Dutch Republic as the centre of the European book trade*, ed. C. Berkvens-Stevelinck, Hans Bots, P.G. Hoftijzer and O.S. Lankhorst (Leiden and New York: Brill, 1992), 251–63.
52 Over a third of the STN's shipments to Geneva, 14,185 copies in total, were STN printings of Rilliet de Saussure's *Planta gagnant sa vie en honnête homme*, the vast majority of which never reached bookstores. See 'Procès Romanesque, offrant un sujet de comédie très riche et très' heureux.
53 Despite their being separated by some seventy-five kilometres, the trade of both Berne and Yverdon (a Bernese territory between 1536 and 1798) was dominated by Fortuné-Barthélemy de Félice and his Société typographique de Berne. The statistics given here, and in the FBTEE database, for the STN's trade with the town of Berne are difficult to employ comparatively because of the extensive traffic of jointly-published volumes during the 'libraires associés' confederation period of 1778–80.
54 Indeed, only 225 (4.1%) of these works can be positively identified as having issued from presses based outside of Neuchâtel.
55 Indeed, only 593 (3.9%) of these works can be positively identified as not having been published in Switzerland.
56 See BPUN STN MS 1160, Dossier François Grasset, 1–579.
57 See Barber, 'The Cramers of Geneva'; Bonnant, *Le livre genevois*; and Corsini, *Le livre à Lausanne*.
58 The trade recorded in the first year of the Cramer Grand Livre is as follows: Germanic (including Austria) clients 1,790 *livres* (six clients) [4.4% of total sales value (11.8% of total clients)]; Avignon 1,565 (1) [3.8% (2%)]; British 713 (1) [1.7% (2%)]; Dutch 668 (3) [1.6% (5.9%)]; French 13,426 (15) [32.8% (29.4%)] of which Paris 8,508 (1) [20.8% (2%)] and Lyon 1,212 (1) [3% (2%)]; Iberian 12,058 (5) [29.4% (9.8%)]; Italian 3,156 (8) [7.7% (15.7%)]; Swiss 5,368 (11) [13.1% (21.6%)]. Totals: 40,960 (51). See AEG, Commerce F57, Grand livre de Gabriel et Philibert Cramer, 1755–67.
59 The volumes of correspondence recorded in the Gosse letter books is as follows. For the period 11 May 1759 to 9 December 1761: Avignon thirty-four letters (to seven

individual clients) [2.4% of total letters (2.6% of total clients)]; Dutch and surrounds 39 (11) [2.8% (4.1%)]; French 286 (56) [20.4% (21%)], of which Paris 6 (2) [0.4% (0.7%)] and Lyon 136 (14) [9.7% (5.2%)]; Germanic (including Austrian Empire) 101 (29) [7.2% (10.9%)]; Iberian 19 (6) [1.4% (2.2%)]; Italian 469 (78) [33.5% (29.2%)]; Swiss 421 (70) [30.1% (26.2%)]; and Unknown 30 (10) [2.1% (3.7%)]. Totals: 1,399 (267). For the period 11 May 1776 to 8 February 1783: Avignon 39 (8) [4.3% (4.4%]; Dutch 7 (6) [0.8% (3.3%)]; Extra-European 3 (1) [0.3% (0.6%); French 267 (55) [29.6% (30.4%)], of which Paris 12 (6) [1.3% (3.3%)] and Lyon 158 (20) [17.5% (11%)]; Germanic (including Austrian Empire) 42 (18) [4.7% (10%)]; Iberian 8 (2) [0.9% (1.1%)]; Italian 59 (16) [6.5% (8.8%)]; Poland 1 (1) [0.1% (0.6%)]; Swiss 465 (71) [51.6% (39.2%)]; Unknown 5 (1) [0.6% (0.6%)]. Totals: 901 (181). For the period 25 February 1783 to 24 March 1791: Avignon 8 (3) [1.1% (1.6%)]; French 149 (54) [20.8% (29.2%)], of which Lyon 79 (17) [11% (9.1%), and Paris 13 (7) [1.8% (3.8%); Germanic (including Austrian Empire) 17 (10) [2.4% (5.4%); Iberian 11 (3) [1.5% (1.6%); Italian 42 (14) [5.9% (7.6%)]; Swiss 475 (98) [66.3% (53%)]; and Unknown 13 (3) [1.8% (1.6%]). Totals: 716 (185). See AEG Fonds de Commerce F61, F63, F63, Copie de lettres: H.A. Gosse. For definitions of the geographic zones used in these statistics, see the FBTEE online dataface interface.
60 See 'Chapter 4 – The Storm Will Pass'.
61 BPUN STN MS 1135, 515 (Chirol to STN, 24 June 1783).
62 No shipments were made to Bardin between June 1785 and May 1787.
63 BPUN STN MS 1135, 558 (Chriol to STN, 21 February 1784). Henri-Albert Gosse died in 1780 and his business was continued by his brother Jean thereafter.
64 Rietje van Vliet, 'Print and Public in Europe, 1600–1800', in *A Companion to the History of Book*, ed. Simon Eliot and Jonathan Rose (London: Wiley-Blackwell, 2009), 247–58 at 247; Selwyn, *Everyday Life in the German Book Trade*, 99.
65 Michel Schlup, 'Sociétés de lecture et cabinets littéraires dans la Principauté de Neuchâtel, (1750–1800): de nouvelles pratiques de la lecture', *Musée neuchâlelois* 1987 [2]: 81–104 at 84.
66 Phillipe Henry, 'L'évolution démographique', in *Histoire du pays de Neuchâtel: De la Reforme à 1815*, ed. Phillipe Henry and Jean-Pierre Jelmini (Hauterive: Attinger, 1991), 140–57 at 146–50.
67 Schlup, 'Sociétés de lecture et cabinets littéraires', 85. From 1780 the Neuchâtelois public could also borrow works from the 'Bibliothèque des Pasteurs', a collection of over 2,000 titles including reference works, philosophy, history, scholarly and classical works and, of course, much theology. See Cecilia Hurley, 'La lecture à Neuchâtel pendant le long XVIIIe siècle', in *Sa Majesté en Suisse: Neuchâtel et ses princes prussiens*, ed. Chantal Lafontant Vallotton, Vincent Callet-Molin and Elisabeth Crettaz-Stürzel (Neuchâtel: Alphil, 2013), 292–7.
68 Schlup, 'Sociétés de lecture et cabinets littéraires', 97.
69 Paul Benhamou, 'La diffusion des ouvrages de la STN à travers les cabinets de lecture', in *Le rayonnement d'une maison d'édition dans l'Europe des Lumières: la Société typographique de Neuchâtel 1769–1789*, ed. Michel Schlup and Robert Darnton (Hauterive: Editions Gilles Attinger, 2005), 299–315.
70 Alas, only the clients J.P. Bernard of Lunéville, the *Cabinet impérial royal de littérature* of Vienna, Jean Gay of Lunéville, Joseph Lex of Warsaw, Mme J. Lossier of Geneva, Pierre Sandoz of Geneva and François Sandré of Lunéville are specifically noted in the STN archives as having operated reading rooms. On this subject see Darnton, *The Business of Enlightenment*, 298, 303.

71 *Feuille d'avis de Neuchâtel*, 18 October 1770.
72 See Schlup, 'Sociétés de lecture et cabinets littéraires', 92.
73 Ibid., 93-4.
74 Schlup, 'Etude d'un processus éditorial et typographique', 272. Schlup cites here the studies and articles of Alexandre Daguet, Charly Guyot, Jean-Pierre Perret and Jean Jeanprêtre as examples of how Samuel Fauche has generally been portrayed as primarily a seller of illegal books.
75 Horace-Bénédict de Saussure, *Voyages dans les Alpes, Précédés d'un essai sur l'histoire naturelle des environs de Genève*, vol. 2 (Neuchâtel: Louis Fauche-Borel, 1803), 48-50.
76 Fauche took 1,307 Bibles and 1,150 catechisms from the STN after 1772. George Sinnet, bookseller in Neuchâtel, also operated largely in the market for devotional works and text books. Between 11 August 1770 and 31 May 1787 Sinnet supplied 345 books and acquired 451 from the STN.
77 The dates given here indicate the periods that these businesses traded with the STN.
78 Indeed, the frequency of book exchanges recorded between Neuchâtel traders more than doubled during the period 1780-4 when compared to the previous five years.
79 *Feuille d'avis de Neuchâtel*, 30 October 1783.
80 See 'Chapter 4: The Storm Will Pass' below.
81 Perret, *Les imprimeries d'Yverdon*, 138.
82 Schmidt, 'Liste des impressions', 236; BPUN STN MS 1050, 7.
83 See Daniel Cahill, 'Abraham Girardet (1764-1823), graveur suisse à Paris sous la Révolution française', *Annales historiques de la Révolution Française* 289 (1992): 434-38.
84 See BPUN STN MS 1103, 163 (STN to Samuel Girardet, 31 March 1777); ibid., 427 (STN to Samuel Girardet, 17 July 1777).
85 Samuel Girardet's shutters are conserved in the Musée d'histoire du Locle. See Caroline Calame, 'Une affiche publicitaire au XVIIIe siècle: les volets de la librairie Girardet', *Nouvelle revue neuchâteloise* 73 (2002): 1-56.
86 Perret, *Les imprimeries d'Yverdon*, 138, 326.
87 Anon., *Histoire de François Wills, ou Le triomphe de la bienfaisance* (Amsterdam and Rotterdam: D.J. Changuion, 1773), 50-9.
88 The English-language first edition of the work appeared as *The Triumph of Benevolence; or, the history of Francis Wills* (London: T. Vernor and M. Chater, 1772). The mystery surrounding its authorship is described in A. Lytton Sells, 'The History of Francis Wills: A Literary Mystery', *The Review of English Studies* 11, no. 41 (1935): 1-27. Lytton Sells found it plausible that Oliver Goldsmith might have written the work, although considered on balance that it should be attributed to a contemporary of lesser standing, Arthur Murphy being the most probable candidate.
89 For an explanation of the categorization systems used in the FBTEE project, see the materials that accompany the online database and Burrows, *Enlightenment Best-Sellers*, Chapter 6.
90 Robert Darnton, 'Reading, Writing and Publishing in Eighteenth-Century France: A Case Study in the Sociology of Literature', *Daedalus* 100, no. 1 (1971): 214-56 at 218-26.
91 Darnton, 'Reading, Writing and Publishing in Eighteenth-Century France', 224.
92 For fuller breakdowns of this data, see Burrows, *Enlightenment Best-Sellers*.
93 Jacques Necker, *Mémoire donné au roi par M. Necker en 1778* (London [Neuchâtel]: [Société typographique de Neuchâtel], 1781).
94 On Brissot, see Frederick A. de Luna, 'The Dean Street Style of Revolution: J.-P. Brissot, jeune philosophe', *French Historical Studies* 17, no. 1 (1991): 159-90; Robert

Darnton, 'The Grub Street Style of Revolution: J.-P. Brissot police spy', *The Journal of Modern History* 40, no. 3 (1968): 301–27.

95 On the anti-*philosophes*, see Mark Curran, *Atheism, Religion and Enlightenment in Pre-Revolutionary Europe* (Woodbridge: Boydell Press, 2012); D. M. McMahon, *Enemies of the Enlightenment* (Oxford: Oxford University Press, 2002); and Didier Masseau, *Les ennemis des philosophes: l'antiphilosophie au temps des Lumières* (Paris: Albin Michel, 2000).

96 This statistic includes the shipments of two works written by the STN director Frédéric-Samuel Ostervald, the *Cours de géographie élémentaire* and the *Cours abrégé de géographie historique, ancienne et moderne, et de sphère*. These textbooks were sold both separately and as a pair by the STN. Alas, because both individual works were sometimes accounted for as 'Ostervald, géographie' or even simply 'géographie' it was impossible to entirely disaggregate their sales for the FBTEE database.

97 Between 1781 and 1788, the STN sold on average 190 works per year by Voltaire. During the period 1770 and 1779, by contrast, the STN had shipped, on average, 1,495 of the patriarch of Ferney's works.

98 Candaux, 'Imprimeurs et libraires dans la Suisse des Lumières', 59.

99 The STN shipped just fifty-three copies of five works by Barthélemy Imbert, despite (or, perhaps, because of) the fact that his writings were in constant production in Paris, Amsterdam and The Hague during the 1770s and 1780s. Joseph-Marie Loaisel de Tréogate had several works published in Amsterdam, Berlin and Paris throughout the two decades. The passage of only five copies of his *Ainsi finissent les grandes passions* (n.p., n.d.) and one of his *Florello: histoire méridionale* can be traced in the FBTEE database. None of Suard's original works appear in the FBTEE database.

100 On translation volumes and foreign language editions in the STN dataset, see also Burrows, *Enlightenment Best-Sellers*.

101 Bonnant, *Le livre genevois*, 272.

102 Works of 'Histoire' (41.9%) and 'Belles Lettres' (38.8%) were still more substantially represented among the STN's translations than among original French-language works.

103 The STN's edition of William Robertson's *The History of America*, likewise, was based on the translation by Marc-Antoine Eidous that had first appeared chez Jean-Edme Dufour and Philippe Roux in Maastricht, and Denné in Paris in 1777 and 1778.

104 See Friedrich Nicolai, *Brief über den itzigen Zustand der schönen Wissenschaften in Teutschland* (Berlin: Kleyb, 1755), 11; Selwyn, *Everyday Life in the German Book Trade*.

105 Citing Hans-Jürgen Lüsesbrink, René Nohr and Rolf Reichardt's evidence that 2,678 works were translated from French to German during the period 1770–88, Freedman concludes that 'the currents of literary transmission flowed thickest between France and Germany'. See Jeffrey Freedman, *Before Nationalism: France, Germany, and the International French Book Trade at the End of the Old Regime*, 70; Hans-Jürgen Lüsesbrink, René Nohr and Rolf Reichardt, 'Kulturtransfer im Epochenumbruch – Entwicklung und Inhalte der französisch-deutschen Übersetzungsbibliothek 1770–1815 im Überblick', in *Kulturtransfer im Epochenumbruch. Frankreich-Deutschland 1770 bis 1815*, ed. Hans-Jürgen Lüsebrink and Rolf Reichardt, vol. 1 (Leipzig: Leipziger Universitätsverlag, 1997), 29–86. Freedman recognizes, however, that these currents never became a flood. Johann Goldfriedrich's analysis suggests that, over a similar period, translations from French represented about 6 per cent of total production in Germany. See Selwyn, *Everyday Life in the German Book Trade*, 47.

106 Christoph Martin Wieland, *Le miroir d'or, ou Les rois du Chéchian* (Paris and Neuchâtel: Société typographique de Neuchâtel, 1774).
107 The STN did not sell a single French-language copy of any work by Goethe or Hamann.
108 The c.1765 trade card of John Wilkie is reproduced in Raven, *The Business of Books*, 272.
109 Despite *The Vicar of Wakefield* having been first translated into French in 1767, the STN only ever traded a few dozen copies of Goldsmith's famous book.
110 BPUN STN MS 1053, Livre de banque, 29 January 1774 to 26 March 74. As *Wills* was being printed, the STN pressmen were simultaneously working on editions of the *Nouveau Journal helvétique* and *Feuille d'avis de Neuchâtel*, a trade catalogue and the following books: Friedrich Nicolai, *La vie et les opinions de maître Sébaltus Nothanker* (Londres [Neuchâtel]: [Société typographique de Neuchâtel], 1774); Louis Godard, *Discours oratoire contenant l'éloge de S.E.M. le chevalier André Tron* ([Neuchâtel]: [Société typographique de Neuchâtel], 1774); Molière, *Oeuvres* (Neuchâtel: Société typographique de Neuchâtel, 1775); Frédéric-Samuel Ostervald, *Cours abrégé de géographie historique, ancienne et moderne et de sphère, par demandes et réponses* (Neuchâtel: Société typographique de Neuchâtel, 1774); Jean-Frédéric Ostervald, *Catéchisme, ou, Instruction dans la religion chrétienne* (Neuchâtel: [Société typographique de Neuchâtel], 1774).
111 Rychner, 'Le travail de l'atelier', 290.
112 The database records 241,104 copies of 210 different works as having been printed by the STN. Exactly half (105/210) of these print runs were explicitly stated in the archives of the STN, while the other half have been reconstructed by the FBTEE project from subsequent sales and stock holdings data.
113 This statistic was calculated by discounting STN editions of less than 200 and more than 4,200 copies.
114 BnF, Département des manuscrits, Français 22019. Archives de la Chambre syndicale de la Librairie et Imprimerie de Paris, aux XVIIe et XVIIIe siècles. Répertoire alphabétique de livres publiés de 1778 à 1788, avec l'indication du chiffre de tirage. See also Henri-Jean Martin, *Le livre français sous l'ancien régime* (Paris: Promodis, 1987), 216–8.
115 BnF, Département des manuscrits, Français 22019, 1–5.
116 Selwyn, *Everyday Life in the German Book Trade*, 42–3.
117 Hernlund, 'William Strahan's Ledgers', 104.
118 See BPUN STN MS 1025, 7.
119 William Strahan charged more for larger orders, as they meant he would have to restock type sooner due to uneven wear. See Hernlund, 'William Strahan's Ledgers', 105.
120 The bookseller Faivre in Pontarlier wrote to the STN in the summer of 1783 to ask for thirty copies of the frontispiece of the *École du Bonheur*, a book he had commissioned from the Society, printed in big characters on a single sheet that could be posted around town. This, he indicated, was common practice in France. See BPUN STN MS 1148, Dossier Faivre, 142 (Faivre in Pontarlier to STN, 21 July 1783).
121 On the *ouvrage de la semaine* initiative, see BPUN STN MS 1030, 21, 25, 28, 33, 44, 50, etc.; BPUN STN MS 1022, Main courante nov 1775-mars 1779, 4, 10, 19, etc.
122 Michel Schlup, 'La STN et l'édition de la Feuille d'Avis de Neuchâtel', in *L'édition nuchâteloise au siècle des Lumières: La Société typographique de Neuchâtel (1769-1789)*, ed. Michel Schlup (Neuchâtel: Bibliothèque publique et universitaire de Neuchâtel, 2002), 157–67 at 157–9.

123 *Feuille d'avis de Neuchâtel*, 10 February 1780, 3.
124 *Feuille d'avis de Neuchâtel*, 4 August 1785, 3.
125 Censer, *The French Press*, 7.
126 For a history of the *Mercure Suisse/Journal helvétique* see Lumières.Lausanne, projet 'Mercure suisse – Journal helvétique (1732–1782)', Université de Lausanne, at http://lumieres.unil.ch/projets/journal-helvetique
127 *Nouveau Journal helvétique*, April 1784, 21–2.
128 BPUN STN MS 1103, 52 (STN to Petitpierre in Basle, 30 January 1777).
129 Schlup, 'Le rêve impossible de la STN', 148.
130 The printers of Lausanne, Geneva and Yverdon all tried to launch journals during the 1770s and 1780s to address this situation. The STL's *Nouvelles de la république des lettres* (1775–77) and the Lausanne based printer Jean-Pierre Heubach's *Nouveau Journal de littérature et de politique* (1784) being prominent examples of these efforts. See Huguenin and Léchot, 'Introduction à l'histoire du Journal helvétique', 64, 70–1.
131 *Année littéraire*, 1774, I, p. 237. See Lytton Sells, 'The History of Francis Wills', 8.
132 Curran, *Atheism, Religion and Enlightenment*, 94–6.
133 See, for example, *Catalogue des livres de la Société typographique de Neuchâtel en Suisse* (Neuchâtel: [Société typographique de Neuchâtel], 1785).
134 For examples of these lists, see BPUN STN MS 1103, 19, 36, 64, 360, 568, 644.
135 This analysis is based on the following STN editions printed in 1773, 1774 and 1775, here given by author surname and short-title only for the sake brevity: Brydone, *Voyage en Sicile et à Malthe*; Arnaud, *Les epreuves du sentiment*; Bauvin, *Arminius ou Les Chérusques*; Bernardin de Saint-Pierre, *Voyage à l'isle de France*; Bertrand, *Elemens d'oryctologie*; Dorat, *Les malheurs de l'inconstance*; Gélieu, *Réflexions d'un homme de bon sens sur les comètes*; Holland, *Réflexions philosophiques sur le Système de la nature* (second STN printing); Pierre le Grand, *Journal de Pierre le Grand*; Riccoboni, *Collection complète des œuvres*; Voltaire, *Nouveautés*; Espagnac, *Histoire de Maurice*; Hawkesworth, *Relation des voyages*; Bertrand, *La morale évangélique*; Mercier, *La brouette du vinaigrier*; Millot, *Elémens d'histoire générale*; Molière, *Œuvres*; Gessner, *Collection complète des œuvres*. For full details of these works see the FBTEE database or Schmidt, 'Liste des impressions', 243–54.
136 See Louis Fauche-Borel, *Catalogue des livres de Louis Fauche-Borel, imprimeur du Roi* (Neuchâtel: 1787), 40. The STN employed several common practices – printing fresh title pages for old works and packaging unsold works together as 'collections' especially – in order to make works appear 'newer' than they really were. For the printing of false title pages see BPUN STN MS 1028, Journal Ci, 458. For an example of another contemporary printer using such practices, see Zachs, *The First John Murray*, 36.
137 The STN printed 2,071 copies of the *Oeuvres completes d'Alexis Piron* on 1 September 1777. On 25 January 1779 1,577 copies were still in stock and even by 1 June 1787, 641 copies were still unsold. The Society printed 805 copies of David Hume's *La vie de David Hume* on 12 October 1777. On 25 January 1779, 548 copies were still in stock, 200 of which remained unsold on 1 June 1785.
138 The STN printed 2,520 copies of Mercier's *La mort de Louis XI* on 16 October 1783. 1,495 of these were still in stock on 1 June 1787.
139 In April 1777, for example, the Society noted to the bookseller Gabriel Décombaz in Lausanne that the batch of 100 copies of the 'Art de coeffer' he had been sent would probably turn out to be a 'garde magasin'. See BPUN STN MS 1103, 203 (STN to Decombaz in Lausanne, 17 April 1777).

140 Denis Diderot, *Lettre sur le commerce de la librairie: la propriété littéraire au XVIIIe siècle* (Paris: L. Hachette, 1861), 11.
141 Mami Fujiwara, 'Diderot et le droit d'auteur avant la lettre: autour de la Lettre sur le commerce de la librairie', *Revue d'histoire littéraire de la France* 105, no. 1 (2005): 79-94.
142 Daniel Roche, 'Lumières et commerces vues de Neuchâtel 1769-1789', in *Le rayonnement d'une maison d'édition dans l'Europe des Lumières: la Société typographique de Neuchâtel 1769-1789*, ed. Michel Schlup and Robert Darnton (Hauterive: Editions Gilles Attinger, 2005), 557-71 at 561.

Chapter 3

1 On the Dotaux affair, see BPUN MS1142, 218-226, Dossier Dotaux, Frédrich.
2 Schlup, 'Coup d'oeil sur les relations commerciales', 109.
3 Jeffrey Freedman, 'La Société typographique de Neuchâtel et l'Allemagne', in *Le rayonnement d'une maison d'édition dans l'Europe des Lumières: la Société typographique de Neuchâtel 1769-1789*, ed. Michel Schlup and Robert Darnton (Neuchâtel: Attinger, 2005), 475-89 at 488.
4 BPUN STN MS 1059, Comte de voyage (unpaginated).
5 Quoted in Selwyn, *Everyday Life in the German Book Trade*, 15.
6 Eisenstein, *Grub Street Abroad*, 3.
7 It is striking that while the 'Cosmopolis' invoked by Eisenstein was indeterminate and essentially boundless, her evidence was drawn predominantly from the Low Countries and its immediate surrounds.
8 For further examination and case studies of some of the STN's European markets, see Burrows, *Enlightenment Best-Sellers*, Chapter 4.
9 BPUN STN MS 1095, 9-12.
10 See 'Chapter 2 - The Myth of the Mountain Dwellers' above.
11 BPUN STN MS 1185, Dossier Jean Mossy, 341 (Jean Mossy in Marseille to STN, 25 December 1771).
12 On *villes d'entrée*, see Rigogne, *Between State and Market*, 59-62. On the numbers of booksellers and printers active in France, see ibid., 171. The figures given here relate to the year 1781.
13 Ibid., 168. This contraction in the number of French publishing houses should not be read as decline, but rather consolidation and concentration, as it was accompanied by increases in both the number of presses operated by each print shop and the efficiency with which these presses were employed. See ibid., 134.
14 Henri-Jean Martin and Roger Chartier, *Le livre triomphant 1660-1830*, Histoire de l'édition française (Paris: Promodis, 1984), 216.
15 Rigogne, *Between State and Market*, 207. The clear under-reporting of connections to foreign presses in the 1764 survey can be confirmed by cross-referencing towns that reported no foreign commercial ties with those actively trading with the Cramers of Geneva. See AEG, Commerce F57, Grand livre de Gabriel et Philibert Cramer, 1755-67.
16 The number and location of France's booksellers used for the statistics in this chapter are taken from Perrin, *Almanach de la librairie*. For a discussion of the difficulty of knowing the exact number of shops and ambulant traders in the kingdom see Rigogne, *Between State and Market*, 164.

17 Rigogne, *Between State and Market*, 69.
18 Avignon and the Comtat Venaissin were not part of the kingdom of France during our period, but were occupied by French troops between 1768 and 1774. Trade restrictions during the rule of Louis XVI dealt a severe blow to the region's printers and booksellers. See Moulinas, *L'imprimerie, la librairie et la presse à Avignon*, 228-71.
19 Nice was part of Piedmont until it was conquered by the armies of the First French Republic in 1792.
20 BPUN STN MS 1150, Instructions et notes de voyage pour J.-F. Favarger, avec ses lettres à la STN. Favarger's letters to the STN serve as a reminder that even in the towns and regions where the Society was relatively successful, the significant majority of booksellers could not be convinced to do business.
21 Between 1773 and 1777, the Veuve Desaint sent 360,603 *livres*-worth of books to the north of France, including 18,975 *livres*-worth in large and near bi-weekly shipments to Gilles Joubert in Coutances and 1,155 *livres*-worth to Charles Monnoyer in Le Mans. See BHVP MS Na 490(4). The network of the Rouen-based bookseller Jacques Besogne in 1784 contrasts equally strongly with that of the STN. See Quéniart, *L'imprimerie et la librairie à Rouen*, 165.
22 Rigogne, *Between State and Market*, 211-2. Like the STN's trade with its regional partners, much of this trade was conducted in the form of exchanges. See Quéniart, *L'imprimerie et la librairie à Rouen*, 158.
23 Frédéric Barbier's study of printing and bookselling in the *ancien régime* towns and villages that now make up the Nord-Pas-de-Calais region also concluded that the STN's failure to make inroads there was not due to a lack of buoyancy in the local market, but came rather because of its inability to compete. See Barbier, *Lumières du Nord*, 175.
24 On 27 January 1780, by printing 1,255 copies of Brissot's *Observations sur la littérature en France* and sending them directly to Versailles on the instructions of the author, the STN took a dramatic strategic turn. Many more editions commissioned by and for Parisian booksellers and authors left the Society's presses during the years that followed. FBTEE database users should be careful not to confuse these large shipments with the normal trading of 'regular' stocks with Paris, which never took place. See 'Chapter 4 – The Storm Will Pass'.
25 BPUN STN MS 1103, 194 (STN to Barré in Paris, 15 April 1777).
26 'Le Nord' is a phrase that crops up at several places in the STN archives to describe, variously, northern France and Paris, The Dutch Republic and its surrounds, and the scattered markets for French books located in England, Scandinavia and Russia. Throughout this volume the term 'The North' is used as shorthand for the vast cross-border zone of production of French books described in the current paragraph.
27 Rigogne, *Between State and Market*, 212. This sea link, of course, also left traders of The North much better placed to serve growing markets for French books in the colonial world, especially North America, than were the Swiss.
28 Karel Davids, *The Rise and Decline of Dutch Technological Leadership: Technology, Economy and Culture in the Netherlands, 1350-1800* (Leiden and Boston, MA: Brill, 2008), 172.
29 Vliet, 'Print and Public in Europe', 250; Eugeen De Bock, *Het nederlandse boek: overzicht van zijn geschiedenis* (Brussel: Vlaamsche Boekwezen, 1939), 92-6.
30 Joost Jakobus Kloek and Wijnandus Wilhelmus Mijnhardt, *Dutch Culture in a European Perspective 2; 1800; Blueprints for a National Community* (London: Palgrave, 2004), 74-6.
31 Baggerman, *Publishing Policies and Family Strategies*, 106-10.

32 On the Dutch press, see ibid., 227–54.
33 Jeremy D. Popkin, *News and Politics in the Age of Revolution: Jean Luzac's Gazette de Leyde* (Ithaca: Cornell Univiversity Press, 1989), 121. See also Goinga, *Alom te bekomen*, 36–7. For a synthesis of work on the international gazettes, see Simon Burrows, 'The Cosmopolitan Press', in *Press, Politics and the Public Sphere in Europe and North America, 1760-1820*, ed. Hannah Barker and Simon Burrows (Cambridge: Cambridge University Press, 2002), 23–47. Gilles Feyel's work on the French post suggests that in 1781, France boasted a relatively modest 45,000 subscribers to newspapers, of which 15,000 were to international gazettes. See Gilles Feyel, 'La diffusion des gazettes étrangères en France et la revolution postale des années 1750', in *Les gazettes européennes de langue française (XVIIe-XVIIIe siècles)*, ed. Henri Duranton, Claude Labrosse and Pierre Rétat (Saint-Etienne: Presses Universitaires de Saint-Etienne, 1992), 81–99. Manuscript newsletters, notably Pidansat de Mairobert's *Mémoires secrets*, Friedrich Melchior Grimm's *Correspondance littéraire* and Louis-François Metra's Neuwied-produced *Correspondance littéraire secrète*, extended this trend to even more privileged influencers learning even more privileged literary news, always remaining the preserve of Paris and the Northern zone.
34 The first known book advertisement in a Dutch newspaper dates from 1724, see B. van Selm, '"Het kompt altemael aen op het distribuweeren". De boekdistributie in de Republiek als object van onderzoek', in *De productie, distributie en consumptie van cultuur*, ed. J. J. Kloek and W. W. Mijnhardt (Amsterdam: Rodopi, 1991), 89–99 at 91.
35 Darnton, *The Business of Enlightenment*, 258.
36 Michel Schlup, 'Un commerce de librairie entre Neuchâtel et La Haye (1769-1779)', in *Le magasin de l'univers*, ed. C. Berkvens-Stevelinck, Hans Bots, P.G. Hoftijzer and O.S. Lankhorst (Leiden and New York, NY: Brill, 1992), 237–50 at 239. Rey's main literary contact in Neuchâtel was not a bookseller or printer, but rather the nobleman and protector of Rousseau, Pierre-Alexandre DuPeyrou.
37 BPUN STN MS 1103, 135 (STN to M. Magerus in Amsterdam, 22 March 1777). For copies of this letter sent to other traders, also see 135–37 and 145.
38 Ibid., 157 (STN to Panchaud, Houlez and Schouw in Amsterdam, 27 March 1777).
39 Schlup, 'Un commerce de librairie', 248.
40 See Bonnant, *Le livre genevois*, 208.
41 This statistic relates to the period 1 July 1769 to 30 September 1771. See 'Chapter 1 – A Printing Shop across the Border' and especially Figure 1.2.
42 Schlup, 'Un commerce de librairie', 239.
43 BPUN STN MS 1033, 19.
44 On Boubers, see Barbier, *Lumières du Nord*, 133–5, 219–27.
45 BPUN STN MS 1033, 112–279. See also Schlup, 'Un commerce de librairie'.
46 BPUN STN MS 1140, Delahaye & Co., 285.
47 The edition was produced in collaboration with Nouffer de Rodon of Geneva.
48 BPUN STN MS 1140, 287 (Delahaye & Co. in Brussels to STN, 3 May 1782).
49 Ibid., 291 (Delahaye & Co. in Brussels to STN, 6 July 1782).
50 Ibid., 294 (Delahaye & Co. to STN, undated [August 1782]).
51 Barber, *Studies in the Booktrade of the European Enlightenment*, 252.
52 BHVP MS Na 490(4), 147. On Nourse see Elena Muceni, 'John/Jean Nourse: un masque anglais au service de la littérature clandestine francophone', *La lettre clandestine* 24 (2016): 203–19.
53 Máire Kennedy, 'The Distribution of a Locally-Produced French Periodical in Provincial Ireland: the "Magazin à La Mode", 1777-1778', *Eighteenth-Century Ireland/Iris an dá chultúr* 9 (1994): 83–98 at 96.

54 Máire Kennedy, 'The Top 20 French Authors in Eighteenth-Century Irish Private Libraries', *The Linen Hall Review* 12, no. 1 (1995): 4–8.
55 Also, see Hugh Gough, 'Book Imports from Continental Europe in Late Eighteenth-Century Ireland: Luke White and the Société typographique de Neuchâtel', *The Long Room* 38 (1993): 35–48.
56 Bonnant, *Le livre genevois*, 277.
57 Zachs, *The First John Murray*, 37.
58 Boinod and Gaillard, *Catalogue des livres qui se trouvent chez Boinod & Gaillard. Les livres éclairent la multitude, humanisent les hommes puissants, charment le loisir des riches, instruisent toutes les classes de la société* (Philadelphia, PA: Printed by Charles Cist, 1784).
59 Darnton, *The Business of Enlightenment*, 318.
60 Bonnant, *Le livre genevois*, 61, 70.
61 Ibid., 32.
62 Ibid., 34–5.
63 Ibid., 18.
64 Darnton, *The Business of Enlightenment*, 312–3.
65 Ibid., 313.
66 Bonnant, *Le livre genevois*, 104.
67 Thirty-one Italian traders, indeed, each bought more than 100 books from the STN.
68 The account books of the Luchtmans of Leiden, for example, show that the firm sold many textbooks to the Italian states.
69 Renato Pasta, 'Les échanges avec l'Italie', in *Le rayonnement d'un maison d'édition dans l'Europe des Lumières: la Société typographique de Neuchâtel 1769-1789*, ed. Robert Darnton and Michel Schlup (Hauterive: Editions Gilles Attinger, 2005), 455–73 at 456.
70 Pasta, 'Les échanges avec l'Italie', 457.
71 Ibid., 465.
72 BPUN STN MS 1145, 297–8 (Durand in Bologne to STN, 21 April 1788).
73 Darnton, *The Business of Enlightenment*, 303.
74 On the STN's difficulties finding a 'solid' trader in Warsaw, see BPUN STN MS 1167, Dossier Joseph Hietzgern, 364 (Joseph Hietzgern in Kraków to STN, 21 August 1784). Shipments to the East European zone also increased dramatically, from 4.3 per cent or total sales to 9.4 per cent, in the period from 8 July 1784 when the STN was winding up its business, often selling works at significant discounts. See 'Chapter 4 – The Storm Will Pass'.
75 Vliet, 'Print and Public in Europe', 248.
76 See Freedman, *Before Nationalism*, 34. Freedman suggests that the booksellers of Berne and Basle, with the possible exception of Serini, for whom little information is available, conducted their French-language wholesale trade mainly (if not exclusively) with, and indeed in, Germany. Swiss-German booksellers would set off for Leipzig in late March or early April and not return until May. This strong link with The North perhaps explains the surprisingly large number of Dutch-printed French-language books available to members of reading societies in contemporary Schaffhausen. See Barney M. Milstein, *Eight Eighteenth-Century Reading Societies. A Sociological Contribution to the History of German Literature* (Berne and Frankfurt: Herbert Lang, 1972), 237–303. Yet there is little in the ordering patterns from the STN's clients in Basle and Berne that suggests the cyclical purchase of works to take to fair, and the number of STN works advertised at Leipzig was always limited. See also Selwyn, *Everyday Life in the German Book Trade*, 121, 25.
77 Selwyn, *Everyday Life in the German Book Trade*, 111.

78 Freedman suggests this dominance was waning. See Freedman, *Before Nationalism*, 13; Selwyn, *Everyday Life in the German Book Trade*, 120–1.
79 Selwyn, *Everyday Life in the German Book Trade*, 131; ibid., 124.
80 Freedman, *Before Nationalism*, 3. Freedman's information comes from the *Tableau des principaux libraires de l'Europe*, which was included in a 1781 edition of the Parisian *Almanach de la librairie*.
81 BHVP MS Na 490(4), 84.
82 BPUN STN MS 1150, 101 (Favarger in Avignon to STN, 2 August 1778).
83 That is, only thirty-five foreign clients took more than 1,000 works from the STN in more than ten different orders spanning at least five years.
84 On the STN's bad debtors, see BPUN STN MS 1044, Livre des Menus débiteurs A (avril 1783–juin 1787).
85 Thierry Rigogne, 'Librairie et réseaux commerciaux du livre en France', in *Le rayonnement d'une maison d'édition dans l'Europe des Lumières: la Société typographique de Neuchâtel 1769-1789*, ed. Robert Darnton and Michel Schlup (Hauterive: Editions Gilles Attinger, 2005), 375–404 at 396.

Chapter 4

1 Mauvelain's crates contained 966 books, 158 of which are flagged in the FBTEE database as having been potentially illegal. The larger part of the contents of these crates was made up of 400 copies of the prospectus for a never realized book, the '*Histoire ancienne et moderne de Châlons-sur-Marne*', printed on commission by the STN, and 200 copies of another commissioned work, Pontus de Tyard, *Histoire de Pontus de Thyard de Bissy; suivie de la Généalogie de cette maison et de la Relation de la campagne de 1664 en Hongrie* (Neuchâtel: [Sociétée typographique de Neuchâtel], 1784).
2 The story of Mauvelain's relationship with the STN is told brilliantly in Darnton, 'Trade in the Taboo'.
3 On the idea that smuggling books through the Jura mountains was a significant and normal part of the STN's business see Darnton, *The Business of Enlightenment*, 39, 159–60; Darnton, *Forbidden Best-Sellers*, 17–20; and Darnton, 'Trade in the Taboo', 68.
4 Darnton, *Forbidden Best-Sellers*, 169–246; Robert Darnton, 'The Forbidden Books of Pre-revolutionary France', in *Rewriting the French Revolution*, ed. Colin Lucas (Oxford: Clarendon, 1991), 1–32 at 32.
5 These 'general stock' statistics exclude commissioned printings, which are discussed in detail later in this chapter.
6 See BPUN STN MS 1027, Copie des comptes, 106–11.
7 On the STN's *grands projets* see, Darnton, *The Business of Enlightenment*; Robert Darnton, 'La Société typographique et les batailles autour de l'Encyclopédie', in *L'édition neuchâteloise au siècle des Lumières: la Société typographique de Neuchâtel (1769-1789)*, ed. Michel Schlup (Neuchâtel: Bibliothèque publique et universitaire de Neuchâtel, 2002), 114–29; Cernuschi, '"Notre grande entreprise des arts"'; Madeleine Pinault Sørensen, 'Les planches de la *Description des arts et métiers*', in *Le rayonnement d'une maison d'édition dans l'Europe des Lumières: la Société typographique de Neuchâtel 1769-1789*, ed. Michel Schlup and Robert Darnton (Hauterive: Editions Gilles Attinger, 2005), 219–55.
8 Darnton, 'La Société typographique et les batailles autour de l'Encyclopédie', 124. Despite many problems, the STN made a profit of about 60,000 *livres* on an investment

of 92,000 *livres* with its *Encyclopédie* project, see Darnton, *The Business of Enlightenment*, 383. Alas, such ventures were risky and difficult to come by.
9. BPUN STN MS 1027, 147.
10. The Brun family, for example, liquidated their investment in the STN in 1782, extracting 20,556.0.8 *livres* of capital. See ibid., 135.
11. Ibid., 106–46.
12. Nicolaus Ernst Kleemann, *Voyage de Vienne à Belgrade et à Kilianova, dans le pays des Tartares Budziacs et Nogais, dans la Crimée et de Kaffa à Constantinople au travers de la mer Noire, avec le retour à Vienne par Trieste, fait dans les années 1768, 1769 et 1770* (Neuchâtel: Société typographique de Neuchâtel, 1780).
13. Danielle Plan, *Un Genevois d'autrefois: Henri-Albert Gosse [1753-1816]* (Paris and Geneva: Fischbacher and Kundig, 1909), 4. The printer and bookseller Henri-Albert Gosse (1712–80) should not be confused with his nephew, the naturalist and pharmacist Henri-Albert Gosse (1753–1816).
14. AEG, Fonds de Commerce F61, F62, F63, 'Copie de lettres H.A. Gosse & Cie'.
15. AEG, Fonds de Commerce F62, 45 (Gosse to Machuel in Rouen, 24 May 1777).
16. Ibid., 384–5 (Gosse to Dufour in Chambery, 1 October 1782).
17. Variations on each of these issues also affected francophone printers and booksellers right across Europe during the 1770s and 1780s and, outside of France, only the strongest houses survived. On the situation in Avignon see Moulinas, *L'imprimerie, la librairie et la presse à Avignon*, 228–71. Pierre Rousseau's successor at the Société typographique de Bouillon, Trécourt, had to save the business from bankruptcy due to bad payers in 1783, reviving it only in a reduced capacity. See Martin, 'La librairie française en 1777-1778', 110.
18. For much of the eighteenth century the French state tolerated, and even at times tacitly encouraged, commercial printing beyond the kingdom's borders. The role played by centres such as Amsterdam and Geneva in enriching French industry, commerce and culture was consequent and recognized by many. Booksellers and printers based in towns like Rouen seldom failed to remind French officials of the mutually beneficial nature of their close ties with foreign presses, and the chaos and hardship likely to ensue if trade was disrupted. In September 1771, having earlier in the year introduced a tax on the sale of paper in France that disadvantaged French book producers, the French government introduced duties on foreign book imports, set at the rate of sixty *livres* the hundredweight. But after complaints concerning the damage being done to French business, these duties were reduced almost immediately to twenty *livres*, then again in 1773 to 6.10.0 *livres*. The duties were abolished altogether in 1775. In 1777 and 1778 significant legislation was introduced that aimed to help France's long put-upon provincial booksellers better compete with their Parisian rivals: limitations were placed on printing *privilèges* (that were largely horded by Parisian dealers); the process of seeking permission to publish was simplified; and existing counterfeit works were allowed, after stamping, to circulate in the kingdom. Robert Darnton has noted that the STN letter books do not betray any great panic on behalf of the Swiss concerning these sweeping regulations. See Darnton, '"What is the History of Books?" Revisited', 501. And the FBTEE database confirms that the immediate consequences for the STN's business were limited. For a summary of French book-trade regulations around this time see Barber, *Studies in the Booktrade of the European Enlightenment*, 172.
19. It is difficult to gauge the effects of edicts on an individual basis for several reasons. First, most important directives provoked remonstrances by disadvantaged parties

that were so melodramatic that even informed contemporaries found it difficult to locate real damage in the sea of crocodiles' tears. Second, few edicts were immediately registered by local *parlemens* creating an inevitable lag before their effects were felt and an uneven and ambiguous legal situation across the kingdom. Third, because *ancien régime* rules were oftentimes very different to enforcement realities, it took some time for book-trade actors on the ground to work out the dedication of central authorities towards new sets of regulations. Practices tended to change only when obvious signs of commitment to enforce new edicts (through confiscations, imprisonments, and so forth) were demonstrated. Fourth, the impact of regulations tended to have less effect on the financial health of the printers and booksellers of any given region than macroeconomic factors, rendering a statistical approach to the issue all but impossible. And fifth, because printing and bookselling circuits were so interconnected, especially in the North, severe damage inflicted anywhere was certain to lead, in the short term at least, to problems across the map. Nonetheless, it is clear from the general situation of the extra-territorial printers during the 1770s and 1780s, and their many complaints about various pieces of regulation, that the STN operated during a period that lacked a clear and stable international regulatory environment conducive to doing good business.

20 See, especially, Ernest Labrousse, *La crise de l'économie française à la fin de l'ancien régime et au début de la révolution* (Paris: Presses Universitaires de France, 1943). See also Peter Michael Jones, *Reform and Revolution in France: The Politics of Transition, 1774-1791* (Cambridge: Cambridge University Press, 1995), 103; Emmanuel Le Roy Ladurie, *The Ancien Régime: A History of France, 1610-1774* (Oxford: Blackwell, 1996), 491; L. M. Cullen, *The Brandy Trade Under the Ancien Régime: Regional Specialisation in the Charente* (Cambridge: Cambridge University Press, 1998), 54; Serge Bonin and Claude Langlois, eds., *Atlas de la Révolution française 10: économie* (Paris: Editions de l'EHESS, 1997); and Joël Félix, 'The Financial Origins of the French Revolution', in *The Origins of the French Revolution*, ed. Peter R. Campbell (Basingstoke and New York: Palgrave, 2006), 107–25.
21 See, especially, Estivals, *La statistique bibliographique*, 391.
22 Inderwildi, 'Acteurs et réseaux commerciaux', 121.
23 After enduring a couple of lean years following his ignominious ejection from the Society, Fauche made a spectacular publishing comeback in 1775 with a re-edition of the works of Rousseau. An eclectic set of popular editions ranging from Du Lauren's *L'Arrétin modern* (1776) to *Les psaumes de David mis en vers* (1777), and stunning trophy books including the quarto first edition of Horace-Bénédict de Saussure's *Voyage dans les Alpes* (1779–86), quickly brought Fauche's operation to notability and renewed sustainability.
24 In Brissot's case, half of the payment was due in advance and the other half within six months of his receipt of the books.
25 STN Commissioned editions are defined by the FBTEE project as works commissioned from the STN by a client, with large numbers of copies (though not necessarily all) distributed to or on behalf of the client. In some cases these works have been identified on the basis of sales data, for example, because a single client took the vast majority of an edition immediately after its publication.
26 Until 26 January 1780 the STN shipped 155,905 books, 12,056 (7.7%) of which have been identified as having been commissioned by third parties. From 27 January 1780, by contrast, the Society shipped 254,169 books, 96,621 (38%) of which were commissioned. If we ignore these commissioned editions, the STNs shipments-per-year

remained relatively steady throughout most of their established trading existence, at around 15–20,000 books per year.
27 1780, 22 per cent; 1781, 15 per cent; 1782, 53 per cent; 1783, 48 per cent; 1784, 27 per cent; and 1785, 17 per cent.
28 Darnton, 'The Grub Street Style of Revolution', 303.
29 See Darnton, ed., 'Brissot's Correspondence with the STN', BRS12 (Jacques-Pierre Brissot de Warville in Paris to STN, 26 January 1780) at http://www.robertdarnton.org/literarytour/brissot. Brissot's Neuchâtel editions were: Jacques-Pierre Brissot de Warville, *Observations sur la littérature en France, sur le barreau, les journaux, &c. ou Lettres d'un Parisien à son ami en province* ([Neuchâtel]: [Société typographique de Neuchâtel], 1780); Jacques-Pierre Brissot de Warville, *Testament politique de l'Angleterre* ([Neuchâtel]: [Société typographique de Neuchâtel], 1680 [1780]); Jacques-Pierre Brissot de Warville, *Recherches philosophiques sur le droit de la propriété considéré dans la nature* ([Neuchâtel]: [Société typographique de Neuchâtel], 1780); Jacques-Pierre Brissot de Warville, *Le café politique de Londres, ou Pasquin dans la loge des Anti-Gallicans à Londres* ([Neuchâtel]: [Société typographique de Neuchâtel], 1780); Jacques-Pierre Brissot de Warville, *Un indépendant à l'ordre des avocats, sur la décadence du barreau en France* (Berlin [Neuchâtel]: [Société typographique de Neuchâtel], 1781); Jacques-Pierre Brissot de Warville, *Théorie des lois criminelles* (Neuchâtel: [Société typographique de Neuchâtel], 1781); Jacques-Pierre Brissot de Warville, *Un Hollandois aux habitans de la Grande-Bretagne* ([Neuchâtel]: [Société typographique de Neuchâtel], 1781); Jacques-Pierre Brissot de Warville, *Le sang innocent vengé, ou Discours sur les réparations dues aux accusés innocens* (Berlin [Neuchâtel]: [Société typographique de Neuchâtel], 1781); Jacques-Pierre Brissot de Warville, *De la vérité, ou méditations sur tous les moyens de parvenir à la vérité dans toutes les connaissances humaines* (Neuchâtel: Société typographique de Neuchâtel, 1782); Jacques-Pierre Brissot de Warville, *Bibliothèque philosophique du législateur, du politique, du jurisconsulte* (Berlin [Neuchâtel]: [Société typographique de Neuchâtel], 1782–85); and Jacques-Pierre Brissot de Warville, *Correspondance universelle sur ce qui intéresse le bonheur de l'homme et de la société* (Neuchâtel: Société typographique de Neuchâtel, 1783).
30 Four of the five Mirabeau works were very short factums and thus do not appear in the FTBEE database. See Schmidt, 'Liste des impressions', 270–71.
31 On Necker see Joël Félix, 'The Problem with Necker's *Compte rendu au roi* (1781)', in *The Crisis of the Absolute Monarchy: France from Old Regime to Revolution*, ed. Julian Swann and Joël Félix (Oxford: Oxford University Press, 2013), 107–25. Félix offers a revisionist alternative to the traditional reading of Necker's work presented here; either way the *Compte rendu au roi* was an unprecedented sensation.
32 The STN accounted for the over 1,700 copies of Necker's *Compte rendu au roi* that they sold under the rubric 'nos editions' and did not record having received any copies from partner houses. Corsini, however, attributes this edition to the 'Libraires associés' confederation of the STN and STB (the STL having left by this point), adding that it was printed in Berne. See Corsini, 'Un pour tous ... et chacun pour soi?', 137.
33 The seven further editions, at least two of which were produced in collaboration with the Société typographique de Berne, were: Necker, *Mémoire donné au roi*; Charles-Alexandre de Calonne, *Les comments* ([Neuchâtel]: [Société typographique de Neuchâtel], [1781]); Philippe-Henri comte de Grimoard, *Lettre du marquis de Caraccioli à M. d'Alembert* ([Neuchâtel]: [Société typographique de Neuchâtel], [1781]); Pierre-Augustin Robert de Saint-Vincent, *Observations modestes d'un citoyen sur les*

opérations de finances de M. Necker, et sur son compte rendu ([Neuchâtel]: [Société typographique de Neuchâtel], [1781]); Charles-Michel [Marquis de] Villette, *Discours au roi* ([Neuchâtel]: [Société typographique de Neuchâtel], [1781]); Bourboulon, *Réponse du sieur Bourboulon,... au Compte rendu au roi par M. Necker* (Londres [Neuchâtel]: [Société typographique de Neuchâtel], 1781); and *Requête au roi sur la retraite de Mr. Necker* ([Berne?]: [Société typographique de Berne?], [1781]). On Quandet de Lachenal, see Charly Guyot, 'Un correspondant parisien de la Société typographique de Neuchâtel: Quandet de Lachenal', *Musée neuchâtelois* 1936: 20–28, 64–74 at 479–83; Robert Darnton, 'Sounding the Literary Market in Prerevolutionary France', *Eighteenth Century Studies* 17, no. 4 (1984): 477–92.

34 On the fascinating publishing history of Mercier's work see Michel Schlup, 'L'édition du Tableau de Paris à Neuchâtel (1781-1783); les éditions du Tableau de Paris, description matérielle', in *Louis-Sébastien Mercier, Tableau de Paris*, ed. Jean Claude Bonnet (Paris: Mercure de France, 1994), XCV–CLXXX. Samuel Fauche had published the first edition of Mercier's work in the spring of 1781, but found himself outbid by his own son and his *commis* Witel for this edition. By comparison, Rousseau obtained only 1,000 *livres* for the manuscript of *La nouvelle Héloïse* and 6,000 *livres* for *Emile*, while Choderlos de Laclos received just 1,600 *livres* for *Les liaisons dangereuses*.

35 Ibid., 133. 7,500 of these copies were printed for Fauche and Witel, with the STN keeping 1,500 for its own account (despite Ostervald having signed a convention limiting the Society to just 750 copies). Fauche and Witel sent the lion's share of their copies to Basle, Frankfurt, Hamburg, Leipzig, London and The Hague. See Alexandre Daguet, 'Mirabeau et ses éditeurs neuchâtelois en 1782', *Musée neuchâtelois* 1887: 233–7 at 235.

36 The STN's Mercier editions were: Louis-Sébastien Mercier, *Le philosophe du Port-au-bled: article du Journal de Paris, pour le 23 octobre 1781, de la lune le 7* ([Neuchâtel]: [Société typographique de Neuchâtel], 1781); Louis-Sébastien Mercier, *La destruction de la ligue, ou La réduction de Paris* (Amsterdam [Neuchâtel]: [Société typographique de Neuchâtel], 1782); Louis-Sébastien Mercier, *L'habitant de la Guadeloupe: comédie en quatre actes* (Neuchâtel: Société typographique de Neuchâtel, 1782); Louis-Sébastien Mercier, *Les tombeaux de Vérone: drame en cinq actes* (Neuchâtel: Société typographique de Neuchâtel, 1782); Louis-Sébastien Mercier, *Zoé: drame en trois actes* (Neuchâtel: Société typographique de Neuchâtel, 1782); Louis-Sébastien Mercier, *La mort de Louis XI, roi de France: pièce historique* (Neuchâtel: Société typographique de Neuchâtel, 1783); Louis-Sébastien Mercier, *Portraits des rois de France* (Neuchâtel: Société typographique de Neuchâtel, 1783); Louis-Sébastien Mercier, *Mon bonnet de nuit* (Neuchâtel and Lausanne: Société typographique de Neuchâtel and Jean-Pierre Heubach, 1784); Louis-Sébastien Mercier, *L'homme sauvage, histoire traduite de ... par M. Mercier* (Neuchâtel: Société typographique de Neuchâtel, 1784); and Louis-Sébastien Mercier, *Portrait de Philippe II, roi d'Espagne* (Amsterdam [Neuchâtel]: [Société typographique de Neuchâtel], 1785). The STN and Fauche family's early 1780s Mirabeau editions (in addition to the five factums) were: Honoré-Gabriel Riqueti comte de Mirabeau, *Des lettres de cachet et des prisons d'état: ouvrage posthume, composé en 1778* (Hambourg [Neuchâtel]: [Jonas Fauche and Jérémie Witel], 1782); Honoré-Gabriel Riqueti comte de Mirabeau, *L'espion dévalisé* (Londres [Neuchâtel]: [Jonas Fauche and Jérémie Witel], 1782); Honoré-Gabriel Riqueti comte de Mirabeau, *Mémoires à consulter pour M. le comte de Mirabeau contre M. le marquis de Monnier* ([Neuchâtel]: [Société typographique de Neuchâtel], 1782); Honoré-Gabriel Riqueti comte de Mirabeau, *Errotika biblion* (Rome [Neu-

châtel]: de l'imprimerie du Vatican [Jonas Fauche and Jérémie Witel], 1783); and Honoré-Gabriel Riqueti comte de Mirabeau, *Le libertin de qualité, ou Ma Conversion* ([Neuchâtel]: [Jonas Fauche and Jérémie Witel], 1784). During this period the Fauche family also printed several other highly illegal books, including Berthélemy-François-Joseph Moufle d'Angerville, *Vie privée de Louis XV* (Londres [Neuchâtel]: John-Peter Lyton [Fauche], 1784). The STN played a role in distributing all of the above works. See also Schlup, 'Entre pouvoir et clandestinité', 79.

37 The top five FBTEE keywords by book sales for the period 1 October 1771 to 26 January 1780 are: Religion (43,560 sales), Literature (42,495), Christianity (38,445), Works of Religiosity (30,101), History (54,484). For the period 27 January 1780 to 7 July 1784 this becomes: France (56,646), Literature (41,265), Politics (39,160), Law (36,820), Current Affairs (35,204). For an explanation of FBTEE keywords, see Burrows, *Enlightenment Best-Sellers*.

38 For reasons of printing process discussed in the chapter 'The Triumph of Benevolence, or The History of Francis Wills', the STN actually achieved a few more copies of each of these work than the targets given here. The Society's printers achieved, for example, 2,036 copies of *Zoé* and 2,045 of *L'habitant de la Guadeloupe*.

39 Schlup, 'Entre pouvoir et clandestinité', 79.

40 After acting like money was no object and winning Ostervald's confidence by promptly paying their initial bills, the likes of Brissot and Rilliet de Saussure typically went on to accrue significant debts. By October 1784 Brissot owed the STN a remarkable 12,301.9.0 *livres*. See Darnton, 'The Grub Street Style of Revolution', 303.

41 See BPUN STN MS 1135, 425 (Barthelemy Chirol in Geneva to STN, 27 February 1782).

42 On this group, and the production of *libels* more generally, see Burrows, *Blackmail, Scandal, and Revolution*; Darnton, *The Devil in the Holy Water*. Charles Gravier, comte de Vergennes, served as the French Minister of Foreign Affairs between 1774 and 1787.

43 '*Les Rois de France dégénérés*' and most other such works of Pelleport's stable were phantoms that were never written. This is clear from the bibliographic record, the attempts of French agents to discover them and above all Brissot's interrogation record. See Simon Burrows, 'The Innocence of Jacques-Pierre Brissot', *The Historical Journal* 46 (2003): 843–71.

44 As an example of threatened pamphleteering, on 7 April Pelleport's broadside *An Alarm Bell Against French Spies* announced (or, rather, threatened) the forcoming appearance of two further scandalous pamphlets, *Les amours et aventures du Vizir Vergennes* and *Les passe-tems d'Antoinette*. See Burrows, *Blackmail, Scandal, and Revolution*, 123–7.

45 The other titles of interest to the police during this mission were: *Confession générale de Madame la comtesse du Barry*; *Le cri de la France contre M. de Maurepas*; *La diligence, ou dialogue entre trois gens qui ne sont pas trop sots sur les affaires du temps*; *Essais historiques sur la vie de Marie-Antoinette*; *Les joueurs et M. Dusaulx*; and two further anti-Necker pamphlets. See Seaward, 'The French Government and the Policing of the Extra-Territorial Print Trade', 333.

46 Ibid., 257–9, 339.

47 Some of this confidence derived from the success that the French authorities had enjoyed neutralisng the illegal trade in Avignon dating from the 1768 invasion and subsequent occupation. See Moulinas, *L'imprimerie, la librairie et la presse à Avignon*, 208–57.

48 Darnton, 'Reading, Writing and Publishing', 227.

49 It was not until April 1782 that the confiscated copies were released back to the STN. On the affair see the letters of Brissot made available by Robert Darnton at http://www.robertdarnton.org/literarytour/brissot, especially BRS21-96.
50 For edition details see notes 33 and 36.
51 BPUN STN MS 1026, Copie de comptes janvier 1780 à mars 1781 et mai-sept 1782, 74. The losses that stemmed from these raids were split between the STN and Chauvet.
52 BPUN STN MS 1180, Dossier Louis-Sébastien Mercier, 240 (Louis-Sébastein Mercier in Paris to STN, 27 August 1782). Mercier informed Ostervald that he had the assurances of Le Noir that the copies would be returned, and that he could pass these assurances on to Witel. It is unclear exactly how many copies of Mercier's book Witel had sent to Paris.
53 See the chapter 'Procès Romanesque, offrant un sujet de comédie très riche et très heureux'. Equally, as Simon Burrows reveals in the companion volume to this book, a large consignment of another STN edition – Jacques Le Scène-Desmaisons, *Contrat conjugal, ou Loix du mariage, de la répudiation et du divorce, avec une dissertation sur l'origine et le droit des dispenses* (Neuchâtel: Société typographique de Neuchâtel, 1783) – were seized at Versailles in 1782. See Burrows, *Enlightenment Best-Sellers*.
54 Le Camus de Néville served as director of the book trade between 1776 and 1784.
55 R. Tresse and M. Daumas, 'La description des arts et métiers de l'Académie des sciences et le sort de ses planches gravées en taille douce', *Revue d'histoire des sciences et de leurs applications* 7, no. 2 (1954): at 166; Schlup, 'Points de repère', 97.
56 Cernuschi, '"Notre grande entreprise des arts"', 186.
57 Dossier Faivre, 133 (Faivre in Pontarlier to STN, 24 July 1780).
58 Ibid., 134 (Faivre in Pontarlier to STN, 27 July 1780). See also, Dossier Charmet, 181 (Charmet in Besançon to STN, 28 July 1780). The French government's crackdown against counterfeit editions of legally circulating books at this time was part of the attempted rebalancing of the French book of the 1777 and 1778 edits (see n. 19). If Paris's printers and booksellers were disadvantaged by limits imposed on their printing *privilèges* and the effective amnesty (through stamping) of existing counterfeit editions, some of their ire was placated by assurances that toughened enforcement policies would be put in place.
59 A final volume of the STN's edition of the *Descriptions des arts et métiers* was printed in 1783, although it lacked the ambitious additions to the original text seen in the rest of the set. By the time that the volumes were ceded to Moutard, the Society was trying to liquidate its vast stock holdings and saw the deal, partially at least, as a relief. See BPUN STN MS 1110, Copies des Lettres L, 1059 (STN to Moutard in Paris, 16 June 1785); see also ibid., 997 (STN to Vergennes in Paris, 1 March 1785).
60 BPUN STN MS 1109, Copies des Lettres I, 347 (STN to Quandet de Lachenal in Paris, 1 March 1781).
61 Schlup, 'Le rêve impossible de la STN', 153–4.
62 BPUN STN MS 1180, 240 (Mercier in Paris to STN, 27 August 1782).
63 Seaward, 'The French Government and the Policing of the Extra-Territorial Print Trade', 234. Attempts were made to confiscate anti-Necker and anti-Miromesnil pamphlets in 1781. See Darnton, *The Devil in the Holy Water*, 109.
64 Seaward, 'The French Government and the Policing of the Extra-Territorial Print Trade', 193–4.
65 The STN handled their first copies of *L'éspion dévalisé* on 18 August 1782 and *Les lettres de cachet* on 5 December 1782. Both editions were taken from Jonas-Samuel Fauche, Ch.S. Favre & Cie in Neuchâtel.
66 Prussian-protectorate Neuchâtel – of strategic importance as a bridgehead towards the Franche-Comté – suffered uncomfortable relations with both France and the

Swiss Confederation of thirteen cantons. Neuchâtel, despite its many efforts, was not even mentioned in the 1777 renewal of the alliance between France and the Swiss Confederation. See Jelmini, 'Politique intérieure et extérieure de Neuchâtel', 103–5.

67 Schlup, 'Entre pouvoir et clandestinité', 81. The Fauche-Witel print shop was again closed down in 1785, at which time Jonas Fauche fled to America. Jérémie Witel set up shop in Les Verrières until 1790, when he was executed for his role in the Genevan Revolution. See Michel Schlup and Pierre-Yves Tissot, eds., *Le livre Neuchâtelois, 1533-1983: catalogue des expositions commémoratives du 450e anniversaire de l'imprimerie neuchâteloise* (Neuchâtel: Attinger, 1983) 40–2.

68 BPUN STN MS 1213, Dossier David-Alphonse de Sandoz-Rollin, 298–9 (Sandoz-Rollin in Paris to STN, 7 May 1783).

69 These books were sent on 3 October 1782, via the forwading agents Revol and Company in Lyon.

70 The diplomatic squeeze around this period was not limited to the printers of Neuchâtel. In December 1783 the Lausannois printer and bookseller Jean-Pierre Heubach was forced to swear an oath in front of Bern's censorship authorities not to print any works by Voltaire and to submit all new works for inspection prior to publication. See Madeleine Bovard-Schmidt, 'Jean-Pierre Heubach, un imprimeur Lausannois du XVIIIe siècle', *Revue historique vaudoise* 74, no. 1 (1966): 1–56 at 40.

71 These regulations had been under consideration for some time and several alternative options, from the re-introduction of the tax on imported books that had been rescinded in 1775 to the state employment of wagon drivers who could be trusted to deliver books without succumbing to corruption, were discounted. See Seaward, 'The French Government and the Policing of the Extra-Territorial Print Trade', 226, 48–9. Rouen's traders, aware of their mutually profitable relationships with the booksellers and printers of Berlin, Copenhagen, London, Liège, Stockholm and a host of other northern European towns, protested vehemently against the project before its implementation. See Quéniart, *L'imprimerie et la librairie à Rouen*, 157.

72 BPUN STN MS 1189, 7–8. Quoted in Dominique Varry, 'Les échanges Lyon-Neuchâtel', in *Le rayonnement d'une maison d'édition dans l'Europe des Lumières: la Société typographique de Neuchâtel 1769-1789*, ed. Michel Schlup and Robert Darnton (Hauterive: Editions Gilles Attinger, 2005), 491–518 at 500.

73 On 14 May 1784 Louis Rosset in Lyon wrote to the STN noting that by the time the Neuchâtelois could get copies of Mercier's *Homme sauvage* to him, it would surely already have been counterfeited in France. See BPUN STN MS 1209, Dossier Louis Rosset, 299 (Louis Rosset in Lyon to STN, 14 May 1784).

74 The STN developed this argument at every opportunity between 1784 and 1786. See, for example, BPUN STN MS 1110, 877 (STN to abbé Mongez in Paris, 14 September 1784), 939 (STN to Baron de Trott in Paris, 21 November 1784), 197 (STN to Mossi in Marseille, 29 November 1785), etc …. The Lyonnais bookseller and printer Jean-André Périsse-Duluc insisted that Vergennes' edict amounted to 'une prohibition totale de la librairie étrangère'. See Seaward, 'The French Government and the Policing of the Extra-Territorial Print Trade', 250.

75 BPUN STN MS 1180, 243–4 (Louis-Sébastien Mercier in Paris to Ostervald, 17 August 1783).

76 Overall the STN's sales to France fell from 21,729 copies in the calendar year leading up to 8 June 1783, to 9,731 in the year that followed. In the year 9 June 1783 to 8 June 1784, the STN managed to ship 1,345 copies to Pontarlier and 345 copies to Marseille.

77 See BPUN STN MS 1110, 1088 (STN to Faivre in Pontarlier, 2 August 1785). See, also Darnton, 'Trade in the Taboo', 20–1.

78 Darnton, 'Trade in the Taboo', 26n.
79 The STN handled its first copies of *Le libertin de qualité*, which it bought directly from Fauche and Witel, on 31 July 1784. The crates also contained other prohibited works. See ibid., 30.
80 See BPUN STN MS 1110, 908 (STN to Rigaud, Pons and Company in Montpellier, 17 October 1784); ibid., 916 (STN to Mauvelain in Troyes, 24 October 1784).
81 An extract from the prospectus for Mauvelain's '*Histoire ancienne et moderne de Châlons-sur-Marne*', proposed for subscription as a two-volume quarto set with each volume totalling 700–800 pages, was published in the *Journal Encyclopédique* in January 1785. The work, however, was never realized. Mauvelain's crates also contained 366 copies of other works, including highly illegal titles like Pelleport's *Le diable dans un bénitier* (six copies) and Servan's *Apologie de la Bastille* (twelve copies).
82 BPUN STN MS 1110, 854 (STN to Mauvelain in Paris, 19 August 1784).
83 Darnton, 'Trade in the Taboo', 36.
84 See, for example, Rigogne, *Between State and Market*, 60; Darnton, *Forbidden Best-Sellers*, 17–20.
85 In one of his earliest and finest articles, Darnton recognized the devastation that Vergennes wrought on the STN with his 12 June 1783 regulations, suggesting that the entire Swiss industry fell into a slumber for at least two years, and perhaps until 1789. See Darnton, 'Reading, Writing and Publishing', 233–5. See also Robert Darnton, 'Le livre français à la fin de l'Ancien Régime', *Annales. Histoire, Sciences Sociales, 28e Année* 3 (1973): 735–44 at 744. It is hoped that the current chapter might reorient our attention away from romantic tales of book smuggling and towards this truth, the implications of which have been little explored. Darnton's suggestion elsewhere that the events of 1783 might have driven the STN and other publishers and book dealers further towards highly illegal works is not corroborated by the FBTEE data. See Darnton, 'Reading, Writing and Publishing', 243–4.
86 BPUN STN MS 1110, 924 (STN to Roland de la Platière in Villefranche, 2 November 1784).
87 Ibid., 1035 (STN to Delinani in Chalon-sur-Saône, 3 May 1785).
88 Ibid., 1103 (STN to Garrigan in Avignon, 23 August 1785).
89 See ibid., 939 (STN to Baron de Trott in Paris, 21 November 1784); ibid., 929 (STN to Blaizot in Versailles, 11 November 1784).
90 Ibid., 1074 (STN to Vve Charmet in Besançon, 7 July 1785); ibid., 1077 (STN to Bontoux in Nancy, 14 July 1785).
91 Pommaret, *Le bon père, ou Le chrétien protestant* (Neuchâtel: Société typographique de Neuchâtel, 1783).
92 Pommaret, *Le chrétien par conviction et par sentiment* (n.p. [Neuchâtel]: [Société typographique de Neuchâtel], 1778); Pommaret, *Le catéchumène instruit sous une forme nouvelle* ([Neuchâtel]: [Société typographique de Neuchâtel], 1779).
93 No evidence has been located that the Society did forward this letter.
94 BPUN STN MS 1198, Dossier M. Pomaret, 1–71. Pommaret's final extant letter to the STN is dated 10 July 1787. After this point the BPUN's archive of letters received by the STN is substantially incomplete.
95 BPUN STN MS 1110, 915 (STN to Pavie in La Rochelle, 24 October 1784).
96 Ibid., 929 (STN to Blaizot in Versailles, 11 November 1784). On the disruption of the trade in books between Rouen and the Dutch Republic see Quéniart, *L'imprimerie et la librairie à Rouen*, 160–4.
97 BPUN STN MS 1124, Dossier D. Bonthoux, 304 (Bonthoux in Nancy to STN, 2 February 1785).

98 See BPUN STN MS 1110, 1071 (STN to Ranson in La Rochelle, 3 July 1785); ibid., 1072 (STN to Chauvet in La Rochelle, 3 July 1785). The principal purpose of the STN's letter to Ranson was to ask if Chauvet could be considered trustworthy.
99 Ibid., 987–9 (STN to Pelloutien 'consul de S.M. le Roi de Prusse' in Nantes, 6 February 1785).
100 Jonas Fauche crossed the Atlantic with a large stock of books around this time. He found readers few and far between, however, and quickly abandoned his plans in bookselling and printing to pursue a (brilliant) military career. See Louis Fauche-Borel, *Mémoires de Fauche-Borel* (Paris: Moutardier, 1829), 34.
101 BPUN STN MS 1135, 558 (Chriol in Geneva to STN, 21 February 1784).
102 John R. Kleinschmidt, *Les imprimeurs et libraires de la république de Genève, 1700-1798* (Geneva: A. Jullien, 1948), 67, 89.
103 Ibid., 148.
104 Ibid., 61.
105 Bovard-Schmidt, 'Jean-Pierre Heubach', 33–6.
106 Darnton, 'The Grub Street Style of Revolution', 303. Brissot was the STN's biggest individual debtor by this point.
107 Schlup, 'Points de repère', 102; BPUN STN MS 1240bis, Acte de cautionnement pour la Société typographique de Neuchâtel du 8 Juillet 1784.
108 BPUN STN MS 1110, 990–3 (13–20 February 1785).
109 See, for example, ibid., 999 (8 March 1785).
110 On the STN's debtors see BPUN STN MS 1042, Bilans. It was not out of the ordinary for accounts overdue by up to five years to be found among the London-based bookseller John Murray's records. See Zachs, *The First John Murray*, 41. On bad debtors in Germany see Freedman, *Books Without Borders*, 43–61.
111 Simply closing the print shop and halting the purchase of new works was not a viable option for the STN. The orders the Neuchâtelois received for older books came almost exclusively alongside those for *nouveautés*, meaning that the Society had to keep its offerings attractive even while it was being wound-up.
112 In legal pleadings published in 1791, Ostervald insisted that Neuchâtel's authorities had not allowed the STN to print any works between the 'Acte de cautionnement' of 8 July 1784 and the summer of 1787, although in reality a few editions did leave the Society's presses. See *Information sommaire pour M. l'A. B. Ostervald, maître-bourgeois, et pour Mad. la veuve Bertrand, sa fille aînée* (n.p. [Neuchâtel]: n.d. [1791]). The bibliographic record suggests that production of French-language books across the entire zone was reduced to a trickle from 1784 until the French Revolution. See Silvio Corsini, *BIBLOS 18: Les presses lausannoises au siècle des Lumières*, Bibliothèque cantonale et universitaire de Lausanne. Available at http://dbserv1-bcu.unil.ch/biblos/intro.php2017.
113 See BPUN STN MS 1110, 902 (STN to Comte de Grimouard in Paris, 10 October 1784).
114 Ibid., 1052 (STN to 'M. Le Prince bibliothécaire du Roi' in Paris, 29 May 1785). An example of another proposal: in the summer of 1785 the STN sought a Parisian bookseller willing to commission a collected edition of the works of Barthélemy Imbert. See ibid., 1072–3 (STN to Legrand in Paris, 5 July 1785). Little came of any such enquiries.
115 BPUN STN MS 1135, 612 (Barthélemy Chirol to STN, 9 December 1785).
116 The itinerary of Durand's 1786 tour has been constructed from the copies of letters that the STN sent to him recorded in BPUN STN MS 1110, 1184, 1187, 1197, 1201, 1205, 1212, 1217, 1220, 1223, 1228, 1238, 1239, 1244, 1255, 1261, 1280, 1294, 1317, 1326, 1339, 1340, 1345, 1346, 1347, 1357, 1372.

117 Ibid., 1335–6 (STN to Le Roy, Barret and Grabit in Lyon, 27 December 1786).
118 From 1785 the printers and booksellers of Avignon were obliged to sell their stamped counterfeit works only outside of France, leaving them much more inclined to cut deals with the traders of the Swiss zone. See Moulinas, *L'imprimerie, la librairie et la presse à Avignon*, 255.
119 Some evidence suggests the contrary was the case. In a blow to the colportage industry that was essential to the plans of the Swiss publishers, on 10 July 1786 the sale of books in France was restricted to recognized booksellers. See Barber, *Studies in the Booktrade of the European Enlightenment*, 172.
120 Durand's letters from his second tour, which form the basis of the following analysis, have been preserved in the STN archive. See BPUN STN MS 1145, 199–373. See also Freedman, *Before Nationalism*, Chapter 3.
121 These statistics include all STN business conducted between 1 February 1786 and 19 November 1788. The remaining sales were to the Iberian Peninsula, Britain and the Dutch and Belgian zones.
122 See, for example, Toscanelli's order of 15 December 1787 and Mangot's 11 June 1788 commission in the FBTEE database.
123 BPUN STN MS 1145, 195.
124 When Toussaint-Bernard Éméric-David made his tour of France between October 1787 and June 1788 he found a string of booksellers in rude health, notably Regnault, Le Roy and the Perisse family in Lyon and Didot, Debure and Panckouke in Paris. His early November detour into Switzerland, however, was another story – the commerce of books in Geneva, he reported, had been cruelly torn apart by the French state's interdiction of imports. See Eboli, *Livres et lecteurs en Provence au XVIIIe siècle*, 133.
125 BPUN STN MS 1009, 18, 81.
126 Schlup, 'Etude d'un processus éditorial et typographique', 303–4.
127 Charles-Godefroy de Tribolet, *Histoire de Neuchâtel et Valangin depuis l'avènement de la Maison de Prusse jusqu'en 1806* (Neuchâtel: H. Wolfrath, 1846).
128 James-Henri Bonhôte, 'Les imprimeurs et les livres neuchâtelois', *Musée neuchâtelois* 3 (1866): 173–81 at 180; Daguet, 'Mirabeau et ses éditeurs neuchâtelois', 239; Louis Junod, ed., *Histoire populaire du pays de Neuchâtel depuis les temps les plus reculés jusqu'en 1815* (Neuchâtel: H. Wolfrath et Metzner, 1863) 350; and Berthoud, 'Les deux Bertrand'. See also Schlup, 'Introduction', 23–5.
129 Charly Guyot, *De Rousseau à Mirabeau: pèlerins de Môtiers et prophètes de 89* (Neuchâtel and Paris: V. Attinger, 1936); Guyot, 'Imprimeurs et pasteurs neuchâtelois'; Charly Guyot, *Le rayonnement de l'Encyclopédie en suisse française* (Neuchâtel: Secrétariat de l'Université, 1955); Guyot, 'Un correspondant parisien'; and Charly Guyot, 'Du baron d'Holbach à Mirabeau: l'activité clandestine des éditeurs suisses-français à la veille de la Révolution', in *Actes du quatrième Congrès international d'histoire littéraire moderne* (Paris: Bovin, 1950), 55–64.
130 Daniel Mornet, 'Les enseignements des bibliothèques privées (1750-1780)', *Revue d'histoire littéaraire de la France* XVII (1910): 449–92.
131 Their arguments were revisited, restated and expanded upon in Darnton's outstanding 1982 collection *The Literary Underground of the Old Regime* (Cambridge, MA and London: Harvard University Press, 1982).
132 Most notably *The Forbidden Best-Sellers* won the National Book Critics Circle award for criticism in 1995.
133 See, for example, Vliet, 'Print and Public in Europe', 257; Carla Hesse, 'Print Culture in the Enlightenment', in *The Enlightenment World*, ed. Martin Fitzpatrick, Peter

Jones, Christa Knellwolf and Iain McCalman (London and New York: Pickering & Chatto, 2007), 366–80 at 374.
134 Jean-Horace Rilliet, *Six siècles d'existence genevoise: les Rilliet (1377-1977)* (Geneva: Editions de la Thébaïde, 1977), 63–72; Béla Kapossy, 'Genevan Creditors and English Liberty: The Example of Théodore Rilliet de Saussure', in *Genève, lieu d'Angleterre, 1725-1814 = Geneva, an English enclave, 1725-1814* (Geneva: Slatkine, 2009), 169–93 at 174–5.
135 Rilliet, *Six siècles d'existence genevoise*, 69.
136 This account of the affair has been put together from an interpretation of the trial briefs cited within, the police and council records of the AEG and a wonderful contemporary summary of the events. Having spoken of the Rilliet–Planta affair in a previous work, and having lamented the difficulty of reconstructing the baroque complexity of events with the Genevan archivist Paul E. Martin, Henri Beraldi was, in 1929, offered a two-volume quarto manuscript by a Parisian book dealer entitled 'EXTRAIT ANALYTIQUE des procédures criminelle et civile suivies entre le S^r. Théodore Rilliet, La D^e Ursule Lion de Planta sa femme, et le Sr Frédéric baron de Planta, colonel, son beau-frère'. The manuscript was apparently written around 1800 by a judge involved in the affair. Printed in octavo, Beraldi judged, this extraordinarily detailed manuscript would run to around 2,000 pages. Beraldi thus offered a summary with some commentary – 'un extrait de l'*Extrait*' – under the title *En marge du Pyrénéisme. Notes d'un bibliophile. L'Affaire Rilliet-Planta* (Paris: 1931). It is a fascinating account that adds detail unrecoverable from the printed record of the trial briefs and the archival evidence in the BPUN and AEG. Alas, it is incomplete since Beraldi died just as he was correcting the proofs for the manuscript and finishing its final section about the lives of Planta and Ursule after the Rilliet affair.
137 See Marc Cramer, 'Les Trente Demoiselles de Genève et les billets solidaires', *Swiss Journal of Economics and Statistics* 82, no. 2 (1946): 109–38.
138 Théodore Rilliet de Saussure, *Lettres sur l'emprunt et l'impôt* ([Geneva]: 1779). See Kapossy, 'Genevan Creditors and English liberty'. *Mémoires secrets* 10 December 1780; *Nouveau Journal helvétique*, November 1779, 19–30.
139 Rilliet, *Six siècles d'existence genevoise*, 70. The Parisian manuscript newsletters the *Mémoires secrets* and *Correspondance secrète* both reported the sum of 70,000 *livres* in damages and 20,000 *livres* in alms, as well as the six months in prison. See *Mémoires secrets* 10 December 1780; *Correspondance secrète* 16 December 1780.
140 Théodore Rilliet de Saussure, *Lettres, pièces et écrits concernant le procès civil en calomnie suspendu de dame Ursule de Planta, demanderesse, et le procès criminel en diffamation personnelle de Monsieur le baron de Planta, chevalier de l'Ordre du mérite, aide-maréchal-général des logis, demander* ([Geneva]: 1780).
141 Some factums were also published during trial on both sides, but it is unclear if the censorship authorities prevented their circulation. See Ami Lullin, *Conclusions. Magnifiques et très-honorés Seigneurs. Je me présente pour spectable Théodore Rilliet, avocat, citoyen et conseiller au Grand Conseil, défendeur dans le procès criminel en diffamation intenté contre lui par le sieur Baron Friedrich de Planta: contre ledit sieur Baron Friedrich de Planta, demandeur audit procès, et je conclus ...* ([Geneva], [1780]); Frédéric de Planta and Rigaud, *Très humble déclaration du baron de Planta, prisonnier, au Magnifique Conseil de la République de Genève* ([Geneva], [1780]); *Quelques pièces postérieures à la clôture de la procédure, données par le baron de Planta, contenant dès la page 11 un relevé de quelques unes des infidélités qui se trouvent dans l'imprimé qui vient de paraître* ([Geneva], [1780]); and *Question: On demande si un*

particulier qui a été poursuivi par une partie formelle, peut, après que l'instruction a été faite dans les prisons, être ... ([Geneva], [1780]).

142 AEG, PCN 13559, Procès Criminels et informations 1780 September 12 Libelle intitule: lettres, pièces et écrits concernant le procès civil Planta Rilliet, 1–13. All documents dated 12 September 1780.

143 No notice concerning the *Lettres, pièces et écrits concernant le procès civil en calomnie* can be found in major contemporary periodicals or manuscripts newsletters. The text is now very rare. One copy was confiscated by the *Chambre syndicale de Paris* on 8 August 1781.

144 The publisher of this work is unknown. According to Béraldi, several thousand copies were printed. See Béraldi, *En marge du Pyrénéisme*, 103. The STN received twelve copies on 8 October 1781 from Samuel Fauche.

145 Théodore Rilliet de Saussure, *Correspondance, ou Défense fondamentale de spectable Théodore Rilliet contre l'ordonnance du conseil de Genève qui, sous le nom de sentence, le dégrade de son état de citoyen, etc., etc., etc.* ([Neuchâtel]: [Société typographique de Neuchâtel], 1782); Théodore Rilliet de Saussure, *Inceste avoué à un mari, ou Exposé rapide de l'innocence & de l'honnêteté, tant absolue que relative, de spectable Théodore Rilliet* ([Neuchâtel]: [Société typographique de Neuchâtel], 1782); Théodore Rilliet de Saussure, *Planta gagnant sa vie en honnête homme, ou Confrontations de M. le baron de Planta & de spectable Théodore Rilliet* ([Neuchâtel]: [Société typographique de Neuchâtel], 1782); and Théodore Rilliet de Saussure, *Requête au Grand conseil de la République de Genève* ([Neuchâtel]: [Société typographique de Neuchâtel], [1782]).

146 Rilliet de Saussure, *Inceste avoué à un mari*, v.

147 Ibid., 25, 43–5.

148 Ibid., 14.

149 Ibid., 31.

150 L. Mettra, *Correspondance secrète, politique et littéraire* (Londres: Adamson, 1788), vol. 13, 272–5.

151 BPUN STN MS 1025, 171; BPUN STN MS 1036, Brouillard D, 315. The Rilliet volumes were shipped with substantial sets of Louis-Sébastien Mercier's plays *Zoé* (500 copies), *L'habitant de la Guadeloupe* (500 copies) and *Les tombeaux de Vérone* (375 copies).

152 BPUN STN MS 1207, Dossier Théodore Rilliet de Saussure, 20 (Rilliet de Saussure in Cologny to STN, 3 October 1782); ibid., 25 (Rilliet de Saussure in Cologny to STN, 11 November 1782).

153 Ibid., 31 (Rilliet de Saussure in Cologny to STN, 10 December 1782).

154 Ibid., 16 (Rilliet de Saussure in Cologny to STN, 1 October 1782).

155 Ibid., 50 (Rilliet de Saussure in Cologny to Spineux [STN prote] in Neuchâtel, 19 February 1783).

156 BPUN STN MS 1209, 301 (Louis Rosset in Lyon to STN, 23 June 1784).

157 BPUN STN MS 1036, 193.

158 BPUN STN MS 1207, 18 (Rilliet de Saussure in Cologny to STN, 1 October 1782).

159 Ibid., Dossier Jacques Rilliet-Plantamour, 5 (Jacques Rilliet-Plantamour in Geneva to STN, 20 May 1783).

160 Ibid., Dossier Théodore Rilliet de Saussure, 14 (Rilliet de Saussure in Cologny to STN, 27 September 1782).

161 Ibid., 22 (Rilliet de Saussure in Cologny to STN, 15 October 1782).

162 Ibid., 32 (Rilliet de Saussure in Cologny to STN, 10 December 1782).

163 Ibid., 16 (Rilliet de Saussure in Cologny to STN, 1 October 1782); ibid., 31 (Rilliet de Saussure in Cologny to STN, 10 December 1782).

164 Ibid., 16 (Rilliet de Saussure in Cologny to STN, 1 October 1782); 22 (Rilliet de Saussure in Cologny to STN, 15 October 82); and 31 (Rilliet de Saussure in Cologny to STN, 10 December 82).
165 Ibid., 7 (Rilliet de Saussure in Cologny to STN, 20 August 1782); 10 (Rilliet de Saussure in Cologny to STN, 3 September 1782; and 12 (Rilliet de Saussure in Cologny to STN, 7 September 1782).
166 Ibid., 33 (Rilliet de Saussure in Cologny to STN, 24 December 1782). Rilliet's letters to the STN were full of contradictions on questions of price and distribution as he tried to simultaneously convince the STN that there was profit in his enterprise, and that the Society must not let profit stand in the way of a broad distribution of his texts.
167 Ibid., 20 (Rilliet de Saussure in Cologny to STN, 3 October 1782).
168 BPUN STN MS 1025, 163.
169 BPUN STN MS 1207, 35 (Rilliet de Saussure in Cologny to Ostervald in Neuchâtel, 27 December 1782).
170 Ibid., 31 (Rilliet de Saussure in Cologny to STN, 10 December 1782).
171 See ibid., 44 (Rilliet de Saussure in Cologny to STN, 21 January 1783).
172 Rilliet, *Six siècles d'existence genevoise*, 71.
173 BPUN STN MS 1207, 58 (Rilliet de Saussure in Cologny to Spineux, 2 April 1783). We should probably not read too much into this. Rillet was excusing himself for an omission from a previous letter, and had a long history of complaining about his health.
174 Ibid., 60-1 (Rilliet de Saussure to STN, 12 April 1783); ibid., 62 (Rilliet de Saussure to Spineux, 12 April 1783).
175 Ibid., Dossier Jacques Rilliet-Plantamour, 1 (Jacques Rilliet-Plantamour in Geneva to M. Spineux, 26 April 1783).
176 BPUN STN MS 1025, 163. The timing of these entries allows us to speculate that once Théodore's fate became clear the STN might have rushed to finish his commission in order to ensure payment from his estate.
177 Rilliet was, initially at least, a good payer. By August 1782 he had sent *billets de change* to the Society totalling over 1,800 *livres*.
178 See BPUN STN MS 1207, 5 (Jacques Rilliet-Plantamour to STN, 20 May 1783). All traces of remaining copies of Rilliet's previous publications also disappeared from the STN's stockroom in the summer of 1783.
179 Schlup, 'Entre pouvoir et clandestinité', 78-9.
180 See Guyot, 'Imprimeurs et pasteurs neuchâtelois'; Schlup, 'Points de repère', 70-7. See also BPUN STN MS 1095, 418-21 (Ostervald in Neuchâtel to Robert Scipio de Lentulus in Schönbeck, 2 July 1771).
181 Seaward, 'The French Government and the Policing of the Extra-Territorial Print Trade', 56.
182 Selwyn, *Everyday Life in the German Book Trade*, 214.
183 Ibid., 245.
184 BPUN STN MS 1157, Dossier Laurent Giraud and Giovine, 509. Quoted in Bonnant, *Le livre genevois*, 130.
185 Works for which no date of publication was given are not counted in these statistics.
186 On censorship in France, see Birn, *La censure royale*; Daniel Roche, 'Censorship and the Publishing Industry', in *Revolution in Print: The Press in France, 1775-1800*, ed. Robert Darnton and Daniel Roche (Berkeley and London: University of California Press, 1989), 3-26; Darnton, *Forbidden Best-Sellers*; Barbara de Negroni, *Lectures interdites: le travail des censeurs au XVIIIe siècle 1723-1774* (Paris: Albin Michel, 1995); Georges Minois, *Censure et culture sous l'ancien régime* (Paris: Fayard, 1995);

Dawson, *Confiscations at Customs*; and Seaward, 'The French Government and the Policing of the Extra-Territorial Print Trade'.
187 Darnton, *The Corpus of Clandestine Literature in France*. For a sometimes similar methodological approach, also see Dawson, *Confiscations at Customs*.
188 For more on how the FBTEE database extends and modifies Darnton's work, see Curran, 'Beyond the Forbidden Best-Sellers'.
189 Irreligious or pornographic works, by contrast, received little attention. See Seaward, 'The French Government and the Policing of the Extra-Territorial Print Trade', 40.
190 Ibid., 76.
191 *La belle Allemande* is equally sometime attributed to Claude Villaret.
192 See Curran, 'Beyond the Forbidden Best-Sellers', 101.
193 See, for example, BPUN STN MS 1103, 135 (STN to Magerus in Amsterdam, 22 March 1777); ibid., 195 (STN to Prevost in Melun, 15 April 1777); BPUN STN MS 1131, 38 (J.-S. Cailler in Geneva to STN, 26 May 1772); and Dossier Jean-Pierre Heubach, 216 (J.-P. Heubach in Lausanne to STN, 6 April 1774).
194 BPUN STN MS 1131, 71 (Cailler in Geneva to STN, 19 December 1774).
195 BPUN STN MS 1103, 73 (STN to Eggendorf in Fribourg, 10 February 1777).
196 Ibid., 91 (STN to Caldesaigue in Marseille, 25 February 1777).
197 The Dole-based printer and bookseller Tonnet, for example, complained to the STN about the extra expense incurred when works were sent to him via Pontarlier rather than Jougne. See ibid., 88–9 (STN to Tonnet in Dole, 25 February 1777). On one technique used to bypass the *chambre syndicale* of Lyon, see Darnton, *The Business of Enlightenment*, 157–8.
198 Darnton, *Forbidden Best-Sellers*, 14–5.
199 Schlup, 'Points de repère', 100.
200 Pommaret, *Le chrétien par conviction et par sentiment*.
201 BPUN STN MS 1103, 437 (STN to Pommaret in Ganges, 22 July 1777).
202 See Bernard Plongeron, 'Aux sources d'une notion faussée: les langages théologiques de la tolérance', *Bulletin de la Société de l'histoire du protestantisme française* 134 (1988): 219–38; Françoise Weil, 'Le marché protestant de la STN', in *Le rayonnement d'une maison d'édition dans l'Europe des Lumières: la Société typographique de Neuchâtel 1769-1789*, ed. Michel Schlup and Robert Darnton (Neuchâtel: Attinger, 2005), 405–13.
203 Jules-Henri Pott, *Catalogue général des livres françois de Jules Henri Pott et comp., libraires à Lausanne en Suisse* (Lausanne: [Jules Henri Pott], 1783).
204 *Vie privée de Louis XV* is also sometimes attributed to Arnoux Laffrey.
205 The reality of widely advertised 'illegal' editions betrayed by Pott's catalogues can be widely replicated, including by using each of the STN's own trade catalogues.
206 *L'espion dévalisé* is also sometimes attributed to Baudouin de Guémadeuc.
207 Darnton, 'Reading, Writing and Publishing', 244.
208 See, for example, Birn, *La censure royale*; Simon Burrows, 'French Censorship on the Eve of the Revolution' in *Censorship and the Limits of the Literary: A Global View*, ed. Nicole Moore (London: Bloomsbury, 2015), 13–31; Jane McLeod, *Licensing Loyalty: Printers, Patrons, and the State in Early Modern France* (University Park: Pennsylvania State University Press, 2011); Seaward, 'The French Government and the Policing of the Extra-Territorial Print Trade'; Charles Walton, 'La liberté de la presse selon les cahiers de doléances de 1789', *Revue d'histoire moderne et contemporaine* 53, no. 1 (2006): 63–87.
209 Curran, *Atheism, Religion and Enlightenment*, 110–4.

Chapter 5

1. William Coxe, *Travels in Switzerland: In a Series of Letters to William Melmoth*, vol. 2 (London: T. Cadell, 1789), 127–9.
2. Noting that the STN did at least correspond with individuals based in 75 per cent of the French kingdom's book trading towns, Rigogne concluded that the question of the STN's representativeness remains unresolved. See Rigogne, 'Librairie et réseaux commerciaux', 400–1. For further thoughts on the question of the representativeness of the Society, see Burrows, *Enlightenment Best-Sellers*.
3. The net result of these issues is that, viewed across time, the STN's sales to an entire region or country can appear to take-off or implode based on the caprices of a single bookseller placing, or failing to place, a large order. Almost the entirety of the society's seemingly healthy trade with Toulouse (1,379 books shipped in total), to take one example, was comprised of four substantial orders delivered during the course of 1777 and 1778 and a baker's dozen copies of Raynal sent in December 1782.
4. Dan Edelstein, *The Enlightenment: A Genealogy* (Chicago: University of Chicago Press, 2010), 13.
5. The STN ceded its last remaining nine copies of *Histoire de François Wills* to Durand, Ravanel and Company in Lausanne on 20 May 1794, when the business was finally wound-up.
6. The STN's printed trade catalogues, published infrequently and always almost immediately out-of-date, served primarily to advertise the size of the business, and thus the confidence that it might be afforded. They were useful to make first contact with foreign booksellers and to garner back-catalogue sales, but were not the primary means by which individuals ordered books from the society.
7. Mornet's case should not, of course, be overstated. For a discussion, see R. A. Leigh, *Unsolved Problems in the Bibliography of J.J. Rousseau* (Cambridge: Cambridge University Press, 1990).
8. The STN sold no works written by Locke or Spinoza, and only forty-four copies of works by Newton. It did, however, sell 325 copies of Bayle's *Dictionnaire historique et critique*, largely the four-volume octavo edition produced by Barret in Lyon in 1771.
9. None among d'Holbach's *La politique naturelle* (London [Amsterdam], 1773), *Système social* (London [Amsterdam], 1773), *Ethocratie* (London [Amsterdam], 1776) and *La morale universelle* (London [Amsterdam], 1776), generated much attention after their initial printings, See Curran, *Atheism, Religion and Enlightenment*, 167–87.
10. Silvio Corsini, 'Quand Amsterdam rime avec Lausanne', in *Le magasin de l'univers*, ed. C. Berkvens-Stevelinck, Hans Bots, P.G. Hoftijzer and O.S. Lankhorst (Leiden and New York, NY: Brill, 1992), 95–120 at 97, 118.
11. Raymond Birn, 'Michel Rey's Enlightenment', in ibid., 23–48 at 25. Of 2,685 almost exclusively French-language works, 774 (28.8%) claimed to be published in Paris, 644 (24%) in Amsterdam, 297 (11.1%) in The Hague, 210 (7.4%) in other Dutch and towns and surrounding territories, 57 (2.1%) in Cologne, 47 (1.8%) in London. A total of 362 (13.5%) titles had no given place of publication and the remaining 303 (11.3%) were shared between a dozen additional places.
12. Bonnant demonstrated that only 105 of the 10,000 titles from the stocks of the Hague bookseller Jean Néaulme that were auctioned in 1765 were printed in Geneva. See Bonnant, *Le livre genevois*, 213.
13. Pierre Conlon, *Le siècle des lumières: bibliographie chronologique* (Geneva: Droz, 1983–2009). These two numbers are not, of course, directly comparable because they

are informed by different methodological approaches. Conlon's study, for example, does not include reprints.
14 Ibid., 84;7, 84;320, 84;683.
15 Ibid., 84;1296–98.
16 BPUN STN MS 1110, 909 (STN to Mauvelain in Troyes, 19 October 1784). The work in question, *Observations historiques sur quelques écarts ou jeux de la nature, pour servir à l'histoire naturelle, par Me E.-J.-P. Housset*, was actually printed in Neuchâtel in 1785 by Jean Pierre Convert using typographical ornaments common in several previous STN editions. The STN never traded the work.
17 François Quesnay, *Physiocratie, ou Constitution naturelle du gouvernement le plus avantageux au genre humain* (Yverdon: [Fortuné-Barthélemy de Felice], 1768).
18 The society had acquired this book in the summer of 1777 from Albert-Emmanuel Haller in Berne, not to sell but to help Bertrand's editorial work on the eighth volume of the *Descriptions des arts et métiers*. It remained forgotten in their storeroom for years, appeared in their 1781 and 1782 stock takes, and was eventually shipped in a discounted bulk order to the Saint Petersburg booksellers Wohak and Company on 22 June 1786.
19 The society handled twenty-four original language copies of unknown editions of Goethe's sensational *Die Leiden des jungen Werthers* between 1775 and 1794. It never traded in works by Herder or Schiller.
20 Curran, 'Beyond the Forbidden Best-Sellers', 94.
21 Pierre Manuel's suppliers included Dufour of Maestricht and Mettra of Neiwied. See Darnton, *The Devil in the Holy Water*, 215.
22 The STN did sell some such works, including around 200 copies of Imbert's *La chronique scandaleuse* (Paris, 1783), which it sourced from C. A. Serini in Basle from 31 October 1783, and later the Société typographique de Neuwied and Munz. The Neuchâtelois largely sold these books outside of France.
23 Commissioned editions account for 108,677 of the 413,710 total sold copies recorded in the FBTEE database.
24 Félix, 'The Problem with Necker's *Compte rendu au roi*', 107.

Epilogue

1 For a wonderful topographical (in the European and older sense of the word) description of much of the Val-de-Ruz, see Samuel de Chambrier, *Description topographique de la Mairie de Valangin* (Neuchâtel: Louis Fauche-Borel, 1795), 55.
2 Schlup, 'Points de repère', 102. The STN's 1788/1789 stocktake finishes with an mysterious entry addition of 5,418 *livres* 10 *sols* added to the value of the STNs stock holdings, 'pour la difference sur 9,482 livres 18 sols dus [*sic*] à Louis Fauche-Borel payable en livres'.
3 BPUN STN MS 1112, 725.
4 See *Information sommaire pour M. l'A. B. Ostervald; Moyens de droit pour M. Frédéric Ostervald, du Petit-Conseil, ancien banneret & moderne maître-bourgeois, & Mad. la veuve Bertrand née Ostervald, membres de la Société typographique de Neuchâtel, appelans : contre MM. les cautions du traité d'attermoiement de ladite Société, intimés* (n.p. [Neuchâtel]: n.d. [c. 1791]).
5 Ostervald's remarks were not simply hyperbole, as this was the route that fellow former STN director Jean-Jaques Bosset has been forced to take. See, *Moyens de droit pour M. Frédéric Ostervald*, 11.

6 Schmidt, 'Liste des impressions', 278–80.
7 The final liquidation of most STN stocks appears to have taken place, among more acrimony, between 1793 and 1795, when the STNs final few transactions took place. The signatures of the 8 June 1784 'Acte de cautionnement', were still drawing interest on invested capital through to 1797. The final entry in the STN ledgers is dated 31 May 1797. See BPUN STN MS 1043, 110, 13. BPUN STN MS 1240bis, Procès cautions contre S.T.N. 1793–179 [sic].
8 Fauche-Borel, *Mémoires de Fauche-Borel*, 37.
9 Ibid., 43–5.
10 Fauche-Borel also appears in a number of trades made by the Society during the 1790s. See, for example, BPUN STN MS 1043, 106.
11 On 11 September 1787, Durand wrote to the STN from Lyon to complain that the wretched Fauches were flooding the market with 'their' catalogues, and showing no discretion concerning whether they were distributed to booksellers or private individuals. See BPUN STN MS 1145, 212. Later during his travels, on 21 April 1788, he wrote from Bologne boasting that despite the fact that the Fauches and Felice were treading the same path as he, they were not doing half as much business. See ibid., 298.
12 Henri-David Chaillet, ed., *Discours qui a obtenu l'accessit au jugement de l'Académie de Besançon, sur la question proposée pour le prix d'éloquence en 1788: Le génie est-il au-dessus de toutes règles?* (Neuchâtel: L. Fauche-Borel, 1789); Schlup, 'Le rêve impossible de la STN', 151.
13 See, for example, Georg Joachim Zollikofer and Jean-Louis-Alexandre Dumas, eds., *Exercices de piété et prières pour l'édification particulière des chrétiens éclairés et vertueux* (Neuchâtel: de l'imprimerie de L. Fauche-Borel, 1791); *Ordonnance concernant l'exercice et les évolutions à l'usage des compagnies de la bourgeoisie de Neuchâtel* (Neuchâtel: de l'impr. de L. Fauche-Borel, 1792); Jacob Vernet, ed., *Abrégé d'histoire universelle: pour la direction des jeunes gens qui commencent cette étude*, Dernière édition, revue & corrigée ed. (Neuchâtel: de l'imprimerie de L. Fauche-Borel, 1791); Isabelle de Charrière, *Eclaircissemens relatifs à la publication des 'Confessions' de Rousseau, avec des réflexions sur la réputation, sur les apologies de MM. Ceruti et d'Holback, sur le moment présent, etc* (n.p. [Neuchâtel]: [Louis Fauche-Borel], n.d. [1790]); Isabelle de Charrière, ed., *Plainte et défense de Thérèse Le Vasseur* (Neuchâtel: chez Louis Fauche-Borel, 1789); Isabelle de Charrière, *Lettre d'un François et réponse d'un Suisse* (Neuchâtel: Louis Fauche-Borel, 1793); and Jean-Jacques Rousseau, *Les Confessions* (Neuchâtel: Louis Fauche-Borel, 1790).
14 Following Waterloo and the Bourbon Restoration, Louis Fauche-Borel returned to Neuchâtel and, after a long and dispiriting struggle for recognition, eventually secured and indemnity of 50,000 *livres* from Versailles and a modest pension from Berlin. His memoirs were published in the spring of 1729, just a few months before he committed suicide by defenestration. For a short biography of Louis Fauche-Borel, see Jean-Daniel Candaux, 'Abraham-Louis Fauche-Borel, libraire-imprimeur et agent contre-révolutionnaire (1762-1829)', in *Biographies Neuchâteloises*, ed. Michel Schlup, vol. 1 (Hauterive: Editions Gilles Attinger, 1996), 91–6.
15 The 'Abrégé choronologique des anciens royaumes, 8o', the two-volume duodecimo edition of 'Les Fastes de Louis XV', the two-volume duodecimo edition of 'Numa Pompilius', and the two-volume octavo edition of 'Zélie dans le désert' count among the survivors. See Auguste Fauche, *Catalogue du cabinet littéraire d'Auguste Fauche* (Neuchâtel: Auguste Fauche, 1798); Louis Fauche-Borel, *Catalogue du cabinet littéraire*

de Louis Fauche-Borel (Neuchâtel: Louis Fauche-Borel, 1793-1796); and See Schlup, 'Sociétés de lecture et cabinets littéraires', 100.

16 The once STN director Abram Bosset de Luze was the proprietor of the spacious 'La Grande Rochette' manor until his death in 1781.

Appendix

1 Authorship of *Histoire de la guerre de Hongrie* is equally often attributed to Friedrich Wilhelm Carl von Schmettau.
2 On Jeanprêtre, see Schlup, 'Introduction', 10.
3 MS1000a is a weak relation of the BPUN STN card index that is crippled by a large number of omissions. Ninety-six clients included in Jeanprêtre's card index, indeed, are absent from the document, including many cases where the BPUN has significant holdings. The library possesses thirty-eight letters sent by the printer–booksellers J. E. Didier & Company of Geneva, for example, that are not recorded in MS1000a.
4 Following standard business practices, as the STN wrote letters to its various correspondents it also recorded copies of these letters in large folio manuscript volumes, noting the date that the missives were sent and their recipients.
5 The FBTEE database, for example, sees individuals and the businesses that they worked for as separate entities, even where individuals were trading under their own names. The trading history of any actor that might have migrated through several partnerships (perhaps first trading with his father, before setting up a series of business ventures with various associates) can be tracked with ease. The database also allows places to be associated with transactions, rather than individuals, ensuring that the location of any given transaction is recorded as stated in the manuscript (rather than simply the default address of the business of the client).
6 See Inderwildi, 'Acteurs et réseaux commerciaux'.
7 See Schmidt, 'Liste des impressions'.

Bibliography

Adams, David, and Adrian Armstrong, eds. *Print and Power in France and England, 1500-1800*. Aldershot: Ashgate, 2006.
Amweg, Gustave. 'L'imprimerie à Porrentruy'. *Actes de la Société jurassienne d'émulation* 20 [2] (1915): 209–75.
Andrey, Georges. 'Madeleine Eggendorffer, libraire à Fribourg, et la Société typographique de Neuchâtel (1769-1788): livre, commerce et lecture dans la Suisse des Lumières'. In *Aspects du livre neuchâtelois*, edited by Jacques Rychner and Michel Schlup, 118–57. Neuchâtel: Bibliothèque publique et universitaire de Neuchâtel, 1986.
Armbruster, Carol. *Publishing and Readership in Revolutionary France and America: a symposium at the Library of Congress*. Westport, CT and London: Greenwood Press, 1993.
Asen, Robert. 'Seeking the "Counter" in Counterpublics'. *Communication Theory* 10 [4] (2000): 424–46.
Baggerman, Arianne. *Publishing Policies and Family Strategies: The Fortunes of a Dutch Publishing House in the 18th and Early 19th Centuries*. Leiden and Boston: Brill, 2013.
Baker, Keith Michael. 'Defining the Public Sphere in Eighteenth-Century France: Variations on a Theme by Habermas'. In *Habermas and the Public Sphere*, edited by Craig Calhoun, 181–211. Cambridge, MA and London: MIT Press, 1992.
Baker, Keith Michael. *Inventing the French Revolution: Essays on French Political Culture in the Eighteenth Century*. Cambridge: Cambridge University Press, 1990.
Bandelier, André. 'La clientèle Neuchâteloise et Jurassienne de la STN'. In *Le rayonnement d'une maison d'édition dans l'Europe des Lumières: la Société typographique de Neuchâtel 1769-1789*, edited by Michel Schlup and Robert Darnton, 317–40. Hauterive: Editions Gilles Attinger, 2005.
Barber, Benjamin R. 'How Swiss is Rousseau?' *Political Theory* 13 [4] (1985): 475–95.
Barber, Giles. 'The Cramers of Geneva and their Trade in Europe between 1755 and 1766'. *SVEC* XXX (1964): 377–413.
Barber, Giles. 'French Royal Decrees Concerning the Book-Trade, 1700-1789'. *Australian Journal of French Studies* 3 (1966): 312–30.
Barber, Giles. 'Pendred Abroad: A View of the Late-eighteenth-century Booktrade in Europe'. In *Studies in the Book Trade, in Honour of Graham Pollard*, edited by Richard William Hunt, I. G. Philip and Richard Julian Roberts, 231–77. Oxford: Oxford Bibliographical Society, 1975.
Barber, Giles. *Studies in the Booktrade of the European Enlightenment*. London: Pindar Press, 1994.
Barbier, Frédéric. 'La libraire française et l'Allemagne rhénane au XVIIIe siècle'. In *Rencontres franco-allemandes dans l'espace rhénan entre 1700 et 1789*, edited by Heinke Wunderlich and Jean Mondot, 177–96. Heidelberg: C. Winter, 1994.
Barbier, Frédéric. *Lumières du Nord: imprimeurs, libraires et 'gens du livre' dans le Nord au XVIIIe siècle (1701-1789): dictionnaire prosopographique*. Geneva: Droz, 2002.

Bauer, Eddy. 'Les imprimeurs d'Yverdon et la Société typographique de Neuchâtel'. *Musée neuchâtelois* 1969: 140–44.
Beales, Derek. *Enlightenment and Reform in Eighteenth-Century Europe*. London: I. B. Tauris, 2005.
Belin, Jean-Paul. *Le commerce des livres prohibés à Paris de 1750 à 1789*. Paris: Belin frères, 1913.
Benhamou, Paul. 'La diffusion des ouvrages de la STN à travers les cabinets de lecture'. In *Le rayonnement d'une maison d'édition dans l'Europe des Lumières: la Société typographique de Neuchâtel 1769-1789*, edited by Michel Schlup and Robert Darnton, 299–315. Hauterive: Editions Gilles Attinger, 2005.
Benhamou, Paul. 'The Reading Trade in Lyons: Cellier's cabinet de lecture'. *SVEC* 308 (1993): 305–21.
Benziger, Karl J. *Geschichte des Buchgewerbes im fürstlichen Benediktinerstifte U.L.F. v. Einsiedeln*. Einsiedeln: Benziger, 1912.
Béraldi, Henri. *En marge du Pyrénéisme. Notes d'un bibliophile. L'Affaire Rilliet-Planta*. Paris, 1931.
Berkvens-Stevelinck, C., H. Bots, P. G. Hoftijzer and O. S. Lankhorst, eds. *Le magasin de l'univers: The Dutch Republic as the Centre of the European Book Trade*. Leiden and New York: Brill, 1992.
Berthoud, Charles. 'Les deux Bertrand'. *Musée neuchâtelois* 7 (1870).
Berthoud, Eric. 'Un commerce de librarie entre Neuchâtel et Prague'. *Musée neuchâlelois* 1969: 134–39.
Billioud, Jacques. *Le livre en Provence du XVIe au XVIIIe siècle*. Marseille: Saint-Victor, 1962.
Birn, Raymond. *La censure royale des livres dans la France des lumières*. Paris: Odile Jacob, 2007.
Birn, Raymond. 'Michel Rey's Enlightenment'. In *Le magasin de l'univers*, edited by C. Berkvens-Stevelinck, H. Bots, P. G. Hoftijzer and O. S. Lankhorst, 23–48. Leiden and New York: Brill, 1992.
Birn, Raymond. 'The Profits of Ideas: privileges en librairie in eighteenth-century France'. *Eighteenth Century Studies* 4 [2] (1970–71): 131–68.
Birn, Raymond. 'Review: Elizabeth L. Eisenstein. Grub Street Abroad: Aspects of the French Cosmopolitan Press from the Age of Louis XIV to the French Revolution'. *The American Historical Review* 99 [2] (1994): 576–77.
Blanning, T. C. W. *The Culture of Power and the Power of Culture: Old Regime Europe, 1660-1789*. Oxford: Oxford University Press, 2002.
Bodenhamer, David J., John Corrigan and Trevor M. Harris, eds. *Deep Maps and Spatial Narratives*. Bloomington: Indiana University Press, 2015.
Boës, Anne, and Robert L. Dawson. 'The Legitimation of Contrefaçons and the Police Stamp of 1777'. *SVEC* 230 (1985): 461–84.
Boës, Anne, and Robert L. Dawson. 'The Legitimation of Piracies and the Police Stamp of 1777'. *SVEC* 230 (1985): 461–84.
Bohnengel, Julia. *'Cette cruelle affaire' Johann Heinrich Mercks Buchhandelsprojekt und die Société typographique de Neuchâtel: mit dem Briefwechsel zwischen Merck und der STN (1782-88)*. Hannover-Laatzen: Wehrhahn, 2006.
Bonhôte, James-Henri. 'Les imprimeurs et les livres neuchâtelois'. *Musée neuchâtelois* 3 (1866): 173–81.
Bonin, Serge, and Claude Langlois, eds. *Atlas de la Révolution française 10: économie*. Paris: Editions de l'EHESS, 1997.

Bonnant, Georges. 'La libraire genevoise dans la péninsule ibérique au XVIIIe siècle'. *Genava* IX (1961): 103–24.
Bonnant, Georges. *Le livre genevois sous l'ancien régime*. Geneva: Droz, 1999.
Bornatico, Remo. *L'arte tipografica nelle Tre Leghe (1549-1803)*. Chur: Gasser and Eggerling, 1971.
Bots, Hans, ed. *La diffusion et la lecture des journaux de langue francaise sous l'ancien régime*. Amsterdam: Holland University Press, 1988.
Bovard-Schmidt, Madeleine. 'Jean-Pierre Heubach, un imprimeur Lausannois du XVIIIe siècle'. *Revue historique vaudoise* 74 [1] (1966): 1–56.
Bowers, Fredson. *Principles of Bibliographical Description*. Princeton: Princeton University Press, 1949.
Boyer, Anne. 'Crédits et faillites: problèmes des financements dans la librairie d'Ancien Régime'. In *L'Europe et le livre: réseaux et pratiques du négoce de librairie, XVIe-XIXe siècles*, edited by Frédéric Barbier, Sabine Juratic and Dominique Varry, 357–69. Paris: Klincksieck, 1996.
Bremme-Bonnant, Florence. 'Considerations sur la libraire genevoise pendant la Guerre de sept ans (1756-1763)'. *Genava* 19 (1971): 131–84.
Brockliss, Laurence W. B. *Calvet's Web: Enlightenment and the Republic of Letters in Eighteenth-Century France*. Oxford: Oxford University Press, 2002.
Brouwer, Han. *Lezen en schrijven in de provincie: de boeken van Zwolse boekverkopers, 1777-1849*. Leiden: Primavera Pers, 1995.
Brown, Andrew. 'Gabriel Grasset éditeur de Voltaire'. In *Voltaire et le livre*, edited by François Bessire and Françoise Tilkin, 67–105. Ferney-Voltaire: Centre international d'étude du XVIIIe siècle, 2009.
Bürger, Thomas. *Aufklärung in Zürich: die Verlagsbuchhandlung Orell, Gessner, Füssli & Comp. in der zweiten Hälfte des 18. Jahrhunderts*. Frankfurt am Main: Buchhändler-Vereinigung, 1997.
Buringh, Eltjo, and Jan Luiten van Zanden. 'Charting the "Rise of the West": Manuscripts and Printed Books in Europe, a Long-term Perspective from the Sixth Through Eighteenth Centuries'. *The Journal of Economic History* 69 [2] (2009): 409–45.
Burrows, Simon. *Blackmail, Scandal, and Revolution: London's French libellistes, 1758-92*. Manchester: Manchester University Press, 2006.
Burrows, Simon. 'Charmet and the Book Police: Clandestinity, Illegality and Popular Reading in Late Ancien Régime France'. *French History and Civilisation: Papers from the George Rudé Seminar* 6 (2015): 32–55.
Burrows, Simon. 'The Cosmopolitan Press'. In *Press, Politics and the Public Sphere in Europe and North America, 1760-1820*, edited by Hannah Barker and Simon Burrows, 23–47. Cambridge: Cambridge University Press, 2002.
Burrows, Simon. *French Exile Journalism and European Politics, 1792-1814*. Suffolk and Rochester, NY: The Boydell Press, 2000.
Burrows, Simon. 'Grub Street Revolutionaries: marginal writers at the Enlightenment's periphary?' In *Peripheries of the Enlightenment*, edited by Richard Butterwick, Simon Davies and Gabriel Sánchez Espinosa, 145–62. Oxford: Voltaire Foundation, 2008.
Burrows, Simon. 'The Innocence of Jacques-Pierre Brissot'. *The Historical Journal* 46 (2003): 843–71.
Cahill, Daniel. 'Abraham Girardet (1764-1823), graveur suisse à Paris sous la Révolution française'. *Annales historiques de la Révolution Française* 289 (1992): 434–8.
Calame, Caroline. 'Une affiche publicitaire au XVIIIe siècle: les volets de la librairie Girardet'. *Nouvelle revue neuchâteloise* 73 (2002): 1–56.

Calhoun, Craig J., ed. *Habermas and the Public Sphere.* Cambridge, MA and London: MIT Press, 1992.
Candaux, Jean-Daniel. 'Abraham-Louis Fauche-Borel, libraire-imprimeur et agent contre-révolutionnaire (1762-1829)'. In *Biographies Neuchâteloises,* edited by Michel Schlup, vol. 1, 91-6. Hauterive: Editions Gilles Attinger, 1996.
Candaux, Jean-Daniel. 'Imprimeurs et libraires dans la Suisse des Lumières'. In *Le rayonnement d'une maison d'édition dans l'Europe des Lumières: la Société typographique de Neuchâtel 1769-1789,* edited by Michel Schlup and Robert Darnton, 51-68. Hauterive: Editions Gilles Attinger, 2005.
Candaux, Jean-Daniel. 'Jérémie Witel, libraire-imprimeur (1754-1794)'. In *Biographies Neuchâteloises,* edited by Michel Schlup, vol. 1, 265-8. Hauterive: Editions Gilles Attinger, 1996.
Candaux, Jean-Daniel. 'Les gazettes helvétiques: inventaire provisoire des périodiques littéraires et scientifiques de langue française publiés en Suisse de 1693 à 1795'. In *L'étude des pédiodiques anciens,* edited by Marianne Couperus, 126-72. Paris: A.-G. Nizet, 1973.
Candaux, Jean-Daniel, and Bernard Lescaze, eds. *Cinq siècles d'imprimerie genevoise: acts du colloque international sur l'histoire de l'imprimerie et du livre à Genève, 27-30 avril 1978.* Geneva: Société d'histoire et d'archéologie, 1981.
Caradonna, Jeremy L. *The Enlightenment in Practice: Academic Prize Contests and Intellectual Culture in France, 1670-1794.* Ithaca: Cornell University Press, 2012.
Carpenter, Edmund Snow, and Marshall McLuhan, eds. *Explorations in Communication: An Anthology.* Boston: Beacon Press, 1960.
Censer, Jack R. *The French Press in the Age of Enlightenment.* London: Routledge, 1994.
Censer, Jack R. 'Remembering the Mémoires Secrets'. *Eighteenth-Century Studies* 35 [ii] (2002): 291-5.
Censer, Jack R., and Jeremy D. Popkin. *Press and Politics in Pre-Revolutionary France.* Berkeley and London: University of California Press, 1987.
Cernuschi, Alain. 'Lectures de l'Encyclopédie d'Yverdon, images d'une œuvre et réflexions méthodologiques à partir des comptes rendus du Journal helvétique'. *Annales Benjamin Constant* 14 (1993): 85-109.
Cernuschi, Alain. '"Notre grande entreprise des arts": aspects encyclopédiques de l'édition Neuchâteloise de la Description des arts et métiers'. In *Le rayonnement d'une maison d'édition dans l'Europe des Lumières: la Société typographique de Neuchâtel 1769-1789,* edited by Michel Schlup and Robert Darnton, 185-218. Hauterive: Editions Gilles Attinger, 2005.
Chartier, Roger. *The Cultural Origins of the French Revolution.* Durham, NC and London: Duke University Press, 1991.
Chartier, Roger. 'Dialogue sur l'espace public: Keith Michael Baker, Roger Chartier'. *Politix-Sciences sociales du politique* 26 (1994): 5-22.
Chartier, Roger. 'L'imprimerie en France à la fin de l'Ancien Régime: l'état général des imprimeurs de 1777'. *Revue française d'histoire du livre* 6 (1973): 253-79.
Chartier, Roger, and Hans-Jürgen Lüsebrink, eds. *Colportage et lecture populaire: imprimés de large circulation en Europe, XVIe-XIXe siècles: actes du colloque des 21-24 avril 1991, Wolfenbüttel.* Paris: IMEC, 1996.
Chevallier, Pierre. 'Les philosophes et le lieutenant de police (1775-1785)'. *French Studies* 17 [2] (1963): 105-20.
Chisick, Harvey, Ilana Zinguer and Ouzi Elyada, eds. *The Press in the French Revolution.* Oxford: Voltaire Foundation, 1991.

Cioranescu, Alexandre. *Bibliographie de la littérature française du dix-huitième siècle*. Geneva: Slatkine, 1969.

Clemens, Th. 'The Trade in Catholic Books from the Northern to the Southern Netherlands'. In *Le magasin de l'univers*, edited by C. Berkvens-Stevelinck, H. Bots, P. G. Hoftijzer and O. S. Lankhorst, 85–94. Leiden and New York: Brill, 1992.

Conlon, Pierre. *Le siècle des lumières: bibliographie chronologique*. Geneva: Droz, 1983–2009.

Cook, Malcolm. 'Review: The Forbidden Best-Sellers of Pre-Revolutionary France by Robert Darnton, The Corpus of Clandestine Literature in France, 1769-1789 by Robert Darnton'. *The Modern Language Review* 92 [1] (1997): 190–1.

Cornaz, Marie. 'Jean-Joseph Boucherie et Jean-Louis de Boubers: deux imprimeurs de musique a bruxelles dans la deuxieme moitie du XVIIIe siecle'. *Revue belge de Musicologie / Belgisch Tijdschrift voor Muziekwetenschap* 46 (1992): 179–88.

Corsini, Silvio. 'L'édition française hors des frontières du royaume: les presses lausannoises sous la loupe'. *Revue française d'histoire du livre* 62-3 (1989): 94–119.

Corsini, Silvio. *La preuve par les fleurons? Analyse comparée du matériel ornemental des imprimeurs suisses romands 1775-1785*. Ferney-Voltaire: Centre international d'étude du XVIIIe siècle, 1999.

Corsini, Silvio. *Le livre à Lausanne, cinq siècles d'édition et d'imprimerie, 1493-1993*. Lausanne: Payot, 1993.

Corsini, Silvio. 'Quand Amsterdam rime avec Lausanne'. In *Le magasin de l'univers*, edited by C. Berkvens-Stevelinck, H. Bots, P. G. Hoftijzer and O. S. Lankhorst, 95–120. Leiden and New York: Brill, 1992.

Corsini, Silvio. 'Un pour tous … et chacun pour soi? Petite histoire d'une alliance entre les Sociétés typographiques de Lausanne, Berne et Neuchâtel'. In *Le rayonnement d'une maison d'édition dans l'Europe des Lumières: la Société typographique de Neuchâtel 1769-1889*, edited by Michel Schlup and Robert Darnton, 115–37. Hauterive: Editions Gilles Attinger, 2005.

Courtney, C. P. *Isabelle de Charrière (Belle de Zuylen): A Biography*. Oxford: Voltaire Foundation, 1993.

Coyecque, Ernest. *Inventaire de la collection Anisson sur l'histoire de l'imprimerie et la librairie, principalement à Paris (manuscrits français 22061-22193)*. Paris: E. Leroux, 1900.

Cramer, Marc. 'Les Trente Demoiselles de Genève et les billets solidaires'. *Swiss Journal of Economics and Statistics* 82 [2] (1946): 109–38.

Cranston, Maurice. *Philosophers and Pamphleteers: Political Theorists of the Enlightenment*. Oxford: Oxford University Press, 1986.

Crossley, Nick, and John M. Roberts. *After Habermas: New Perspectives on the Public Sphere*. Oxford: Blackwell Publishing/Sociological Review, 2004.

Cullen, Louis M. *The Brandy Trade Under the Ancien Régime: Regional Specialisation in the Charente*. Cambridge: Cambridge University Press, 1998.

Curran, Mark. *Atheism, Religion and Enlightenment in Pre-Revolutionary Europe*. Woodbridge: Boydell Press, 2012.

Curran, Mark. 'Beyond the Forbidden Best-Sellers of pre-Revolutionary France'. *Historical Journal* 56 [1] (2013): 89–112.

Curran, Mark. 'Mettons toujours Londres: Enlightened Christianity and the Public in Pre-revolutionary Francophone Europe'. *French History* 24 [1] (2010): 40–59.

Curran, Mark. 'The Société typographique de Neuchâtel and Networks of Trade and Translation in Eighteenth-Century Francophone Europe'. In *Cultural Transfers: France* and *Britain in the Long Eighteenth Century*, edited by Ann Thomson, Simon Burrows and Edmond Dziembowski, 257–67. Oxford: Voltaire Foundation, 2010.

Daguet, Alexandre. 'Mirabeau et ses éditeurs neuchâtelois en 1782'. *Musée neuchâtelois* (1887): 233–7.

Darnton, Robert. 'Books and Border Crossings in the Age of Enlightenment'. In *Lumières sans frontières: hommage à Roland Mortier et Raymond Trousson*, edited by Daniel Droixhe and Jacques-Charles Lemaire, 187–97. Paris: Hermann, 2016.

Darnton, Robert. *The Business of Enlightenment: A Publishing History of the 'Encyclopédie', 1775-1800*. Cambridge, MA and London: Belknap Press, 1979.

Darnton, Robert. *The Case for Books: Past, Present, and Future*. New York: PublicAffairs, 2009.

Darnton, Robert. *The Corpus of Clandestine Literature in France, 1769-1789*. New York and London: Norton, 1995.

Darnton, Robert. 'An Early Information Society: News and the Media in Eighteenth-century Paris'. *American Historical Review* 105 (2000): 1–35.

Darnton, Robert. *Édition et sédition: l'univers de la littérature clandestine au XVIIIe siècle*. Paris: Gallimard, 1991.

Darnton, Robert. 'The Encyclopédie Wars of Prerevolutionary France'. *The American Historical Review* 78 [5] (1973): 1331–52.

Darnton, Robert. 'An Exemplary Literary Career'. In *André Morellet (1727-1819) in the Republic of Letters and the French Revolution*, edited by Jeffrey Merrick and Dorothy Medlin, 5–26. New York: P. Lang, 1995.

Darnton, Robert. 'Finding a Lost Prince of Bohemia'. *The New York Review of Books* 55 [5] (2008).

Darnton, Robert. *The Forbidden Best-Sellers of Pre-Revolutionary France*. New York and London: W. W. Norton, 1995.

Darnton, Robert. 'The Forbidden Books of Pre-revolutionary France'. In *Rewriting the French Revolution*, edited by Colin Lucas, 1–32. Oxford: Clarendon, 1991.

Darnton, Robert. *Gens de lettres, gens du livre*. Paris: Editions Odile Jacob, 1992.

Darnton, Robert. *George Washington's False Teeth: An Unconventional Guide to the Eighteenth Century*. New York and London: W. W. Norton, 2003.

Darnton, Robert. *The Great Cat Massacre: And Other Episodes in French Cultural History*. London: Allen Lane, 1984.

Darnton, Robert. 'The Grub Street Style of Revolution: J.-P. Brissot police spy'. *The Journal of Modern History* 40 [3] (1968): 301–27.

Darnton, Robert. 'The High Enlightenment and the Low-Life of Literature in Pre-Revolutionary France'. *Past and Present* 51 (1971): 81–115.

Darnton, Robert. 'La STN et la librairie française: un survol des documents'. In *L'édition neuchâteloise au siècle des Lumières: la Société typographique de Neuchâtel (1769-1789)*, edited by Michel Schlup and Robert Darnton, 211–32. Neuchâtel: Bibliothèque publique et universitaire de Neuchâtel, 2002.

Darnton, Robert. 'The Life of a "Poor Devil" in the Republic of Letters'. In *Essays on the Age of Enlightenment in Honor of Ira O. Wade*, edited by Jean Macary, 39–92. Geneva: Droz, 1977.

Darnton, Robert. 'The Life-Cycle of a Book: A Publishing History of d'Holbach's Système de la nature'. In *Publishing and Readership in Revolutionary France and America*, edited by Carol Armbruster, 15–43. Westport, CT: Greenwood Press, 1993.

Darnton, Robert. *The Literary Underground of the Old Regime*. Cambridge, MA and London: Harvard University Press, 1982.

Darnton, Robert. 'The Memoirs of Lenoir: Lieutenant of the Police of Paris, 1774-1785'. *The English Historical Review* 85 [336] (1970): 532–59.
Darnton, Robert. *Mesmerism and the End of the Enlightenment in France*. Cambridge, MA: Harvard University Press, 1968.
Darnton, Robert. 'Police Writers in Paris Circa 1750'. *Representations* 5 (1984): 1–31.
Darnton, Robert. 'Publishing d'Holbach's Système de la nature'. *SVEC* 265 (1989): 1706–9.
Darnton, Robert. 'Reading, Writing and Publishing in Eighteenth-Century France: A Case Study in the Sociology of Literature'. *Daedalus* 100 [1] (1971): 214–56.
Darnton, Robert. 'The Science of Piracy: A Crucial Ingredient in Eighteenth-century Publishing'. *SVEC* 12 (2003): 3–29.
Darnton, Robert. 'Sounding the Literary Market in Prerevolutionary France'. *Eighteenth Century Studies* 17 [4] (1984): 477–92.
Darnton, Robert. 'Trade in the Taboo: The Life of a Clandestine Book Dealer in Pre-revolutionary France'. In *The Widening Circle: Essays on the Circulation of Literature in Eighteenth-century Europe*, edited by Paul J. Korshin, 11–83. Philadelphia: University of Pennsylvania Press, 1976.
Darnton, Robert. 'Two Paths Through the Social History of Ideas'. In *The Darnton Debate*, edited by H. T. Mason, 251–94. Oxford: Voltaire Foundation, 1998.
Darnton, Robert. '"What is the History of Books?" Revisited'. *Modern Intellectual History* 4 [3] (2007): 495–508.
Darnton, Robert, and Daniel Roche. *Revolution in Print: The Press in France, 1775-1800*. Berkeley and London: University of California Press, 1989.
Darnton, Robert, and Michel Schlup, eds. *Le rayonnement d'une maison d'édition dans l'Europe des Lumières: la Société typographique de Neuchâtel 1769-1789*. Hauterive: Editions Gilles Attinger, 2005.
Davids, Karel. *The Rise and Decline of Dutch Technological Leadership: Technology, Economy and Culture in the Netherlands, 1350-1800*. Leiden and Boston: Brill, 2008.
Dawson, Robert L. *Confiscations at Customs: Banned Books and the French Booktrade During the Last Years of the Ancien Régime*. Oxford: SVEC, 2006.
Dawson, Robert L. *The French Booktrade and the 'Permission Simple' of 1777*. Oxford: Voltaire Foundation, 1992.
De Bock, Eugeen. *Het nederlandse boek: overzicht van zijn geschiedenis*. Brussels: Vlaamsche Boekwezen, 1939.
Donato, Clorinda. 'From Switzerland to Europe Through Leipzig: the Swiss book trade and the Leipziger Messe (1770-1780)'. *Leipziger Jahrbuch zur Buchgeschichte* 4 (1994): 103–33.
Donato, Clorinda 'The Letters of Fortunato Bartolomeo De Felice to Pietro Verri'. *MLN* 107 [1] (1992): 74–111.
Droixhe, Daniel. *Une histoire des lumières au pays de Liège: livre, idées, société*. Liège: Université de Liège, 2007.
Dubosq, Yves Zacharie. *Le livre français et son commerce en Hollande de 1750 à 1780: d'après des documents inédits*. Amsterdam: H. J. Paris, 1925.
Dutens, Joseph. *Histoire de la navigation intérieure de la France: avec une exposition des canaux à entreprendre pour en compléter le système*. Paris: A. Sautelet, 1829.
Easley, David, and Jon Kleinberg. *Networks, Crowds, and Markets: Reasoning About a Highly Connected World*. Cambridge: Cambridge University Press, 2010.
Eboli, Gilles. *Livres et lecteurs en Provence au XVIIIe siècle: autour des David, imprimeurs-libraires à Aix*. Méolans-Revel: Atelier Perrousseaux, 2008.
Edelstein, Dan. *The Enlightenment: A Genealogy*. Chicago: University of Chicago Press, 2010.

Eisenstein, Elizabeth L. 'Bypassing the Enlightenment: taking an underground route to revolution'. In *The Darnton Debate*, edited by H. T. Mason, 157–77. Oxford: Voltaire Foundation, 1998.

Eisenstein, Elizabeth L. *Grub Street Abroad: Aspects of the French Cosmopolitan Press from the Age of Louis XIV to the French Revolution*. Oxford: Clarendon Press, 1992.

Eisenstein, Elizabeth L. *The Printing Press as an Agent of Change: Communications and Cultural Transformations in Early-modern Europe*. Cambridge: Cambridge University Press, 1979.

Eisenstein, Elizabeth L. 'An Unacknowledged Revolution Revisited'. *The American Historical Review* 107 [1] (2002): 87–105.

Estivals, Robert. *La statistique bibliographique de la France sous la monarchie, au XVIIIe siècle*. Paris: Editions de l'EHESS, 1965.

Fajn, Max. 'Marc-Michel Rey: Boekhandelaar op de Bloemmark (Amsterdam)'. *Proceedings of the American Philosophical Society* 118 [3] (1974): 260–8.

Falk, Henri. *Les privilèges de librairie sous l'ancien régime: étude historique du conflit des droits sur l'oeuvre littéraire*. Geneva: Slatkine, 1970.

Farge, Arlette. *Dire et mal dire. L'opinion publique au XVIIIe siècle*. Paris: Le Seuil, 1992.

Feather, John P. 'The Book in History and the History of the Book'. In *The History of Books and Libraries: Two Views*, edited by John P. Feather and David McKitterick, 1–16. Washington: Library of Congress, 1986.

Febvre, Lucien, and Henri-Jean Martin. *L'apparition du livre*. Paris: A. Michel, 1958–59.

Félix, Joël. 'The Problem with Necker's *Compte rendu au roi* (1781)'. In *The Crisis of the Absolute Monarchy: France from Old Regime to Revolution*, edited by Julian Swann and Joël Félix, 107–25. Oxford: Oxford University Press, 2013.

Feyel, Gilles. 'La diffusion des gazettes étrangères en France et la revolution postale des années 1750'. In *Les gazettes européennes de langue française (XVIIe-XVIIIe siècles)*, edited by Henri Duranton, Claude Labrosse and Pierre Rétat, 81–99. Saint-Etienne: Presses Universitaires de Saint-Etienne, 1992.

Finkelstein, David, and Alistair McCleery. *The Book History Reader*. Abingdon: Routledge, 2006.

Fortuny, Claudette. 'La troisième edition de l'Histore des deux Indes et ses contrefaçons: les contributions de Genève et Neuchâtel'. *SVEC* 12 (2001): 269–97.

Francillon, Roger. *Histoire de la littérature en Suisse romande*. 4 vols. Lausanne: Payot 1996–99.

Fraser, Nancy. 'Rethinking the Public Sphere: A Contribution to the Critique of Actually Existing Democracy'. *Social Text* 25/26 (1990): 56–80.

Freedman, Jeffrey. *Books Without Borders in Enlightenment Europe: French Cosmopolitanism and German Literary Markets*. Philadelphia: University of Pennsylvania Press, 2012.

Freedman, Jeffrey. 'La Société typographique de Neuchâtel et l'allemagne'. In *Le rayonnement d'une maison d'édition dans l'Europe des Lumières: la Société typographique de Neuchâtel 1769-1789*, edited by Michel Schlup and Robert Darnton, 475–89. Neuchâtel: Attinger, 2005.

Freedman, Jeffrey. 'Lumières in the North: a French bookshop on the Elbe (1775-1785)'. *Leipziger Jahrbuch zur Buchgeschichte* 4 (1994): 49–102.

Freedman, Jeffrey. 'Zwishen Frankreich und Deutschland: Buckhändler als Kulturvermittler'. In *Kulturtransfer im Epochenumbruch: Frankreich-Deutschland 1770 bis 1815*, edited by Hans-Jürgen Lüsebrink and Rolf Reichardt, 445–98. Leipzig: Leipziger Universitätsverlag, 1997.

Fujiwara, Mami. 'Diderot et le droit d'auteur avant la lettre: autour de la Lettre sur le commerce de la librairie'. *Revue d'histoire littéraire de la France* 105 [1] (2005): 79–94.
Furbank, Philip Nicholas. *Diderot: A Critical Biography*. London: Secker & Warburg, 1992.
Furet, François. 'La « librairie » du royaume de France au 18e siècle'. In *Livre et société dans la France du XVIIIe siècle*, edited by François Furet, vol. 1, 3–32. Paris: Mouton et Cie, 1965.
Furet, François, and Jacques Ozouf, eds. *Reading and Writing: Literacy in France from Calvin to Jules Ferry*. Cambridge: Cambridge University Press, 1983.
Gaskell, Philip. *A New Introduction to Bibliography*. Oxford: Clarendon Press, 1972.
Gay, Peter. *The Enlightenment: An Interpretation: The Rise of Modern Paganism*. New York: Knopf, 1966.
Germann, Martin. *Johann Jakob Thurneysen der Jüngere 1754-1803, Verleger, Buchdrucker und Buchhändler in Basel*. Basle and Stuttgart: Helbing und Lichtenhahn, 1973.
Gervais, Pierre. 'A Merchant or a French Atlantic? Eighteenth-century Account Books as Narratives of a Transnational Merchant Political Economy'. *French History* 25 [1] (2011): 28–47.
Gibbs, Graham C. 'The Role of the Dutch Republic as the Intellectual Entrepôt of Europe in the Seventeenth and Eighteenth Centuries'. *Bijdragen en Mededelingen betreffende de Geschiedenis der Nederlanden* 86 (1971): 323–49.
Gingerich, Owen. *The Book Nobody Read: Chasing the Revolutions of Nicolaus Copernicus*. New York: Walker, 2004.
Goinga, Hannie van. *Alom te bekomen: veranderingen in de boekdistributie in de Republiek 1720-1800*. Amsterdam: Buitenkant, 1999.
Goodman, Dena. 'Enlightenment Salons: The Convergence of Female and Philosophic Ambitions'. *Eighteenth-Century Studies* 22 (1989): 329–50.
Goodman, Dena. 'Public Sphere and Private Life: Toward a Synthesis of Current Historical Approaches to the Old Regime'. *History and Theory* 31 [1] (1992): 1–20.
Goodman, Dena. *The Republic of Letters: A Cultural History of the French Enlightenment*. Ithaca and London: Cornell University Press, 1994.
Gordon, Daniel. 'Philosophy, Sociology and Gender in the Enlightenment Conception of Public Opinion'. *French Historical Studies* 17 [4] (1992): 882–911.
Gough, Hugh. 'Book Imports from Continental Europe in Late Eighteenth-Century Ireland: Luke White and the Société typographique de Neuchâtel'. *The Long Room* 38 (1993): 35–48.
Graham, Lisa Jane. *If The King Only Knew: Seditious Speech in the Reign of Louis XV*. Charlottesville and London: University Press of Virginia, 2000.
Grant, Hugh. 'Bookkeeping in the Eighteenth Century: The Grand Journal and Grand Ledger of the Hudson's Bay Company'. *Archivaria* 43 (1997): 143–57.
Gregory, Ian N. *A Place in History: A Guide to Using GIS in Historical Research*. Oxford: Oxbow Books, 2003.
Gregory, Ian N. 'Time Variant GIS Databases of Changing Historical Administrative Boundaries: a European comparison'. *Transactions in GIS* 6 [2] (2002): 161–78.
Gregory, Ian N., and Alistair Geddes. *Toward Spatial Humanities: Historical GIS and Spatial History*. Bloomington: Indiana University Press, 2014.
Gunn, John Alexander Wilson. *Queen of the World: Opinion in the Public Life of France from the Renaissance to the Revolution*. Oxford: Voltaire Foundation, 1995.
Guyot, Charly. *De Rousseau à Mirabeau: pèlerins de Môtiers et prophètes de 89*. Neuchâtel and Paris: V. Attinger, 1936.

Guyot, Charly. 'Du baron d'Holbach à Mirabeau: l'activité clandestine des éditeurs suisses-français à la veille de la Révolution'. In *Actes du quatrième Congrès international d'histoire littéraire moderne*, 55–64. Paris: Bovin, 1950.

Guyot, Charly. 'Imprimeurs et pasteurs neuchâtelois: l'affair du Système de la nature 1771'. *Musée nuechâtelois* 1946: 74–81, 108–16.

Guyot, Charly. *La vie intellectuelle et religieuse en Suisse française à la fin du XVIIIe siècle: Henri-David de Chaillet, 1751-1823*. Neuchâtel: La Baconnière, 1946.

Guyot, Charly. *Le rayonnement de l'Encyclopédie en suisse française*. Neuchâtel: Secrétariat de l'Université, 1955.

Guyot, Charly. 'Relations intellectuelles franco-neuchâtelois vers 1780'. *Musée neuchâlelois* 1940: 97–105.

Guyot, Charly. 'Un correspondant parisien de la Société typographique de Neuchâtel: Quandet de Lachenal'. *Musée neuchâtelois* (1936): 20–8, 64–74.

Guyot, Charly. 'Voltaire et l'édition neuchâteloise des Questions sur l'Encyclopédie'. *Musée neuchâtelois* 1969: 123–33.

Habermas, Jürgen. 'Further Reflections on the Public Sphere'. In *Habermas and the Public Sphere*, edited by Craig Calhoun, 421–61. Cambridge, MA and London: MIT Press, 1992.

Habermas, Jürgen. *The Structural Transformation of the Public Sphere: An Inquiry into a Category of Bourgeois Society*. Cambridge, MA: MIT Press, 1989.

Hampson, Norman. *The Enlightenment*. Harmondsworth: Penguin Books, 1968.

Hanley, Ryan Patrick, and Darrin M. McMahon, eds. *The Enlightenment: Critical Concepts in Historical Studies*. London: Routledge, 2010.

Hardman, John. *French Politics, 1774-1789: From the Accession of Louis XVI to the Fall of the Bastille*. London and New York: Longman, 1995.

Hellinga, Lotte. *The Bookshop of the World: The Role of the Low Countries in the Book-trade, 1473-1941*. Goy-Houten: Hes & De Graaf, 2001.

Henry, Phillipe. 'Le pays de Neuchâtel à l'époque de la naissance de la STN'. In *Le rayonnement d'une maison d'édition dans l'Europe des Lumières: la Société typographique de Neuchâtel 1769-1789*, edited by Robert Darnton and Michel Schlup, 33–49. Hauterive: Editions Gilles Attinger, 2005.

Henry, Phillipe. 'L'évolution démographique'. In *Histoire du pays de Neuchâtel: De la Reforme à 1815*, edited by Phillipe Henry and Jean-Pierre Jelmini, 140–57. Hauterive: Attinger, 1991.

Hernlund, Patricia. 'William Strahan's Ledgers: Standard Charges for Printing, 1738-1785'. *Studies in Bibliography* 20 (1967): 89–111.

Hesse, Carla. 'Print Culture in the Enlightenment'. In *The Enlightenment World*, edited by Martin Fitzpatrick, Peter Jones, Christa Knellwolf and Iain McCalman, 366–80. London and New York: Pickering & Chatto, 2007.

Holub, Robert C. *Jürgen Habermas: Critic in the Public Sphere*. London and New York: Routledge, 1991.

Hont, Istvan. *Jealousy of Trade: International Competition and the Nation-state in Historical Perspective*. Cambridge MA: The Belknap Press of Harvard University Press, 2005.

Huguenin, Séverine, and Timothée Léchot. 'Introduction à l'histoire du Journal helvétique'. In *Lectures du 'Journal helvétique', 1732-1782: actes du colloque de Neuchâtel 6-8 mars 2014*, edited by Séverine Huguenin and Timothée Léchot, 23–82. Geneva: Slatkine, 2016.

Hulliung, Mark. *The Autocritique of Enlightenment: Rousseau and the Philosophes*. Cambridge, MA and London: Harvard University Press, 1994.

Hurley, Cecilia. 'La lecture à Neuchâtel pendant le long XVIIIe siècle'. In *Sa Majesté en Suisse: Neuchâtel et ses princes prussiens*, edited by Chantal Lafontant Vallotton, Vincent Callet-Molin and Elisabeth Crettaz-Stürzel, 292–97. Neuchâtel: Alphil, 2013.
Hurley, Cecilia. 'L'ouverture aux Lumières: la Bibliothèque des Pasteurs et son essor dans la deuxième moitié du XVIIIe siècle'. In *Sa Majesté en Suisse: Neuchâtel et ses princes prussiens*, edited by Chantal Lafontant Vallotton, Vincent Callet-Molin and Elisabeth Crettaz-Stürzel, 286–91. Neuchâtel: Alphil, 2013.
Im Hof, Ulrich. *The Enlightenment*. Oxford: Blackwell, 1994.
Inderwildi, Frédéric. 'Géographie des correspondants de libraires dans la deuxième moitié du 18e siècle: la Société typographique de Neuchâtel, Cramer et Gosse à Genève'. *Dix-huitième siècle* 40 (2008): 503–22.
Infelise, Mario. *I libri proibiti: da Gutenberg all'Encyclopédie*. Rome: Laterza, 1999.
Innis, Harold Adams. *The Bias of Communication*. Toronto: University of Toronto Press, 1951.
Israel, Jonathan. *A Revolution of the Mind: Radical Enlightenment and the Intellectual Origins of Modern Democracy*. Princeton, NJ: Princeton University Press, 2010.
Israel, Jonathan I. *Democratic Enlightenment: Philosophy, Revolution, and Human Rights 1750-1790*. Oxford: Oxford University Press, 2011.
Israel, Jonathan I. *The Dutch Republic: Its Rise, Greatness and Fall, 1477-1806*. Oxford: Clarendon Press, 1995.
Israel, Jonathan I. *Enlightenment Contested: Philosophy, Modernity, and the Emancipation of Man, 1670-1752*. Oxford: Oxford University Press, 2006.
Israel, Jonathan I. *Radical Enlightenment: Philosophy and the Making of Modernity, 1650-1750*. Oxford: Oxford University Press, 2001.
Jacob, Margaret C. 'The Mental Landscape of the Public Sphere: A European Perspective'. *Eighteenth Century Studies* 28 [1] (1994): 95–113.
Jacob, Margaret C. *The Radical Enlightenment: Pantheists, Freemasons and Republicans*. London: Allen & Unwin, 1981.
Jacob, Margaret C. *Strangers Nowhere in the World: The Rise of Cosmopolitanism in Early Modern Europe*. Philadelphia: University of Pennsylvania Press, 2006.
Jeanprêtre, Jean. 'Histoire de la Société typographique de Neuchâtel, 1769-1798'. *Musée neuchâtelois* 70-9, 115–20, (1949): 48–53.
Jelmini, Jean-Pierre. *Neuchâtel 1011-2011: mille ans - mille questions - mille et une réponses*. Hauterive: G. Attinger, 2010.
Jelmini, Jean-Pierre. 'Politique intérieure et extérieure de Neuchâtel, de 1707 à la veille de la Révolution française'. In *Histoire du Pays de Neuchâtel: De la Reforme à 1815*, edited by Philippe Henry and Jean-Pierre Jelmini, 91–105. Hauterive: Attinger, 1991.
Johns, Adrian. 'How to Acknowledge a Revolution'. *The American Historical Review* 107 [1] (2002): 106–25.
Johns, Adrian. *The Nature of the Book: Print and Knowledge in the Making*. Chicago: University of Chicago Press, 1998.
Jones, Colin. *The Great Nation: France from Louis XV to Napoleon 1715-99*. London: Allen Lane, 2002.
Jones, Howard Mumford. 'The Importation of French Books in Philadelphia, 1750-1800'. *Modern Philology* 32 [2] (1934): 155–77.
Jones, Peter Michael. *Reform and Revolution in France: The Politics of Transition, 1774-1791*. Cambridge: Cambridge University Press, 1995.
Jost, Hans-Ulrich, and Stéfanie Prezioso, eds. *Relations internationales, échanges culturels et réseaux intellectuels. Actes du colloque du 3e cycle romand d'histoire moderne et contemporaine, Lausanne-Fribourg, 8-23 février 2001*. Lausanne: Antipodes, 2002.

Junod, Louis, ed. *Histoire populaire du pays de Neuchâtel depuis les temps les plus reculés jusqu'en 1815*. Neuchâtel: H. Wolfrath et Metzner, 1863.

Kapossy, Béla. 'Genevan Creditors and English liberty: The Example of Théodore Rilliet de Saussure'. In *Genève, lieu d'Angleterre, 1725-1814 = Geneva, an English enclave, 1725-1814*, edited by Valérie Cossy, Béla Kapossy and Richard Whatmore, 169–93. Geneva: Slatkine, 2009.

Keighren, Innes M. *Bringing Geography to Book: Ellen Semple and the Reception of Geographical Knowledge*. London: I. B. Tauris, 2010.

Keighren, Innes M. 'Bringing Geography to the Book: Charting the Reception of Influences of Geographic Environment'. *Transactions of the Institute of British Geographers* 31 [4] (2006): 525–40.

Kennedy, Máire. 'The Distribution of a Locally-Produced French Periodical in Provincial Ireland: the "Magazin à La Mode," 1777-1778'. *Eighteenth-Century Ireland / Iris an dá chultúr* 9 (1994): 83–98.

Kennedy, Máire. 'The Top 20 French Authors in Eighteenth-Century Irish Private Libraries'. *The Linen Hall Review* 12 [1] (1995): 4–8.

Kennedy, Máire. 'The Trade in French Books in Eighteenth-Century Ireland'. In *Ireland and the French Enlightenment, 1700-1800*, edited by Graham Gargett and Geraldine Sheridan, 173–96. London and New York: Palgrave, 1999.

Kessler, Amalia D. 'A Revolution in Commerce: The Parisian Merchant Court and the Rise of Commercial Society in Eighteenth-century France'. New Haven, Connecticut: Yale University Press, 2007.

Kirschenbaum, Matthew G. *Mechanisms: New Media and the Forensic Imagination*. Cambridge, MA: MIT Press, 2008.

Kirsop, Wallace. 'Following the Money Trail: Selling Books Before, During and After the Revolution'. *Australian Journal of French Studies* 29 (1992): 266–87.

Kleinschmidt, John R. *Les imprimeurs et libraires de la république de Genève, 1700-1798*. Geneva: A. Jullien, 1948.

Kloek, Joost Jakobus, and Wijnandus Wilhelmus Mijnhardt. *Dutch Culture in a European Perspective 2; 1800; Blueprints for a National Community*. London: Palgrave, 2004.

Labrousse, Ernest. *La crise de l'économie française à la fin de l'ancien régime et au début de la révolution*. Paris: Presses Universitaires de France, 1943.

Laevan, A. H. 'The Frankfurt and Leipzig Book Fairs and the History of the Dutch book Trade in the Seventeenth and Eighteenth Centuries'. In *Le magasin de l'univers*, edited by C. Berkvens-Stevelinck, H. Bots, P. G. Hoftijzer and O. S. Lankhorst, 185–98. Leiden and New York: Brill, 1992.

Lamb, Jonathan. 'Fantasies of Paradise'. In *The Enlightenment World*, edited by Martin Fitzpatrick, , Peter Jones, Christa Knellwolf and Iain McCalman, 521–35. London and New York: Pickering & Chatto, 2007.

Landes, Joan B. *Women and the Public Sphere in the Age of the French Revolution*. Ithaca: Cornell University Press, 1988.

Lavandier, Jean-Pierre. *Le livre au temps de Joseph II et de Leopold II: code des lois de censure du livre pour les pays Austro-Bohemiens (1780-1792)*. Berne: Peter Lang, 1995.

Le Roy Ladurie, Emmanuel. *The Ancien Régime: A History of France, 1610-1774*. Oxford: Blackwell, 1996.

Le Roy Ladurie, Emmanuel, Yann Fauchois, Anette Smedley-Weill and André Zysberg. 'L'édition francophone (1470-1780): Paris – province – 'étranger' par tranches diachroniques'. *Histoire, économie et société* 15 [4] (1996): 507–23.

Leigh, Ralph. 'Une balle qu'il eût fallu saisir au bond: Frédéric-Samuel Ostervald et l'édition des Œuvres de Rousseau (1778-1779)'. In *Aspect du livre neuchâtelois*, edited by Jacques Rychner and Michel Schlup, 89–96. Neuchâtel: Bibliothèque publique et universitaire de Neuchâtel, 1986.

Leigh, R. A. *Unsolved Problems in the Bibliography of J.J. Rousseau*. Cambridge: Cambridge University Press, 1990.

Lepetit, Bernard. *Les villes dans la France moderne (1740-1840)*. Paris: Albin Michel, 1988.

Livet, Georges. *Histoire des routes et des transports en Europe: Des chemins de Saint-Jacques à l'âge d'or des diligences*. Strasbourg: Presses universitaires de Strasbourg, 2003.

Lopez, François. 'Stratégies commercials et diffusion des idées: les ouvrages français dans le monde hispanique et hispano-américain à l'époque des Lumières'. In *L'Amérique espagnole à l'époque des Lumières*, 353–62. Paris: Centre National de la Recherche Scientifique, 1987.

Lovejoy, Arthur O. *The Great Chain of Being: A Study of the History of an Idea*. Cambridge, MA: Harvard University Press, 1936.

Luna, Frederick A. de. 'The Dean Street Style of Revolution: J.-P. Brissot, jeune philosophe'. *French Historical Studies* 17 [1] (1991): 159–90.

Lüsesbrink, Hans-Jürgen, René Nohr and Rolf Reichardt. 'Kulturtransfer im Epochenumbruch—Entwicklung und Inhalte der französisch-deutschen Übersetzungsbibliothek 1770-1815 im Überblick'. In *Kulturtransfer im Epochenumbruch. Frankreich-Deutschland 1770 bis 1815*, edited by Hans-Jürgen Lüsebrink and Rolf Reichardt, vol. 1, 29–86. Leipzig: Leipziger Universitätsverlag, 1997.

Lytton Sells, A. 'The History of Francis Wills: A Literary Mystery'. *The Review of English Studies* 11 [41] (1935): 1–27.

MacDonald, Bertrum H., and Fiona A. Black. 'Using GIS for Spatial and Temporal Analyses in Print Culture Studies: Some Opportunities and Challenges'. *Social Science History* 24 [3] (2000): 505–36.

Machet, Anne. 'Clients Italiens de la Société typographique de Neuchâtel'. In *Aspects du livre neuchâtelois*, edited by Jacques Rychner, 159–85. Neuchâtel: Bibliothèque publique et universitaire de Neuchâtel, 1986.

Mah, Harold. 'Phantasies of the Public Sphere: Rethinking the Habermas of Historians'. *The Journal of Modern History* 72 [1] (2000): 153–82.

Martin, Angus, Vivienne G. Mylne and Richard Frautschi. *Bibliographie du genre romanesque français: 1751-1800*. London: Mansell, 1977.

Martin, Henri-Jean. 'Comment mesurer un succès littéraire: le problème des tirages'. In *La bibliographie matérielle*, edited by Roger Laufer, 25–42. Paris: Editions du centre national de la recherche scientifique, 1983.

Martin, Henri-Jean. 'La librairie française en 1777-1778'. *Dix-huitième siècle* 11 [1] (1979): 87–112.

Martin, Henri-Jean, and Roger Chartier. *Le livre triomphant 1660-1830*. Histoire de l'édition française. Paris: Promodis, 1984.

Mason, H. T., ed. *The Darnton Debate: Books and Revolution in the Eighteenth Century*. Oxford: Voltaire Foundation, 1998.

Mason, Haydn T., ed. 'The European Enlightenment: Was it Enlightened?' *The Modern Language Review* 94 [4] (1999): xxvii–xxxviii.

Masseau, Didier. *Les ennemis des philosophes: l'antiphilosophie au temps des Lumières*. Paris: Albin Michel, 2000.

May, Georges. *Le dilemme du roman au XVIIIe siècle, étude sur les rapports du roman et de la critique (1715-1761)*. New Haven and Paris: Yale University Press and Presses Universitaires de France, 1963.

Maza, Sarah C. *The Myth of the French Bourgeoisie: An Essay on the Social Imaginary, 1750-1850*. Cambridge, MA and London: Harvard University Press, 2003.

Maza, Sarah C. *Private Lives and Public Affairs: The Causes Célèbres of Prerevolutionary France*. Berkeley and London: University of California Press, 1993.

McKenzie, F., and J. C. Ross, eds. *A Ledger of Charles Ackers, Printer of the London Magazine*. Oxford: Oxford Bibliographical Society, 1968.

McKitterick, David. *A History of Cambridge University Press. Volume 2, Scholarship and Commerce 1698-1872*. Cambridge: Cambridge University Press, 1998.

McKitterick, David. *Print, Manuscript, and the Search for Order, 1450-1830*. Cambridge: Cambridge University Press, 2003.

McLeod, Jane. *Licensing Loyalty: Printers, Patrons, and the State in Early Modern France*. University Park: Pennsylvania State University Press, 2011.

McMahon, Darrin M. 'The Counter-Enlightenment and the Low Life of Literature in Pre-Revolutionary France'. *Past and Present* 159 (1998): 77–112.

McMahon, Darrin M. *Enemies of the Enlightenment*. Oxford: Oxford University Press, 2002.

Mellot, Jean-Dominique. 'Qu'est-ce qu'un livre? Qu'est-ce que l'histoire du livre?' *Histoire et civilisation du livre: revue internationale* 2 (2006): 4–18.

Mellot, Jean-Dominique. 'Rouen et les libraires "forains" à la fin du XVIIIe siècle: le veuve Machuel et ses correspondants (1768-1773)'. *Bibliothèque de l'Ecole des chartes* 147 (1989): 503–38.

Mellot, Jean-Dominique, Élisabeth Queval and Antoine Monaque, eds. *Répertoire d'imprimeurs-libraires (vers 1500-vers 1810)*. Paris: Bibliothèque nationale de France, 2004.

Milstein, Barney M. *Eight Eighteenth-Century Reading Societies. A Sociological Contribution to the History of German Literature*. Berne and Frankfurt: Herbert Lang, 1972.

Minois, Georges. *Censure et culture sous l'ancien régime*. Paris: Fayard, 1995.

Mornet, Daniel. 'Les enseignements des bibliothèques privées (1750-1780)'. *Revue d'histoire littéaraire de la France* XVII (1910): 449–92.

Mornet, Daniel. *Les origines intellectuelles de la Révolution française*. Paris: Armand Colin, 1933.

Moulinas, René. *L'imprimerie, la librairie et la presse à Avignon au XVIIIe siècle*. Grenoble: Presses Universitaires de Grenoble, 1974.

Moureau, François, ed. *Les presses grises. La contrefaçon du livre (XVIe-XIXe siècles)*. Paris: Aux amateurs de livres, 1988.

Muceni, Elena. 'John/Jean Nourse: un masque anglais au service de la littérature clandestine francophone'. *La lettre clandestine* 24 (2016): 203–19.

Munck, Thomas. *The Enlightenment: A Comparative Social History 1721-1794*. London: Arnold, 2000.

Negroni, Barbara de. *Lectures interdites: le travail des censeurs au XVIIIe siècle 1723-1774*. Paris: Albin Michel, 1995.

Ogborn, Miles, and Charles W. J. Withers. *Geographies of the Book*. Farnham: Ashgate, 2010.

Outram, Dornida. *The Enlightenment*. Cambridge: Cambridge University Press, 1995.

Pasta, Renato. *Editoria e cultura nel Settecento*. Firenze: L. S. Olschki, 1997.

Pasta, Renato. 'Les échanges avec l'Italie'. In *Le rayonnement d'un maison d'édition dans l'Europe des Lumières: la Société typographique de Neuchâtel 1769-1789*, edited by Robert Darnton and Michel Schlup, 455–73. Hauterive: Editions Gilles Attinger, 2005.

Pasta, Renato. 'Prima della Rivoluzione: il mercato librario italiano nella carte della Société typographique de Neuchâtel (1769-1789)'. *Mélanges de l'Ecole française de Rome. Italie et Méditerranée* 102 [2] (1990): 282–320.

Pasta, Renato. 'Towards a Social History of Ideas: The Book and the Booktrade in Eighteenth-century Italy'. In *Histoires du livre: nouvelles orientations*, edited by Hans Erich Bödeker, 101-38. Paris: IMEC, 1995.
Pelet, Paul Louis. *Le Canal d'Entreroches, histoire d'une idée*. Lausanne: F. Rouge, 1946.
Perret, Jean-Pierre. *Les imprimeries d'Yverdon au XVIIe et au XVIIIe siècle*. Lausanne: F. Roth, 1945.
Petitpierre, Olivier, ed. *Histoire abrégée des troubles de Neuchâtel pendant les années 1766, 1767, et 1768, suivie de divers autres documens historiques*. Neuchâtel: Petitpierre et Prince, 1832.
Pettegree, Andrew, and Flavia Bruni, eds. *Lost Books: Reconstructing the Print World of Pre-Industrial Europe*. Leiden: Brill, 2016.
Plan, Danielle. *Un Genevois d'autrefois: Henri-Albert Gosse [1753-1816]*. Paris and Geneva: Fischbacher and Kundig, 1909.
Popkin, Jeremy D. *News and Politics in the Age of Revolution: Jean Luzac's Gazette de Leyde*. Ithaca: Cornell University Press, 1989.
Popkin, Jeremy D. 'Pamphlet Journalism at the End of the Old Regime'. *Eighteenth-Century Studies* 22 (1999): 315-67.
Popkin, Jeremy D., and Hans-Jürgen Lüsebrink, eds. *Enlightenment, Revolution and the Periodical Press*. Oxford: Voltaire Foundation, 2004.
Porret, Michel. 'Édition combustion: les circonstances de la censure à Genève au XVIIIe siècle'. *Annales Benjamin Constant* 18-9 (1996): 281-90.
Porret, Michel. 'La feu de la censure dans la Genève des lumières: écrits séditieux, "bagatelles de Monsieur Voltaire" et "livres remplis d'obscénités"'. In *Swiss made: la Suisse en dialogue avec le monde*, edited by Beat Schläpfer, 35-47. Geneva: Zoé, 1998.
Porter, Roy. *Enlightenment: Britain and the Making of the Modern World*. London: Allen Lane, 2000.
Porter, Roy, and Mikuláš Teich, eds. *The Enlightenment in National Context*. Cambridge: Cambridge University Press, 1981.
Pothion, Jean. *Dictionnaire des bureaux de poste français, 1575-1904*. Paris: Poste aux lettres, 1976.
Pottinger, David Thomas. *The French Book Trade in the Ancien Régime, 1500-1791*. Cambridge, MA: Harvard University Press, 1958.
Quéniart, Jean. *L'imprimerie et la librairie à Rouen au XVIIIe siècle*. Paris: C. Klincksieck, 1969.
Raven, James. *The Business of Books: Booksellers and the English Book Trade, 1450-1850*. New Haven and London: Yale University Press, 2007.
Raven, James. 'Selling Books Across Europe, c.1450-1800'. *Publishing History* 34 (1993): 5-19.
Ravier, Louis. *Répertoire de librairie, contenant toutes les lois rendues sur la librairie et l'imprimerie depuis le règlement de 1723*. Paris: Crapart, Caille et Ravier, 1807.
Reymond, Anne. 'Le libraire Samuel Girardet et ses relations commerciales avec la Société typographique de Neuchâtel, 1769-1777'. In *Aspects du livre neuchâtelois*, edited by Jacques Rychner and Michel Schlup, 99-115. Neuchâtel: Bibliothèque publique et universitaire de Neuchâtel, 1986.
Rigogne, Thierry. *Between State and Market: Printing and Bookselling in Eighteenth-century France*. Oxford: Voltaire Foundation, 2007.
Rigogne, Thierry. 'Librairie et réseaux commerciaux du livre en France'. In *Le rayonnement d'une maison d'édition dans l'Europe des Lumières: la Société typographique de Neuchâtel 1769-1789*, edited by Robert Darnton and Michel Schlup, 375-404. Hauterive: Editions Gilles Attinger, 2005.

Rilliet, Jean-Horace, ed. *Six siècles d'existence genevoise: les Rilliet (1377-1977)*. Geneva: Editions de la Thébaïde, 1977.
Robertson, John. 'The Enlightenment Above National Context: Political Economy in Eighteenth-century Scotland and Naples'. *The Historical Journal* 40 [3] (1997): 667–97.
Roche, Daniel. 'Censorship and the Publishing Industry'. In *Revolution in Print: The Press in France, 1775-1800*, edited by Robert Darnton and Daniel Roche, 3–26. Berkeley and London: University of California Press, 1989.
Roche, Daniel. *France in the Enlightenment*. Cambridge, MA and London: Harvard University Press, 1998.
Roche, Daniel. 'La censure'. In *Histoire de l'édition française, t. ii: Le livre triomphant*, edited by Henri-Jean Martin, Roger Chartier and Jean-Pierre Vivet, 76–83. Paris: Promodis, 1984.
Roche, Daniel. *Les républicains des lettres: gens de culture et Lumières au XVIIIe siècle*. Paris: Fayard, 1988.
Roche, Daniel. 'Lumières et commerces vues de Neuchâtel 1769-1789'. In *Le rayonnement d'une maison d'édition dans l'Europe des Lumières: la Société typographique de Neuchâtel 1769-1789*, edited by Michel Schlup and Robert Darnton, 557–71. Hauterive: Editions Gilles Attinger, 2005.
Rychner, Jacques. 'Alltag einer Druckerei im Zeitaler der Aufklärung'. In *Buch und Buchhandel in Europa im achtzehnten Jahrhundert*, edited by Giles Barber and Bernhard Fabian, 53–80. Hamburg: E. Hauswedell, 1981.
Rychner, Jacques. 'Espaces de l'atelier d'imprimerie au XVIIIe siècle'. In *Le livre et l'historien: études offertes en l'honneur du professeur Henri-Jean Martin*, edited by Frédéric Barbier, Annie Parent-Charon, François Dupuigrenet Desroussilles, Claude Jolly and Dominique Varryet, 291–318. Geneva: Droz, 1997.
Rychner, Jacques. 'Fonctions et tribulations d'un prote au XVIIIe siècle: Jacques-Barthélemy Spineux, 1738-1806'. In *Aspects du livre neuchâtelois*, edited by Jacques Rychner and Michel Schlup, 187–269. Neuchâtel: Bibliothèque publique et universitaire de Neuchâtel, 1986.
Rychner, Jacques. *Genève et ses typographes vus de Neuchâtel, 1770-1780*. Geneva: C. Braillard, 1984.
Rychner, Jacques. 'Le travail de l'atelier'. In *Histoire de l'édition française, t.ii: Le livre triomphant*, edited by Henri-Jean Martin, Roger Chartier and Jean-Pierre Vivet, 42–61. Paris: Promodis, 1984.
Rychner, Jacques. 'Les archives de la Société typographique de Neuchâtel'. *Musée neuchâtelois* 1969: 99–122.
Rychner, Jacques. 'A l'ombre des Lumières: coup d'œil sur la main-d'œuvre de quelques imprimeries du XVIIIe siècle'. *Revue française d'histoire du livre* 5 [16] (1977): 611–42.
Rychner, Jacques. 'Running a Printing House in Eighteenth-Century Switzerland: The Workshop of the Société typographique de Neuchâtel'. *The Library, sixth series* 1 [1] (1979): 1–24.
Sayce, R. A. 'Compositional Practices and the Localization of Printed Books: 1530-1800'. *The Library* 31 (1966): 1–45.
Schlup, Michel. 'Aperçu de l'imprimerie et de l'édition Neuchâteloise avant 1769'. In *L'édition neuchâteloise au siècle des Lumières: la Société typographique de Neuchâtel (1769-1789)*, edited by Michel Schlup, 29–59. Neuchâtel: Bibliothèque publique et universitaire de Neuchâtel, 2002.
Schlup, Michel. 'Diffusion et lecture du Journal helvétique au temps de la Société typographique de Neuchâtel, 1769-1782'. In *La diffusion et la lecture des journaux de*

langue française sous l'ancien régime, edited by Hans Bots, 59–71. Amsterdam and Maarsen: APA/Holland University Press, 1988.

Schlup, Michel. 'Entre pouvoir et clandestinité: l'édition neuchâteloise des Lumières'. In *Le rayonnement d'une maison d'édition dans l'Europe des Lumières: la Société typographique de Neuchâtel 1769-1789*, edited by Michel Schlup and Robert Darnton, 69–86. Hauterive: Editions Gilles Attinger, 2005.

Schlup, Michel. 'Etude d'un processus éditorial et typographique: l'impression des œuvres de Charles Bonnet par Samuel Fauche, 1777-1783'. In *Aspects du livre neuchâtelois*, edited by Jacques Rychner and Michel Schlup, 271–335. Neuchâtel: Bibliothèque publique et universitaire de Neuchâtel, 1983.

Schlup, Michel. 'Introduction'. In *L'édition neuchâteloise au siècle des Lumières: la Société typographique de Neuchâtel (1769-1789)*, edited by Michel Schlup, 7–13. Neuchâtel: Bibliothèque publique et universitaire de Neuchâtel, 2002.

Schlup, Michel. 'Introduction'. In *Le rayonnement d'une maison d'édition dans l'Europe des Lumières: la Société typographique de Neuchâtel 1769-1789*, edited by Michel Schlup and Robert Darnton, 17–32. Hauterive: Editions Gilles Attinger, 2005.

Schlup, Michel. 'L'achat mouvementé des papiers de la Société typographique de Neuchâtel (1931-1932)'. In *L'édition neuchâtelois au siècle des Lumières: la Société typographique de Neuchâtel (1769-1789)*, edited by Michel Schlup, 171–7. Neuchâtel: Bibliothèque publique et universitaire de Neuchâtel, 2002.

Schlup, Michel. 'L'édition de Mon Bonnet de nuit'. In *Mercier, Louis-Sebastien: Mon Bonnet de nuit, suivi de Du Théâtre*, edited by Jean Claude Bonnet, xlviii–lxxix. Paris: Mercure de France, 1999.

Schlup, Michel. 'L'édition du Tableau de Paris à Neuchâtel (1781-1783) ; les éditions du Tableau de Paris, description matérielle'. In *Louis-Sébastien Mercier, Tableau de Paris*, edited by Jean Claude Bonnet, xcv–clxxx. Paris: Mercure de France, 1994.

Schlup, Michel. 'La bibliothèque et les lectures d'un "gentilhomme" Neuchâtelois à la fin des Lumières: Pierre-Alexandre DuPeyrou (1729-1794)'. In *Usages du livre à la fin de l'ancien régime: autour de la bibliothèque Castella*, edited by Thomas Hunkeler, Simone de Reyff and Lucas Giossi, 237–52. Gollion: Infolio, 2015.

Schlup, Michel. 'La diffusione des libro francese in Russia vista da Neuchâtel: 1775-1788'. In *Gli spazi del libro nell'Europa del XVIII secolo*, edited by Maria Gioia Tavoni and Rossella Sassi, 35–45. Bologne: Pàtron, 1997.

Schlup, Michel. 'La Société typographique de Neuchâtel (1769-1789): Points de repère'. In *L'édition neuchâteloise au siècle des Lumières: la Société typographique de Neuchâtel (1769-1789)*, edited by Michel Schlup, 61–105. Neuchâtel: Bibliothèque publique et universitaire de Neuchâtel, 2002.

Schlup, Michel. 'La Société typographique de Neuchâtel et ses auteurs: rapports de force et affaires de dupes'. In *Le rayonnement d'une maison d'édition dans l'Europe des Lumières: la Société typographique de Neuchâtel 1769-1789*, edited by Robert Darnton and Michel Schlup, 139–60. Hauverive: Editions Gilles Attinger, 2005.

Schlup, Michel. 'La STN et l'édition de la Feuille d'Avis de Neuchâtel'. In *L'édition nuchâteloise au siècle des Lumières: La Société typographique de Neuchâtel (1769-1789)*, edited by Michel Schlup, 157–67. Neuchâtel: Bibliothèque publique et universitaire de Neuchâtel, 2002.

Schlup, Michel., ed. *Le mangeur Neuchâtelois et quelques voisins au temps des Lumières (1730-1800)*. Neuchâtel: Bibliothèque publique et universitaire de Neuchâtel, 2003.

Schlup, Michel. 'Le rêve impossible de la STN: un Journal helvétique et "parisien"!' In *L'édition neuchâteloise au siècle de Lumières: la Société typographique de Neuchâtel,*

1769-1789, edited by Robert Darnton and Michel Schlup, 143–55. Hauterive: Editions Gilles Attinger, 2005.

Schlup, Michel., ed. *L'édition neuchâteloise au siècle des Lumières: la Société typographique de Neuchâtel (1769-1789)*. Neuchâtel: Bibliothèque publique et universitaire de Neuchâtel, 2002.

Schlup, Michel. 'Samuel Fauche, libraire-imprimeur et éditeur (1732-1803)'. In *Biographies Neuchâteloises, t. 1: De saint Guillaume à la fin des Lumières*, edited by Michel Schlup, 83–9. Hauterive: Editions Gilles Attinger, 1996.

Schlup, Michel. 'Sociétés de lecture et cabinets littéraires dans la Principauté de Neuchâtel, (1750-1800): de nouvelles pratiques de la lecture'. *Musée neuchâlelois* 1987 [2]: 81–104.

Schlup, Michel. 'Un commerce de librairie entre Neuchâtel et La Haye (1769-1779)'. In *Le magasin de l'univers*, edited by C. Berkvens-Stevelinck, H. Bots, P. G. Hoftijzer and O. S. Lankhorst, 237–50. Leiden and New York: Brill, 1992.

Schlup, Michel. 'Un indicateur de la vie économique et sociale au XVIIIe siècle: la Feuille d'Avis de Neuchâtel, 1769-1782, édition et diffusion'. In *C'est la faute à Voltaire, c'est la faute à Rousseau*, edited by Roger Durand and Jean-Daniel Candaux, 155–66. Geneva: Droz, 1997.

Schmidt, Michael. 'Liste des impressions et éditions de la Société typographique de Neuchâtel'. In *L'édition neuchâtelois au siècle des Lumières: la Société typographique de Neuchâtel (1769-1789)*, edited by Michel Schlup, 233–85. Neuchâtel: Bibliothèque publique et universitaire de Neuchâtel, 2002.

Seaward, Louise. 'Censorship Through Co-operation: The Société Typographique de Neuchâtel (STN) and the French Government, 1769-1789'. *French History* 28 (2014): 23–42.

Seaward, Louise. 'The Small Republic and the Great Power: Censorship Between Geneva and France in the Later Eighteenth Century'. *The Library: The Transactions of the Bibliographic Society* 18 [2] (2017): 191–217.

Selm, B. van. '"Het kompt altemael aen op het distribuweeren." De boekdistributie in de Republiek als object van onderzoek'. In *De productie, distributie en consumptie van cultuur*, edited by J. J. Kloek and W.W. Mijnhardt, 89–99. Amsterdam: Rodopi, 1991.

Selwyn, Pamela E. *Everyday Life in the German Book Trade: Friedrich Nicolai as bookseller and publisher in the Age of Enlightenment, 1750-1810*. University Park: Pennsylvania State University Press, 2000.

Sgard, Jean. *Dictionnaire des journalistes, 1600-1789*. Grenoble: Presses Universitaires de Grenoble, 1976.

Sgard, Jean. *Dictionnaire des journaux, 1600-1789*. Paris: Universitas, 1991.

Sonenscher, Michael. *Before the Deluge: Public Debt, Inequality, and the Intellectual Origins of the French Revolution*. Princeton: Princeton University Press, 2007.

Sonenscher, Michael. 'The Nation's Debt and the Birth of the Modern Republic: The French Fiscal Deficit and the Politics of the Revolution of 1789'. *History of Political Thought* 18 [11] (1997): 64–103.

Sørensen, Madeleine Pinault. 'Les planches de la *Description des arts et métiers*'. In *Le rayonnement d'une maison d'édition dans l'Europe des Lumières: la Société typographique de Neuchâtel 1769-1789*, edited by Michel Schlup and Robert Darnton, 219–55. Hauterive: Editions Gilles Attinger, 2005.

Strehler, Hermann. *Die Buchdrunkerkunst im alten St. Gallen: die Geschichte der Offizin Zollikofer*. St. Gallen: Verlag Zollikofer, 1967.

Sutherland, John. 'Publishing History: A Hole at the Centre of Literary Sociology'. *Critical Inquiry* 14 [3] (1988): 574–89.

Svensson, Patrik. 'The Landscape of Digital Humanities.' *Digital Humanities Quarterly* 4 [1] (2010): http://digitalhumanities.org/dhq/vol/4/1/000080/000080.html.
Swann, Julian. *Politics and the Parlement of Paris under Louis XV, 1754-1774*. Cambridge: Cambridge University Press, 1995.
Tanselle, G. Thomas. *Literature and Artifacts*. Charlottesville: Bibliographical Society of the University of Virginia, 1998.
Taylor, Charles. *Philosophical Arguments*. Cambridge, MA: Harvard University Press, 1997.
Tecoz, René-Maurice. 'L'imprimerie à Nyon au XVIIIe siècle: J.L. Nathey, ses publications et leurs auteurs'. *Schweizerisches Gutenbergmuseum / Musée Gutenberg suisse* 52 (1966): 159–79.
Thomson, Ann, Simon Burrows and Edmond Dziembowski, eds. *Cultural Transfers: France and Britain in the Long Eighteenth Century*. Oxford: Voltaire Foundation, 2010.
Tissot, Pierre-Yves. 'Les débuts de l'imprimerie dans les montagnes neuchâteloises, des origines à 1848'. In *Aspects du livre neuchâtelois*, edited by Jacques Rychner and Michel Schlup, 453–72. Neuchâtel: Bibliothèque publique et universitaire de Neuchâtel, 1986.
Tissot, Pierre-Yves. 'Premiers éditeurs et imprimeurs dans les montagnes neuchâteloises'. *Librarium* 26 (1983): 87–99.
Towsey, Mark. 'First Steps in Associational Reading: Book Use and Sociability at the Wigtown Subscription Library, 1795-9'. *Proceedings of the Bibliographical Society of America* 103 [4] (2009): 455–95.
Tresse, R., and M. Daumas. 'La *Description des arts et métiers* de l'Académie des sciences et le sort de ses planches gravées en taille douce'. *Revue d'histoire des sciences et de leurs applications* 7 [2] (1954): 163–71.
Tribolet, Charles-Godefroy de. *Histoire de Neuchâtel et Valangin depuis l'avènement de la Maison de Prusse jusqu'en 1806*. Neuchâtel: H. Wolfrath, 1846.
Tucoo-Chala, Suzanne. *Charles-Joseph Panckoucke et la librairie française, 1736-1798*. Pau: Marrimpouey jeune, 1977.
Valeri, Stefania. *Libri nuovi scendon l'Alpi venti anni di relazioni franco-italiane negli archivi della Société typographique de Neuchâtel, 1769-1789*. Macerata: Eum, 2006.
Van Horn Melton, James. *The Rise of the Public in Enlightenment Europe*. Cambridge: Cambridge University Press, 2001.
Van Selm, B. 'Johannes Van Ravesteyn, "Libraire Européen" or Local Trader?' In *Le magasin de l'univers: The Dutch Republic as the centre of the European book trade*, edited by C. Berkvens-Stevelinck, H. Bots, P. G. Hoftijzer and O. S. Lankhorst, 251–63. Leiden and New York: Brill, 1992.
Varry, Dominique. 'La diffusion sous le manteau: la Société typographique de Neuchâtel et les Lyonnais'. In *L'Europe et le livre: réseaux et pratiques du négoce de libraire, XVIe-XIXe siècles*, edited by Frédéric Barbier, Sabine Juratic and Dominique Varry, 309–32. Paris: Klincksieck, 1996.
Varry, Dominique. 'Le commerce du livre 'philosophique' à Belfort à la fin de l'ancien régime'. *Revue d'Alsace* 121 (1995): 97–110.
Varry, Dominique 'Les gens du livre à Lyon au XVIIIe siècle: Quand de 'loyaux sujets' sont aussi des 'maronneurs''. In *Le peuple des villes dans l'Europe du Nord-Ouest de la fin du Moyen Age à 1945*, edited by Philippe Guignet, vol. 2, 229–42. Lille: Université Charles-de-Gaulle, 2003.
Varry, Dominique. 'Pour de nouvelles approches des archives de la Société typographique de Neuchâtel'. *SVEC* 359 (1997): 235–49.
Varry, Dominique. 'Une géographie de l'illicite: les espaces du livre à Lyon au temps des Lumières'. *La lettre clandestine* 8 (1999): 113–33.

Ventre, Madeleine. *L'imprimerie et la librairie en Languedoc au dernier siècle de l'ancien régime, 1700-1789*. Paris and The Hague: Mouton, 1958.

Vercruysse, Jeroom. 'Joseph Marie Durey de Morsan chroniqueur de Ferney (1769-1772) et l'édition neuchâteloise des Questions sur l'Encyclopédie'. *SVEC* 230 (1985).

Vercruysse, Jeroom. 'L'édition neuchâteloise du Système de la nature et la libraire bruxelloise'. In *Aspects du livre neuchâtelois*, edited by Jacques Rychner and Michel Schlup, 77–88. Neuchâtel: Bibliothèque publique et universitaire de Neuchâtel, 1986.

Via, Rachele. *Il libro e la storia delle idee: le società tipografiche di Napoli e di Neuchâtel alla fine del '700*. Soveria Mannelli: Rubbettino, 1995.

Vliet, Rietje van. 'Print and Public in Europe, 1600-1800'. In *A Companion to the History of Book*, edited by Simon Eliot and Jonathan Rose, 247–58. London: Wiley-Blackwell, 2009.

Walton, Charles. 'La liberté de la presse selon les cahiers de doléances de 1789'. *Revue d'histoire modern et contemporaine* 53 [1] (2006): 63–87.

Warner, Michael. 'Publics and Counterpublics'. *Public Culture* 14 [1] (2002): 49–90.

Weber, Ernst. 'Sortimentskataloge des 18. Jahrhunderts als literatur- und buchhandelsgeschichtliche Quellen'. In *Bücherkataloge als buchgeschichtliche Quellen in der frühen Neuzeit*, edited by Reinhard Wittmann, 209–57. Wiesbaden: O. Harrassowitz, 1984.

Weedon, Alexis. 'The Uses of Quantification'. In *A Companion to the History of the Book*, edited by Simon Eliot and Jonathan Rose, 33–49. London: Wiley-Blackwell, 2009.

Weil, Françoise. 'Le rôle des libraires hollandais dans la diffusion des livres interdits en France dans la première moitié du XVIIIe siècle'. In *Le magasin de l'univers*, edited by C. Berkvens-Stevelinck, H. Bots, P. G. Hoftijzer and O. S. Lankhorst, 281–88. Leiden and New York: Brill, 1992.

Weil, Françoise. *Livres interdits, livres persécutés 1720-1770*. Oxford: Voltaire Foundation, 1999.

Weil, Françoise. 'Une 'secte' de colporteurs venus du Dévoluy (1764-1780)'. *Australian Journal of French Studies* 37 [2] (2000): 165–202.

Yamey, Basil. 'Diversity in Mercantile Accounting in Western Europe, 1300-1800'. In *The Development of Accounting in an International Context*, edited by T. E. Cooke and C. W. Nobes, 12–29. London: Routledge, 1997.

Yamey, Basil. *Double-Entry Bookkeeping in Western Europe, 1300 to 1800*. New York and London: Garland, 2000.

Yamey, Basil. 'Scientific Bookkeeping and the Rise of Capitalism'. *The Economic History Review* 1 [2/3] (1949): 99–113.

Yamey, Basil. 'Some Seventeenth and Eighteenth Century Double-Entry Ledgers'. *The Accounting Review* 54 [2] (1959): 534–46.

Zachs, William. *The First John Murray and the Eighteenth-Century London Book Trade*. Oxford: Oxford University Press, 1998.

Zurbuchen, Walter. 'Une famille tragique: les Witel'. *Revue du Vieux Genève* 14 (1984): 54–63.

Index

Alembert, Jean le Rond d' 57
Algarotti, Francesco 25–6, 68, 73, 90
archives of the Société typographique de Neuchâtel 4
   comparable collections 33–4
   day books 39–41
   discovery 33
   lacunae 38
   ledgers 37–8
   order books 43–4
   stock books 41–2
Auzière, George 25, 27

Barde, Manget and Company 31, 110
Bardin, Isaac 61, 110
Barret, Jean-Michel 28
Barret *veuve* 112
Bassompière, Jean François de 110, 119
Berthoud, Charles 114
Bertrand, Elie 71, 78
Bertrand, Jean-Elie 22–3, 57
Bible 30–1
Birn, Raymond 141
Black, Fiona 5
Bluche, François 66
Bonhôte, James-Henri 114
Bonnant, Georges 5, 141
Bonthoux, D. 109
Borel, Henry-Louis and François-Béat 63
Bosset de Luze, Abram 32, 90
Bosset, Jean-Frédéric 110
Boubers, Jean-Louis de 3, 90–1
Bovet, André 33, 34, 38
Boyve, Abraham 20
Brissot de Warville, Jacques-Pierre 49, 69, 102, 104, 110, 114
Brun, Anne-Marie 32
Bruzard de Mauvelain 97, 107

café Dardel 62
Cailler, Jean-Samuel 16, 28, 53, 60, 127–8
Catalogue des livres défendus par la commission impériale et royale, jusqu'à l'année 1786 125
Chaillet, Henri-David de 57, 153
Chaillet d'Arnex, J. H. de 110
Charrière, Isabelle de 15, 19, 49, 71, 114, 153
Chauvet, P. L. 109
Chauvet (lawyer) 116
Chirol, Barthélemy 54, 60–1, 109, 111
circulating libraries 19, 62
Compte rendu au roi (Necker) 102, 144–5
Condillac, Étienne Bonnot de 71
Condorcet, Jean-Antoine-Nicolas de Caritat, marquis de 71
Conlon, Pierre 142
Convert, Jean-Pierre 62
Correspondance, ou défense fondamentale de spectable Théodore Rilliet (Rilliet de Saussure) 119–21
Correspondence secrète, politique et littéraire (Mettra) 120
Corsini, Silvio 5, 56, 80, 141, 158
Coxe, William 15–16, 19, 20, 22, 135
Cramer, Gabriel and Philibert 27, 31, 33, 49, 60, 85, 93, 94, 110

Daguet, Alexandre 114
Darnton, Robert 3, 23, 66, 143
   and 'floating stock' 8, 50–2, 67, 135, 141
   'Grub Street' thesis 114–15, 126, 131–2
   and Mauvelain case-study 97, 107
Décombaz, Gabriel 110
Delahaye and Company 90–1

Deluc, Jean-André   55–6
De Luze, Jean J.   110
De Mairan, Jean-Jacques Dortous   66
De Meuron, Daniel and Henri   63
Desaint, *veuve*   33, 88, 92, 95, 137, 147
Descriptions des arts et métiers (Academy of Science)   3–4, 30–1, 105
Des lettres de cachet affair   106, 114, 124
de Tournes (family)   110
Diderot, Denis   71, 79–80, 101
Dotaux, Frédrich   83
double-entry accounting
  capture of trading events   36–7
  limitations   45–7
  manuals and guides   35–6
  relationship between ledgers   37
  value to merchants   35
Dufart, François   110
Dufour, Jean-Edmé and Roux, Philippe   90–1
Dugast De Bois-Saint-Just, Jean-Louis-Marie   49
Du Peyrou, Alexandre   19, 54
Durand, Victor   44–5, 52, 54, 94, 99, 111–13, 130–2, 139, 151, 153, 155

Eisenstein, Elizabeth   23
Encyclopédie (Diderot and d'Alembert)   4, 21–2, 30–1, 114
the Enlightenment
  fabric of the Enlightenment   137–8
  grands hommes   140
  manipulation by power and wealth   144–5
  pace of change   139–40
  unevenness across space   141–2
Essai philosophique sur le plaisir   78
Extrait du journal d'un officier de la marine de l'escadre de M. le comte d'Estaing   102, 103, 106

Faivre (smuggler in Pontarlier)   97, 106–8
Fauche, Jonas   101, 102–7, 114
Fauche, Samuel   20, 29, 36, 49, 54, 101, 102, 124, 153
  career and background   21–2, 63
  Le gazetier cuirassé affair   29
Fauche-Borel, Abraham-Louis   62, 101

Fauche-Borel, Louis   45, 63, 101, 131, 151, 153–4
Fauche-Borel, Marianne   154
Favre, Charles-Samuel   101, 105
Febvre, Lucien   5, 114
Félice, Fortuné-Barthélemy de   54, 64
Feuille d'avis de Neuchâtel   16, 20, 22, 63, 75–6, 151
The Forbidden Best-Sellers of Pre-Revolutionary France (Darnton)   7, 115, 149
Freedman, Jeffrey   3, 45
French book trade
  12 June 1783 regulations   106–9
  cosmopolitanism   52, 72–3, 84–5
  flow of books   5, 7, 96
  government enforcement   104–7
  haulage costs   83–4, 85
  historiography   5, 114
  importance of *nouveautés*   7, 28, 53, 71, 75–9, 139, 142, 146–7
  legal frameworks   79–80, 86, 101
French Book Trade in Enlightenment Europe Database   1
  'born digital' resource   2
  'clients' tables   157–7
  data spine   4, 38–47, 155
  data structure   6
  'editions' tables   157–60
  insights into the Enlightenment   137–47
  limitations   3, 4, 8, 45–7, 137–8
  reception   2
Furet, François   66, 114

Gaudot, Claude affair   23
Gautier, Moyse   20
Gibbon, Edward   49
Girardet, Abraham   64
Girardet, Abraham-Louis   64
Girardet, Samuel   63–4
Goëzman, Louis-Valentin de   25, 27
Gosse, Henri-Albert   31, 32, 33, 60–1, 85, 100, 110, 111
Gosse, Pierre junior and Pinet, Daniel   25, 27, 32, 90–1, 120–1
Grasset, François   16, 21, 27, 54, 55, 59, 93
Grasset, Gabriel   16, 28, 49
Griesser, Jean David   20
Guyot, Charles   114

Hardouin, Robert-André 103
Heilmann, Jean-Christophe 27
Hellen de Boligen, Jean-Jacques 64
Heubach, Jean-Pierre 28, 31, 55–6, 93, 151
Hiribarren, Vincent 1
Histoire de François Wills (Murphy ?) 65–6, 70, 78, 139
Hoftijzer, Paul 5

illegal publishing
    demise of *ancien régime* 131–3
    differences across space and over time 128–9
    diplomatic activity 126–7
    efficacy of censorship 132, 145
    historiography 114–5
    interception of works 121
    in 'The North' 104, 143
    legal frameworks 124–5
    lists of illegal works 126
    livres philosophiques 127
    as negotiation between stakeholders 132–3
    policing 125
    pricing 127–8
    progressive closure of the French border of 1783-7 60–1
    Protestant works 128
    STN printings 124, 143
    trading patterns 129–30
Inceste avoué à un mari (Rilliet de Saussure) 119–21

Jaquet-Droz, Pierre 20, 33, 46
Jeanneret, Susanne 20
Junod, Louis 114

Kattau, Sarah 1
Kirschenbaum, Matthew 2
Kleemann, Nicolaus Ernst 98, 99–100

La banque rendue facile aux principales nations de l'Europe (Giradeau) 36
La Mettrie, Julien Offray de 71
L'an deux mille quatre cent quarante (Mercier) 27
La Noue (Mme) 104
La Porte, Mathieu de 35–6
L'apparition du livre (Febvre and Martin) 5, 114
La science des négocians et teneurs de livres (La Porte) 35–6, 38, 39, 41, 42, 43, 47
Le bon père (Pommaret) 108–9
Le Camus de Néville, François-Claude-Michel-Benoît 88, 105–6
Leipzig book fair 28, 61, 95
Le libertin de qualité 107
Lenoir, Jean-Charles-Pierre 104–6, 125
Le nouvel Abeilard 75
Lepagnez cadet 53–4
Le Scène-Desmaisons, Jacques 70
Létourmy, Jean-Baptiste 152
Lettres du comte Algarotti sur la Russie (Algarotti) 25–6, 68, 73, 90
Lettres physiques et morales sur les montagnes (Deluc) 55–6
Lettres sur l'emprunt et l'impôt (Rilliet de Saussure) 116–17
'Lettre sur le commerce des livres' (Diderot) 79–80, 101
Linguet, Simon-Nicolas-Henri 88, 104, 127
Livre de comptes-faits (Barrême) 36
Luchtmans (firm) 33–4, 38, 137, 147
Lullin, Ami 118, 119, 120

MacDonald, Bertrum 5
Marat, Jean-Paul 49
Martin, Henri-Jean 5, 114
Mercier, David 83
Mercier, Louis-Sébastien 49, 70, 71, 102, 105, 106, 114
Merivale, Henry 1
Mettra, Louis 120
Meyer, Jean 66
Mirabeau, Gabriel-Honoré de Riquetti, comte de 49, 102, 106
Montesquieu 71
Mornet, Daniel 66, 114, 140
Mossy, Jean 85
Moutard, Nicolas-Léger 105

Necker, Jacques 102
Neuchâtel
    development 15, 19–20, 61
    location 17–18

print industry 20
topography 15–16
Nicolai, Friedrich 31, 34, 57, 61, 73, 75, 95
Normandie, Lucrèce-Angélique de 116
'The North' 31
Nouffer, Jean Abram 61, 105–6, 110
Nouveau Journal helvétique 16, 19, 22, 23, 25, 51, 57–8, 62, 76–9, 104–5, 153

Ostervald, Frédéric-Samuel 22, 70, 151–4
Ostervald, Jean-Frédéric 70

Pasta, Renato 3
Pavie, Louis-Victor 109
Pelleport, Anne-Gédeon de La Fite de 104
Pellet, Jean Léonard 119
Pelloutien (diplomat) 109
periodicals 58, 89
Philibert, Claude and Chirol, Barthélemy 28, 45, 54, 57, 60, 61, 109–11
Pistorius, Jean 20
Planta, Ursule de 116–23
Planta gagnant sa vie en honnête homme (Rilliet de Saussure) 119–21, 122–3, 133
Plantamour, Jacques Rilliet 122
Poinçot, Claude 103
Pommaret (pastor) 108–9
Pott, Jules-Henri 28, 51, 128–9
printing in the Swiss Romand
  advertisement 75–6, 77
  alliances 55–7, 96, 101
  distinctiveness of editions 50, 66–74, 142–4
  edition sizes 74–5
  intertextuality 143
  liquidity risk 20–1
  nouveautés 53, 142
  orientation 73–4
  pricing 26, 53–4, 75
  trading conditions 100–1, 110
  vertical integration 58–9
  wholesale model 18, 28, 51–5, 60, 127–8

Procès romanesque, offrant un sujet de comédie très-riche & très-heureux (Rilliet de Saussure) 119–21
public sphere 9, 80, 138–9

Quandet de Lachenal 103, 105, 114, 120
Questions sur l'encyclopédie (Voltaire) 27, 77, 90, 123, 127, 140, 143
Quiby, Jaques and Boisselier, Joseph 119

reading rooms 31, 45, 62
Requête au Grand Conseil de la République de Genève (Rilliet de Saussure) 119
Restif de la Bretonne, Nicolas-Edmé 75
Revillod, veuve 118–9
Rey, Marc-Michel 54, 141
Reycends *frères* 28
Riccoboni, Marie-Jeanne 70, 71
Rigaud, Pons and Company 87, 107, 121
Rigogne, Thierry 5, 31
Rilliet de Saussure, Théodore 69, 70, 102
  Rilliet-Planta affair 115–23, 133
Roche, Daniel 66
Rohan, Louis René Édouard de 121
Rousseau, Jean-Jacques 15, 49, 153
Rychner, Jacques 3

St Clair, William 13
Sandoz-Rollin, David-Alphonse de 105
Saussure, Horace-Bénédict de 49, 54, 63, 71
Schlup, Michel 3
Schmid, Jean-Jacques 20
Société du jardin 62
Société littéraire (de Neuchâtel) 62, 75
Société typographique de Berne 28, 101
Société typographique de Lausanne 55, 101
Société typographique de Neuchâtel
  acquisitions 51
  advertisement 75–6, 77
  displaced distribution printing 100–4, 144–5
  early development 25
  edition exhaustion rates 78–9, 139
  edition sizes 74–5

ephemera 30, 45–6
establishment 21, 23–4
exchange partnerships 28–9
financial issues 26, 95–6, 98–9
growth 30
leadership 21–2
liquidation 110–11, 113, 151–4
previous scholarship 3, 4
pricing of works 75
representativeness 8–9, 67, 136–7
sales by author 71–2
sales by category 67–70, 142
sales by title 70–1
sales overview 30
sales to Britain and Ireland 91–2
sales to Eastern Europe 94–6
sales to extra-European territories 92
sales to France 86–8
sales to Neuchâtel 61, 63–4
sales to Paris and Versailles 88, 103
sales to Southern Europe 93–4
sales to Swiss Romand 59–60
sales to 'The North' 88–91
size of establishment 31
split with Samuel Fauche 29
stock fragmentation 79
strategic shifts 24, 26
transition to wholesaling 27–9
translations 72–3
Sturm und Drang 73
Swiss Romand 19
Système de la nature (Holbach) affair 27, 114, 123, 124, 139

Tableau de Paris (Mercier) 102–3
Théorie des lois criminelles (Brissot) 104
Trattner, Johann Thomas von 31
Tribolet, Charles-Godefroi de 114
Trim, Nicolas 119

Varry, Dominique 3
Vergennes, Charles Gravier comte de 104–6
Vingle, Pierre de 20
Voltaire 33, 49, 71, 140
Voyage de Vienne à Belgrade et à Kilianova (Kleemann) 98, 99–100

Wilkie, John 73
Witel, Jérémie 54, 63, 101, 102–7, 110, 114, 124
Wolfrath, Chrétien-Henri 154

www.ingramcontent.com/pod-product-compliance
Lightning Source LLC
Chambersburg PA
CBHW052036300426
44117CB00012B/1842